'Here is a book of compassion, wisdom and skill that brings new textures and insights to those practising CFT with troubled minds.'
Professor Paul Gilbert OBE

Compassion Focused Group Psychotherapy

An Exploratory Programme for People who Could Have a Diagnosis of 'Personality Disorder'

Kate Lucre

Compassion Focused Group Psychotherapy

An Exploratory Programme for People who Could Have a Diagnosis of 'Personality Disorder'

© Pavilion Publishing & Media

The author has asserted her rights in accordance with the Copyright, Designs and Patents Act (1988) to be identified as the author of this work.

Published by:
Pavilion Publishing and Media Ltd
Blue Sky Offices, 25 Cecil Pashley Way
Shoreham by Sea, West Sussex
BN43 5FF

Tel: 01273 434 943
Email: info@pavpub.com
Web: www.pavpub.com

Published 2025

All rights reserved. No part of this publication may be reproduced, stored in a retrieval system, or transmitted in any form or by any means, electronic, mechanical, photocopying, recording or otherwise, without prior permission in writing of the publisher and the copyright owners.

A catalogue record for this book is available from the British Library.

ISBN: 978-1-803883-28-1

Pavilion Publishing and Media is a leading publisher of books, training materials and digital content in mental health, social care and allied fields. Pavilion and its imprints offer must-have knowledge and innovative learning solutions underpinned by sound research and professional values.

Author: Kate Lucre
Editor: Mike Benge
Cover design: Tony Pitt, Pavilion Publishing and Media Ltd
Page layout and typesetting: Emma Dawe, Pavilion Publishing and Media Ltd
Printing: Independent Publishers Group (IPG)

'If you are interested in how to use CFT with complex trauma, attachment and interpersonal difficulties, this is the book for you. Filled with great insight, wisdom and clinical examples. Dr Lucre's book is both inspiring and practical. Highly recommended.'

Dr Chris Irons
Clinical Psychologist and Director of Balanced Minds

'In this intelligent, helpful, very personal book, Kate Lucre generously shares, not just the wisdom she has gathered over many years, but the flaws that have got her into trouble and mistakes she has made along the way. Her compassionate approach to herself, as well as to her patients and indeed her readers, is there on every page and makes her a highly readable and supportive guide and creative comrade.'

Dr Penny Campling
NHS psychiatrist and psychotherapist

'This is such an important book. The ideas and methods described here should be taken up by practitioners far and wide. Kate Lucre describes the model she has developed to work with perhaps the most challenging client group in adult mental health services, a model influenced by Compassion Focused Therapy, psychodrama, psychodynamic thinking, ancestral traditions and more, all melded into a way of working she has made very much her own. What shines through is Kate's commitment, compassion and ability to learn, and the effectiveness of the work as her research has shown. On top of that, perhaps surprisingly, it's a very human book and a cracking good read.'

Graham Music
Adult, child and adolescent psychotherapist

'Kate Lucre's book is an absolute treasure in the world of clinical psychology and Compassion Focused Therapy, which has proven its profound effectiveness over the years. This is not just a guide – it's an inspiring, hand-in-hand journey that makes you feel like a co-creator in building transformative group CFT interventions. With Kate's unmatched expertise, sparkling humor, boundless compassion, and deeply personal touch, every page brims with wisdom and heart. Kate, thank you for this extraordinary gift – you've truly outdone yourself!'

Niki Petrocchi, Ph.D., Psy.D.
Professor of Psychology, John Cabot University, Rome

Dedication

This book is humbly dedicated to all my patients, group members, co-travellers and fellow conspirators, whose compassionate courage, wisdom and strength have enabled Compassion Focused Group Psychotherapy to be. I am indebted to you all.

About the author

Dr Kate Lucre is a Birmingham-based Consultant Psychotherapist and Supervisor specialising in the use of Compassion Focused Therapy (CFT) for complex attachment and relational trauma for groups and individuals. She has over 25 years' experience working in statutory, NHS and social care organisations in the UK and overseas. She also runs workshops across the UK and internationally in CFT for Groups and Compassion Focused Staff Support and Supervision. Kate is the founder of Compassion Focused Group Psychotherapy (CFGP) for people who would attract a diagnosis of personality disorder and has published the only data in this model, recently completing a 7-year follow-up study to this original research programme. Kate has also developed Compassion Focused Staff Support and offers her model to staff in various settings in the UK and internationally, and is also involved in a number of UK-wide research projects, evaluating this model.

Acknowledgements

I am most grateful to my supervisors, Dr Chris Jones and Prof Alex Copello, who have advised, counselled and at times pulled me out of a number of holes as I completed the formal evaluation of this programme. Chris' attention to detail has been a source of joy, humour and ultimately learning (often the hard way). Alex's gentle approach has provided a consistent source of soothing, often just when I needed it most.

Susie Taylor and Jeni Goodfellow-Pemsel have brought energy and enlivening to this programme as supervisors, trainers and close allies. Their understanding of the attachment bonds which sit within the supervisory relationship have been both a source of comfort and enrichment.

Chris Irons and Graham Music have held a space for me to explore what this book could be and, more importantly, what I wished it be, and encouraged me to do it my own way.

Dion, my co-traveller, has supported, cajoled, challenged and ultimately proofread all my work; without him not only would this not have been possible, it would not have been nearly so much fun. My children Affi and Tane have given me space to work when I needed and stopped me from taking this book or myself too seriously.

My co-facilitators and supervisors have, with me, coaxed Compassion Focused Group Psychotherapy into life and often been the rather noisy voice of my conscience. I am grateful.

Sarah Theaker has been alongside me in this for so many years, inspiring me with her courage, wisdom and tenacity to develop and expand this programme.

I am deeply indebted to all those who travel with me on this journey as part of my many supervision groups. You provide inspiration and so many new ideas, many of which are contained in this book. It is your immense courage, humour and authenticity which continually inspire and enliven me and the programme.

Neil Clapton and Lucy Courtney Brisbane have proofread this book, offering suggestions, encouragement and an invitation to bring the 'fierce' into compassion and some 'bang' into my sentences!

Last but most definitely not least, Professor Paul Gilbert has inspired, supported, questioned and provoked me to make Compassion Focused Group Psychotherapy accessible to those who are truly at the 'edge of therapeutic opportunity'. It is his unwavering support and dedication to CFT that has made all this possible.

Finally, I am thankful to rock climbing and all those who climb with me. It makes everything else possible.

Contents

About the author vi
Acknowledgements vii
Foreword 3
   Professor Paul Gilbert OBE
Preface 7
Glossary 14
Introduction 17
   The Guidebook for Compassion Focused Group Psychotherapy 27

Phase One: Assessment and Formulation 39
   Chapter 1.1: The practicalities of the assessment 41

Phase Two: The Waiting List Group (tea and biscuits!) 63
   Chapter 2.1: Waiting... waiting... and waiting... 65
   Chapter 2.2: Role of the therapist/conductor 73

Phase Three: The Preparation and Engagement Group (PEG) 85
   Chapter 3.1: To prep or not to prep? That is the question 87
   Chapter 3.2: How it works 95
   Chapter 3.3: The Modules – an overview 115
   Chapter 3.4: Module One – Our Tricky Brains 119
   Chapter 3.5: Module Two – Compassion 129
   Chapter 3.6: Module Three – The Compassionate Kitbag 139
   Chapter 3.7: Closed and Online Groups... 169

Phase Four: Compassion-Focused Trauma Group (CFTG) 177
   Chapter 4.1: Transitions and conflict 179
   Chapter 4.2: Getting ready.. 191
   Chapter 4.3: Compassionate transformation in action
      Part 1 – Action methods 205
   Chapter 4.4: Compassionate transformation in action
      Part 2 – Chairwork 229

Chapter 4.5: Compassionate transformation in action
Part 3 – Sharing, talking and gathering 245

Chapter 4.6: Integration, endings and homemade brownies 261

Phase Five: The Moving On Group 279

Chapter 5.1: Moving on 281

The final words 289

Appendices 297

Appendix 1.1: Example Assessment Summary

Appendix 3.1: Example Safe Space Agreement

Appendix 3.2: How the body responds to threat

Appendix 3.3: Pros and cons of a compassionate being

Appendix 3.4: Compassion Postcard

Appendix 3.5: Job description of the inner critic

Appendix 3.6: Compassionate roles map

Appendix 3.7: Calm Place Imagery Script and link

Appendix 3.8: Role-taking

Appendix 4.1: Word cloud

Appendix 4.2: Compassion-Focused Therapy Threat Formulation – 'this is how I survived…'

Appendix 4.3: Multiple selves map

Appendix 4.4: Whirlpool of Grief

Appendix 4.5: Rosa!

References 315

Case study characters 330

Online resources are available at
www.pavpub.com/compassion-focused-group-psychotherapy-resources
from where they can be downloaded and printed.

Foreword

Professor Paul Gilbert OBE

I'm delighted to write the foreword for Kate's important book on Compassion Focused Group Psychotherapy (CFGP). Our first major research study on the effectiveness of Compassion Focused Therapy (CFT) was a group therapy one in around 2002, which was eventually published some years later (Gilbert & Procter, 2004). It was shortly after this first study that Kate came to various workshops on CFT and explored how to contextualise therapy within the psychophysiology of evolved care systems.

Crucial to CFT group therapy is the relational process we call *the social mentality of caring*. This is because caring behaviours, like many other forms of social behaviour, have to co-evolve. In order for an individual to be capable of caring behaviour, their brain must be capable of detecting not only the need to be caring (such as picking up forms of distress) but also caring signals and have the ability to physiologically react to them. When an infant detects caring signals they will respond to them with a calming or positive affect. Clearly, if these signals are not detected or are interpreted as threat signals, the infant's response will be very different.

At the heart of this book is the importance of understanding social mentalities and the concept of the co-regulation of states, a concept central to CFT and one which Kate expertly navigates. From the day we are born to the day we die, our interactions with others plays a fundamental role on a range of physiological systems, our values and health outcomes. Also central to the CFT therapeutic process is the importance of steering that co-regulating dynamic through a motivational system of caring-compassion, because human evolution created brains and bodies that are highly regulated through experiences of caring. Kate puts the group's co-regulating dynamic at the centre of the therapeutic process.

Kate draws on the work of Darcia Narvaez, attachment theorists and many others. Indeed, we now know that it's not just family-based attachment that matters but our experience of being embedded within supportive communities. Indeed, in our hunter gatherer past children were cared for by relatives and communities, not just by individuals. Neglect and abuse would be rare. So, in addition to the closeness of family-attachment relationships we also all seek a sense of belonging and to be part of a community; to have friends, allies and lovers. This ability to share and care between peers is called community-based attachment, and it can be essential for well-being and group success in CFT.

Research has also shown that it is not just the caring that we receive from others that can be crucial, but it is also the relationships we have inside our own heads; the way we think and feel about ourselves. This is the basis of social mentality theory: that social mentalities can both send signals (e.g., of threat, desire or care) and respond to those signals in mentality appropriate ways. Social mentalities can also have more harmful effects as they allow us to feel hostility and anger to ourselves in the same way we might to others. When others are critical of us, parts of our threat system light up in the brain. These same systems light up when we are being harshly self-critical because we are tapping into a social mentality that has both sending and receiving functions. Therefore, if we have experienced a lot of external shaming, that can become a template for our internal self-relating.

When the competitive and social threat mentality becomes the lens by which people relate to the world, the therapeutic task is to not so much modify that mentality as to switch them out of it and into one rooted in caring and sharing, because this has a very different physiological architecture and brain state. Hence, if we are struggling and we become harshly self-critical and view ourselves as inadequate or deficient in some way, we generate angry and hostile emotions to ourselves and cause ourselves a lot of pain and suffering. It follows that, if we learn to be sensitive to our distress, empathic and understanding, then our brains and our bodies will respond quite differently.

Understanding these processes also helps us understand why CFT is an ideal fit for group-based therapies. However, it is crucial that the therapist has the awareness and, ideally, training in the process of facilitating group therapy. As Kate makes clear in this book, this has always been one of her central interests. The model works so well due to the fact she has not only undertaken group psychotherapy training, but she has also weaved those wisdoms into the delivery of CFT.

For all kinds of reasons, Kate also indicates how she has been very interested in helping those individuals who perhaps have not being able to utilise some of the shorter term therapies; individuals that are sometimes written off as too complex or too resistant; people who can pick up a pocket full of labels that describe symptom clusters but not the deeper psychological fractures they give rise to them. Kate highlights the importance of seeing past the symptom clusters into the deeper psychological fractures of a self that is lost in the mind that hasn't been able to mature, cultivate or utilise crucial care-evolved psychophysiological systems necessary for the regulation of mind for the finding of connection love and joy.

Whilst kindness, gentleness and support can be ways of being compassionate, they're not necessarily the basis of compassion because that depends on the context one is being compassionate about. CFT is not a therapy just about kindness or being gentle, but also about positioning compassion as an active motivation and a dedication to pay attention to suffering, even if that can be painful, and then to find the wisdom and courage to act and bring healing, even if such an action is very painful and difficult to do. It is about creating the competencies to engage with what is hard, frightening and painful: descending into suffering to heal from it, not to escape from it. Such compassionate actions can be frightening and dangerous and require wisdom and courage, like a firefighter risking their life to save people. Confronting trauma and learning how to be compassionate, supportive, empathic and validating is not an easy journey for those with who have been harmed by others' inadequacies and so find ways to tolerate the rage, fear and sadness that they experience. In CFT it is not only important to find new relationships with ourselves, but also to find a new self-experience in relationships.

I offer this background because Kate has pioneered this psychodynamic texturing of CFT to work with people who others may choose not to, and to highlight that her understanding of the complexities of the evolutionary model guide her in how to conceptualise CFT group dynamics. This book is full of experience-gained wisdoms and will guide those interested in CFT therapy to the heart of the process. Kate outlines in detail many interactions with clients and how they have both challenged, but also informed, her practise. She is open about the clients that sometimes we ourselves find difficult to trust and engage with, and how to work with them within the CFT process. Equally however, the book unfolds a story of great hope and the potential for change if we can create the right contexts for people.

CFT is not just a set of technical skills one can learn – they need practise. One has to understand that the evolving nature of the mind is inherently tricky, prone to cause great harm to self and others in certain contexts, and that is not anybody's fault. This is why human history is full of the horrors that it is: the wars of conquest and vengeance, slavery, the holocausts, the tortures, the treatment of women and children and so on. Encountering minds that can be full of narcissistic entitlement, or rage and hate, is not easy, but the more we can recognise these shadows within ourselves the easier it might be to tolerate. Kate skilfully navigates us through the constant process of the therapist as an active participant within the group dynamic.

Foreword

When Kate asked me about my view of whether or not to have open groups where people could join at different periods, frankly I was sceptical. However, until we get the evidence we should never close down ideas, and that's exactly what Kate has done. So, after many years of chipping away, developing, growing and bringing together good evidence, here is a remarkable book outlining her journey with a wealth of case discussions and the sharing of client personal experiences on their journey. CFT offers what we hope is the scientific biopsychosocial evolutionary approach to the nature of the human mind in all its various complexities and potentials for helpfulness and harmfulness. Here is a book of compassion, wisdom and skill that brings new textures and insights to those practising CFT with troubled minds.

Preface

I would like to take you on a journey through the phases and stages of compassion, but first I would like to share a little of my journey with you.

My story begins at the age of seven, with the idea that every 'show off' needs a stage. This, of course, could not have been truer in my case, but for such different reasons. The stage offered an opportunity for self-expression, a place to play and, over time, a place for self-discovery. This passion took me to Shakespeare, a lifelong love affair of mine. Cordelia in King Lear, Lady Macbeth, more opportunities to take on roles that were full of life even in death. So I learned about our 'multiple selves' from the inside out. I could take on a role, develop it, play with it, and in so doing, let other overdeveloped roles go. Rebellion became an admirable attribute, something that could bring fire to a role, and not something to be extinguished.

Amidst the drama came an introduction to the mountains, which, in truth, are most effectively climbed in your mind. The discovery of another source of peace – that to be in a state of slow, purposeful, mindful motion could bring quiet to the chaos. Nothing to think of but the next place to put your hands and feet. A performance where no one is watching. One-hundred metres from the ground, there is no one to call on but yourself. In those moments, every role you have taken on or had thrust upon you becomes deeply relevant. There is an authentic and true discovery of the self, with all your vulnerabilities and strengths, in a way like directing or performing on the stage. You may have auxiliaries, someone holding the rope, but you have to summon something from within you at that moment and take the risk. Your co-therapist, like your climbing partner, can offer support and encouragement through minute and imperceptible gestures, but only you can decide about the next step.

I was therefore going to be an actress who did rock climbing, right up to the point that I understood that I would require a back-up profession – a 'proper job' – to subsidise these passions. Many dear friends and fellow accomplices entered the world of drama ahead of me and were unceremoniously spat out again. I knew that I did not have a role even under construction to buffer me against the rejection and cruelty that came with this profession. So I went travelling, met my co-traveller, gave up acting and set about building myself a career.

Drama lay dormant for a while, replaced perhaps with climbing, another kind of peaceful enactment. I travelled, climbed, worked. I couldn't be an actress who climbed, but then, equally, I couldn't be a climber who acted. Looking back, I needed something that connected both.

Around this time, I began to work with young people in the care leavers system, who were only a few years younger than I was at the time. Back then, I had no idea of the stigma associated with the diagnostic label of 'personality disorder', but I felt acutely aware that those leaving the care system were often written off before they got a foothold. Many, of course, would indeed later get that label of personality disorder, with all its pejorative associations. At the same time, I was horrified by the treatment many of the patients I worked with in the old asylums were subjected to, before all the hospitals were unceremoniously closed and the institutionalised patients were shoved into the community. It was called 'Care in the Community', which was in my experience mostly a bad joke. Many of these patients had been locked up for decades, over medicated, given a label of personality disorder which meant they were considered untreatable.

What seemed to bind these two seemingly disparate groups of humans together, those being ejected from the care system and those being ejected from the old asylums, was early trauma and tragedy. This tragedy had marred their lives and halted their emotional, psychological and spiritual development. In those early days, I was angered by my powerlessness to change the system; I felt like I was stamping my feet and shouting from the sidelines, so I had to roll up my sleeves and get involved.

The subsequent decades as a social worker, probation officer and then psychotherapist taught me that significant early relational trauma, tragedy or adverse early relationship experiences generate a series of responses that can place these people at the 'edge of therapeutic opportunity'. This 'edge' is arguably largely created by healthcare services and treatment providers and is most definitely not the fault of those being labelled. At times it has been a lack of our imagination which has prevented these patients from receiving the care and treatment they need. We may have officially ceased the use of the term 'untreatable', but this group continue to be denied appropriate treatment, care and understanding.

My journey into group therapy has taken many twists and turns – from short-term, time-limited, heavily structured and manualised group programmes, where participants sat at tables with workbooks, through to largely unstructured, exploratory and analytic group programmes with a slow, open membership and much in between. I have always seen the merits of both approaches, but I wondered if we actually need a combination of structured and unstructured components to support people whose therapeutic capacity is limited.

Halfway through my cognitive behavioural psychotherapy training, Paul Gilbert came to give a talk on compassion-focused therapy (CFT) and I realised in a moment of clarity that I was on the wrong course! But there was no full CF psychotherapy training that I could switch to. Discovering compassion-focused therapy arrived at just the right moment. This was a model of therapy which had some substance, rooted in neuroscientific practice, attachment and evolutionary psychology research, with a personal practice component that felt like a good fit.

My first job after qualifying as a psychotherapist was with Dr Penny Campling in one of the few remaining UK residential therapeutic communities. This experience really did change everything for me. I had left forensic social work frustrated by the limitations of the role and my capacity to support people with attachment and relational trauma (A&RT). I found that, as a social worker, I often spent my time driving my patients to various places. In my car, with us both facing forward, ostensibly focusing on a different task, my patients would tell me some of the horrors they had been subjected to. I had no idea how to respond and often absorbed much of their angst, leaving me burned out and exhausted. Many of my patients would say that they didn't want to talk to the forensic psychologist and would rather speak to me – classic splitting – but even so, the relationship was often with me. Back then, I didn't have the skills or training to be truly helpful.

This environment of the therapeutic community was deeply challenging – there was no hiding, you could be called out by anyone! I recall my first community meeting. There were over 30 people in the room and I had sat in one of the senior resident's chairs. It felt like being back at school – nerve racking. But as the meeting unfolded, I could see the benefits of the shared responsibility and accountability and the 'living learning' experience, which combines structured work groups, small exploratory psychotherapy groups and community meetings. During those five years, I worked with others to bring some structured behavioural interventions to the programme, but I was moving away from these ideas and towards a compassion and process-focused approach. One of my esteemed colleagues during that time reminded me that, even if we are supporting a cake baking group with people with A&RT, we will need highly experienced psychotherapists for the work, and they were right.

With these experiences in mind, I started my first 16-week closed group back in 2006. It was compassion-focused therapy with strands of therapeutic community practice, with the check in and sharing of space and an intention towards democracy. Our group members taught us a great deal and made good use of the therapeutic experience, and even after 12 months many had maintained the therapeutic change and continued to flourish.[1] I added a few weeks, then a few more, offered a men's group and tried a 12-month closed group. Not to mention the unsustainable waiting lists. It felt like there was something missing. The dynamic in a closed group seemed to get set and stuck quite quickly. The roles that we took up in the group seemed to be repeating those of early childhood (perhaps for us all).

It was around this time that I completed a foundation course in group analysis. This was my first introduction to the therapeutic principles of group analysis. It was reassuring to be able to connect with my experiences in the therapeutic community. There were a few more years during which I turned my attention to bringing the theory and practice of compassion-focused therapy to the therapeutic day programme provision that we offered in the complex needs outpatient service where I worked. It was here that I encountered action methods and psychodrama for the first time, and as I have said previously a few things came together in my mind about therapeutic opportunity.

Creating a model for people with complex relational trauma required increasing creativity. Some people couldn't even sit in a circle, let alone breathe together, so we had to evolve. It was at this point that I was reminded of the theatre, the games, ice-breakers, props and the offering of another focus. The model that emerged was compassion focused and had some rudimentary elements of something like action methods, with a fair smattering of play therapy. The therapy room would often resemble a preschool classroom by the end of a session, with art materials, cloth and chairs scattered around the room. But the good news was that they stayed, shared, and began to take small forays into the idea and practice of compassion for themselves and for the others in the group.

This work took me on a gradual transition from being an individual therapist to a group therapist – another uneasy transition which I never imagined I would make. It was almost like moving from climbing with fixed protection and bolts in the rock, to traditional climbing, accepting the terrifying reality that the only thing holding you 100 metres above the ground is a bit of metal you shoved in a crack in the rock. But once this terror subsides, it can become difficult to go back to the safer way. I wonder if my transition to groups has been similar. Within individual therapy, there are only two minds to consider, but within a group setting the number of minds that you are required to mentalise with, make sense of and explore with compassion, grows exponentially.

---

1   Lucre, K. M., & Corten, N. (2013). An exploration of group compassion-focused therapy for personality disorder. *Psychology and Psychotherapy: Theory, Research and Practice*, **86**(4), 387–400.

There have been times, particularly in the early days, when the terror of the group mind and its vagaries felt too much. When anxious, I tend to speed up. There were some groups in that time when I could scarcely catch my breath as I attempted to keep the group moving, almost jollying them along at times with relentless activity.

My intuitive and attuned group very quickly picked up on this and, with trepidation, I stopped focusing on the content and shifted my attention to pacing and tone. This has over time become the bedrock of all my teaching, trying to demonstrate how slowing the pace can create space for our group members to begin to connect with their feelings. The same process of course occurs in us, so I was often confronted with my own feelings. These still regularly take me by surprise, and I am often moved to tears. The difference is that now I let them be… well, perhaps that is a work in progress. Although these feelings in the early days were terrifying and the image of myself sobbing uncontrollably could pop into my mind at any given moment, plunging my nervous system in a downward spiral.

My own slowly developing practice in self-compassion, incredible supervision and painful personal therapy were part of the solution, aided in immeasurable ways by climbing on a weekly basis. Climbing, again like therapy, requires a steady hand. I learn this lesson very regularly when I rush into my climbing practice still full of the day's preoccupations. Quite simply, I fall off very quickly and unceremoniously, and then I remember that my body cannot do both, and that rumination and climbing are not possible for me. So, as I pick myself up off the mat or steady myself on the rope, I wake up and shift my focus back solely to the task at hand, slowing my breathing and my pace. So, in therapy, the personal practice breathing before the group starts became a non-negotiable aspect of the developing model. I also attempt to stretch out my body and my mind. I know this now to be a specific version of the warm up. I skip it at my peril. Lurching into the group space while weighed down with the other 'stuff' sets a tone for the group, which I could feel, and I believe without doubt the group could feel too. As I write this, I am taken back to our warm-ups before a performance, no chocolate – blocks your throat – stretching, laughing at our own vocal iterations, coming together and developing an affiliative space in our minds for the work ahead. As facilitators, we come together in this way, another place where the roads meet.

I have been fortunate to have met many co-travellers on this journey towards self-compassion, as a model of therapy and perhaps most importantly as a way of being. But there are a small number whose presence has led me to this point, reflecting on the journey so far. Together we have mobilised compassion; moved the therapy from a vague manual into a living and breathing process-driven intervention which my edge-of-therapeutic-opportunity-folk tell me really does work. This is, of course, a huge relief given how much is riding on this!

I have always had quite a belligerent part of me that is ignited if someone tells me that 'they' can't be helped. This has motivated me to work at the edge of therapeutic opportunity for my whole career. But it hasn't always ended well, and my belligerence, which has bordered on showing off at times, has got me into considerable trouble. At times, my passion turns to arrogance and blinds me to the reality of a situation, and at other times it helps me to take a risk. I am still working on distinguishing between the two. Slowing down and learning to use my wise compassionate mind remains a work in progress.

I therefore stand by my choice – those who no one else wants, those who have either had everything and it didn't work or had nothing. I have no doubt that I have also been bringing attention and care to the girl who felt that no one really wanted her, and that care was conditional. But I am no paragon of virtue. I wonder if another part of what draws me to this group is an affinity with a difficult, prickly nature, coupled with a deep yearning for that which is so difficult to take: emotional connection. I have often wondered, in group therapy, about a version of me for whom things turned out differently, perhaps without climbing. I could easily have been sitting in the patient's and not therapist's chair.

So to offering a rolling compassion-focused group psychotherapy, combining principles and practice from group analysis within a compassion-focused framework and structure, animated by action, movement and, most importantly, play. The play bit has been most straightforward. My accomplices have brought play in buckets, and as Piaget said, 'play is the answer to how anything new comes about'. I like this idea as I love to play; I cannot imagine life without it. I return again to acting and climbing – both, I think, attract playing and playfulness. I laugh louder and longer with climbing buddies, as I did with my acting buddies, than in any other place. If you fail on a climb, you are likely to be greeted with derision and a suggestion that if you weren't so weak you might be able to make the move, but given from a place of deep compassion, care and belief in you.

We share the metaphor of climbing with the group, we are journeying, and we need sustenance on the way, a Compassionate Kitbag to hold what you need to develop your new identity. We need climbing buddies, to enable us to do this joyful and terrifying activity with safeness. There will be times when you don't feel like leading, but the wisdom comes from knowing whether it is avoidance or a much-needed rest. The group can help with the wisdom, hold you to it when needed, and let you sit back on the off days.

Writing this book has afforded me the opportunity to 'bivvy' on my journey – to slow down, take a breath, enjoy the view and reflect on my journey so far. I can be a climbing psychotherapeutic actress or an acting climbing therapist, or even a psychotherapeutically acting climber, and I can add any new roles which I find on my journey.

From a deep awareness and sensitivity to the suffering of people who have traditionally been excluded from longer-term psychological therapies, I have been motivated to develop a therapy and now to share it. My intention is to offer a practical, helpful and illuminating guide to all aspects of developing a compassion-focused group psychotherapy programme. I also hope that an infusion of playfulness and a light touch demonstrates how enlivening this psychotherapeutic work can be for us all. My compassionate wish to all who read this book is that you find it helpful in supporting your own journey in compassion and compassion-focused group psychotherapy.

Glossary

Dynamic Administration
The seemingly mundane but immensely important. These are the tasks associated with setting up the group, from arranging the chairs to communication with the group about time and place. It all matters.

Process
Paying close attention to what is happening in us and between the group members as the group session unfolds. This involves letting go of a strict adherence to content and being prepared to follow what emerges in the room.

Antigroup
The destructive and potentially creative forces that arise in any group process, which can manifest at any time and can feel like members attacking the group. This will all need to be attended to, to ensure the continued function of the group.

Safeness
Where there is no threat; a state of calm connection in the present moment. Different from safety, which describes the act of seeking safety in the context of running away from a threat.

Transference
These are the unprocessed and unresolved feelings that we might have for someone in our past. These feelings then get transferred onto someone in the present, but they do not belong to that person or the situation.

Projection

We all have disowned feelings and parts that we cannot tolerate. Unconsciously we can push these feelings into others in the group, which can be tricky to notice and work with.

Projective identification

When we feel the projected feelings as if they are our own, and act them out.

Introduction

To begin, I want to be very clear that compassion-focused group psychotherapy (CFGP) is a model which is underpinned by interconnected aspects of psychotherapeutic theory and practice. This model is rooted in the evolutionary theory and practice of compassion-focused therapy, with necessary adaptations to make it accessible for people who might attract a diagnosis of personality disorder. The search for the adaptations has taken me to psychodrama, group analysis, and into therapeutic communities. I have had the good fortune to learn from, work with and train in all these models over the course of my career, and hope is that CFGP is a respectful blend.

Beginning to weave these strands together, I need to acknowledge the key influences in the development of this programme. There is a sequence to the evolution of this which I hope will offer the reader an insight into how it came to be as it is. But before that, my starting point is the patient group. Working with those at the outer reaches has been my interest and passion from the outset. This model only makes sense if we first consider those it was developed for.

The very edge of therapeutic opportunity

There are those who have suffered ruptures, absence and intrusion in their primary attachment relationships, in that those who were supposed to love and care for them couldn't or wouldn't. From Bowlby's eloquent description of the human need for attachments, these experiences can rob the child of their confidence to seek proximity, while the experience of both a safe haven and a secure base are fundamentally undermined. In other words, the child learns that calling for help is ineffective, that seeking comfort is pointless or dangerous, and that the experience of safeness cannot be found in a relational context. Therein lies the paradox for this group – often the care and support they need most, they find hardest to tolerate.

Surviving these experiences often results in complex and self-defeating patterns of relating to others which guide their style of interaction throughout life. This in turn makes accessing appropriate psychological therapy difficult. Often, the therapeutic opportunity to make new connections is not available to this group of patients. Sloman and Taylor poignantly suggest the 'early relationship therefore influences the ability to self sooth and regulate emotions later in life'.[2]

Tragically, these survival strategies and behavioural manifestations will often attract a diagnosis of personality disorder, and with it, stigma, judgement and condemnation.

> *'Personality Disorder appears to be an enduring pejorative judgement rather than a clinical diagnosis. It is proposed that the concept be abandoned.'*[3]

Lewis and Appleby made this claim over 35 years ago and this has been followed by repeated and numerous calls for change. However, despite the significant concerns about the use of the term, it remains in common use in health and social care settings as a means of describing a set of behavioural manifestations which are often not connected with their traumatic origins. The diagnosis is often used instead of thinking with, exploring and making sense of the person's difficulties.

Reworking the diagnosis through an evolutionary lens

The science and practice of compassion has been deeply helpful in the reconceptualising of this group of troubled and troubling patients. A more reflective perspective on the role of inherited characteristics is essential in enriching our understanding of these patients. There is value in considering the role of epigenetic influences on gene expression[4] and the role of evolution in shaping which characteristics remain within the genome.

> *'Why do we stigmatise people if evolution is perfecting the work, scanning our needs and adjusting the responses?'*[5]

---

2   Sloman, L., & Taylor, P. (2016). Impact of child maltreatment on attachment and social rank systems: Introducing an integrated theory. *Trauma, Violence, & Abuse*, **17**(2), 172–185. https://doi.org/10.1177/1524838015584354

3   Lewis, G., & Appleby, L. (1988). Personality disorder: The patients psychiatrists dislike. *British Journal of Psychiatry*, **153**(1), 44–49. https://doi.org/10.1192/bjp.153.1.44

4   Gilbert, P., & Bailey, K. G. (2014). *Genes on the Couch: Explorations in Evolutionary Psychotherapy*. Routledge.

5   Ali, A. Y. (2015). Personality & Personality Disorders: Evolutionary Entrances and Exits. *Psychological Bulletin*, **140**(5), 1303–1331.

From this perspective, a range of problematic behavioural manifestations can be understood as 'complex adaptations to early adversity' which have, or at least had, an important function to regulate stress.[6] I am a huge fan of the work of Martin Brune who suggests that, given the often dangerous and unpredictable nature of the early environment, these 'adaptations' were functional. However, in the absence of new learning, these strategies remain fixed and can become incongruent and out of context in a seemingly less-hostile environment.

From this behavioural ecological perspective, which borrows from evolutionary ideas of adaptation and survival, we can begin to consider the experience of the child and the response of the child to these adverse (disordered) early environments. It is of course of note that this maltreatment can also take a psychological and less-visible form, and can manifest in an absence of care and affection rather than just the application of harm and abuse. The work of Sheridan and McLaughlin describes these two traumatising pathways, recognising both the distinctive and shared aspects of each pathway.[7] In essence, they highlight the way early life experiences shape our emotional, behavioural and relational ways of being, all of which are sustained by our maturing neurological architecture.

So let us be clear that those who we might find at the outer reaches of therapeutic opportunity are better described as having suffered attachment and relational trauma (A&RT). This is a more accurate and honest way to cluster this group of patients who truly are in need of care.

Mobilising compassion and weaving threads

It was the early learning about compassion-focused therapy (CFT) which got me thinking about how much this could help my shame-drenched patients to begin to normalise their experiences and develop an evolutionary understanding of survival strategies. CFT is an integrated and multi-modal approach that draws on evolutionary, social and developmental psychology and neuroscience, with a particular emphasis on the importance of affiliative processing to mental health and well-being. A central focus in CFT is to help people access and stimulate care-orientated motives, affiliative emotions and various competencies underpinning compassion that play important roles in threat regulation, well-being and prosocial behaviour. To put this another way, CFT

---

6   Brüne, M. (2016). Borderline Personality Disorder: Why 'fast and furious'? *Evolution, Medicine, and Public Health*, **2016**(1), 52–66. (p.61)
7   Sheridan, M. A., & McLaughlin, K. A. (2020). Neurodevelopmental mechanisms linking ACEs with psychopathology. In *Adverse Childhood Experiences* (pp. 265–285). Elsevier. https://www.sciencedirect.com/science/article/pii/B9780128160657000136

focuses on the importance of cultivating reciprocal role relationships in the caring social mentality both intra- and inter-personally. This focus on motivational-level rather than symptom-level change is often part of what is missing for this group of patients.

I had become frustrated with the focus on symptoms change as a measure of success during my brief foray into CBT. I was also very aware that those with A&RT generally did not 'achieve' symptomatic change without focusing on the underlying causes. Working within one of the few remaining UK residential therapeutic communities showed me that 'It goes beyond the eradication of symptoms into the area of interpersonal reconstruction'.[8] The unit seemed to be offering and supporting the residents to learn how to play and be engaged with others, to build new relationships. I also experienced how living and learning together enabled residents to slowly increase their capacity to be held in mind by each other, another missing element from their early lives.

So I began to weave this strand into the emerging model of compassion-focused group psychotherapy by offering an opportunity for reconstruction through the explicit and implicit cultivation of compassion across three interconnected flows. At the same time, I was moving the groups into a more process-driven way of working, where there is an emphasis on understanding the complex interactions between therapists and group members and the links with experiences in the past. There seemed to be something incredibly important about the authority and autonomy which the group members were being invited to develop. This seemed fundamental to the process of recovery, as they developed new ways of relating to each other.

My time working within the community also introduced me to group analysis, another place where the group is at the centre of the therapeutic process. Sigmund Foulkes (about whom we will learn more in a moment) was very clear about his wish to move away from what he perceived to be several dyadic exchanges in a group to a collective treatment process involving everyone including the therapist. He asserted that all communication should be understood in the context that the group is set, lessening the centrality of the individual group members.

Subsequent group analytic training and group psychotherapy taught me some hard lessons about the value of surrendering to the collective treatment process, where we become vulnerable and dependent on the others in the group. I recall many hours spent defending against this as a group member and then feeling the therapeutic opportunity which stemmed from relinquishing the need to go it alone. I find myself with a wry inner smile when I see this played in my groups. Someone said to me recently, *'Don't think I will ever need any of you'*… suffice to say that this sentiment lost conviction over time.

---

8   Behr, H., & Hearst, L. (2008). *Group-analytic Psychotherapy: A meeting of minds*. John Wiley & Sons.

As I have delved into the group analytic model, I was intrigued to learn that both NHS therapeutic communities and group analysis emerged from the Northfield experiments in Birmingham, a city very close to my heart.[9] These were therapeutic 'experiments' with soldiers returning from the front line during the early 1940s, who we now understand were suffering with post-traumatic stress. The experiment involved psychiatrists and psychotherapists being invited to engage with and offer treatment. The story of this involved both Sigmund Foulkes and Wilfred Bion and others who were motivated to make a therapeutic offer to these soldiers, but I think that perhaps the military wanted a quick fix and so the initial projects floundered.

I have often wondered why Foukes and Bion never spoke of each other or collaborated despite what seems to have been significant overlap in their practice and ideas from their time as part of the Northfield experiments. Psychotherapeutic models are shaped by the circumstances and the life experiences of those who have developed them. This is of course not chosen. There was most certainly significant attachment and relational trauma in the narratives of those who developed these models. Foulkes escaping the devastation of his homeland and the persecution of his people. Bion's active service in the First World War earned him high commendation but no doubt brought traumatic experiences, which sat alongside the loss of his wife in childbirth. There is some talk that Bion was deeply wounded by his experience at Northfield and that is why, beyond his seminal work, *Experiences in Groups*, he never returned to groupwork of any kind.

The story of these therapeutic modalities emerging from the post-war devastation in the UK and intergenerational trauma, I feel has shaped both models in particular ways. Sigmund Foulkes was influenced by Gestalt Therapy in Europe and developed the idea of the group as a matrix, a network of communications at multiple levels analogous to the neural networks of the brain. This seemed to be a great fit for me with the neuroscientific underpinning of CFT. I often sit in the group programme imagining the new neural pathways being made as the members learn to give and receive compassion. This is entirely consistent with Foulkes' ideas of a web of communication in group spaces with stretches beyond the talking, into the realms of the collective unconscious and into the spiritual joining which can happen in groups. Phase Four will illustrate the ways that we have adapted and extended the ideas from Gestalt Therapy about using chairs as a medium for psychotherapeutic change and growth.

Another central theme that joins therapeutic communities and group analytic theory is the facilitator as conductor, supporting the orchestra to play. This is particularly pertinent for this group of people whose experience of authority has invariably been toxic. I will explore this further in Phase Two, but suffice to say that this idea supports

---

9   Harrison, T., (2000) *Bion, Rickman, Foulkes, and the Northfield Experiments*. Jessica Kingsley Publishers.

letting go of the need to be 'leading from the front'. In fact, Tom Harrison has in the title of his book about the Northfield experiments, put forward the idea of 'advancing on a different front', referencing the military roots of the work of Sigmund Foulkes, Wilfred Bion and Maxwell Jones.

Working with those who at times could barely tolerate being a room with others, let alone share something of themselves with a group, required more than a talking space. Developing therapeutic day programmes for people with a diagnosis of personality disorder who had been unable to make use of any other therapeutic interventions offered an opportunity to train in and begin to integrate action methods and sociometry. Psychodrama and play seemed to provide something much needed in the group psychotherapy space. But as we will explore later, play is often much feared and scorned by those who have not learned how, or been allowed, to play.

Jacob Moreno, like Foulkes, changed his name, left his home and moved to start his 'theatre of spontaneity' practice in the USA. Foulkes and Moreno were both of the view that the group could be the therapeutic agent for change and flourishing, a distinct move away from the more dyadic ideas that prevailed about the possibilities of group work. Within both models there was an explicit invitation for group members to project aspects of their inner world onto and into the group to enable the development of new meaning. Of course, the method was generally verbal for one and in action for the other, as Zerko Moreno reminds us, 'Don't tell me, show me'.

Moreno's interest has always been in the roles that people inhabit and the consequent impact on their basic functioning. This was underpinned by a move away from more traditional psychoanalytic thinking about pathology and symptomatology and towards a model of understanding the significance of role development as a precursor to personality development:[10]

> *'Moreno's idea is that the concept of role is, above all practical, aimed at helping people to reflect on and change the beliefs they have about themselves.'*[11]

The concept of role-taking was designed within psychodrama as a means of exploring, expanding and strengthening the more functioning aspects of self, via an explicit intentional process. Over time, I have added the explicit practice of compassion, as you

---

10   Moreno, J. L. (1987). *The Essential Moreno: Writings on psychodrama, group method, and spontaneity*. Springer Publishing Company. https://books.google.co.uk/books?hl = en&lr = &id = dIAJWORz1JIC&oi = fnd&pg = PR5&dq = moreno + 1987&ots = NzPt3GySqx&sig = mvMvaDOLo44HN_BOgFr-W0hVtzo

11   Blatner, A. (1991). Role dynamics: A comprehensive theory of psychology. *Journal of Group Psychotherapy, Psychodrama & Sociometry*, **44**(1), 33–40. P.34

will see in later chapters, to form a Compassionate Self. It is therefore congruent as a method for psychological exploration and change, particularly for those whose experience of themselves has been distorted by misattuned, absent or intrusive caregivers.

Moreno's ideas about roles fit well with Paul Gilbert's social mentality theory, which highlights the fact that all living things have certain roles and tasks to perform in life that centre around survival and reproduction.[12] Part of these tasks is to develop social roles with members of the same species. For example, many mammals compete with each other for resources, engage in sexual reproductive behaviour, build alliances, create status hierarchies and engage in caring for offspring. These motivational systems come with their own neurophysiological architectures and physiological mediators. Understanding, enacting and changing roles, multiple selves or parts has come to form the basis of the CFGP programme, based on the weaving of this way of thinking about the self.

Linked to this were Moreno's keen observations of play and spontaneity in children, which are so often lost through the process of ageing and 'maturation'. His intention was to harness this childlike spontaneity and creativity within the psychotherapeutic process. Kipper is keen to differentiate between 'spontaneity' as it is used in common parlance, which implies a level of impulsivity, and the psycho-dramatic concept of 'spontaneity', which describes the energy of action in the present moment.[13] He introduces the concept of 'spontaneity training' as a metaphor for the psychotherapeutic practice which links to Moreno's belief in the positive correlation between capacity for spontaneous and creative action and emotional well-being. This has become a bedrock of my therapeutic work as I have come to the realisation that most of my group members are deeply fearful and mistrusting of play, as we will explore later in the phases. Through action, group members are invited to begin to train their minds in compassion with the use of spontaneous creativity, supported by their fellow group members in an affiliative process of understanding and repair.

Last, but most definitely not least, we turn to Irvine Yalom; you will hear his words of wisdom resonate throughout this book.[14] Bion, Foulkes and Moreno were the architects of defined theoretical models of group psychotherapy, with all the inherent blind spots. But Irvine Yalom has been the gatherer of stories from all these and more to offer sound, helpful and practical advice in setting up and running groups. Yalom's ideas about authenticity, honesty, self-disclosure and, ultimately, compassionate courage sit as a circle of strength around the whole of compassion-focused group psychotherapy. My

---

12 Gilbert, P. (2005). *Compassion: Conceptualisations, research and use in psychotherapy*. Routledge.
13 Kipper, D. A. (1986). *Psychotherapy Through Clinical Role Playing*. Brunner/Mazel.
14 Yalom, I. D. (1995). *The Theory and Practice of Group Psychotherapy*. Basic Books (AZ).

motivation to share honestly the stories of failure and frustration have been inspired by his work. I recall reading *Love's Executioner* and being moved to tears of connection and a deep gratitude for someone who could share their struggles with such grace.

As we move through the book, I will introduce many of the key ideas from all these theoretical models which I have borrowed and imbibed with compassionate purpose.

Storytelling and our ancestral history

To round off, I turn to stories and storytelling which is the last thread of influence I would like you to consider as we move towards the nuts and bolts of this book. If we are to consider groups and why they might be helpful, we must turn back to our ancestral roots and consider the experiences of hunter gatherer societies, who were successful through connection and cooperation. I think our ancestors got a bad reputation for brutality and a lack of sophistication, however in the absence of moralising gods they demonstrated a highly cooperative way of being towards the whole community.[15] They co-parented children who were passed around societal groups with great freedom and mutual responsibility.[16] Paul Gilbert reminds us that this way of raising children offers the child multiple secure adults to seek proximity with, rather than relying on a flawed nuclear family ideal. Yuval Harari, in his brief history of mankind, suggests that agriculture brought a lot more hardship and a move towards competing and withholding, and he playfully suggests that the crops domesticated us and not the other way round.[17]

Our human history, regardless of race or culture, is full of the rich oral storytelling traditions, from Odysseus in Greek mythology to 'The Wife of Bath' in *The Canterbury Tales* and all the way back to our ancestors who told stories to keep the cold out and prepare their young ones for the world outside the cave. We have sat around fires jostling for space, laughing, sighing and ultimately shaping cultures and transmitting knowledge for perhaps almost as long as there have been humans. We have often created the ancestral fire in our group room, with scarfs and our imagination, to tell the untold stories of sadness and joy.

---

15   Smith, A., Pedersen, E. J., Forster, D. E., McCullough, M. E., & Lieberman, D. (2017). Cooperation: The roles of interpersonal value and gratitude. *Evolution and Human Behavior*, **38**(6), 695–703.

16   Topa, W., & Narvaez, D. (2022). *Restoring the Kinship Worldview: Indigenous voices introduce 28 precepts for rebalancing life on planet earth*. North Atlantic Books. https://books.google.co.uk/books?hl=en&lr=&id=ffE3EAAAQBAJ&oi=fnd&pg=PR17&dq=darcia+narvaez+kinship+worldview&ots=vtMbiJjqJd&sig=DRLeNslQEHKeZeHJWAOaDouBxKY

17   Harari, Y. N. (2014). Sapiens: A brief history of humankind. *Harvill Secker*. https://books.google.co.uk/books?hl=en&lr=&id=B4ARBAAAQBAJ&oi=fnd&pg=PP9&dq=sapiens+a+brief+history+of+humankind&ots=tQgtmgHsBK&sig=LUvVbPluJxS_tVYPKJQGNlJsTzM

Some of us have forgotten about this fundamental aspect of our common humanity, but the inspirational work of Darcia Narvez and her concept of the Evolved Nest has connected me with how fundamental this is in our psychotherapy programmes.[18] Nature-based cultures have most definitely not forgotten that humans have evolved in cooperative bands and groups who survived based on their capacity to cooperate and work together. Darcia makes a distinction between the competitive detachment which is afflicting our society with the consequent impact on physical emotional and spiritual well-being. She suggests ways that we can develop cooperative companionship and a compassionate culture in which we are more careful about where we direct our attention. This, I believe, fits well with all the models I am weaving together: collective responsibility, compassionate courage, living and learning together, and ultimately turning back to and not away from difficulty, pain and suffering.

I have adopted some of these ideas explicitly and implicitly into the developing compassion-focused group psychotherapy programme and we will hear later about the ways that we cultivate this compassionate capacity and how this then manifests in the group experiencing themselves as a tribe with a shared language and common compassionate purpose.

In conclusion

What emerged from all the blending, weaving and mobilising was compassion-focused group psychotherapy which integrates a process-driven group psychotherapy format with more structured components to foster a sense of social safety and safeness, a secure base and safe haven between group members.[19] Dyadic and small group tasks, with careful attention to the development of the capacity of group members to tolerate the shared group space, aim to foster affiliative connections and shared experiences between group members.[20]

CFGP has elements of group analytic theory and practice delivered through a medium of action methods and psychodrama. 'Action methods' describes the use of visual, tactile and role based psychological interventions which were derived from psychodrama to support perspective taking, conflict resolution and the development of new meaning to past events.

---

18 Topa, W., & Narvaez, D. (2022). *Restoring the Kinship Worldview: Indigenous voices introduce 28 precepts for rebalancing life on planet earth*. North Atlantic Books. https://books.google.co.uk/books?hl = en&lr = &id = ffE3EAAAQ BAJ&oi = fnd&pg = PR17&dq = darcia + narvaez + kinship + worldview&ots = vtMbiJjqJd&sig = DRLeNslQEHKeZe HJWAOaDouBxKY

19 Kalleklev, J., & Karterud, S. (2018). A comparative study of a mentalization-based versus a psychodynamic group therapy session. *Group Analysis*, **51**(1), 44–60.

20 Bateman, A., & Fonagy, P. (2006). *Mentalization-based Treatment for Borderline Personality Disorder: A Practical Guide*. OUP Oxford.

Within the psychotherapeutic process of CFGP, the issues of ruptured attachments are addressed initially through explicit teaching – training in the cultivation of compassion for the self and for others, and learning to tolerate receiving it from others. The Compassionate Mind Training (CMT) focus of this aspect of the work is to develop a safe haven within the therapy space to enable habituation to the experience of social safeness and, in time, to enable the movement to a secure base.

On a very basic level, people with A&RT often experience somatic memories of early trauma which are triggered by being in group settings. The combination of CMT practices, with movement and play-based activities, is designed to offer participants practical ways to feel safe and contained in the group space. In doing so, the programme was developed as a model to rebuild some of the functions of attachment such as 'safe-relating' as a secure base, proximity seeking and safe haven, these being primary functions of the early attachment system to enable a process of growth and development.

The cultivated capacity for compassion is then used to turn back to early traumatised attachment relationships and rebuild, change endings, and let go of painful restimulating memories and people.

The Guidebook for Compassion Focused Group Psychotherapy

So hopefully it is now clear who this programme is for and how and why it was developed. This book is designed to be something of a guidebook for the mountain climb that has now been running for over ten years, without a break. We will start with the first contact with group members, the beginning of the programme, through all the twists and turns, to the ending and beyond.

This group programme is run within an NHS tertiary psychotherapy service in the UK, offering long term psychodynamically informed psychotherapies to people with complex emotional needs and those who may attract a diagnosis of personality disorder. Other versions of this are offered in community outpatient services, prisons and private practice.

| Phase 1 Assessment and formulation | Phase 2 Waiting list group | Phase 3 Preparation and engagement group | Phase 4 Compassion focused trauma group | Phase 5 Moving on group |

Flowchart of the programme

Phase and chapter overview

Compassion-focused group psychotherapy has five consecutive phases, shown above in the flowchart and explained in more detail in the table below. We split the 12-week psychoeducation phase from the 12-month exploratory phase to ensure that the group members did not end up doing 12 months of psychoeducation! In practice, the programme is 15 months long with two component parts, a 12-week Preparation and Engagement Group followed by a 12-month compassion-focused trauma group. Group members complete the PEG, Phase Three, on week 12, and start the CFTG on week 13, so there is no break between the two elements of the programme.

My intention is to create a flow in the book which replicates the flow of the five phases of the programme. The unintended consequence of this will be a variation in the lengths of the phases, with some being much longer than others. Each phase will be subdivided into chapters as needed. For example, phase 1.1, 1.2, 1.3 etc. Each section of this book will cover a single phase with the following structure:

- A brief overview of theoretical material.
- A description and explanation of the unique components of the CFGP model.
- Relevant quotations from the qualitative study.
- Case studies and material to illustrate.
- Practical examples of the way the mod el works in action.

The five phases of compassion-focused group psychotherapy

Programme element	Format	Function
1. Assessment and Formulation Process	■ Three individual sessions with one of the psychotherapists from group programme ■ Opportunity for final group-based assessment session	■ Initial engagement with patient ■ Establishing trust ■ Safe haven function in the room ■ Commencement of narrative-based formulating and sense making process ■ Containment for the therapeutic work ■ Commencement of psychoeducation phase of treatment ■ Provision of a consistent containing informal space
2. Waiting List Group Psychoeducation	■ Monthly one-hour drop-in sessions ■ Facilitated by Lived Experience Practitioner (a service user who has completed the CFGP) and a psychotherapist ■ Informal setting, amplified by the offer of tea and biscuits	■ For patient to feel 'held in mind' by group facilitators ■ Offering information about programme ■ Opportunity for connection with other patients, pre therapy ■ Continuing development of safe haven function ■ Exposure to an experience of being in a group setting ■ Managing risk during pre-therapy phase of treatment
3. Preparation and Engagement Group (PEG) Psychoeducation and Compassionate Mind Training	■ 12 weekly sessions ■ Two hours in duration (no break)	■ Continuation of psychoeducation phase ■ Introduction of compassionate mind training practices and rationale ■ Early exposure to CFGP model and the experience of compassion across the three flows

Programme element	Format	Function
(Continued)	■ Slow paced, experiential, play-based group intervention ■ Facilitated by two highly trained compassion-focused psychotherapists	■ Continuing development of safe haven and proximity seeking function
4. Compassion-Focused Trauma Group (CFTG) Compassion-focused Therapy	■ 52 weekly sessions ■ Two hours (no break) 'putting compassion to work' ■ Facilitated by the same two highly trained compassion-focused psychotherapists	■ Using the capacity for compassion developed in the PEG to turn back towards early ruptured attachment relationships ■ Using the group as a secure base to begin to explore past and present relationships ■ Bringing compassion to shame-based trauma memories ■ Using the group process to develop new attachment relationships ■ Working with conflict (internal and in the group) ■ Using the group process to explicitly and implicitly stimulate the care giving and care receiving social mentalities
5. The Moving On Group Individuation	■ 12 monthly one-hour drop-in sessions ■ Patients not discharged if they do not attend	■ Supporting the gradual process of individuation ■ Enabling the grieving process to be resolved ■ Providing a platform for patients to engage in peer led support

Programme element	Format	Function
(Continued)	■ Facilitated by Lived Experience Practitioner (a service user who has completed the CFGP) and a psychotherapist ■ Slow-paced group that is member led	

The voices from the Group

We will stop off on our mountain climb and take in the view, hearing from the group members who have shaped the programme with their generous and sometimes painful feedback. These words of wisdom from the group are taken from a qualitative research study that invited 11 graduates from the programme to share their experiences, and these transcripts were analysed using thematic analysis methodology. The full study is reported in Lucre et al (2024) and Lucre *et al* (in press).[21] The group members who contributed to this research and who gave their permission for their words to be used, will not be named and no identifying details about them will be given in this text. The words, however, are a verbatim account of their experience.

Introducing Louie, Adam, Sherelle, Dalvinder and Jane

As we move through the five phases of the programme, the key components and practical application of the model will be illustrated with examples and case studies of group members. We will particularly focus on the journeys of five group members, their struggles and triumphs through the CFGP programme. All circumstantial material, background history and presenting issues will be based on actual events and people, but each case study is an amalgamation of multiple people, a composite character. It is important to note, however, that all the scenarios presented are factually accurate and did indeed occur in the way described.

---

21 Lucre, K. (2022). Compassion Focused Group Psychotherapy for people who could attract a diagnosis of personality disorder. *In Compassion Focused Therapy: Clinical practice and applications*. Routledge/Taylor & Francis Group.

Significant changes in the personal and historical details have been made and key information mixed up to protect the confidentiality of each of the group members whose journey in compassion will provide the foundation for this book. It is my wish that the illustrative material you read is authentic and represents the complexity, struggles and perseverance of the group members in this programme. So it may be that group members who read this book may recognise a scenario described but all the identifiable information will have been changed.

The phases will also be illustrated by case vignettes of other group members whose stories will be reported accurately with significant details changed. But first, let us turn to the characters whose psychotherapeutic journey we will be following.

The short biographies of these five group members are at the back of the book (p.330) for ease of checking back for more detail as you read.

Louie

Louie is a 54-year-old man of mixed heritage, referred to psychotherapy services after many years of short-term cognitive behavioural interventions, mainly focused on managing anger. Most had been reportedly unsuccessful as it has been difficult for Louie to tolerate being challenged.

Louie grew up in a large family as one of the youngest of seven siblings, all of whom suffered with significant emotional and mental health difficulties. Both parents had significant alcohol dependency, and by the time I met Louie, his parents had both died from alcohol related illness. There was brutal, cruel and instrumental violence within the family where parents and siblings used violence indiscriminately. Louie had not managed to complete his education, having been excluded from school in the context of repeated absence and violent incidents.

He was involved with criminal gangs from a young age, but avoided prison, stating that he 'got away with it'. Louie had been diagnosed with narcissistic and paranoid personality disorder, with reports indicating that he presented with little or no remorse or his actions. There was a general sense of therapeutic pessimism about Louie's capacity to engage with any therapeutic work.

There was some suggestion that his previous partner had fled taking their son with her, out of concern for her safety. Although it was not clear at the time of assessment, there was some suggestion in his notes that he may have posed a risk to his intimate partners. He came to CFGP stating that this was the 'end of the road' and he had been told by his care team that it was his last chance. No pressure there then!

Adam

Adam, a white English man, came to psychotherapy services at the age of 35 as a new referral to mental health services. At this point after an initial meeting with a psychiatrist, he was diagnosed with borderline and paranoid personality disorder.

He had been in the prison system but had never been assessed or offered any form of psychotherapy or mental health care. Despite a significant history of physical abuse, neglect and sexual trauma (at the hands of an individual known to his family), he never came to the attention of services. He was groomed over many years and sexually abused. This continued despite disclosing the abuse to his mother. This was in the context of prolonged neglect and physical abuse from his mother which teachers at school 'turned a blind eye' to. Adam had no siblings and never knew his father, and despite requests, was never given any information about him by his mother.

He had struggled significantly with addiction to substances and had been convicted of multiple offences related to possession and distribution, which had involved a number of prison sentences. The ways in which he hurt and punished himself included starving himself, pulling the hair from his beard and hitting himself, often with objects. This did not come to light until much later in his journey. Adam had been in a committed relationship in his early adulthood and had a daughter. This relationship had ended abruptly in the context of a serious incident of domestic violence. We were not aware of any of this until much later in the therapeutic work. He came to psychotherapy services perhaps quite unclear about what, if anything, could be offered or would be helpful, or even if he had the right to ask for anything.

Sherelle

Sherelle, of mixed heritage, was referred to psychotherapy services at the age of 38 having been involved in social care and health services her entire life. Sherelle's notes indicate that she was diagnosed with dependent and borderline personality disorder in her late teenage years, but this was not communicated to her. She tells a story about her mother screaming in a courtroom holding Sherelle as a newborn baby when the family court decision was made to remove her from the care of her parents. Her early life was scattered across multiple failed foster and care home placements, separation from her siblings and sporadic contact with her parents, which generally ended in re-entry into the care system until their early alcohol-related deaths. She had two younger siblings who were placed in different homes and eventually adopted by the same family. She lost touch with them after this.

Sherelle's young life was characterised by repeated experiences of intrusion and abuse. Her parents were both neglectful, intrusive and abusive, at times coming to the care homes to try to forcibly remove her, often resulting in violent exchanges with the home staff, Sherelle and her parents. Sherelle started her therapy journey with a fixed belief that she and her parents had been wronged by the system and that they had always had her best interests at heart.

Sherelle's adult life followed a similar pattern, with many violent and controlling partners, and five children who were all taken into the care system, which she has fought tirelessly. She has had many admissions to inpatient services following impulsive overdoses and taking herself to a local car park where she considered jumping. All these events have been connected with significant decisions made in relation to her children. Two of her children are in the care of her ex-partner's family, despite her disclosure of domestic violence and abuse in the relationship.

Dalvinder

Dalvinder, of Pakistani heritage, came to the psychotherapy service at age 28, in the midst of a conflict and rupture with their mental health care team, whom they perceived had been withholding care. This had led to a complaint which had taken many months to resolve, which had further delayed their access to an assessment and subsequent treatment. This experience seems to be a mirror of Dalvinder's early life, which had involved being a carer for their mother without any recourse to support (formal or informal). In their early life, their own needs had been subjugated and feelings of anger or injustice were not permitted. They spoke of constantly being reminded of how much their mother was suffering and that they ought not to complain. This suppression also included Dalvinder's gender identity, as non-binary, which was also denied and evoked disgust and anger from within their community. Dalvinder's father had been authoritarian and harsh, abdicating all responsibility for the care of his wife to Dalvinder before leaving the family in dire financial straits.

The sexual abuse they suffered from a school support teacher created further fragmentation with the approach-avoidance conflict, with this teacher being one of the first people to take an interest in and provide support for Dalvinder.

Dalvinder had struggled with intimate relationships and seemed to be unsure of their sexual orientation. Within their social network, it seemed that they were either pulled into a caring role or in a battle to be cared for by friends. Their broader social network evolved around campaigning for change in the community, but this seemed generally unsatisfying to Dalvinder. Often Dalvinder was caught in a battle with services and external agencies to ensure that services met their needs, perhaps replacing friendships and partners with care coordinators and support workers.

Dalvinder had been given a diagnosis of borderline personality disorder but they did not agree and had raised a formal complaint and demanded a second opinion.

Jane

Sixty-year-old Jane, a retired white English woman who lived alone for all of her adult life, was referred to psychotherapy services following the completion of 12 sessions of CBT to treat depression. Jane was diagnosed with a depressive disorder, but this did not take into account the significant early trauma that marred her childhood. Her early life had been characterised by heavily critical and physically harmful parents who had insisted on her admission to inpatient services at the age of 14 years, where she remained on and off until the age of 17. It was difficult to establish the reasons for the long admission beyond an impulsive overdose at the age of 14 years.

Jane had one young sister who she had felt was the favourite. She had been heavily involved in caring for her sister, with a wish to protect her from the overly punitive and harsh treatment she had received. Jane's sister Joanne went on to have healthy, stable relationships, and she married and had children. Conversely, Jane has avoided intimate relationships and close friendships of any kind throughout her life. The understandable threads of resentment that she carried did not emerge until later in the therapeutic work.

Despite graduating from her medical training with honours, she was never able to sustain work as a doctor and sought part-time work in a local library. Jane struggled with binge-eating difficulties and found it almost impossible to throw anything away, to the point where only one room in her home was accessible (we didn't know this about Jane until much later in the group process).

I will remind the reader of the details of each character prior to their first appearance in the text.

The use and importance of language

Although I will be introducing you to the idea of therapists as 'conductors' of the group, I will use the term 'facilitator' to describe the therapists who run the group. During the assessment phase, they are referred to as 'therapists'.

I will refer to our group members as either 'patients' or 'group members' depending on which phase they are in within the psychotherapy programme. The use of word 'patient' is important as this links to the original meaning of the term from the Latin, meaning 'one who suffers'. Recent studies involving patients have also indicated a preference for this term which is understood and familiar, over 'client or service user'.[22] This

---

22   Adil, J. (2010). Ancient origins of the term patient. *The Psychiatrist*, **34**(3), 117–118. https://doi.org/10.1192/pb.34.3.117b

resonates with the model of compassion-focused group psychotherapy, supporting a process whereby those who suffer can be supported to turn back to and not away from suffering, and find healing and growth.

Once in group, patients become 'group members', with the inferred collective responsibility that accompanies this term. They move from being singular often isolated and alone, to becoming part of (the) group, 'family' or 'tribe'. As one group member described, 'I went from being all on my own, very much just me, to being like we were all a bunch of warriors'.

> *'It only worked when we all put in something it's like full group full room, it's like the group was the catalyst kind of thing but what made the substance of the work and what helped was us all being the participants in it, definitely, if we hadn't done what we done together, joined in it wouldn't have worked.'*

This quote describes the importance of the group and everyone being in the room together, with a shared intention towards themselves and each other, which we will return to throughout the book.

The development of a shared language for the group programme is essential to ensure that everyone is clear about what compassion is and, more importantly, what it is not. It takes huge courage to turn back to and not away from the suffering caused by others. It is therefore equally important that we start with a shared understanding of compassion and how this underpins the compassion-focused group psychotherapy programme and my reason for writing this book and doing this work.

Final thought

> *'Everyone wants to live on top of the mountain, but all the happiness and growth occur while you are climbing it.'*

Climbing, I believe, is a lot like psychotherapy. It is during the journey towards discovery, change and growth that we learn the most about ourselves, not when we reach the summit. Often there is no summit, as the journey is lifelong. Change and compassion are not something we 'nail', tick off or complete. They are goals we commit to journeying towards for the rest of our lives. I will take you on a journey, which is inextricably linked with the science and practice of compassion. This path first invites us to turn back to, and not away from, suffering and difficulty, and to do so courageously and with strength, before moving into wise action to alleviate and prevent.

So too it is for compassion-focused group psychotherapy. Members are invited to join and support each other through the psychotherapeutic process and beyond. But as Yalom reminds us, 'If you want to choose the pleasure of growth, prepare yourself for some pain'. Group psychotherapy is not for the faint hearted, as one of our programme graduates reminds us:

> 'Compassion was an alien concept ... scared the crap out of me ... but feeling compassion for everybody understanding that it was compassion for everybody and that they were feeling compassion towards me without any strong ... without any other motives... It was very, very strange. You were with a group you were asking for help and they're asking for help and you were helping each other ... asking for help in the beginning was hard.'

I am constantly reminded of the immense courage and commitment required to keep turning up week after week, to tolerate the ruptures, manage the repairs, and slowly use the group to develop new attachment relationships, with compassion at their core:

> 'Compassion is not a relationship between the healer and the wounded. It's a relationship between equals. Only when we know our own darkness well can we be present with the darkness of others. Compassion becomes real when we recognize our shared humanity.'[23]

This is certainly true for all elements of the programme. Group members are invited to join up with the facilitators and each other to co-create safeness for a space for therapeutic change and growth to be possible. The facilitators are guides on the journey, not the leaders, and will learn much about themselves in the process.

---

23 Chodron, P. (2018). *Becoming Bodhisattvas: A Guidebook for Compassionate Action*. Shambhala Publications. https://books.google.co.uk/books?hl = en&lr = &id = dQBlDwAAQBAJ&oi = fnd&pg = PT7&dq = pema + choden + buddhism&ots = zDmlD_0gVh&sig = sG5_g1LxHGX2V6jAsq5Ujz9s6Ks

Phase One:
Assessment and Formulation

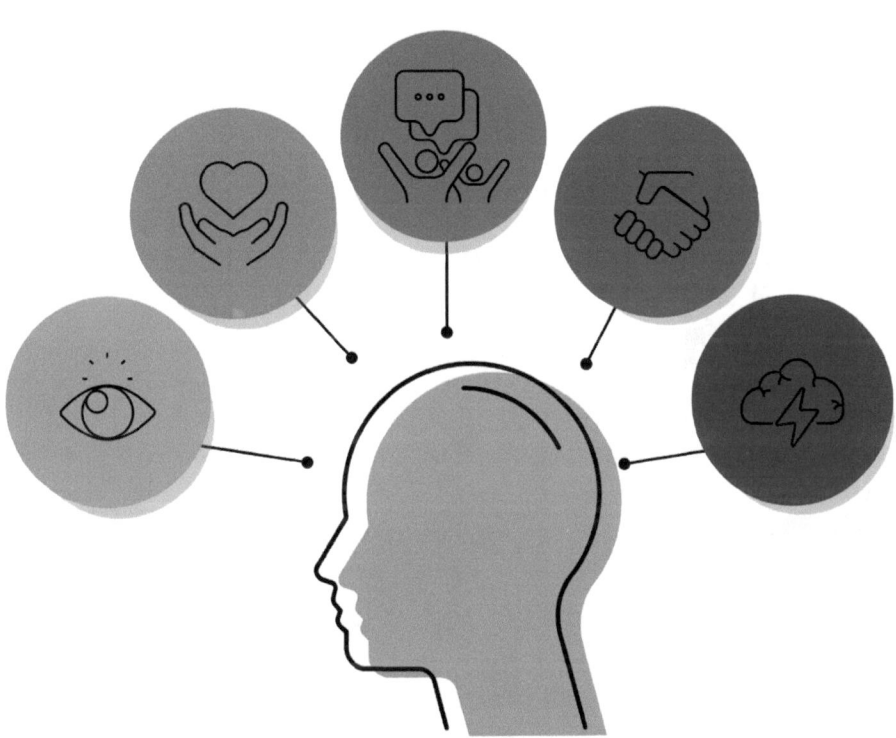

Programme element	Format	Function
1. Assessment and Formulation process	■ Multiple individual sessions with one of the psychotherapists from the group programme. ■ Opportunity for a final group-based assessment session.	■ Initial engagement with the patient. ■ Establishing trust. ■ Provides a safe haven, secure base and proximity function in the room. ■ Commencement of narrative-based formulating and sense-making process. ■ Containment for the therapeutic work. ■ Commencement of psychoeducation phase of treatment.

Chapter 1.1: The practicalities of the assessment

Cultivating the conditions for safeness

Compassion-focused group psychotherapy is a group programme developed specifically to rebuild some of the functions of the attachment system, such as a secure base and safe haven. The therapeutic space can offer empathic engagement, connectedness, validation, confidence-building and an opportunity to work through unprocessed emotions and traumatic memories. Before any of this can take place, however, we must work quite hard to get our patients into the assessment room. It is only once they have landed with us that we can begin to cultivate the conditions for safeness. We will explore the myriad ways that this can be done and supported, including some of the pitfalls I have encountered on the way.

I liken this process to the essential and mindful time needed to gather everything you need for a journey into the mountains. Checking the weather, the terrain and your maps, and ensuring you've got the right gear. This is not nearly as exciting as the actual climbing part, but you don't want to find yourself halfway up the first pitch having forgotten your water bottle! I have actually arrived at the base of a mountain with only one climbing boot – this was a very short expedition. I have similarly sat in many assessment rooms wondering how I was going to address the fact that I do not have a watch and the clock is behind my head! Slowing down and using our personal practice in compassion is a good starting point.

I am often asked about the ideal duration, frequency etc. of a group programme. My response is always to invite people to consider why they want to run a group in the first place. Is it a service requirement or deep and long-held passion, or, if you are lucky, both? Starting with some clarity about our own compassionate intention towards the work will be deeply helpful on what can often be a dark and arduous journey. Like being clear why you are setting off up the side of a mountain or cliff, the glory of the end may not be not enough to sustain you through the cold hours, stiff limbs and dehydration!

For many, these questions will be answered by service need and requirements. But where there are choices, I am keen for the group programme to replicate as much as possible the real world your group members will return to. Single issue or gendered groups can offer a strong experience of cohesion but may not help the group to translate their experiences in group to their lives outside.

So, developing and understanding your own compassionate intention towards the work may take some time and practice, as Tobyn Bell and colleagues encourage us to explore as a basis on which to build our therapeutic work.[24] Using the practice of compassion to support ourselves is vital to cultivating embodied distress tolerance and therapeutic courage, as Neil Clapton and Syd Hiskey remind us in their work exploring the utility of martial arts for compassion-focused therapists.[25]

Tobyn Bell also invites us to consider how we might develop an internal compassionate supervisor to 'act as a role model for their own compassionate enactments as therapists'. This seems to be good place to start, coupled with a supportive actual supervisor to guide the process.

---

24 Kolts, R. L., *et al.* (2018) *Experiencing Compassion-Focused Therapy from the Inside Out.* Guilford Publications.
25 Clapton, N. E., & Hiskey, S. (2023). The way is in training: martial arts-informed compassionate mind training to enhance CFT therapists' compassionate competencies. *OBM Integrative and Complementary Medicine*, **8**(1), Article 1. https://doi.org/10.21926/obm.icm.2301001

Imbibed with our compassionate intention, and with an internal compassionate supervisor and our real compassionate supervisors all on board, we can begin to consider who we might like to invite to our group programme. This will also help guide the length and duration of the group programme.

Getting started

'Transforming [a] twinkle into the reality of a group' is a practical process, involving many 'apparently mundane tasks' which are associated with ensuring that the group is a safe, containing and consistent space for members to join and engage with.[26] The initial setting and then holding of the therapeutic frame provides a supportive boundary for the therapeutic work as it unfolds.

Cynthia Rogers speaks about the clear significance of the 'behind the scenes' preparation and ongoing work, which is focused on the development of the psychological functions of evolved caring, a secure base and a safe haven within the therapeutic space. It seems that the explicit and implicit process of administrating the group weaves together practical elements with a deeper understanding of the meaning of such matters for the group. Irvine Yalom also advises us that this early work will decide the 'fate' of the group, whether it flourishes or flounders. All this before anyone has stepped foot in the room. This can be collectively described as 'dynamic administration', fundamentally important and often overlooked when we are setting up a group.

The development and facilitation of the overlapping attachment functions of a secure base, a safe haven and proximity seeking within the group, require administration and attention from therapists from the outset. Your patients will likely not have had this fundamentally important and repeated experience of predictable, reliable caring others, and this lack, over time, becomes internalised. Many parents have been unable to create a safe haven for their infants to cling to in times of distress or to provide a secure base from which to explore the world. This means that these infants learn not to seek proximity to their primary caregivers, and their internal working model, or 'blueprint', carries a low expectation of receiving care or understanding from others.

First contact

The process of cultivating safeness begins at the outset of engaging with the patient, even before the first assessment appointment. Let us begin by paying close attention to the initial contact that a patient might receive from the service: what is it like to receive their invitation letter? Is the tone welcoming? Does the letter offer helpful information?

---

26 Behr, H., & Hearst, L. (2008). *Group-analytic Psychotherapy: A meeting of minds.* John Wiley & Sons.

Does the patient know what they are coming for and what to expect? It is important to consider these questions. Although dropout before initial contact has not been explored with any academic rigour, there is some suggestion that that many patients (20-40%) do not attend first appointments, but we can only guess the reasons why.[27] It may be that a more personal and less standardised approach to initial contact may facilitate and support the initial engagement process. I would like to invite you to spend some time looking at the standard communications that are sent to patients where you work. Perhaps bring some curiosity about how you would feel if you were to receive this as your first contact from a psychotherapy service.

Spend time walking through the entrance and waiting room of your building, imagining yourself as a patient coming for the first time. This will guide you into considering what might be needed to make your waiting room more welcoming or warm. How we greet our patients, introduce ourselves – those early moments of the assessment process will likely determine whether they come back and also what they feel able to share with you. Good working relationships with those who administrate the place where you work are of vital importance. These staff are the very first physical contact with your patient and the experience matters. Many patients speak about experiences of being greeted by the administrative staff on first arrival and how much it meant to them to be treated with respect and kindness.

The next step is to consider how we respond when patients don't attend their appointments with us. Do we send a standard Did Not Attend (DNA) letter? I invite you to wonder how this is experienced. Many of our patients have had repeated experiences of punitive and critical interactions with authority figures, often stretching all the way back into early childhood. In such situations, it may become difficult to disentangle past and present. I am always sorry when people do not come to the initial assessment appointment with me, so I express this in my letters and invite them to contact me.
In some cases, it may be helpful to reach out with a phone call, but this can be tricky when we do not have a relationship with the person.

Introducing Jane's experience of misattunement in the assessment process

Sixty-year-old Jane, is a retired English woman who has lived alone for all of her adult life. She was referred to psychotherapy services following the completion of 12 sessions of CBT to treat depression. Jane's early life had been characterised by heavily critical and physically harmful parents who had insisted on her admission to inpatient services at the age of 14 years, where she remained on and off until the age of 17. It was difficult to

---

27 Mitchell, A. J., & Selmes, T. (2007). Why don't patients attend their appointments? Maintaining engagement with psychiatric services. *Advances in Psychiatric Treatment*, **13**(6), 423–434.

establish the reasons for the long admission beyond an impulsive overdose at the age of 14 years. Despite graduating from her medical training with honours, she was never able to sustain work as a doctor and sought part-time work in a local library.

Jane was referred to the psychotherapy services with a very brief letter stating that she found CBT unhelpful and so perhaps needed something of longer duration. This pattern was then repeated by the psychotherapy service, in that she was not given very much information about the service and what she could expect. She attended the appointment and, when she arrived, was unable to park in the disabled bay (she was a blue badge holder) as someone had blocked access to it. She advised the staff about her accessibility needs but somehow this was overlooked. During the assessment, she spoke a lot about the room being cold and finding the chairs uncomfortable, leaving her feeling pain after the sessions. It was not possible to connect her physical discomfort with her experience of coming to the assessment. The assessment summary that was sent to Jane, which was written to the referrer, was long and very detailed (seven pages of A4). This was perhaps an attempt to make sense of and conceptualise what had happened in the assessment room, but was experienced by Jane as another example of her being overlooked.

By attending closely to the early stages of Jane's contact with the service, it may have been possible to engage with her about her actual experience and what this meant to her. Also, some space to acknowledge where we may have made errors or overlooked her in the preparation for the assessment may have been helpful and was a missed opportunity. It is hoped that, during early sessions, we can try to join up the patient's experience in the external world with their internal processes. In practice for Jane, this may have meant a gentle enquiry about the possible connections between being unable to find a space to park and the feeling that there may not be space for her in the therapy or the mind of the therapist. For Jane, it took many months in the therapy group to support her to name, and for us to work through, the ruptures which had occurred in the assessment process and how this had repeated her early life tragedy

Once they are in the room

Compassion-focused group psychotherapy specifically addresses difficulties with shame-based trauma, self-criticism and how they manifest within interpersonal and intrapersonal relationships. The assessment should therefore focus on exploring the following areas:

- Motivation to engage in therapy.
- Reflective function and capacity.
- Issues of risk to self and others.
- Capacity to form a therapeutic alliance.

- Tolerance of challenge.
- Capacity to work within a frame of psychotherapeutic intervention.

This all seems very sensible, but it is also a great challenge to accurately establish in a short period of time, when the conditions for safeness have not been established. We may therefore need to accept that assessment is an imprecise science and relies on honest, authentic communication to support the gathering of as much information as we can.

Paul Gilbert advises us that the process of 'formulating' with your patient should always come after the basic assessment. The assessment therefore requires multiple sessions which are spaced out over several weeks to allow time for a therapeutic alliance to be established, and some initial understanding and trust to be developed. Perhaps some more time with Jane in those early weeks may have made it possible to explore the repeating pattern of feeling ignored and overlooked and the connections with her early life in an institution. This slow unfolding process is also designed to facilitate and promote a trusting relationship between therapist and patient, which is understood to be integral to the establishment of a working therapeutic alliance. Essentially, we are slowing the pace to allow time for familiar patterns of relating and being with others to be explored and understood, rather than just noted.

It is a source of some curiosity to me that we expect our deeply hurt and traumatised patients to come and meet with a stranger in a place they have never been before. Surely these are all the conditions for the activation of the threat system? Then we expect (and often require) our patients to offer a coherent, emotionally connected narrative of their early life experiences, including what they might want and need from psychotherapy. This narrative is invariably infused with shame, guilt and all the tragedy which accompanied these experiences. It is therefore quite likely in such situations that our patients will have a reactive threat response, which is either mobilised angry, sad or frightened, or immobilised shut down or submissiveness. Put simply, our attempts to be helpful and provide a space for our patients to tell their stories can become deeply re-traumatising experiences. Therefore, we must lower our expectations.

This is the therapeutic work, to support the cultivation of a space of safeness to facilitate the co-construction of a shared language and subsequently a narrative of the patient's early life tragedy. So, attending closely to the pacing and tone of these early sessions is incredibly important if we are to support the early development of a secure base and safe haven in the therapeutic process. This lays the foundations for the long process of repairing and restoring trust and cooperation that has often been so compromised and broken by our patient's (repeated) early relational experiences.

Why kindness isn't enough...

> *'I will do this compassion-focused stuff,
> if I really have to, but if you could just kick me
> at the end of every session... it would help.'*

This playful statement sheds light on a fundamentally important dynamic which will and does emerge in the context of much of the compassion-focused therapeutic work for people with attachment and relational trauma (A&RT). The underlying implication of this statement indicated the limitations of the patient's capacity to tolerate the experience of warmth and care from another, in this case, the therapist. This is likely to show up in the early stages of the assessment process and will need to be addressed to reduce the risk that our patients will become overwhelmed and withdraw.

When our patient's attachment systems are activated and they will be in the context of experiencing validation, understanding and compassion from others – this can stimulate a powerful threat-focused response. Our attachment systems are coded with all our sensory memories of early bonding, or lack thereof. When others exhibit attachment behaviours towards us, whatever is coded in the system will be activated, deep below conscious awareness. See Figure 1.1 below for an illustration. Giovani Liotti highlights the 'paradoxical fear of much desired emotional closeness and compassionate feelings'.[28] Sadly, our patients often hold a deep yearning for closeness and connection, coupled with an equally deep-seated fear and resistance. Paul Gilbert encourages us to see 'resistance as wisdom', something to be validated and understood in the context of adverse early life experiences and not as a reason to exclude someone from psychotherapy.

> ### Introducing Louie
>
> Louie is a 54-year-old man of mixed heritage, referred to psychotherapy services after many years of short-term cognitive behavioural interventions mainly focused on managing anger. Most had been reportedly unsuccessful as it has been difficult for Louie to tolerate being challenged.
>
> Louie grew up in a large family as one of the youngest of seven siblings. Both parents had significant alcohol dependency and by the time I met Louie, his parents had both died from alcohol-related illness. There was brutal, cruel and instrumental violence within the family, where parents and siblings used violence indiscriminately. Louie had not managed to complete his education, having been excluded from school in the context of repeated absence and violent incidents.

---

28 Liotti, G. (2012). Disorganized attachment and the therapeutic relationship with people in shattered states. In *Shattered States: Disorganised attachment and its repair* (pp. 127–156). Karnac Books.

Louie came for his first psychotherapy assessment and from the outset he began to describe horrifying details of the abuse he suffered at the hands of both his parents and siblings. With his head down and speaking in a low, flat tone, he started with his earliest memory and moved through years of tragedy. I was overwhelmed and deeply moved with feelings of sympathy for him and his story of being rejected at the time when he most needed care. I found myself leaning towards him as he spoke, trying to make a connection with him. He looked up, saw my face and, with a mixture of anger and confusion, stormed out of the room. At the time, I didn't understand, but upon reflection, it was perhaps too much for him to bear my concern and feelings for him. Therapy can provide a bridge to integrate the terror of early experience, but this has to be a slow and careful process.

So we may need to invite our patients to give a voice to this adverse reaction to their experience of care and normalise this and other reactions as understandable survival strategies, and not maladaptive coping strategies. In the case of Louie, I went and found him and we spent the rest of the assessment appointment sitting next to each other on the wall outside the building looking at the pigeons eating leftover sandwiches! On reflection, I think that this was my attempt to dilute the intensity of our earlier interaction and pave the way for a return to a state of regulation, and eventually to the assessment space.

Gathering in the life stories of our patients, as we have established, must be a slow-paced exercise. This gathering must come with an understanding that a coherent narrative is often not possible due to the devastating impact of early tragedy on a developing brain. It is now well understood that excessive cortisol production, which occurs in the context of prolonged exposure to neglectful, abusive and intrusive caregiving, has a significant detrimental effect on hippocampal functioning. So our patients may not be able to access the sequential memories of their experience. In his extensive work in this area, Giovani Liotti invites us to consider that the result of these adverse childhood experiences seems to be generalised fragmentation, dissociation and memory loss.[29]

Compassion-focused formulations – creating a de-shaming narrative

There is much talk of formulation as a trauma-sensitive way of responding to and making sense of our patient's difficulties. We need to be cautious, however, to ensure that formulation does not fall into the same trap as diagnosis, essentially categorising people according to preset notions and ideas.

---

29   Liotti, G. (2012). Disorganized attachment and the therapeutic relationship with people in shattered states. In *Shattered States: Disorganised attachment and its repair* (pp. 127–156). Karnac Books.

Let us begin with a gentle curiosity about presenting difficulties, bringing with us a compassionate lens and moving into formulation as the trusting relationship is established. We must support the understanding and contextualising of all experiences. Russell Kolts invites us to ask our patients, 'Knowing what you know about your life and experiences, how much does it make sense to you that you thought/felt/behaved in that way, in that situation?' Many will say 'not much'. In that case, we may need to support this co-produced autobiographical process more explicitly with how it might make sense to us.

An initial, tentative and collaborative formulation process starts at this stage, but it is then a template to return to within the psychotherapeutic process, rather than a concrete representation of the patient's pathology. If we follow and match our patient's capacity with our expectations, then the whole formulation may not be completed during Phase One.

The compassion-focused therapy formulation was devised to offer 'de-shaming' and sense-making of the threat system, with a particular focus on understanding shame and its many facets. Paul Gilbert explains the process thus:

> *'Formulation in these terms focuses first and foremost on people's efforts at self-protection, empathically validating them as understandable (if undesirable and problematic) whilst at the same exploring options to go beyond them and re-construct a sense of self and engage with self and others in warmer and more compassionate ways.'*

Having trained in CBT and been slightly baffled by the dizzying array of complex formulation diagrams, I have found it incredibly helpful and reassuring to discover the simplicity of the CFT formulation. This process can be used to support the normalising and validation of the patient experience. This replaces 'dysfunctional assumptions' and 'maladaptive coping strategies' with 'understandable survival strategies' which were developed in the context of extreme threat. The term 'unintended consequences' is used to describe the problems that the patient experiences as a consequence of their survival strategies, in that they are not intentional and often deepen the key fears. Bringing awareness and understanding is the first stage in the journey towards cultivating a compassionate intention, turning towards and not away from difficulty.

Figure 1.2: Compassion-focused therapy formulation – 'This is how I survived'

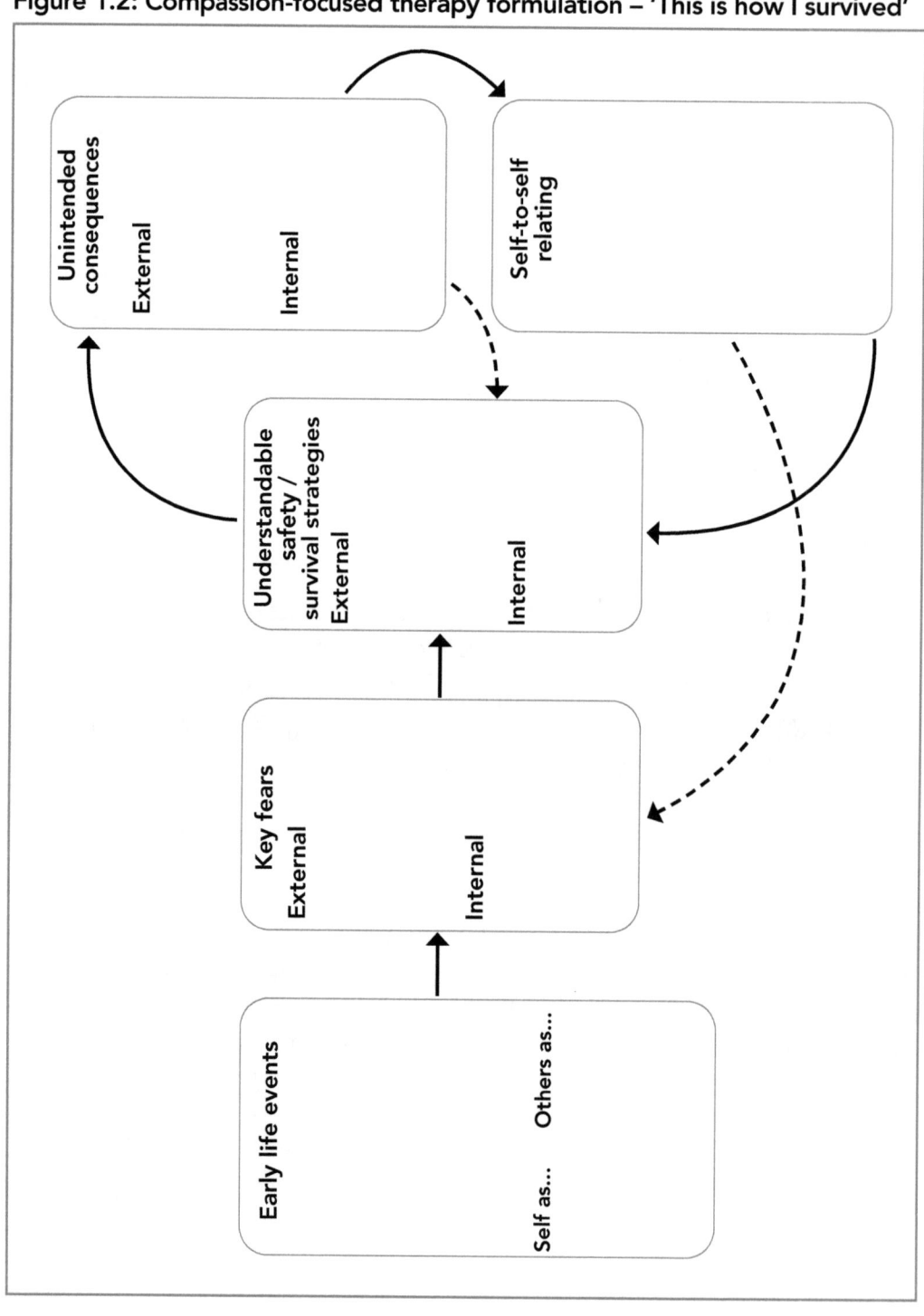

There are so many ways into this process and how we approach it will depend on the capacity of our patient to tolerate making connections with past tragedies and current difficulties. Some of our patients may find it more helpful to follow a diagrammatic process using the framework in Figure 1.2. Equally, for others who have not yet made sense of the connections between their early life experiences and their problems in the present, the formulation process may be more informal and discursive. Here, we would hold in mind the elements of the formulation and use them as a guide during our conversations in assessment. Introducing the de-shaming language of survival strategies and unintended consequences lays the foundation for developing a new understanding of the nature of our tricky brains, which comes later, in Phase Three.

This formulation then informs the future therapeutic work. Some elements that have been discussed are included in the summary, which is written explicitly *to* the patient and not *about* them, to aid the process of collaboration. It is important to ensure that the language and format are accessible for the patient, using a shared language which has been developed during the sessions.

The beginning of Adam's journey

Adam, a white English man, came to psychotherapy services at the age of 35 as a new referral to mental health services. He had been in the prison system but had never been assessed or offered any form of psychotherapy or mental health care. Despite a significant history of physical abuse, neglect and sexual trauma (at the hands of an individual known to his family), he never came to the attention of services. He had struggled significantly with addiction to substances and had been convicted of multiple offences related to possession and distribution, which had involved a number of prison sentences. Understandably, he came to psychotherapy services quite unclear about what, if anything, could be offered or be helpful, or even if he had the right to ask for anything.

It was a difficult and slow process for Adam to engage with the psychotherapy services and he missed many of his early appointments. Often in such situations, patients are discharged from the service due to non-engagement or lack of commitment to the therapeutic process. I reached out to Adam to explore the blocks to engaging with the assessment process, trying to remain curious and open to making adaptations, while maintaining a clear sense of what could not be negotiated (for example, I would not offer a home visit).

Before the sessions, he would stand in the corner of the hallway, refusing the offer to sit in the waiting room. The fear of exposure also played out in the room and in the early assessment sessions Adam clearly felt threatened, avoiding eye contact. I carefully noticed how hard it was for Adam to feel OK in the room with me and I wondered what would help. We agreed to move the chairs so that we were not directly opposite each other, reducing the intensity and exposure. This enabled him to take a seat in the session. Adam kept his coat, hat and gloves on, as this allowed him to feel more protected in the space with me. Having this as part of the conversation seems to allow Adam to develop some tentative trust that I would not push him further than he could tolerate.

Over the course of the five assessment sessions, which were spread over a number of months, we began to develop a shared understanding of how parts of his early life had affected him. He had never felt a sense of safeness with others, linked to the multiple abusive intrusions, against a backdrop of neglect and denial.

The formulation process began with observations from the room:

Therapist: *'I notice you have taken your hat off today; I wonder what has made this possible?'*

Adam: *'Something you said last week made me realise that you had been listening to what I was saying.'*

Therapist: *'So when you feel listened to, that makes it easier to let a little of your defences down?'*

Adam: *'Yes, I guess so. No one's ever listened to what I said. When the teachers at school saw the bruises and I tried to tell them what had happened, they turned away and said I must have deserved it.'*

The ending of the assessment process was a shared formulation (see Figure 1.2), which then formed part of the summary letter which we discussed before it was sent. The letter was addressed to Adam, not the referrer, with careful attention to the language, ensuring that it was consistent with what had been discussed in the sessions. The length of the letter also felt important – we can probably say everything that is helpful and tolerable on two sides of A4! I have imagined receiving such a letter about my own life, and I feel that any more than two sides might be too much. This requires us to be concise and thoughtful with what we report back through the summary letter and how it is said. I find that it is often a source of disappointment when patients receive letters containing multiple factual inaccuracies, as distinct from differences of opinion. We can of course all make mistakes in what we hear, but being willing and available to correct our errors is important (Appendix 1.1 Sample Assessment Summary).

Adam then had an opportunity to meet with me again and discuss any elements of the letter that he wished. This process sat alongside the next steps of being invited to join the compassion-focused group psychotherapy programme (Phase Three and Phase Four) and the Waiting List Group (Phase Two), while he was waiting.

Chapter 1.1: The practicalities of the assessment

Figure 1.2: Compassion-focused therapy threat formulation completed

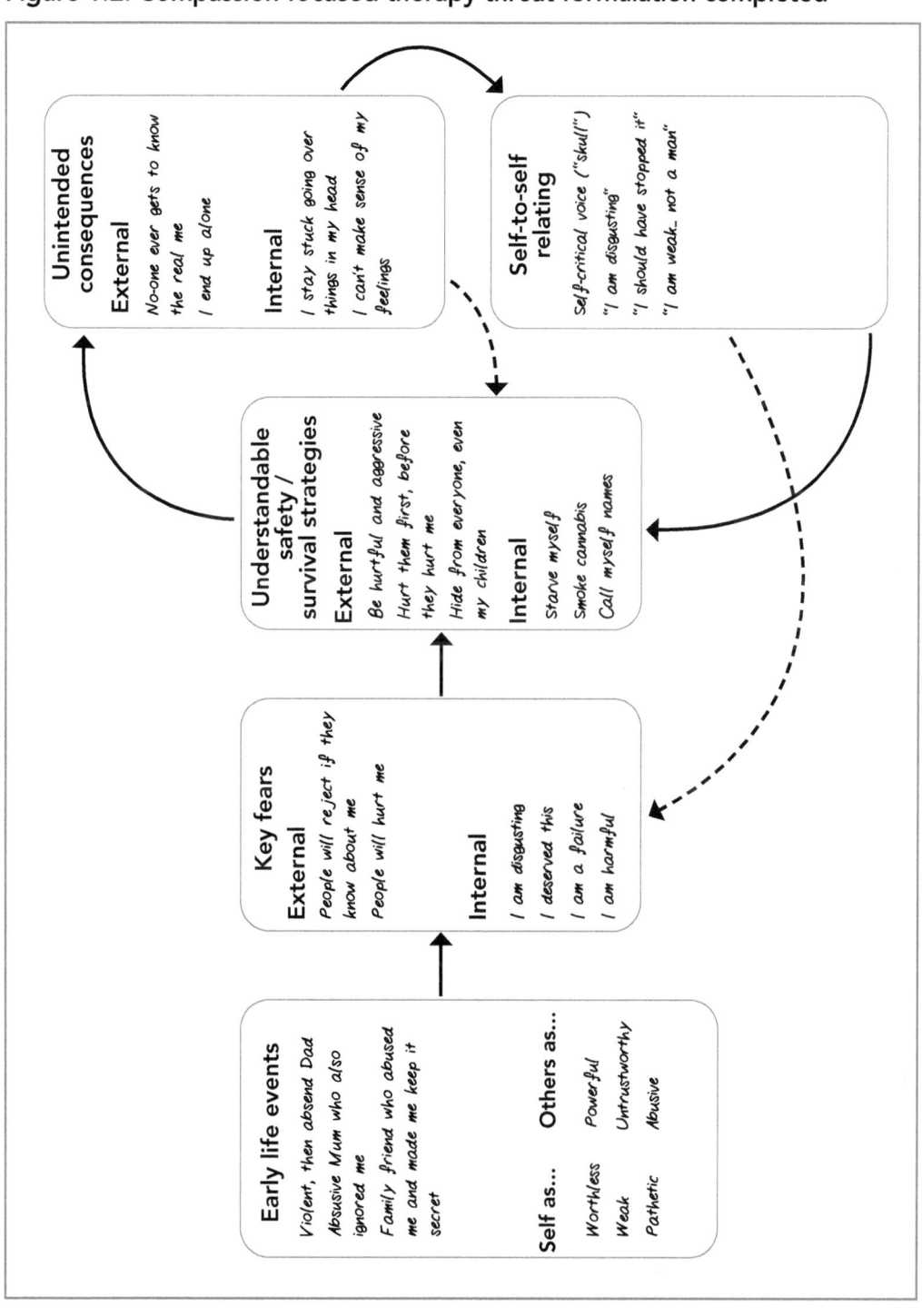

Rolling with the resistance

We have focused on the ways in which we might work explicitly with blocks to engaging with the process of assessment. But this may not be the only challenge we face in developing a compassion-focused group psychotherapy programme. Myths, misconceptions and misunderstandings abound in relation to group psychotherapy. I have lost count of the number of times I have been informed that a group member was only referred to the group because the waiting list was too long for individual psychotherapy. The decision to refer someone to group therapy invariably has nothing to do with the expediency of getting to treatment and is carefully considered as the most appropriate option to meet the needs of the individual:

> *'I think most people have got an idea of group therapy as not for them anyway, sharing personal stuff in a group it's a bit of a no and if you're talking about compassion and you're naturally an empath, you think I'm struggling so much with myself I cannot take anybody else stuff on and if I'm in a group I'm naturally gonna be their sponge and I can't afford to be that way.'*

This is, I believe, a commonly held view about what group therapy will look like. So we can expect and anticipate a great deal of resistance to the idea of joining a group. This is of course understandable and highlights the need to be really clear about why you are suggesting group psychotherapy. I find Judith Herman's words very helpful in the first instance:

> *'The core experiences of psychological trauma are disempowerment and disconnection from others. Recovery, therefore, is based upon the empowerment of the survivor and the creation of new connections. Recovery can take place only within the context of relationships; it cannot occur in isolation.'*[30]

If the traumatic experiences that we are hoping to heal have occurred in the context of the patient's familial setting, the group can then provide the healing through what Yalom

---

30 Herman, J. L. (1992). Complex PTSD: A syndrome in survivors of prolonged and repeated trauma. *Journal of Traumatic Stress*, **5**(3), 377-391.

describes as the 'corrective recapitulation of the primary family group'. Put more simply, the group setting is a safe place to rework old family patterns and dynamics to enable a corrective emotional experience and to lay down new attachment codes and memories. Explaining this to someone who is deeply fearful and suspicious of what the group will look like takes some work.

Sherelle and the case for individual therapy

Sherelle, of mixed heritage, was referred to psychotherapy services at the age of 35 having been involved in social care and health services her entire life. Her early life was scattered across multiple failed foster and care home placements, and marked by separation from her siblings and sporadic contact with her parents. This contact generally ended in re-entry into the care system until their early alcohol-related deaths.

Sherelle's adult life followed a similar pattern, with many violent and controlling partners. All her five children had been taken into the care system, which she has fought tirelessly.

Sherelle remained quite guarded during the assessment and formulation sessions and spoke of being unsure if she could even be in the room with the therapist without her support worker present. The support worker was invited in during the early sessions and had some discussions about what might be needed. It was subsequently agreed that she could manage without her support worker, as long as they waited in the building. The conclusion of the assessment came with a recommendation for compassion-focused group psychotherapy. This was based on the repeating patterns for Sherelle of struggling to hold boundaries and have any meaningful or supportive relationships with peers. Her only sources of support had been mental health care staff, which was also complicated by the transference material from unresolved relationships with care home staff, and child protection social workers. There had been some discussions with Sherelle about a wish for her to have a different experience with groups and peers, and also to build a new relationship with herself through the group.

Sherelle's response to the summary letter was to ask her support worker to contact us and say that she did not want group therapy and instead wanted individual therapy. She stated, through her support worker, that she could not share personal things in a group and would only trust an individual therapist. She was therefore offered a further appointment to think this through, as it was beginning to emerge that Sherelle was inviting her support worker to intercede on her behalf. There was a suggestion in the communication that we might be treating Sherelle unfairly.

Support worker (Jo): *'So, Sherelle is not keen on the group and feels that she was pushed into it. Is this because of waiting lists? Really, she wants individual therapy, do you offer that here?'*

Therapist: *'Sherelle, are you able to say a bit more about what is happening for you here?'*

Sherelle (long pause and very quiet): *'It's like Jo said, not sure I really want it.'*

Therapist: *'I am sorry if you didn't feel able to share this with me when we met for our final session. Perhaps I was a little too enthusiastic about the group?'*

Sherelle: *'No, it wasn't that... Bad things happened in groups before.'*

Therapist: *'In the care home? (Sherelle nods.) And you worried that the group here wouldn't be safe either? (Sherelle nods again.) That makes sense to me that you would be worried about this and prefer individual therapy.'*

Sherelle: *'Well, I don't really want that either, bad things happened there too in the kid's home.'*

Therapist: *'It is tricky, isn't it, to imagine that you might be able to trust people to keep you safe when things have been so unsafe and scary in the past? (Sherelle nods.) I wonder if you might need to try some of this out and see if we can be trusted? Like you have done by coming to see me and tell me a bit about what has happened to you.'*

Sherelle: *'Maybe, but what if I don't like it, can my support worker come in with me?'*

Therapist: *'How about trying the Waiting List Group? I am sorry, but Jo won't be able to come in but she could wait for you like before when you met with me. I will be in the group and you can come along for an hour once a month and try us out.'*

Sherelle 'tried us out' with the Waiting List Group and decided to continue with the programme. Reflecting on the process with Sherelle, there are a number of strands to consider. The pacing of the assessment seemingly allowed Sherelle to return and think further about her decision with support from someone she trusted. I wonder if this made it possible for Sherelle to make connections with her early life and how this may have been influencing her thinking about group therapy. I am also mindful of the teachings of Bob Hobson and Psychodynamic Interpersonal Therapy, who invites us to consider that some people do not find questions that helpful, in that they do not know the answer.[31] So offering statements and hypotheses to be considered together can be much more helpful and therapeutic.

But that is not the end of the story with myths and misconceptions, particularly on the subject of compassion. For many, compassion is mis-associated with soft, fluffy ineffectual niceness, which understandably puts many off. It will take work in those early stages to ensure that your patients understand that compassion is actually associated with strength, wisdom, courage and commitment. The following quote below shows the journey in therapy towards a new understanding: 'I realised that compassion isn't necessarily all about fluffy kind of ... of yeah, you know, we love ourselves, it's not like that it was quite tough, a tough kind of passion'.

---

31 Hobson, R. F. (2013). *Forms of Feeling: The heart of psychotherapy.* Routledge.

'Showing your working'

When I was at school, I recall the frequent refrain from my teachers to 'Show your working!' This instruction was, of course, to remind us to ensure that we showed in our tests how we got our answers. This idea stayed with me, as I was always well aware that I would need all the marks I could muster! This concept has returned to my mind as I have grappled with how to demonstrate my compassionate motivation towards my patients without overwhelming them and 'blowing fuses', as described above.

I have no desire to be a 'blank slate' for my patients. I wish for them to have an understanding of what I am holding in my mind, and most importantly, to give them a sense of my intention towards them and the process. Edward Tronick's well-known 'still face' experiment demonstrates that a neutral face is not actually neutral and is instead deeply disturbing to young minds. My suggestion is that many of the minds you will be meeting in the early stages of assessment will also be very young, developmentally. Many of our patients will also have had repeated experiences of depressed and disconnected caregivers whose faces and dispositions will have been 'neutral' or 'still', with little offered in the way of reassurance or sense-making. Let us not repeat this, and instead offer a warm, clear and explicated version of ourselves to our patients. There are many occasions when my intention is not clear to my patients as they are clouded by their own experiences of opaque and absent caregivers. So it is my job to spell it out and show my thinking. This is of course within reason. I would not share everything that I am thinking, as this would not be in the best interests of the patient. If I am wondering if I have been misunderstood, having tuned in to the feeling I am getting with my patient in the room, I might invite a conversation about this.

Choosing group members

Much has been written about membership of a group and the importance of carefully considering the dynamic in the room. However, for many, the choices are limited to the requirements of the services we work in or who funds our programmes. Caution is advised when setting up group programmes, as we can easily become caught up in the threat-based drive and the need to 'fill' the programme with sufficient numbers. This can overshadow a thoughtful assessment of the capacity of those who have been referred and the mix in the room, particularly in the early stages. Many a group programme has ended prematurely or suffered excessive dropout, when group members have been thrust together without sufficient time taken to consider whether the members will be able to tolerate each other.

It can be helpful to take some time to consider who is on your waiting list, and whether they will be able to work together and make adjustments to the group members who are invited to join the programme accordingly. A slow-paced, attuned, supportive therapeutic group process is likely to be helpful to anyone presenting with psychological difficulties and overwhelming emotions.

Again, I am often asked for inclusion and exclusion criteria, and these can be helpful. However, perhaps what is more important is to match our expectations to the capacity of the patient. If there are only 12 sessions in your programme, and your feeling is that your patient will likely require a number of months to tolerate the group space, then your group programme may not be a good fit. The assessment of capacity is of course an imprecise science and often Phase Two (Waiting List Group) offers an opportunity to continue to assess the capacity of your patient to tolerate a group space.

Should we exclude those who are caught in a cycle of addiction, or those who use self-harm as a means of communication and other behaviours which might be on a standard exclusion list? Maybe, but might that be like suggesting that a man who has broken his leg walk to the hospital to get treatment and a cast? Matters of risk must always be attended to and some people are just not ready to replace the addiction with the experience of compassion from the group. I can recall many occasions on which we have had to ask people to leave the group temporarily and direct them to addictions services, to receive some practical support. But with the understanding that they would be welcome back in the future. Many have returned, but of course not all. There have also been many groups where I have had to ask someone to leave who has arrived, swinging their half-finished six-pack of Special Brew or staring off into the middle distance, clearly having taken some substances. I remind them to come back next week when they have straightened out and we will try again. Creating a firm, welcoming and non-judgemental space is, for some, their first experience of compassion as a flow from others.

Saying no

We have considered some of the ways that we can work to support those whose capacity to engage with services is compromised by early ruptures and intrusions. This model offers an opportunity to those who may not traditionally be considered appropriate for exploratory psychotherapy. There are, however, occasions when we may need to say no to people. Again, I do not believe that there is a precise formula for this. Careful consideration of how your patient responds to the assessment process may offer an indication of whether they could tolerate the group.

Tuning into the intention towards the therapeutic work that sits behind what your patient might be telling you in the session can aid this process. I have said a gentle but clear no to many patients who have been seeking group psychotherapy with an ulterior motive, often in relation to court proceedings, family court processes etc. I would also always so no to compassion-focused group psychotherapy being part of a court disposal, in that they are obliged to attend or face a custodial sentence. This creates a split in the group with those who have chosen to be there and those who have not, which interferes with the group process and often results in envy on both sides.

There are some messages from our patients that we need to listen to with extra care. Those with a significant history of instrumental violence towards others may not be able to manage the challenges of this kind of group process. Inviting those who present with strong and well-honed defences, will need to be tempered by establishing whether there is also a motivation to work with such defences. This was the case with Louie, but he expressed a clear motivation to work to understand himself and learn to tolerate others, which we tested in the assessment process. I will often use the end of the assessment process to explore in more depth what being challenged in a group setting might look like. Group-based assessments can be a helpful part of the process at this stage, recruiting the help and support of existing or past group members.

Ideally, when it is necessary to say no, there is a consensus between you and the patient that this is not the right time or even the right kind of therapy. I am always keen to think of it in this way rather than inadvertently putting blame or responsibility onto the patient. When this is not possible, I will try within reason and considering personal safety, to be as honest and clear as I can be about the reasons.

Concluding thoughts

The first steps in the journey towards compassion-focused group psychotherapy requires a slow pace and careful attunement to the individual needs of the patient. Time spent paying attention to the details of the therapeutic space and the way that patients are welcomed can support and improve engagement for those who are particularly sensitive and predisposed to feeling rejected and uncontained.

Adam's story shows us that engaging with and bringing compassion to what you see in the room can help to begin the process of cultivating safeness. This is instead of possibly re-traumatising them by requiring them to retell their story over and over with a stranger in an unknown and unsafe place. Jane's experience also reminds us how easily we can become misattuned and recreate the experience of neglect and absence.

Paul Gilbert encourages us to consider the formulation as 'not one process', but instead as a series of stages along which we may move back and forth. It is also important to remember that the formulation does not need to be completed at the outset of therapy. The process is best understood as a repeated and organic process of turning back towards, making sense of, validating and integrating.

Essential to the process of cultivating safeness during this phase is establishing and holding a healthy boundary and frame around the work. On one level, this may be keeping to the agreed time for the session, as well as offering clear and consistent communication. Honesty and transparency are some of the ways that we can begin to establish a trusting relationship that fosters a commitment to the programme. There will be occasions when we need to be able to say no, hopefully collaboratively, but sometimes not. Safeness is created through us holding and maintaining our authority with our own compassionate wise mind front and centre.

Phase Two:
The Waiting List Group (tea and biscuits!)

Programme element	Format	Function
2. Waiting list support group Psychoeducation	■ Monthly, one-hour drop-in sessions. ■ Facilitated by Lived Experience Practitioner (a service user who has completed the CFGP) and psychotherapist. ■ Informal setting, amplified by the offer of tea and biscuits.	■ For patient to feel 'held in mind' by group facilitators. ■ Offering information about the programme. ■ Opportunity for connection with other patients before therapy. ■ Continuing development of the safe haven function. ■ Exposure to an experience of being in a group setting. ■ Managing risk during the pre-therapy phase of treatment. ■ Provision of a consistent, containing and informal space.

Chapter 2.1:
Waiting... waiting... and waiting...

The volume of research evidence supporting the negative impact of waiting for psychotherapy is dizzying, and it would be impossible to share it all here. However, the key messages that can be helpful in developing programmes relate to the level of dropout while waiting, which sadly remains very high. Patients are generally referred for psychotherapy at the point of need and generally would not be assessed without said need first being identified, which results in a paradox in the modern NHS and the appallingly long wait for psychotherapy.

Let's consider a scenario. You have survived the assessment process and agreed that you will join a group, which generally is understood to be a terrifying prospect. Then you are told you must wait for two years. This feels completely unacceptable but is sadly the reality for so many.

The context

In the service where I work, like so many of you, I am sure, there is a long wait for therapy. Despite the steps we have taken with the rolling programme, over the years, the wait for the programme for many has stretched to over 12 months.

I have noticed that the longer the wait, the more people seem likely not to come to the first session. Many speak of feeling forgotten by the service or forced to seek an alternative therapy. I worry that the work undertaken in Phase One, beginning to build a therapeutic bridge into the experience of our patients, crumbles as the months roll by. We can then become just another person in a long line of people who promised to help but let them down. I don't have any solid evidence for this assertion, but it is a strong feeling that has been supported by conversations with those who have had to wait.

Drawing again on the wisdom from the theory and practice of therapeutic communities, we decided to introduce a Waiting List Group. Groups of this nature are commonplace in therapeutic community programmes and provide preparatory work as well as a much-needed holding function. This was designed to offer a further level of containment and support through the monthly one-hour supportive space for those waiting to commence the group programme. For many, CFGP will be their first experience of group psychotherapy and so this group offers a gentle introduction to the experience of being in a group. It is also hoped that the group can extend the work that has begun in Phase One to provide an opportunity for seeking proximity to a consistent safe haven. The group space is offered to each patient without expectation that they attend, in that their place in the CFGP programme will not be affected. They don't even need to tell us if they are coming. The emphasis is on the idea of an invitation rather than an obligation, with respect and recognition that this offer would be helpful for some but not all.

I recall a conversation with Adam, long after he had graduated from the programme. He had been clear that he was never able to attend the Waiting List Group as he had spoken of feeling unable to come to the group and not 'do the therapy thing'. But he was also able to articulate the sense of being held in mind by the monthly invitation letters, which we hoped this group could offer some of our patients.

The practicalities of the Waiting List Group

The group is held at the same time and in the same room each time, to begin to create the safeness and familiarity with the therapeutic space. This group is an hour long, offering a 'sub-therapeutic dose', to reduce the pull into therapeutic sharing. This is the intention, however there will of course always be a need to steer the group away from the choppy waters of therapeutic depth and keep the discussions light and informative. We have tea and biscuits as a direct and intentional separation from the formal therapy space where there are no breaks or refreshments. We also hoped that the tea and biscuits would mark this as an informal and perhaps more welcoming space. We have created as much flexibility as we feel is possible, but it is not a 'drop-in' session, where people can stop by at any point during the hour. We invite the group members 'in waiting' to come for the whole hour once a month. If only one person attends the group, however, we cut the group short and set a length of about 20 minutes. This is to ensure that the person who has attended is offered some time, which is also contained. When there are a few attendees and a lot of curiosity, I am often pleasantly surprised how quickly an hour passes.

There is no specific structure to this group and we try to make the space as informal and welcoming as possible. We invite group members to bring questions about all aspects of the programme. This is particularly helpful for those who have had their assessment with other clinicians in the service. The group is run in the building and the room where the therapy will take place. The intention behind this is to offer a 'dry run', a rehearsal of as much of the experience of coming to the group for the first time as possible. Finding the building, seeing the room, assessing the journey and noticing the experience.

When planning for a big climbing trip, I am always grateful for the opportunity to go and scope out the climb. I have found myself at the base of many mountains squinting up at the line I hope to follow. Does it look good? Will I find it again in the near dark of early morning? But equally important is the wisdom of my fellow climbers, often gleaned in the local pub. Have you tried this line? Is it good? What should I look out for? Such questions can make all the difference (we call it 'beta'), but the idea translates well into preparing people for group psychotherapy. Would I trust someone to give advice who had never climbed and who had never tried this particular line? Probably not. With this in mind, the Waiting List Group is supported and co-facilitated by one of the programme psychotherapists and a Lived Experience Practitioner (LEP). Lived experience practitioners go by many names, but LEPs, I believe, most accurately describes the fundamentally important role offered by such staff.

The importance of the lived experience practitioners

> 'Lived experience practitioners are uniquely situated to understand the difficulty involved in engaging in therapy and may use their experiential knowledge to connect with patients. Their insights into suffering allow them to become highly understanding, compassionate, and empathetic practitioners.'

I think this quote from Cleary and Armour articulates clearly and simply one of the many benefits of having people with lived experience support the ongoing work.[32] Especially considering the worrying trends in drop out before the therapeutic work has commenced. Perhaps if they knew a little more about what they were waiting for, it might support them to 'hang in there' for their place in the programme to become available.

In the case of our CFGP programme, LEPs have graduated from the programme and work in a variety of different contexts in our mental health trust. This might be bringing compassion to the staff in the form of teaching and reflective groups, engaging in research or supporting the group psychotherapy programme. The opportunities for employment for LEPs in our trust vary from full-time, permanent contracts, through to therapeutic-earning payments to coordinate with sickness-benefit payments.

All our LEPs will have at least two to three years following graduation from CFGP before coming to join our LEP training programme, which has been developed and is delivered by Sarah (our first LEP). She blazed the trail and got us all thinking about how much lived experience could support our programmes at the beginning, middle and end. She has also shown us that LEPs are uniquely placed to offer authentic compassion-focused staff support[33] to the staff in our trusts, and the feedback from these projects supports this. She supports and prepares people who have graduated from CFGP to prepare for this new role. We will hear more about Sarah's journey at the end of this book, so read on...

The support from staff with lived experience of CFGP has multiple benefits for all those involved, including us therapists. In the first instance, the involvement of LEPs in the Waiting List Group reinforces the important message that this group will be informative but is not a therapy space. There have been many occasions where Sarah has gently but firmly pulled me back from the easy slide into therapy, and her mere presence in the group reminds me what we are here for.

I would never invite our LEPs to be involved in the formal therapeutic work. Many LEPs will have a potential affinity for this work, but there is a risk of overidentification with the group members, connection with residual unprocessed material and the difficulty with the change in relationship with the co-facilitator. All this makes this transition untenable and therefore not safe. That said, I wholeheartedly support LEPs to train as therapists if this is their wish, but to choose carefully their area of work to ensure that their career's flourish.

---

32 Cleary, R., & Armour, C. (2022). Exploring the role of practitioner lived experience of mental health issues in counselling and psychotherapy. *Counselling and Psychotherapy Research*, **22**(4), 1100–1111. https://doi.org/10.1002/capr.12569

33 For more details of CFSS, see Lucre K & Taylor J (2020) To suffer with: Compassion focused staff support as an antidote to the cost of caring in forensic services. In *Sexual Crime and Trauma* (pp143–174). Springer.

Our LEPs also benefit from supporting people at the beginning of their journey. Sarah will often reflect that seeing people at this stage reminds her how far she has come. She can also offer authentic and heartfelt advice based on her own journey. I have sat many times with the tea cooling, deeply moved by what Sarah has to offer those still considering whether they will 'give it a try', as Sherelle did. This opportunity to come and be in a group before the actual therapy starts is a little like 'try before you buy'.

I recall one session where Sarah worked with strength and sensitivity with a particularly prickly group member, who was 'not convinced' that she would ever share anything in a group. She only took off her mask (long after the COVID-19 days) because we all assured her that we did not have any germs and she certainly was not going to be accepting anything from me. Sarah spoke with some passion about remembering feeling very similarly about the idea of group therapy, and that this feeling did not dissipate the first day or even the first week of the programme. Her honesty seemed to melt something in this group member, who turned to her with more questions about how she managed the intensity of other people. I tried to fade into the background to allow this exchange to unfold.

I generally endeavour to sit back in this process and support my co-facilitator to take the lead, as what they have to offer has far more value to the prospective group members. I try not to invite a lot of exploration which will be the foundation of the psychotherapeutic offer. I often busy myself with pouring the tea or coffee, allowing the space to unfold. This is not an easy task. I metaphorically need to sit on my hands and stay away from the allure of therapeutic territory, hence busying my hands with tea preparation! It is important for us to employ a light, conversational style to modulate the potential intensity of the intervention.

Sarah and I have toyed with the idea of having this group being run by two LEPs and taking out the therapist-holding function. On one level, this would protect against the pull into the therapeutic work, but I wonder if one of the LEPs would end up on the receiving end of the maternal transference material. I believe that the transference material will be in the room regardless of whether the therapist is there or not, and it may be most helpful for this to be navigated by the therapist.

Jane and her difficult assessment

Jane attended the Waiting List Group for the first time after completing her assessment. As we discussed in Phase One Jane had a difficult assessment process which repeated and reinforced the neglect of early life. She brought some of her dissatisfaction with the assessment process and unhappiness with her assessment summary letter, described in Phase One, to the Waiting List Group.

> As soon as we entered the room, Jane began with what felt like a tirade of things that had been 'done wrong'. These ranged from inaccuracies in the assessment summary, the parking, the room and the service in general. Having some knowledge of Jane, and the underlying transference process, I was able to apologise which diffused some of the tension. The role of the therapist here was to calm the situation, using psychotherapeutic skills and competencies. Jane was given some space to talk about her dissatisfaction, which was then held by the therapist for further exploration in Phase Three. This was named explicitly:
>
> 'It seems like a lot has come up for you, Jane, that we will be able to explore and support you with when you join the Preparation and Engagement Group'. This served a dual function of gently moving on from Jane's grievances, through validating the difficulty she faced, and also offered some hope for the future.

This should not be an expected or helpful part of the LEP role and could take them outside the boundary of safe practice. There have also been moments in these groups where group members have disclosed feeling at risk, in particular of harming themselves. Again, I would not view managing this kind of situation to be solely the task of LEPs. Particularly pre-therapy, our knowledge of the group members is much more limited and joining up with other services may be needed.

I find that I am often quite conflicted as to how much to find out about the group members before they attend their first Waiting List Group. The issue of risk needs to be attended to, but I also want to give everyone an opportunity to be seen clearly in that first group. The LEP co-facilitator also has a unique role which can be supported by not having the full assessment formulation from the assessing therapist, but rather an overview. So, with all this in mind, we have opted to continue as we are, which offers me an opportunity to practice sitting on my therapy-hands, but also to hold the space with my therapy-head on!

Another benefit of the LEP role is that, while my co-facilitator is engaging with the questions, explanations and the offer of feedback, I have space to be curious about the new group members. The decision about entry into the programme is a delicate process and one which requires careful consideration and an assessment of capacity. Observations of the interactions between the group members in this informal group can offer some insights into how they will manage Phase Three. The rolling nature of Phase Three offers the opportunity for group members to join in pairs and have a 'therapy buddy', so named by the group members. In essence, group members are always invited to join the programme with at least one other person, in the hope that this person will be on their journey with them from start to end. With this in mind, I have sat in many Waiting List Groups trying to imagine the pairings and how they will work. We have then on occasion shuffled the arbitrary pairings on the waiting list, to try and create some lasting partnerships. This is my hope, but of course it does not always work out in the way.

I am also aware that this is the place where I meet some prospective group members for the first time. There will be patients who have been assessed by others in a service and put on your waiting list. There is a good argument for always offering a meeting in such circumstances, but I have found that the Waiting List Group offers a less formal and intense opportunity to meet with those waiting. I also find that this can avoid a potential rehashing of the assessment process, which sometimes emerges when we meet individually with patients following the completion of the assessment. In this setting, we can also casually acknowledge where there is prior knowledge or connections and where there isn't: 'So, just for the rest of the group, Louie, you and I met for assessment a few months ago', or 'It is good to meet you and put a face to the name on the waiting list'.

The group serves to ensure that prospective group members can find out where they are on the waiting list and give them a likely start date. The rolling programme means that drop outs can shift the positioning of the waiting list, so group members will be given the latest date but with the understanding that this could change and we could offer an earlier start date. The Waiting List Group is a place where group members can meet each other casually, knowing they will meet again in the same space but with a different purpose. They will also know that they will only meet Sarah (LEP) again at the end of the programme in the Moving On Group (Phase Five).

Cultivating safeness

The group is designed to offer a continuation of the unfolding work in cultivating safeness for prospective group members. We have an informal discussion about safeness in this group but tend to leave the formal Safe Space Agreement until the start of the Programme in Phase Three, but there may be an argument for creating a formal agreement at this stage that is returned to each session.

> ### Introducing Dalvinder
>
> Dalvinder, age 28 of Pakistani origin, came to the psychotherapy service in the midst of a conflict and rupture with their mental health care team, whom they perceived had been withholding care. This had led to a complaint that had taken many months to resolve, which had further delayed their access to an assessment and subsequent treatment. This experience seems to be a mirror of Dalvinder's early life, which had involved being a carer for their mother without any recourse to support (formal or informal). In their early life, their own needs had been subjugated and feelings of anger

or injustice were not permitted. They spoke of constantly being reminded of how much their mother was suffering and that they ought not to complain.

Chance encounters

Dal had been a regular attender at the Waiting List Group and had also been an active participant, particularly seeming to engage with Sarah. Outside work, Dal and Sarah happened to bump into each other. Sarah acknowledged Dal and thought nothing more of it, but Dal attempted to engage Sarah in conversation about aspects of the programme that she remained unsure of. The encounter was quite uncomfortable and left me wondering if we needed to be more specific about the parameters of the group and the professional role of LEP in the group. This is still a work in progress but perhaps the lesson from this encounter is the need for clarity about roles within this informal space and the boundaries.

Concluding comments

We hope that this informal, information-focused phase of the programme offers a preliminary container for prospective group members to try out various elements of the programme before joining, from the practical journey to the emotional experience of being in a group with others. For those who choose not to come (and many don't), the set-up of the group is designed to help people feel that they are being held in mind while they wait, and at the same time not judged or sanctioned.

Crucially, we have explored how the role of the LEP is key to diluting some of the intensity and the pull into the choppy waters of therapy, as well as providing the 'beta', or inside knowledge about the next phases of the therapeutic programme.

Chapter 2.2:
Role of the therapist/conductor

Co-facilitation is the 'glue' that holds CFGP and all its phases and stages together. We start developing our capacity as co-facilitators, parental transference objects and holders of the therapeutic space, with the Waiting List Group. Holding this space together with an LEP who has themselves been a group member, will at require first an acknowledgement of this previous relationship. Following this, there is a journey to be undertaken to implicitly and explicitly change roles and responsibilities. This can be a challenge, and I have worked with many LEPs who did not know that they weren't ready to take the leap until we were in the room together. I recall one occasion on which I shared a facilitated training space with an LEP perhaps too soon after finishing therapy. As we stood up together to introduce ourselves, I caught something in his eye that I could not translate. It was not until the break that he told me he wasn't ready to move into a different role and that he couldn't get beyond 'Kate – my therapist'. He made his excuses and left the training, and I learned a valuable lesson about the time and space that is required to make a transition from patient/group member to co-facilitator. Equally, we have to be prepared to work through and tolerate being vulnerable in a different way with someone who has been in a transference relationship with us. Some might say that it is not advisable, but I hope that the previous section makes the necessary case for the value of the role, and therefore the need to work through the difficulties and complexities.

I have generally found it helpful to invite and model honest communication about the changing role that is being navigated. I have often explicitly aimed to dilute or dissolve the transference with a greater level of self-disclosure. I will share my own vulnerabilities in this different facilitation role and seek support to stop straying into therapy. Collaboration is key and the deep understanding that, regardless of seniority outside the group, in the group you are equal partners. This is true of all co-facilitation relationships, but perhaps most pertinent when the transitions are on this kind of scale.

Co-facilitation and conducting your orchestra

Foukes' idea of the group facilitator as a conductor is one of the many inspired contributions to our understanding of the way to effectively support and develop a group. He invited us to move from the role of 'leader' in the group, to becoming a conductor, guiding rather than instructing the orchestra how to play, and when they are playing, 'stepping back' and allowing the process to unfold. I have observed many conductors in action with this metaphor in mind and it seems to have so many helpful layers. There will be times when the conductor, perhaps in the earlier days of an orchestra coming together, may need to be more directive. But this need diminishes over time as the capacity of the orchestra develops, and the conductor may instead just need to give a nudge here and there – a little lighter on the strings, a little more bassoon! So it is for us in the CFGP programme as it unfolds. This first group experience in the Waiting List Group may be like the early rehearsals: where do I sit? What is OK to say? Moving on to Phase Three and then Phase Four of the group, there is the opportunity to sit back and just watch the group play. Over time, the group develop the capacity to nurture, challenge and support each other. I will be sharing some of these moments with you in Phase Four. There is something deeply satisfying in becoming superfluous in a mature group. That said, I am not convinced that my presence in such moments is redundant. I am holding a space of safeness, but lightly.

One of my favourite books describing the setting up and running of a psychoanalytic psychotherapy group is by Behr and Hearst.[34] They have some great advice about

---

34 Behr, H. & Hearst, L. (2008) *Group-analytic Psychotherapy: A meeting of minds*. John Wiley & Sons.

co-facilitation and how the 'couple dynamic' can influence the group and provide helpful material in the group process to enable the group to reflect on their own experience of coupling, parental dyads or the lack thereof. We will see in Phase Three and Phase Four the ways that we can use group members' experience of the parental pairing in the group:

> *'I suppose it was there from the beginning you have the group... [you have] Kate and Graham, and then there's us, so when one of them is missing it's a bit like when your dad's away on business or your mum's out with her friends... it just like... someone's missing.'*

Here we can see the explicit experience of the facilitators in parental roles and what it felt like when one of them was missing. I recall a group I had been running solo for a while and there had been a complaint about the breathing practice being a bit 'samey and boring'. I responded by inviting the group to consider how often a single parent might cook beans on toast for tea. The group responded with smiles, acknowledgement and a deeper understanding of the potential limitations of my role as a solo facilitator. At the same time, I took the message about how we can all get a little stale with the practices that we offer on a regular basis. I went away and found a deeply humorous (well, I thought so) and also irreverent spin on the standard breathing practice, entitled 'Fuck That: An honest meditation'. It caused much hilarity and served as a reminder that, even when flying solo, we can keep the practices fresh[35].

It can also be a helpful 'dispersal' of the transference on a single facilitator, which often comes with it a tendency for splitting by the group members, into good and bad, playful and harsh. If this can be named and worked through, it offers a rich therapeutic opportunity for reworking old attachment patterns. We will explore in Phase Three the implications for the group when group members are not able to acknowledge or work with the transference material and consequent splitting. We will need to read on to Phase Four for the example of how co-facilitation can be a vehicle for reworking attachment patterns in an adaptive way: *'I had to tell him that he [facilitator] had been the most significant male figure in my life ever... because I grew a bond'*.

Co-facilitation pairings that seem to be the most successful rely on clarity about roles and understanding the role you play in the group. We don't need to try and be the same; as the following quote demonstrates, the different ways of being are welcome:

---

35 https://www.youtube.com/watch?v=92i5m3tV5XY

> '[The male facilitator] was a bit more challenging...
> provocative whereas [the female facilitator] had a more gentle
> approach, not too gentle, the contrast was empathic... I liked
> the combination they were just different and it worked.'

The movement into a conducting role in the group can also enable a shift in the group, moving it into a more horizontal transference position. In the early stages of a group, its members, as articulated above, are more likely to relate to the facilitators in a vertical/parental transference, looking for leadership. But over time, the group take on some of the leadership functions, thus allowing for more flattened sibling-orientated ways of relating:

> '...it was good the way... they [the facilitators] used to interact
> with each other, you know, it was only sometimes, you know,
> it was... it was friendly banter with each other which made
> you think are they brother and sister and stuff like that, but
> you know but obviously they were not, that would lighten the
> mood it as it would make people feel comfortable and how they
> would relate to things that had happened, erm, so that we were
> in a safe environment, you know.'

> '...they were very compassionate people and very sneaky
> [laugh]; they were able to see through the bullshit and draw
> out the real side of things... being light-hearted in stressful
> moments but also having the understanding and care that
> they have... don't change.'

Co-facilitation is a *lot* like rock climbing

It will come as no surprise that I see many overlaps between the mindset and skills required to rock climb with another person and those needed to co-facilitate with someone! I have learned many hard lessons over the years about the importance of choosing your climbing partner carefully. I even have a scar to remind me what happens if your climbing partner fails to tell you they have dislodged a rock! Once your partner is chosen, you work out the route together based on your strengths and you take turns. I much prefer a fingery, technical face climb, whereas my burly climbing partner likes a big laid-back flake, so we plan it out based on whatever we have gleaned about the terrain ahead of us. I remember one route on which we got the order wrong and I found myself leading up a powerful flake of rock. Feeling out of my depth, it helped to know that he had the rope. And so it is in therapy: you need to know your co-facilitator has your back. One will lead off up the mountain and the other will hold the rope, shouting encouragement and advice as needed. The leader will then find a place to stop, make themselves safe and bring you up. The metaphor may not match exactly, but the important point is that you both cannot lead at the same time. It would not be safe or productive.

Take a moment and consider how many groups you have sat in, internally berating your co-facilitator for taking the group in the 'wrong direction', interrupting you or generally not feeling joined up or in sync. When training, I always ask for a show of hands for those who have never had a problem with a co-facilitator. No one ever puts their hand up, and there is always a burst of laughter. It doesn't surprise me that group analytic and psychodrama psychotherapy colleagues opt to fly solo! That being said, in this kind of multi-faceted programme, if you are solo, then be mindful of not going too high. So many climbers over the years have learned the hard lesson about what can happen when no one is holding the rope. Having flown solo many times over the years, I have also had to learn to adapt to how far I can take a group with no one to support, observe, and pull me out of a hole when needed.

When you are 100 metres above the ground, it becomes really clear that you do not need a polished performance. It doesn't have to look like 'Mission Impossible'! Similarly, we do not need perfection in the co-facilitation pairing – quite the reverse, in fact.

There is an opportunity here to model collaboration and conflict resolution in a healthy way. Like climbing, it takes time to develop the kind of bond needed to enable the kind of safeness that the quote above articulates. I recall reaching a point, after much teeth gnashing and frustration, where I could feel confident saying more of what I was thinking:

> **Kate (therapist):** *'So, I have an idea of a way that we could work with what Dal has shared with us. I am wondering what you are thinking, Graham?'*
>
> **Graham (therapist):** *'That is an interesting idea. I also had a thought about a slightly different direction.'*
>
> **Kate (therapist) [with a smile]:** *'Of course you did, Graham, so what to do…? Maybe we can find a way to combine both ideas and see where we get to?'*
>
> **Graham:** *'Yes, let's see what the group are feeling, too?'*

I hope that this short script illustrates how we can keep a light touch and model working things through in an adaptive way without one needing to dominate the other or a pretending that we are in total agreement. The group will know when you don't agree, they will be already attuned to it and feel it in the unconscious material in the group. It is generally a source of relief for all to put words to it and lighten the impact. My hope is that we can offer the group an opportunity for new learning about pairings and working together. I think we have already established that there will be times when your group members react to you 'as if' you were their parental figures and transfer feelings to you that actually belong with those early attachment figures. So we can use this to support the work of reshaping the attachment systems of the group through offering new learning and experiences. My own experiences of therapy as a patient and group member, coupled with learning from my group members, have taught me that sometimes the most important capacity that we have is to pay attention and be attuned:

> *'Things were said made me realise that they were paying attention... that means a lot if you have a negative self-image... when somebody pays attention two or three months later and they remember something you said... that is worth a lot.'*

I hope that all this metaphorical chatter illustrates that co-facilitation is an attachment relationship, which, like all relationships, takes time, compromise and hard work. Making time before each group to come together, breathe and be connected to each other can help a great deal with this. This is separate from group preparation, where you might be deciding what you will be doing; this is checking in and sharing how you are doing, before the doing! This is fundamental to developing a relationship with all the ups and downs and solid co-supervision.

Co-supervision

There has been a great deal written about supervision and the importance of having a space to process the projections and work with the transference material, which is the grit of psychotherapeutic work. Fundamental to any co-facilitation relationship is a shared space to come together with an elder, keeping in mind the ideas about nature-based communities from the introduction.

Choosing a supervisor is a task that requires wisdom and courage to consider what is needed and to ensure that the equality in the relationship is maintained and encouraged. Ideally, you and your co-facilitator, particularly the LEP, should choose together and both hold veto rights if it is not a good fit.

This coming together can feel in certain moments like an opportunity to practice before thrusting a new idea onto your group, and at other times it feels like couple's therapy. Our first CFGP facilitator offered us supervision on the large couch in her back room (this is the same room that CFGP was born in). I can recall, with a smile, how the distance between us on the sofa was an indication of how the group had gone the previous week. This ranged from cosily conspiratorial, full of excitement to share the week's adventure, to frostily occupying opposite ends of the couch. Our supervisor would also have a cup of herbal tea for each of us, cooling on the coffee table. She would often comment with a light touch on the positions we were occupying. In this space, we 'role reversed' with our group members and each other, and in doing so, we shifted perspectives. We challenged each other to try out new ways of working; we laughed and cried together, and in time we came to a mutual understanding and respect, which I do not believe would have emerged on its own.

It was my relationship with our supervisor which still burns brightly in my mind, that led me to conclude that 'a supervisor is for life, not just for Christmas'. This supervisory relationship is, as many notable therapists have concurred, indeed an attachment relationship and acts as a container for all our messy enactments and shadowy stuff![36] She was there when we celebrated our fantastic data and positive feedback, and was also there when one of our graduates took their own life. Over six years after she retired, my clear memory of the minute details of the room – the pictures on the wall, the fluffy cushions on the sofa and her inimitable style – reminds me how important she was, and still is.

Therapist's therapy

Another important consideration as we prepare for co-facilitation is personal therapy. There is a wealth of published material on this topic, which takes us all the way back to the early beginnings of psychoanalytic psychotherapy. Personal therapy has been mandatory for all those engaging in psychoanalytical training, whereas within humanistic and cognitive behavioural traditions there is an emphasis on self-reflection without a requirement for therapy. That said, many therapists of all disciplines will choose to access personal therapy to support their own personal therapeutic journey and enhance their awareness and reflexivity.

Within the CFGP programmes, therapists are required to engage in their own self-practice in compassion, which mirrors the Compassionate Mind Training process. This enables therapists to learn about compassion from the inside out, rather than on a purely

---

[36] Pistole, M. C., & Watkins, C. E. (1995). Attachment theory, counseling process, and supervision. *The Counseling Psychologist*, **23**(3), 457–478. https://doi.org/10.1177/0011000095233004

theoretical basis. Additionally, this also supports therapists to attend to their own responses within their therapeutic work. A number of close colleagues and dear friends have written a fantastic book on this topic and I would strongly recommend checking it out. [37]

I would also strongly recommend accessing personal therapy and group therapy if this is your interest. It is deeply helpful to have your own experience as a patient in a group. On one level, this supports the compassionate wisdom that you then bring to your group members. This process is also deeply helpful to work through our own shadowy parts, which, if left unchecked, can emerge in unhelpful ways in the group programme. I could fill the rest of this book with such moments, where my own unprocessed and unresolved attachment material has emerged underneath my awareness and caused me to react rather than respond. I shall resist this urge, however, and instead offer a brief example of the ways in which personal therapy and supervision can coalesce to support our developing awareness.

There was a member in one of my early groups who I really struggled to form a strong connection with. I found him frustrating, grandiose, and I was a little disgusted by him. There was a particular story that had stayed with me. He was living in a shared house and was having difficulties with the other tenants, seemingly linked to his insistence that he kept his shoes outside his room. His shoes by all accounts were highly malodorous (there was some evidence of this in the group also). He was incredibly angry and defensive, and it was not possible to explore with him why his housemates may have taken exception to him and his shoes.

I felt deeply provoked by this situation and grappled with an urge to 'out' him and what seemed to be the obvious reason for the conflict. My co-facilitator urged restraint and together we took this to supervision. I was keen to focus on the symbolism of the smelly shoes, which he could not bear to have in his intimate space and forced onto others. With some support, I instead turned my attention to trying to be curious about what sat underneath my own feelings of contempt and disgust. My supervisor benignly inquired who he reminded me of and, with a jolt, I realised it was me. I spent much of my early life drenched in shame, working hard to defend myself against this, likely leaving my own metaphorical 'smelly shoes' outside the door. Personal therapy offered some space to explore and unpack the terror which sat underneath my contempt. Another version of me could have been this group member, socially difficult, excluded and unaware. Over time and with help, I discovered compassion for this man, which coincided with my own therapeutic work finding compassion for my shamed and denied young self. I have found the work of Irving Yalom deeply helpful in his willingness to acknowledge moments of fragility and errors of judgement, and I invite all those who resonate with this to do the same.

---

[37] Kolts, R. L., Bell, T., Bennett-Levy, J., & Irons, C. (2018). *Experiencing Compassion-focused Therapy From The Inside Out: A self-practice/self-reflection workbook for therapists*. Guilford Publications.

Let's be really clear, though: this is not an easy task. Some of us will find it more challenging than others to be in a group as a member rather than a group leader. I am speaking very much from personal experience, as I alluded to in the Preface, in that tolerating my own vulnerability continues to be a big part of my journey in compassionate courage and wisdom.

Despite signing up for group psychotherapy seemingly voluntarily, I recall with some discomfort the months of resistance that I experienced being a 'group member'. I found myself sitting with crossed arms and legs and listening to others with a level of detachment, which manifested in what I perceived to be wise and helpful suggestions. But these were in fact strategies designed to distance myself from my fellow group members and my own connections to their stories. I was fortunate to have a wise and patient group conductor who, when I was ready, gently but firmly held up the mirror to my defences and helped me back myself out of the corner.

It's all about the chairs!

To conclude this section, which has focused on what we need to pay attention to in preparing for the therapeutic work to begin, it feels important to talk about chairs. Chairs so often hold symbolic meaning relating to many other elements of the group therapeutic process, in that their presence, absence or layout can heavily impact a group. Ensuring that the chairs are equidistant, of the same type, and in a near-perfect circle is a fundamental part of the dynamic administrative responsibility of any group facilitator. I find myself uncomfortable as I write this, recalling times when I have 'forgotten' someone in my counting of the chairs. It has felt like a significant rupture as the last person in the room realises that they do not have a chair. As I touched on in the previous section, there is often something for us to understand about what has happened in us to result in the chair error. Another reason why having a co-facilitator is so important is to have your back, hold the rope, and check the chairs! I have often found myself arranging and re-arranging the chairs to ensure they are equidistant and that there is the right number. Ensuring that everyone has a chair, even if you know that they are not coming that week, helps to keep the whole group in everyone's mind. It also becomes a visual representation of each member of the group, and often a way into the conversation and feelings when members are absent. The removal of someone's chair from the circle is also discussed in the context of a pause or ending of their time in the programme. We will come back to this and how it is managed in Phase Three. But at this stage of the programme, Sarah and I will put out chairs for all those on the waiting list, to indicate everyone who has been invited.

NHS chairs are, in my experience, generally uncomfortable, with the necessity of prioritising fire safety regulations over comfort. The space you have in your room will also dictate the size of the chairs. Many years ago, we had lovely bucket chairs with arms and sides, but I then realised that some of our group members may not be able to fit comfortably into these chairs, so armless stiff chairs resulted. I purchased cushions which some have spoken of appreciating, as they can also be used as props in the later work. I think that the attention that we pay to trying to make the room comforting and welcoming is generally appreciated. Uplighters, a coffee table, a rug on the floor – these small gestures can demonstrate that you have the group in mind. Recently, a few of my group members had a small-scale mutiny, stating that there was no way they would be doing any kind of exploratory work in the group unless I got some plants. Again, a reminder that attending to the room is important. I duly went and bought plants and we got down to the 'work'. We will come back to the topic of chairs with the 'folding chairs of doom' in Phase Four, where it is important that the chairs for chairwork and the like are different from the others.

Concluding comments

Co-facilitation becomes an attachment relationship built on tolerating and resolving inevitable ruptures and misattunements and eventually reaching a point of trust. The feeling of having someone to 'hold the rope' while navigating the group process is deeply reassuring and containing for everyone.

Let's not underestimate the support needed to nurture and support the co-facilitation relationship. Shared supervision and personal therapy can provide the foundations for self-reflection and personal growth. So, we are ready to begin Phase Three, the Preparation and Engagement Group.

Phase Three:
The Preparation and Engagement Group (PEG)

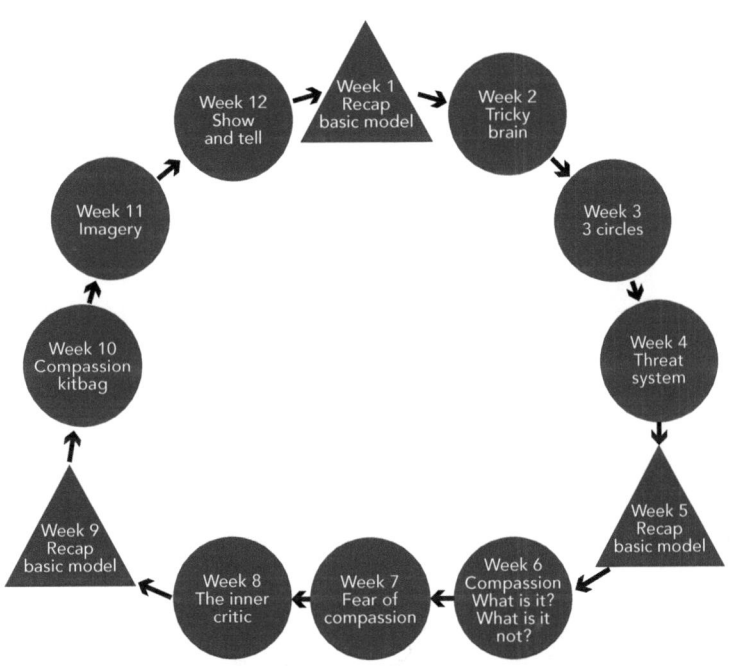

Programme element	Format	Function
3. Preparation and Engagement Phase Group (PEG). Psychoeducation and Compassionate Mind Training.	■ 12 weekly sessions. ■ Two hours in duration (no break). ■ Slow-paced, experiential, play-based group intervention. ■ Facilitated by two highly trained Compassion-Focused Group Psychotherapy Facilitators.	■ Continuation of psychoeducation phase. ■ Introduction of Compassionate Mind Training practices and rationale. ■ Early exposure to CFGP model and the experience of compassion across the three flows. ■ Continuing development of safe haven and proximity seeking function.

Chapter 3.1:
To prep or not to prep? That is the question

'The core experiences of psychological trauma are disempowerment and disconnection from others. Recovery therefore is based upon empowerment of the survivor and the creation of new connections.' (Herman, 2002, p.s98)

As we move into Phase Three of the programme, we have already begun to facilitate the development of some tentative connections, both with the facilitator through the assessment and perhaps with co-travellers and 'group members to be' in the Waiting List Group (Phase Two). But here the work of compassion-focused group psychotherapy really begins.

The motivation to split the programme in this way is twofold. First, to separate the Compassionate Mind Training (psychoeducation and practices) from the exploratory trauma processing component of the programme (Phase Four). Second, to attempt to address the difficulty with currently high attrition rates in group psychotherapy for people with a diagnosis of personality disorder, particularly in the first three months.[38] It is well understood that the social and emotional implications for those who drop out of therapy prematurely are significant. But over the past 20 years, research has identified that psycho-educative, preparatory interventions can reduce the dropout rate substantially and therefore improve outcomes for this marginalised and often overlooked group of patients. The split also allows for the pacing of the two groups to be slightly different, with an initial lighter touch appreciating a more vertical parental transference with group members often looking more explicitly to the facilitators to lead the group. I have sat in many early groups with multiple pairs of eyes fixed on me or my co-facilitator, waiting and hoping for something to soothe the anxiety.

What is the purpose of the Preparation and Engagement Group (PEG)?

During the 12-week PEG, three modules are introduced to slowly introduce the group to the psychoeducation and Compassionate Mind Training (CMT). The group has an open rolling format, in that members join at specified time points within a rolling continuous 12 weeks cycle. This would mean that group members would all spend 12 weeks in the PEG group but would receive the sessions in a different order (see Figure 3.1). In practice, members are invited to join a group, usually in pairs, and then have a 'therapy buddy' to journey with them through the following phases of the programme. This joining with another or others is also designed to reduce the anxiety associated with joining a group that is already running or rolling.

This aspect of the model is intended to promote a process whereby new group members are supported and welcomed by existing 'senior' members to begin to make sense of the process and content of the groups, thereby encouraging a sense of cohesion.

In explaining the basic model to new members, senior group members can rehearse and explore their own learning, including reflecting on their journey in self-compassion, while being empowered by the opportunity to support those at the commencement of their journey. This group structure, content and process has been designed to cultivate compassion in the participants across the three flows of compassion, explicitly through teaching participants about the meaning of

---

38 Arntz, A. (2015). Imagery rescripting for personality disorders: Healing early maladaptive schemas. Working with Emotion in *Cognitive-Behavioral Therapy: Techniques for Clinical Practice*, 175–202.

compassion, and implicitly through the design of the programme which encourages turn-taking and mutual support. Thus, it facilitates and supports developing the capacity of group members to experience compassion from others, offer compassion to others and to begin to practice giving compassion to themselves:

> '...so having that rolling programme is a great benefit if we had all started on the same day ... a room full of frightened silent people wouldn't have been of great benefit but where some had been there for months and were ready to move on ... seeing people at different stages of development, that kind of gave me hope.'

Figure 3.1: Format of the 12-Week Preparation and Engagement Group

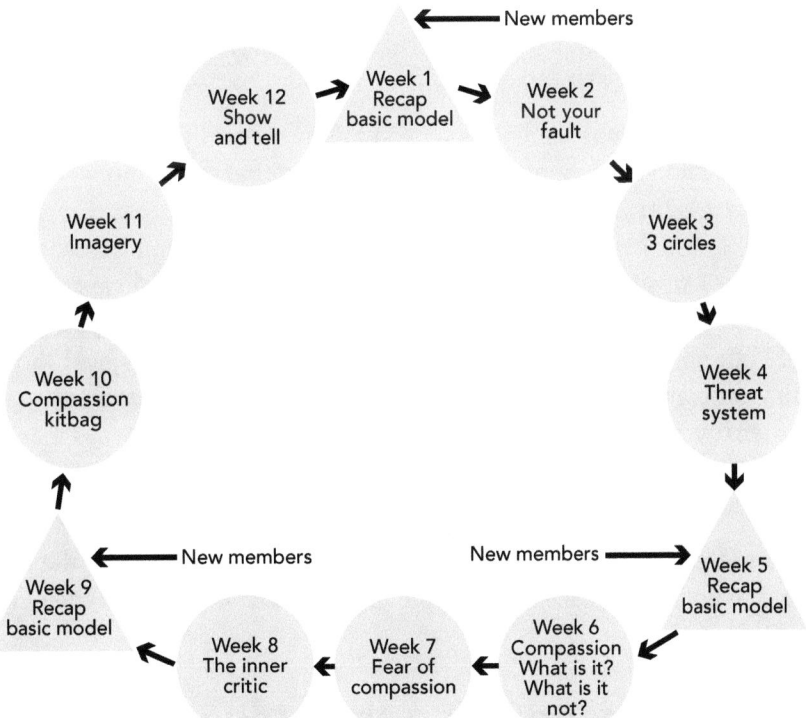

The set up

The group runs for two hours on the same day and at the same time each week, in the same room, with the same set up of chairs and other furniture. Unexpected changes to the room have been likened to returning home to find your house rearranged, and brings with it all the understandable distress and consternation which would accompany this. It has also suggested to me that a two-hour group might be too long for some folk, particularly those who struggle to maintain concentration. This may be true, and adaptations can be made to support the group, but my experience over the years of taking breaks in this kind of exploratory psychotherapy programme is that people do not return, metaphorically and actually. Often in the early days with a ten-minute comfort break in the group, I would enquire where Louie was as we returned from the break, only to be told he had 'gone home'! Also, trying to return the group to the material from the previous segment can be challenging and takes time to re-establish the connection and ability to tolerate the intensity. Day therapeutic communities are a different process whereby milieu and group-based breaks are built into the programme, but with only two hours, maintaining some intensity of connection in the work is imperative.

The thorny issue of sustenance has also been raised many times over the years by both facilitators and group members. Many have said that the group would feel more manageable with a break and cup of tea, and I know of many programmes that have started out with this. I try to remain curious about the motivation that sits underneath what may seem like a benign and soothing warm drink. Of course we can look at this as a way of creating the conditions for safeness with a compassionate gesture towards the group. I am not so convinced, having explored this many times over the years. My sense is that a break and a drink serves to dilute the discomfort for many associated with the intensity of group psychotherapy. I believe that there are ways that we can work with the intensity within the group process which develops the capacity to tolerate it, rather than swerve it.

I will return to the occasions where we explicitly and deliberately dilute the transference and intensity with tea and cake, but group members have to wait until their ending for this. As will you!

Facilitating or conducting the group

I discussed the benefits of co-conduction and the links with rock climbing in the previous chapter, but I would like to add to these ideas with some further thoughts on co-facilitation and the practicalities of running the programme with another. I would strongly suggest that the facilitators do not change, without spending time preparing the group for the departure and entry of new facilitators. As mentioned previously, the parental transference will be implicit in the relationships between the facilitator and the group members, which can be positive and negative. But most importantly, we are not interchangeable. Co-facilitation also enables us to cover for each other in times of absence. This helps to create consistent, reliable, good-enough parental transference objects who can support with the work of repairing early attachment ruptures and provide a new experience of dependency.

Dependency, I think, gets a bad rap in services providing care for those with A&RT. I recall being told many years ago that I needed to be careful as my patients might become dependent on me. I was told that this had negative implications for me and them, in that I had somehow made my patients dependent on me and that this would be deleterious and hamper their recovery. Many years ago, I took this issue to my supervision with Paul Gilbert to ask for strategies to manage and reduce dependency. His response has been a guiding principle of my work since that time. Paul smiled and asked why I thought dependency was problematic, given the early attachment ruptures and absences for the group members. I didn't have an answer to his question and we went on to explore what it would mean to support a healthy dependence as part of a reparative attachment experience, which group members could individuate from in time. Paul went as far as to invite me to consider that dependency for this group would be a sign of progress, as they had attached to the group and to me – for many, possibly for the first time. This reminds me of a time when a group member asked if they could bring and leave their slippers in the group room. This example is full of possible interpretations, about being held in mind, but importantly also about this space being something to depend on and settle into. Gwen Adshead also invites us consider that all psychiatric staff will become attachment figures for their patients, it is only the quality of the attachment relationship that we can influence.[39] Kelly Steele writes helpfully about the importance of addressing accepting and enabling dependency in the context of working with dissocation.[40] Dependency will of course also be a source of terror for many of your group members, whose unmet attachment needs will likely be activated if any feelings of reliance or dependency emerge (as we explored in Phase One). We will return to ways of supporting the group to slowly over time tolerate this experience.

With this in mind, I have found that it is generally quite tricky and counter-productive to draft in substitute co-facilitators to support when one or both are absent. This is likely linked to issues already raised about healthy dependency and connection with

---

39 Adshead, G. (1998). Psychiatric staff as attachment figures: Understanding management problems in psychiatric services in the light of attachment theory. *The British Journal of Psychiatry*, **172**(1), 64-69.
40 Steele, K., Van Der Hart, O., & Nijenhuis, E. R. S. (2001). Dependency in the Treatment of Complex Posttraumatic Stress Disorder and Dissociative Disorders. *Journal of Trauma & Dissociation*, **2**(4), 79-116. https://doi.org/10.1300/J229v02n04_05

the established facilitators and the trust that inevitably develops. Group members over the years have likened this experience to the substitute teacher who generally cannot hold the class in a space of safeness and often finds that they are taken for a ride by the class! Having been a substitute group facilitator over the years, I would concur with this, and my experience has been generally flying blind, with a group who are not keen to have me for a session and instead tend towards finding ways to trip me up!

That said, there will inevitably be a need for change, and this can be a deeply helpful opportunity to practice what is being taught and learned implicitly about turning back to and not away from suffering and difficulty. Our group members have invariably experienced traumatic changes – people leave without warning, trust is breached, repairs and apologies never come. So it unsurprising that there is a lot of resistance to any form of change.

> **The case of the invisible facilitator**
>
> A new facilitator was introduced into an established CFGP programme where there were ruptures between the group members which the group were struggling to address. It seemed that the arrival of the new facilitator offered a distraction from the ingroup conflict. One group member, Clara, often challenged the structure of group, typically by criticising the facilitators and other group members (she had even interrogated another patient waiting for therapy in the waiting room about why they had a blue disabled badge on their car). This situation had left her isolated and alone in the group, with limited capacity for her to see her part in this process and to pull back. The tension in the group had been building for some weeks around whether these repeated issues could be worked with.
>
> The new facilitator's arrival was felt deeply by the group, as the previous facilitator had not been able to have a planned ending with the group and the pain of this was still felt by some. Clara seemed to find the presence of the new facilitator difficult and repeatedly claimed to have forgotten the new facilitator's name. She would often refer to the facilitator with a variety of different names, never making eye contact or responding to comments or questions, insisting that she could not hear what she was saying. This went as far as Clara saying to the other facilitator, 'I really cannot hear anything that *she* is saying, do you think she has a problem?' Invitations by both facilitators to be curious about what was happening were met with an absolute defence and insistence that the name forgetting was an oversight and her voice was just too quiet. The group were also invited into wondering about this apparent difficulty and someone quietly suggested that it might be hard to accept the authority of another facilitator.

This case vignette highlights the delicate process of change in a rolling group programme and the time needed to explore and unpack the transferential material which can emerge in such contexts. We will return to Clara, the anti-group process and the ingroup conflict, in Phase Four.

Attention to pacing and tone is a key component of cultivating and maintaining safeness. I made reference earlier to my experience of myself in the early days in threat-based drive trying to keep everything moving. Incredible and painful supervision from Paul Gilbert and others has supported me to slow down and really pay attention to what is happening in the room. A wise colleague once advised me to try to be the milk float and not the fire engine. This advice has stayed with me over the decades, working towards a gentle, unknowing curiosity and a willingness to be wrong.

It is often painful and shame-based material that pushes us all into hyperdrive. I often find in such moments that group members can switch into 'problem solving mode', with helpful but often overwhelming advice that serves to dilute the intensity of the distress and often shuts it up altogether. This can feel similar to someone quickly passing tissues to a person who is showing signs of becoming tearful. Your group member will tell you that they intended to be helpful, but often the struggle to tolerate distress sits underneath this.

Gently inviting the group to notice what they are feeling as they launch into practical advice, carefully navigating the tendency for group members to feel; that they have got it wrong. Some groups have put in the Safe Space Agreement that they will try not to problem solve and instead try and sit with each other's suffering.

Concluding comments

I hope to have offered a rationale for the separation of the programme into two parts, with the first part slow-paced and generally smaller, aimed at addressing the problems with attrition in the early stages of psychotherapy. The need for a predictable and consistent therapy space is coupled with a rolling programme which introduces change, not always welcomed, but necessary to create the conditions to test the developing compassionate capacity.

We will now move on to the practical components of the PEG.

Chapter 3.2: How it works

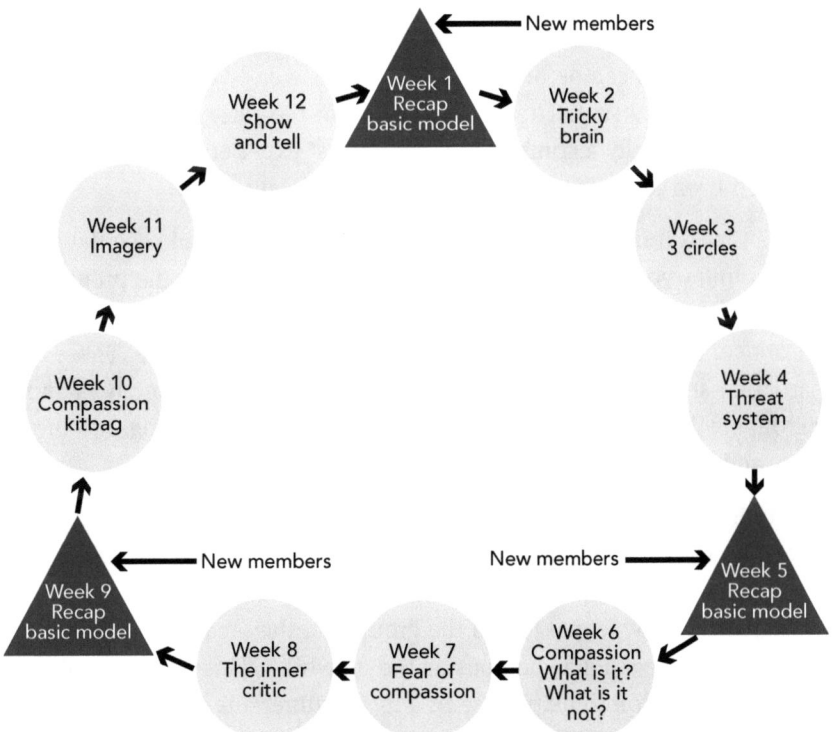

The First Session

'First part, first session, I will never forget… absolutely terrifying… I… I barely looked up all session. I remember sitting huddled up with coat pulled up and my hat on, not wanting to make eye contact with anybody in a very full room… that day… of complete

> *strangers not knowing what was going to happen, not knowing what was going to be asked of me... I was terrified... absolutely terrified, but I felt like I settled in quite quickly ... by the time the first six weeks were over I felt like I'd found my feet in the group ... and listening to other people who were slightly further ahead in the process I could ... I could see that perhaps when I am six weeks further ahead I will be where they are.'*

We have our work cut out to support our group members to hold on in those first few sessions, given that the experience described in the quote above is very common.

There appears to be a consensus within the literature that providing a structure to the therapeutic intervention can be helpful to those whose early attachment relationships have been ruptured or absent. The psychotherapy in the early stages is predictable and reliable, which is generally a contrast to participants' experiences of parental figures who have often been absent, chaotic, intrusive and abusive.

The structure that is introduced during the 'triangle' joining week, see the chapter image, is then followed for every subsequent session throughout the programme. During the 12-week cycle of PEG, there are three joining sessions, depicted by the triangles in Figure 5.1 above. This is when new participants join the programme. These sessions have a particular structure designed to introduce the new group members and explain how the groups will be run. The intention is to offer a gentle landing into the group programme, and an explanation of the structure also supports this.

Again, the rolling programme is helpful at this point, as your existing 'senior' group members can be recruited to offer an authentic explanation of the structure and purpose and also to reflect on their own journey so far. Group members have often reported that it was not until new people joined the group that they realised that something had shifted, in that they were not as anxious as the 'newbies'. This also prompted for many a compassionate motivation to help those in a more vulnerable place.

> *'The older ones showed us the ropes... Then you look after the newbies; you just take on that role and, I don't know, it naturally shifts.'*

The change in group membership can also shift the dynamic in the room in other ways. I can recall many groups which had become a little stuck, with members rolling their eyes and sucking their teeth about this 'group' which made them worse and most definitely wasn't working. Then new members would join and there would be a dramatic shift, the complaints about the group stopped and were replaced with proclamations about how great 'their' group was. There are many ways, I think, we can understand this process: from something territorial and linked to ownership, which we can understand in the context of our shared ancestral roots in tribes and small social groupings, through to the change in the self only being visible to the existing group members when newer, more fearful members joined. However we make sense of this, it is often very helpful for new people to join in those early weeks and keep the dynamic fluid and individual change visible. I also feel strongly that the rolling programme offers a more authentic representation of 'real life', in that you will meet new people and things will change.

I will explicitly invite the existing group members to recall how they felt on their first session. This has multiple functions to remind the existing group how much they have changed and also to provide much-needed reassurance to the new members. Many report that this light touch instillation of hope is what made them decide to come back the next week.

There are also moments in those joining sessions when the new members may not be so welcomed. The group will become settled into a rhythm and the arrival of new people disrupts this. I recall a joining group session when one existing group member spoke of feeling furious for reasons she could not identify. She spoke of sitting in the car park feeling enraged by a car that had parked outside the lines. She had even taken a photo of it, which she wanted to share with the group. I wondered if this car belonged to the new member who may have been perceived as 'out of line' by coming to the programme. It felt much too early to be inviting discussion of this directly, not least for the new highly anxious group member. But instead, I invited the furious group member and the rest of the group to be curious about what else might feel 'out of line' or off kilter. In this way there could be a tentative discussion about symbolic meaning without jumping straight into what was perhaps resentment towards the new member. The furious group member settled and was able to talk about her resentment towards her children who seemed not to acknowledge how much she was struggling.

However, during the triangle or joining week, the ordering of the session is slightly different in order to acknowledge new people coming into the group. There are some very basic introductions, such as stating names and where individuals are on the programme (i.e. 'my name is Sherelle and is this is my fifth week in the group'). This is designed to orientate everyone without too much pressure and exposure. The facilitators will offer a summary of the PEG what and why, as much as possible drawing on the expertise of the existing members to avoid long monologues by the facilitator. The Safe Space Agreement comes after this, followed by a discussion and introduction to the breathing practice, before then proceeding to the breathing practice, feedback and check in. This allows new people to understand the 'what and why' of the group process before being plunged into it. The final stage of this initial or joining session is an opportunity for the group to recap the previous three sessions, reminding themselves and also bringing the new members into the work.

The Safe Space Agreement

An essential component of this 'joining session' is the 'Safe Space Agreement', which is a group-based behavioural contract that everyone agrees to abide by, designed to create a clear, predictable and consistent space. This is reviewed each time new members join, thus ensuring the key principles of the therapy contract are co-produced, agreed and held in mind by each member[41].

> *'It's the people that you respect and trust and all the rest of it and because the ground rules stay the ground rules and they are the ground rules we came up with and all that trust and shared history is still there.'*

The group are invited to explore what they need from themselves, from each other, and from the facilitators to cultivate and maintain a space of safeness in the room. Time is spent exploring what is meant by this with suggestions to get the conversation started (see Appendix 3.1: Space Safe Agreement for an example). This process is perhaps more explicitly collaborative, with the intention of ensuring that the agreement around conduct in the group is shared and can be used to hold and reinforce the group boundaries. This becomes a 'live' document that is returned to and adapted each time new people join. We also return to this in the event of ruptures or conflict in the group and remind ourselves what we agreed to. In this way, accountability is shared and hierarchy is flattened at the outset of the group.

Group members are also offered a variety of options for contact with the group facilitators and the service in general, with a shift from a more traditional expectation of telephone contact. Text and email messaging are available to support those whose capacity to use the phone is compromised by the manifestations of trauma, such as those for whom leaving a message or communicating with someone other than the facilitator may not feel possible in the early days of therapeutic engagement.

---

[41] Lucre, K., & Clapton, N. (n.d.). The Compassionate Kitbag: A creative and integrative approach to compassion-focused therapy. *Psychology and Psychotherapy: Theory, Research and Practice*, e12291.

Within this, the limitations of this means of communication are made explicit, in that messages outside 9–5pm will not be responded to until the following day, and also the expectation that all contact will be brought back into the group process.

This part of the group also offers an opportunity for a discussion about 'between-group contact'. Many therapies have strict rules to ensure that no between-group contact takes place, but, in my mind, this takes the responsibility for bringing compassionate wisdom away from the group. If it does not come up, I will invite the group to consider what between-group contact might look and feel like.

Here's a script that may help guide such a conversation:

> **Facilitator:** *'So, what do we think about having contact with each other outside of group?'*
>
> **Group member 1:** *'I don't see a problem with it, I was in a therapy before and we had a WhatsApp group for support between the sessions.'*
>
> **Facilitator:** *'What do others feel about this?'*
>
> **Group member 2:** *'I'm not too sure…'*
>
> **Facilitator:** *'I wonder if we can think about what it would be like if you knew that other group members were chatting between the sessions…'*
>
> **Group member 2:** *'I would be wondering if they were talking about me and what I had said.'*
>
> **Group Member 3:** *'Yeah, me too.'*
>
> **Facilitator:** *'This feels really important because we want to make sure that everyone feels OK to share personal things in the group and know that it won't be discussed outside. I would also worry that it might stop people from sharing or feeling connected to each other. So maybe we make sure that we keep all our conversations and contact inside the group?'*

Let's be really clear that, despite these conversations, this does not always go to plan. There was a group many years ago when two group members were in contact with each other between the sessions and a difficult situation emerged. One of the group members was Louie:

> *'Yeah there was a boundary issue coz he wanted... to see me outside of the group although the rules weren't... we did discuss it at the beginning and it probably wasn't a good idea to see members of the group outside of the group because it can affect the group and I agreed with that ... I like rules, but I've got one part of me that's all kind of like, yeah, whatever, and another part of me likes my rules I feel comfortable so I liked the fact that we set those rules ... and so I said no, we can't do that because that's breaking the rules and he said oh he said oh... you know f*** the rules ... I don't follow rules... Well, I said, well, I do follow them ... erm... but we did meet up once outside of the group and I thought oh god we shouldn't have met up outside the group... It did change things a little bit... erm... I felt a bit bad .. and I felt like I felt I dunno it... it changed the atmosphere within the group for me.'*

This example demonstrates how tangled and conflicted our group members can become in relation to the Safe Space Agreement. Also, how something that seems benign, like meeting up outside the group, can have a significant impact on everyone in ways that are often not anticipated. I believe that allowing the group to have some autonomy in the development of the agreement then leads to the group being invited to work with the inevitable ruptures. We will return later, in Phase Four, and look at the work in that group which was undertaken to repair this rupture.

The structure of a group

> *'The breathing practice to get everyone in the flow of the group session ... and gather yourself in really ... then we'd do a check in... then you'd pass it on to someone else and it's a way of bonding as well, and you also got to learn people's names.'*

This quote offers a great summary of the predictable structure of the group, which was designed to support the development of ritual and routine. The importance of this emerged as a key theme in the qualitative study and was closely linked to the cultivation of safeness as a necessity for therapeutic engagement.[42]

---

42   Lucre, K., Ashworth, F., Copello, A., Jones, C., & Gilbert, P. (2024). Compassion Focused Group Psychotherapy for attachment and relational trauma: Engaging people with a diagnosis of personality disorder. *Psychology and Psychotherapy* **97**(2).

This makes me think of how important rituals are for us all. I was raised within the Catholic faith. I am no longer a practicing Catholic, or even a Christian, however I find it deeply reassuring that I can go into any Catholic church anywhere in the world and know what to do, follow the service and feel connected to what is happening. Steve Porges takes us further back to the links, or 'portals', to compassion with ancient rites and rituals.[43]

Each group follows the same structure as outlined below, with the rationale for the inclusion of each component provided.

Table 5.1: Structure of the weekly group session – Preparation and Engagement Group

Component	Purpose
Soothing breathing rhythm practice	Creating predictable ritual for the group Introducing Compassionate Mind Training and self-practice Creating a Safe haven and secure base in the therapy room
Feedback from the breathing practice	Turn-taking Social skills training Informal teaching and validation around soothing breathing rhythm (SBR)
Check in with participants	Turn-taking Social skills training Gathering information for taught components
Introduction of module-specific topic using participant examples from the check in	Delivery of basic compassion-focused therapy model Opportunities for group discussion/engagement Normalising and validating emotional distress Preparing the group for the ending
Closing of the group, checking out	Inviting the group to 'park' difficult feelings

The latecomers

There will inevitably be occasions when members will arrive late, for a variety of different reasons. I am always on the lookout for patterns forming. One group member was always late, arriving just in time for the end of the practice. Over time, we worked

---

43   Porges, S. W. (2017). Vagal pathways: portals to compassion. *The Oxford Handbook of Compassion Science*, 189-202.

with her to acknowledge that she was avoiding a regular part of the session she disliked, but also missing the meeting in the waiting room, the banter on the way into the room and the sense of being part of something (rather than on the outside). There is a great deal of therapeutic opportunity in the waiting room, and this unstructured social space has been described by many as their 'pre-group'! This is as much a part of the work as making sure the chairs are set out and your watch tells the right time.

Lateness is an important consideration to be attended to and addressed with compassion. I remember with a smile a group member reacting to my invitation to consider the impact on his therapy and others' by his persistent lateness – 'I thought this was compassion-focused therapy, but you are a real bitch!' What was clear to me in that moment was that he had confused compassion with being 'nice', perhaps expecting that a 'compassionate' response would be, 'Oh, don't worry, never mind, I know it is hard'. But in fact what he got was, 'I know that is difficult to come and be part of this group but we need to understand what is getting in the way of being here on time; I wish for you to have the whole therapy and for us to benefit from having you here with us'. My hope was to be clear about the intention that sat underneath my challenge, drawing on my own compassionate wisdom that those who persistently come late will eventually be excluded from the group on many different levels.

There is of course a view held by some that, if you are late you cannot come in. I understand this view but do not subscribe to it. Time management is a skill that we learn through our lives in school, work, and family life. But if you don't have those life opportunities, then it is another deficit that gets punished. So we teach it instead, gently and carefully, while holding the boundary and attending to the needs of all the group members.

With that dual attention in mind, we have noticed over the years the practical ramifications of people coming into group after the start have been quite disruptive. There were so many groups in the early days of the programme, where someone would rush in late, flustered, berating themselves, apologising profusely and, of course, completely disrupting the breathing practice. The group then have an impossible choice: give authentic feedback and deepen the guilt of the interrupting group member, or avoid it and give dishonest feedback. Either way, it created chaos, so we came up with the idea of 'the Notice'. Just before we start our practice, if anyone was still missing, this (literal) notice would be pinned to the door outside. The poster had a calming image and the words 'We are just breathing, take a moment and we will come and get you'. This meant that the group members knew 'the breathe' (see below) was in progress and that we would check after the practice and let them know to come in. This has generally worked well, but there was an occasion when

I forgot to go and get the sign and a group member sat furiously outside for half an hour, believing that I was punishing him for his lateness! Another rupture to be acknowledged and repaired.

The breathe

The breathing practice is introduced during the first session of every intake to the group with a detailed rationale for the practice to ensure that its purpose is understood. Each group then commences with a guided soothing breathing rhythm practice (SBR), designed to create a predictable and consistent starting point for the group and an opportunity for group members to settle into the group space at the outset.

> *'Then the breathe... It was almost like a trigger for the group that's when the work started.'*

This practice is consistent with Steve Porges' Polyvagal Theory.[44] An emphasis is placed on an increased postural awareness, a straight, slightly concave back, grounded, upright posture, a gentle facial expression and a warm and friendly inner voice tone, as this can facilitate the activation of the vagal nerve which is associated with the activation of the social engagement system and the neurobiological benefits of co-regulation in groups.[45]

Some of your group members will be very interested in the science that underpins this part of the group structure, others not so much! But what is perhaps more important is the emphasis on the experimental nature of the practice, and this process takes time and work.

> *'...but oh my god it took work and this is something that the group brought for me, yes, I fall on and off the band wagon with it, but, yes, it so helpful.'*

It is the collective work of the group to support everyone to find their own way to make the breathing practice meaningful and helpful. Group members are invited to share ideas, bring practices and/or objects to the session to support the collective work. I invite the group to think of this practice as a set of ingredients to be adapted to whatever kind of 'vagal' cake you wish to put together, rather than a prescription to be

---

[44] Porges, S. W. (2011). *The Polyvagal Theory: Neurophysiological foundations of emotions, attachment, communication, and self-regulation (Norton Series on Interpersonal Neurobiology).* WW Norton & Company.
[45] For recorded practices Stream Kate Lucre music at https://soundcloud.com/kate-lucre.

followed in a rigid way. The intention is to bring a light touch to this practice and invite creativity and individuality. One group member found closing her eyes too terrifying and triggered flashbacks, so she would focus her attention on the movement of the trees outside the window. Over time, she found that she could regulate her breathing with the movement. Once she had established this practice in the group, she used this strategy in other areas of her life, such as focusing on the movement of wind through the trees as she sat on the bus. This intuitive discovery become the foundation for her practice and how she developed the capacity to regulate and manage problematic anger.

The group are also invited to use objects which are available on the table in the group room – beanbags, stones, cubes – which have the dual purpose of providing a sensory focus and also a connection to the group. We will explore this in more detail later in the chapter:

> *'The stones that can help you focus... You have that visual form that is great to go back to... refresh it for yourself ... something physical there that brings you back to the group in a way.'*

I will return to the significance of gifts and transitional objects from the group when we explore the Compassionate Kitbag later in this chapter.

The function of this practice is also to stimulate personal practice between the sessions:

> *'It's like the breathe we did once a week and everybody practised it at home... and that just became natural... it formed a habit.'*

This practising at home has, in my experience, always been a thorny issue. I recall my early days as a Cognitive Behavioural Therapist struggling with the idea of setting homework. I often felt a little that I was patronising people. It is likely that my concern made its way into the unconscious material in the room and I found that my patients rarely 'did' their homework. I found that some group members whose survival strategies generally involved appeasing would 'do' the homework in a complicit way, which would activate threat and not drive or soothing. Others would become angered and insulted by the school associations and perhaps feel infantilised by this, and so refuse practices that may have been helpful. So, over time, I developed the confidence to drop it.

However, the benefits of between-session practice are indisputable. The incredible work of Marcela Matos is now beginning to show changes at an epigenetic level following regular practice, in addition to the decades of research demonstrating that:

> *'Cultivating a compassionate mind/self-identity through the core components of CMT may stimulate vagal regulatory activity and positively impact one's ability to experience and be open to compassion, and thus promote emotion regulation, well-being and mental health.'*[46]

This is not to mention the benefits to physical health and the immune system.

So, we are faced with a tricky question: how to encourage practice compassionately? The language here is important. Dropping the idea of homework, with all its associated burden of compulsion, will help. Instead, invite the group to consider what would happen if they practised at home and then support them with the means to achieve this (sound clouds and CDs can also be offered to support home practice). Inviting the group to record the in-session practice has also been very popular over the years. It seems that the coughing, door slamming, foot shuffling rather than just a distraction becomes part of what the group associate to the slowing down and settling into the session. Group members are also invited to set compassionate challenges for each other in a spontaneous way and this must always include you as the facilitators. I was issued a compassionate challenge recently, which involved just being still, no activity whatsoever. It was indeed a challenge, and the group received my feedback the next week with humour and understanding!

Creating the conditions for spontaneous practice as the group develops can be linked to the cultivation and mobilising of a compassionate mind and motivation. I often use Paul Gilbert's simple but effective question, 'Would you wait until overboard in a storm before learning to swim?', to which, hopefully, your group will respond in the negative. This again becomes part of the shared language of the group, gently reminding and supporting regular practice. Inviting the group to 'learn to swim' together in and between sessions, so that the capacity has been developed when it is needed, is well worth the effort.

Adam and the Pebble

Adam has been quite clear from the outset that the breathing practice made no sense to him and instead he would sit during the practice thinking and worrying about what he was going to say in the check in. Other group members would make suggestions and encourage Adam to try the practice, perhaps with an object from the table. Adam was always very clear that that he would not be taking anything from the table ever, as he could not bear to touch anything without his gloves on, fearing being contaminated and also contaminating the objects on the table. At the beginning of a session in the

---

[46] Matos, M. et al (2022). Cultivating the Compassionate Self: An exploration of the mechanisms of change in compassionate mind training. *Mindfulness*, 13(1), 66–79. https://doi.org/10.1007/s12671-021-01717-2

> PEG, another group member took a pebble from the table that he noticed that Adam had perhaps had his eye on, he wiped it with antibacterial cloth and handed it in the cloth to Adam. To everyone's surprise, Adam took the pebble and held it during the practice. The next week, he returned to group and shared a difficult experience with his mother who had come to his home unannounced and criticised him in front of his family. He described using the pebble in his pocket to ground himself and connect to the group, which he noticed calmed him down. He was practising using his own compassionate wisdom. The work for facilitators in such moments was (and is) to slow down and notice what has happened and invite comment from the group.

What happens when things don't go to plan?

It is helpful to anticipate the likely adverse reactions that often accompany the practices, as they are inevitable. Many group members in the early stages of the programme will find the whole idea of breathing, mindfulness and meditation abhorrent on many different levels.

> *'If anybody had said to mediation to me, I would have gone. I am not sitting on a flower power rug doing kumbayah and meditating. I'm not doing it, in tie dye kaftan, I'm not meditating listening to someone with a gong.'*

Again, the invitation to slow down and be still in a group context is important here. For many, groups can be experienced as threatening, particularly by those who are prone to emotional dysregulation because these individuals have often not learned (or more importantly not been taught) how to regulate their emotions. It can be helpful therefore to pre-empt this reaction by offering information in the Waiting List Group (Phase Two) about what to expect in group and also inviting your senior group members to recall and share their own journeys with the practice. As Yalom and others remind us, it is the group members whose opinions and interventions hold the greatest sway and should therefore be woven into your group structure.

We can anticipate, therefore, that our intention to support the cultivation of compassion through slowing down the mind and body may not be how these practices are experienced in the early stages. We may instead trigger a threat response for many of our group members who have experienced attachment and relational trauma at the hands of others who were in positions of authority and expected to provide care. So, a fundamental part of the work is to offer validation to the experience of each individual group member.

The 'check in': Feedback from the practice and gathering

> *'The stuff that happened that was good …*
> *happened in the round the room check in.'*

This 'check in' follows the practice and is an invitation for each group member to offer some feedback about what they noticed in the practice. Other group members are invited to ask questions and be curious with each other. The role of the facilitator in this part of the group is to support the curiosity and connection between the group members, encouraging them to see the ways in which their experiences are similar.

Feedback is therefore vital for each group member after each breathing practice, to ensure that the common misunderstandings of the practice and the inevitable critical dialogues can be explored and understood. If we do not elicit feedback after each and every practice, I would suggest that we do not offer the practice in the first place. We need to know how the practice that we offer has been experienced: some may dissociate, others misunderstand the process, and for many, the practice in the early stages is likely to trigger self-criticism, which, left unchecked, could lead to drop out. Setting up the expectation that everyone will contribute something to this part of the group and bringing our own curiosity can be deeply helpful. The group member who tells you that they found the practice helpful as they 'zoned out', would likely benefit from your curious enquiry about what 'zoning out' actually means to them. Many will use the practice as a way of 'unplugging' from the anxiety and exposure associated with the early experience of group therapy. The 'seniors' can again be recruited to share their ideas and suggestions which has multiple benefits, bringing an authentic voice of lived experience and can foster a sense of hope. This experience of helping is also a key component of the implicit cultivation of compassion across all three flows, which is a one of the unique benefits of CFGP, in that your group members are practising receiving and giving compassion simultaneously:

> *'…but I don't think any of us would have tried it if we hadn't been in that situation, other people saying this, you don't feel it as constructive criticism, they're not telling you what to do and you can honestly take it on board, genuinely try this or I'm finding this is working for me this week, staring at the clock. This was a real breakthrough for me, being still staying present, the whole idea of meditation, it wasn't about drifting off it was being present with your thoughts.'*

We have already explored the benefits of co-facilitation. However, a further benefit is modelling in relation to the practice and feedback. If you are leading a practice, it is important that your co-facilitator engages in the practice and (within reason) offers genuine feedback to the group. This enables us to model in a light and gentle way the common humanity that we all share and the universal struggle with training our minds in compassion. This can also give permission to the group to also offer authentic and honest feedback about what they noticed.

> ### The case of KFC
> During the beginning of a PEG group, I led the practice and my co-facilitator (Graham) was invited to offer some feedback on what they noticed. The turn-taking ritual was observed as usual, and as it often the case, group members were keen to hear the experience of the facilitator. I wonder if there is something in this about getting 'inside information' about the facilitator who at times may keep themselves on the periphery of the group process. The co-facilitator was invited by one of the group members to feedback what they noticed in the practice. Graham said, 'I was wondering…', and then paused for a moment. It seemed as though the group 'leaned in', waiting for some significant disclosure. But he finished his sentence with '…are they still doing two-for-one at Kentucky Fried Chicken?' The group burst into laughter, the feedback was genuine and the group learned something valuable about our common humanity. It is these small but important examples of authenticity in the group that can flatten the hierarchy in meaningful ways and create the conditions for safeness within and between the members. Graham's preoccupation with KFC became part of the language of the group and a shorthand to describe the importance of honesty.

Group members are also invited to offer something of a 'check in' about their week and what they were bringing to the group that week. In the early days, we went around the room twice, firstly to gather feedback from the practice then to check in about the week. As you can imagine the group process slowly ground to a halt with almost two hours of the talk. So we put to the two components together, but remained mindful that we must gather the feedback from the practice, as this is often the element of the check in that can get missed or forgotten. This is of course unsurprising, as it is much easier to share the minutia of your week than to try and articulate where your mind went in the practice.

There are many implicit elements to the check in that relate to gathering information for the psychoeducation component and, importantly, skills training. Many group members will not have had positive experiences in familial, social and educative groups, where many of us learn the social skills of active listening and turn-taking. So we are implicitly teaching these skills through mirroring curiosity with each individual and inviting resonance and connection between the members. Group members learn each other's names without the need for name badges, and if they forget, they can just point. One group member once told me that they had come to group determined to 'punish the group with my silence, but then someone passed me the check in, used my name and I melted'. I think what this group member could not 'resist' was the experience of being attended to explicitly, invited in by name.

The social skills acquisition component of the group, enabled through turn-taking and expectations regarding contribution, are designed to teach and encourage mentalising capacity, altruism through listening to others, and the reparative experience of other's curiosity and connection. Over time, group members are encouraged to take responsibility for time keeping the check in and supporting each other to manage the time boundary. See Table 5.1 Structure of the weekly group session on page 65.

That said, I would not recommend 'checking in' as a facilitator as this is quite problematic, to offer genuine check in without either falling into something quite trite ('I've had a busy week') or too deep ('my cat just died'). Yalom offers some really helpful advice on the subject of self-disclosure and invites us to consider whether the disclosure is in the service of the group. It is hard to see how facilitators checking in about their week is in the service of the group, whereas limited spontaneous self-disclosure can be deeply meaningful to group members and the process.

The check in, as many can imagine, could fill the whole two-hour group space. Managing those who talk and those who don't in the check in can be arduous and delicate work. It reminds me of traversing on a crumbly slab with not very good protection in the rock. One slip and you will swing violently sideways, smashing into everything in your path. In such moments, slow and careful movements are required. Such is the work to gently encourage your reluctant members while simultaneously interrupting those who threaten to dominate the whole group. I have found that a less provocative way to interrupt a monologue is something like this, 'I am just going to stop you there; I am sorry but I am getting a little lost in the story and I really want to understand how you are doing and your feelings.'

This can invite the group member to refocus their attention on the emotions rather than the narrative, which is often a well-rehearsed defence. This does not always go well and there are times where my well-intentioned intervention is experienced as another authority figure shutting them down. There is often gentle work to be done to support group members with the sharing of the space.

Here's a script that may help guide such conversations:

> ### Dalvinder and their unmet needs
>
> Dalvinder joined the PEG group and, in the early stages, spoke of feeling aggrieved by the process they had been through to access the group. This was played out in long check ins, full of details about what they had not been given and how much they had to fight for everything.
>
> **Dalvinder:** *Nobody listens to my needs; I am constantly calling my care team to let them know how let down I feel. I get passed to duty and no one calls me back. I have really had enough. I tried to call to let the group know I was going to be late today and again no one got back to me and I don't even know if the message was passed on. It is always the same and I don't know why I am bothering.*
>
> *Long silence...*
>
> **Dalvinder:** *Well, this isn't helping me, I feel worse after coming here.*
>
> *A long silence with everyone looking at their feet...*
>
> **Facilitator:** *I wonder if it is hard to find a way to respond to Dal in a way that you think will be helpful to them?*
>
> *Another long silence...*
>
> **Group member:** *Yes, I don't know what to say.*
>
> **Group Member 2:** *Neither do I and I feel guilty.*
>
> **Facilitator:** *I wonder if is helpful to know what people are feeling when they do not respond to what you have brought Dal? I also wonder if you can hear that there is a compassionate intention in the room towards you today, Dal? Maybe we can use this to support you to think about what happens with your care team. Maybe they don't know what to say either?*
>
> **Dalvinder:** *I hadn't thought about it like that ... but I'm still upset.*
>
> **Facilitator:** *Of course you are, Dal, and we can see that today in this room.*

This was the very beginning of a process to bring the minds of the group members into Dal's mind and to support a gentle process of learning to mentalise (to use our minds to explore and make sense of the minds of others). Dal has of course not learned how to do this as they had not had an experience of being held in the mind of another person. This work needs to be undertaken carefully to avoid triggering a very patterned shame response, and to foster a sense of exploration rather than blame.

Working with those who find it difficult to contribute or even respond when invited in requires other forms of attunement. At these and other times, it can be helpful to turn to the body which Bessel Van De Kolk, in the great book of the same name, reliable informs us 'Keeps the Score'.[47] There is a wealth of literature, science and psychotherapeutic practice which supports attunement to the communications from the body – ours and other's.
We can start this conversation with the body with a light touch and some preliminary invitations to be curious about the idea of our body as a barometer of our inner world. A group member in the early stages may nod, head down, that they are OK, while their foot or leg is shaking or tapping violently. In such moments, I might gently inquire what their leg might have to say. This can, of course be met with derision, confusion and or shame. So I would mirror the leg movement or the wrapped body posture and try and stay with the curiosity and name my intention: 'I just noticed that your leg is doing this, and I wondered if it might be able to help us to understand how things are for you today.'

As we talk about a lot in this book, knowing when to back off is of course important here, and we may need to 'drop a pebble' of an idea and return to at another time.
It is also a great opportunity to broaden out to the whole group to invite curiosity about what all our bodies might be saying, including our own. Once established in the group, we can have whole conversations with parts of our bodies to explore the other communications, enriching the material in the room. I noticed that one group member was holding her body so tightly during the practice that I was surprised she could breathe at all. When I lightly commented on this, she spoke of her body feeling that it might disappear altogether if she didn't hold onto it. This was a way in to explore and normalise dissociation triggered by the breathing practice. She was supported to use tactile objects and smell to hold her during the quiet moments of the practice.

Generally, in the early days of the group, there will be a preference for sitting and talking together, but there are other ways to check in with the group. I will sometimes invite the group to stand in a circle and make a shape with their bodies or hands to demonstrate to the group how they are doing that day. This has many functions, firstly to get the group out of their chairs and warmed up for using the space in a different way. It also offers a way into embodied action and movement, inviting the members to become more comfortable with checking in and using their bodies to communicate explicitly. Another option is to invite group members to step into the circle with something they are bringing to group, wanting or needing from the session, e.g. 'I am struggling with exhaustion today'. Other group members who feel the same way are invited to step in with them. This exercise is designed to support the group to notice their connections with each other and, again using movement and embodied practices, prepares the way for Compassionate Mind Training.

---

47   Van der Kolk, B. A. (2015). *The Body Keeps the Score: Brain, mind, and body in the healing of trauma.* Penguin Books.

At one point, I had an idea that I could use this exercise to 'short cut' the check in and get us onto the material of the session more quickly. I was mistaken... I recall with a smile sitting down after an 'action check in', only for the group to resume the usual ritual of passing the check in around the circle. When I gently questioned this, 'Haven't we already done our check in?', I was greeted with laughter, 'No, of course not, we need to talk to each other'. So I learned a lesson about the importance of the ritual that we had created and how fundamental it is to cultivate safeness.

The Escape Pod

> *'There was a safe chair... You could put yourself and sit there until you felt comfortable enough to come back...'*

The escape pod is an idea that an early cohort of CFGP came up with and it has become part of the culture. There will be times when group members do not feel up to coming to group; they may feel they have nothing to offer or could not manage the rigours of the two-hour session. It is at these moments when we encourage people most to come, but without the expectation of full engagement or participation. The escape pods are a collection of chairs around the edge of the room which members know they can step into or start the group sitting in. This lets everyone know what their capacity is for the session. We will always acknowledge that someone is in the escape pod chair and invite them to say something or nothing, but remind them that they will be held in mind by the group. We might check in with the person or just acknowledge them throughout the session, but also remind them that there is no expectation of participation.

> *'So you could actually remove yourself from the group but still be part of the group and go and calm yourself and then come back.'*

Sometimes people ask, what if group members sit in the escape pod every week? What then? Like everything in the group, it becomes part of a conversation and maybe that this group member is communicating that they cannot manage the group at this time and may need a break or to restart. But this has not been my experience.

When there is nowhere else to hide

This was Sherelle's third week in PEG: she came into the room, looked around, and walked out again. Before she reached the door she turned and took her chair. After the initial breathe, as someone was about to pass her the check in, she shifted in her chair and moved to one of the escape pod chairs.

Here's how the conversation went:

> **Facilitator:** *I see Sherelle has moved to the escape pod. Does everyone remember this and what it means?*
>
> **Group member:** *I think it means she's here but that is about it. I know when I used the pod I wanted people to know I couldn't offer much that week*
>
> **Facilitator:** *Thank you for that, it is really helpful to know how you felt when you used the pod. So we understand that Sherelle is with us today, but may not be able to say or do too much, but this is absolutely OK. Sherelle I just wanted to check in with you. I hope you heard that we understand that things are tricky today*
>
> Sherelle nodded with her hair pulled all the way over her face.
>
> **Facilitator:** *If you do decide you want to say anything, we are here.*
>
> Sherelle again shook her head.
>
> Sometime later in the group, the conversation came back to Sherelle:
>
> **Facilitator:** *I just wanted to check in with Sherelle – again, no pressure, but I wanted you to know that you are in my mind and I see how much you are struggling today.*

Sherelle returned the next week and shared that this has been a big moment for her, as she had never before felt permitted to just be upset.

Weaving in the psychoeducation

The material from the check in is then used to explore a particular theme for each session. There will be discussions, activities and therapeutic tasks. The group is then closed with a discussion about the material explored and sometimes a guided imagery practice or game:

> *'It wasn't just go there and pour your heart out...*
> *It was educational which you need because without*
> *understanding how you can even begin really on that path.'*

The introduction of the basic evolutionary psychology model takes place gradually, with shared discussions, games and pairs work. This experiential learning is designed with careful attention to the development of the capacity of group members to tolerate the shared group space/processes. The evolutionary psychology model is introduced in the 12-week PEG in three distinct modules which we will come to in the next chapter. Although given the slow, open and 'rolling' nature of the programme, group members will receive the modules in a different order. This potential difficulty with making sense of the model has been overcome by recapping the previous weeks, which takes place on each intake weeks (the triangle sessions in the session diagrams). During these sessions, part of socialising the new group members to the programme involves recapping the main topics and ideas from the previous three weeks. This provides an opportunity for senior group members to return to and recap their learning and at the same time introduce new members to the basic model. Given the length of the group programme, it is also possible to return to and explore further the basic elements of the model that are introduced in the PEG, thus removing any pressure to fully integrate the learning at the beginning of the programme.

Concluding comments

This chapter has offered a step-by-step guide to introducing, setting up and rolling the initial preparatory stages of the group. As the title implies, it explains how to get started with CFGP and ensure that the pacing matches and is attuned to your group's capacity. The feedback from our group members has informed and shaped the group process, with time spent explaining and sharing our thinking about each aspect of the group before we start.

Making space in the structure for the inevitable objections, reactions and misunderstandings will support the group to develop cohesion within and between the group members, including us as facilitators.

So, onwards to the content, which sits within the framework of PEG.

Chapter 3.3:
The Modules – an overview

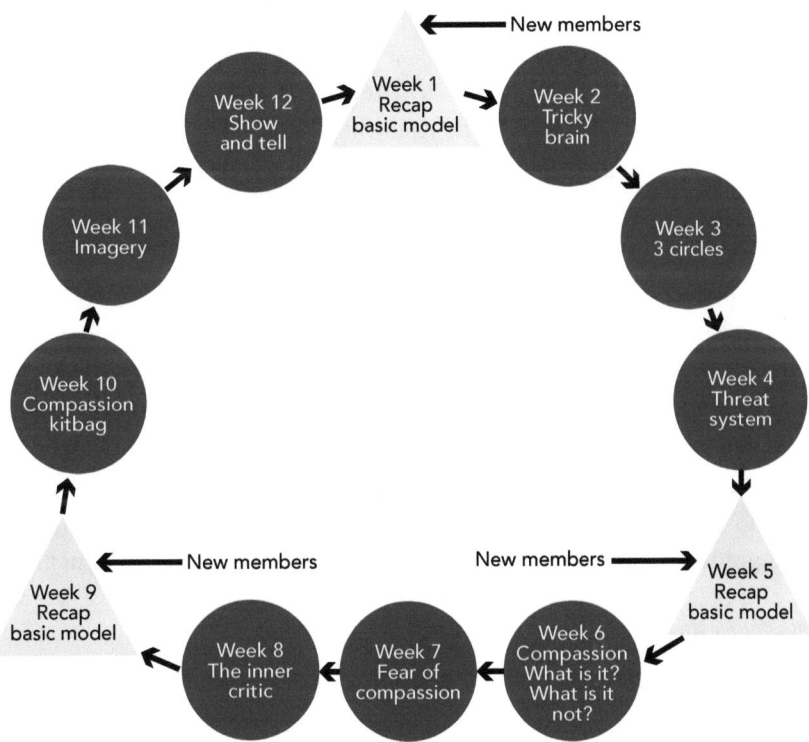

Three modules are introduced over these 12 weeks of the PEG (see Table 6.1). There is an emphasis on collaborative psychoeducation and Compassionate Mind Training. The development of these modules has been informed by the substantial published work on CFT as a modular short-term intervention.[48]

---

48 Petrocchi, N., et al. (2024) The impact of compassion-focused therapy on positive and negative mental health outcomes: Results of a series of meta-analyses. *Clinical Psychology* **31**(2).

Each module has three sessions followed by a 'joining week', where new members join and there is a short recap. These joining-week sessions follow the same slightly altered format described above to introduce the new group members to the group process and offer the existing members an opportunity to review what they have learned so far.

The key components of the psychoeducation are explained with the use of the material that the group members share about their current difficulties, rather than delivering the materials in a more traditional didactic teaching format. The design of the sessions is focused on normalising, creating shared connections, and de-shaming the experience of the group. In practice, group members are invited to talk a little about their week and it is this material that is used to explain the basic model. The material is therefore 'woven' around the individual experiences shared by the group members:

> *'Before I'd think I'm an idiot, there's somit [sic] wrong with me, but it [the old brain new brain teaching] got rid of that and the feeling of helplessness.'*

Most importantly for me, the content of these preparatory sessions is minimal and space is made for the discussion and playful engagement with the ideas. I often invite people who are training in CFGP, to write on a piece of paper the content that they feel they *should* be covering in the group programme, then fold it and keep folding it until they have a tiny square. That is how much content I feel that group members can tolerate in those early sessions. If you are not sure, cast your eye back over the quote on pp.95-96 (First group). We understand that when our threat systems are activated, our capacity to take in new information and retain it is severely compromised. So time spent slowing down, both ourselves and our group members, inviting them to learn to take turns and listen to each other, will create the capacity for learning. We will come back to the centrality of play later in this chapter.

One of the key ideas (see above) is introduced using group members' own experiences and narrative, and the group are then encouraged and given space to use creative means to explore their personal connections to and associations with the ideas presented. In these sessions, bring and develop the shared language from the formulation in the assessment phase: invite your group to explore key fears, redefine dysfunctional or maladaptive coping into understandable survival strategies and bring awareness to the unintended consequences. I turn to the incredible work of Bob Hobson who created The Conversational Model (now known as Psychodynamic Interpersonal Therapy), but who sadly died before he could finish his work. His words have been a guide for me in working to create compassionate conversations, where we mix questions with wondering, and remain open to be corrected until we have found some shared meaning. I think this quote gets right to the heart of Bob's message and it resonates for me with the message of compassion:

> *'I can only find myself in and between me
> and my fellows in human conversation.'*[49]

Alongside the conversation, we are offering activities which could be embodied movement and games using art materials to represent or externalise an aspect of the self, to allow for emotional distance and an alternative perspective.

Another important part of the group structure is for the facilitators to leave the room, allowing the group to work independently. There are multiple layers to this:

> *'...but I do think one of the benefits of that was having the facilitators leave the room briefly... was seeing how the group began to interact more and more together without being held ... so you know there were some people who would creatively guide the activity... I'm thinking of one person in particular who would quite often step in and say ... if people were struggling he would say well why don't you try doing it this way or that way ... so the group took on a different dynamic once the facilitator had left and that was quite nice.'*

This quote highlighted the opportunity for group members to begin to move into a horizontal transference relationship with each other and take on a sibling role. Group members over the years have often likened the group process to a familial relationship, but a corrective one, as Yalom describes. Learning to play and trust the facilitators gives way to learning to play and trust the other group members.

But this process can take some time and I am minded of many groups where I have got up to leave the group with a task and been met with terror on the faces of the members and a strong resistance. This has been explored and understood as the group not being ready for me to leave, because, without the presence of the maternal object, the group has not felt safe. This reminds me of a playground where the children can play as long

---

49 Hobson, R. F. (2013). *Forms of Feeling: The heart of psychotherapy*. Routledge.

as the parent is in close proximity, to be used as a secure base and safe haven. In these groups, I would stay in the room but try to distance myself from the activity to allow the capacity for the group to use each other to develop.

Table 6.1: Overview of the Preparation and Engagement Group modules

Module Title	Material covered
Module 1 **The brain, how it works and our threat systems**	An introduction to the neuroscientific complexity of underlying everyday human experience and emotional difficulties, the inevitable nature of suffering coupled with a predisposition to threat-based emotional processing, is offered to normalise and validate difficulties.
Module 2 **Compassion. What it is, what it isn't , and why we might need it**	The second module introduces the concept of compassion in greater depth, although the understanding of compassion is discussed explicitly during every group. Time is spent exploring what compassion is, more importantly perhaps what it is not, and why we might need it. This translates into an exploration of the fears of compassion and an introduction to the concept of internal critical self to self-shame-based dialogues.
Module 3 **The Compassionate Kitbag**	The third module formalises the Compassionate Mind Training, which has been gradually introduced through the preceding weeks. The focus of this module is the development of the sensory and imaginal Compassionate Kitbag, including harnessing diverse sensory objects and items that can be powerful and rapid nonverbal ways of stimulating compassionate processes of both self-soothing and courage innervation.

Chapter 3.4:
Module One – Our Tricky Brains

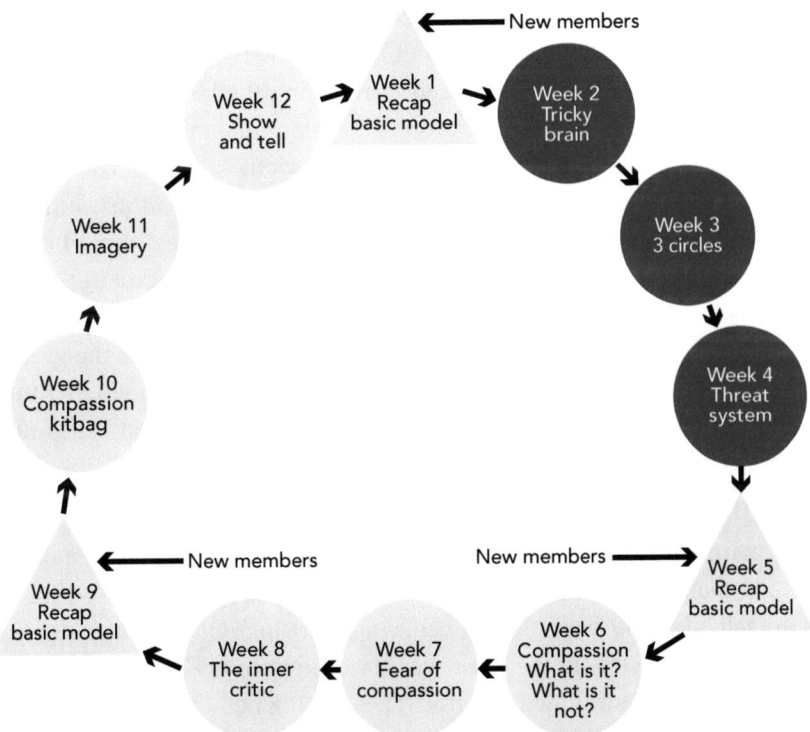

Session 1 will always be a joining week, as described in the previous chapter. The first module will therefore always start with Session 2.

Session 2: Our tricky brains

Using the material from the check in, the evolutionary psychology model of compassion-focused therapy is introduced[50]. Over the years, I have adapted the traditional lion and antelope story, which is a feature of all CFT introductory trainings, with a group-specific variation. Inviting the group to imagine an antelope grazing on the savanna, and their neurobiological response to an oncoming lion remains the same. Keeping this story Socratic, encouraging the group to respond and work together, helps to build the sense of group cohesion. Then I introduce the uniquely 'sapiens' version of the story – I have often invited the group to imagine they are on their way to group and there is a catastrophic delay, when they also discover they have no charge on their phone to make a call. We can make this element tailored to the particular presenting issues in the group and follow the story of the new brain bringing the tendency for rumination and introducing the idea of loops in the mind. I have also used my mobile phone as a prop to have an imaginary conversation with a mythical police officer who is advising me of the 'serious incident' which is happening outside. This is then the basis of an exploration with the group, illustrating the understandable and functional nature of rumination and looping of old brain to new brain and back. The key here is to de-shame and normalise the experience of group members. This is a good opportunity for some limited self-disclosure, checking that what you share is, firstly, processed and, secondly, in the service of the group. I have found myself on many occasions oversharing unprocessed and potentially upsetting material, as well as sharing what is in the service of me rather than the group. These painful experiences have taught me, with help from Yalom, to take a breath before sharing anything and check in with myself first.

I will often share a thoroughly processed story, intended to be used as a model to normalise and make sense of phobias. The story is offered Socratically, with humour, and tells the tale of my 17-year-old self believing that siphoning petrol into my broken down car would be like it is in the films, yet discovering to my horror that it is actually very hard to do without swallowing petrol! The ensuing body memories which haunted me for many years are also shared, with the hope that group members will share their own versions of this experience, which they often do. Creating this connection between the group and me included sharing our common and fragile humanity, and the reality of loops in the mind that cause much of our human distress and suffering. This story is designed to illustrate how we can get caught in loops where our emotional and sensory

---

50 For more details on the evolutionary psychology model of CFT cf Gilbert, P., & Simos, G. (2022). *Compassion focused therapy: Clinical practice and applications*. Routledge. https://books.google.co.uk/ books?hl = en&lr = &id = m99aEAAAQBAJ&oi = fnd&pg = PT14&dq = gilbert + and + grigoris + compassion + focused + therapy&ots = sDSOX7s6Bi&sig = skmX0VafHkuIRHDe713FgOEkg00

memory systems can get activated causing problems long after the traumatic incident. Our thinking, evaluating capacities are then recruited to critically examine our old brain reactions, restarting the whole process again, hence the loop.

The group are then invited – either individually or as a group – to explore an old brain new brain loop which has emerged for them in the last week. Keeping the task in the present will support your group to engage, as this can be less exposing.

Art materials, pens, paper, objects and scarfs should be made available for the group to use, but also it is important to be mindful that many group members will find the use of such materials very challenging. This brings to mind a group in which I had laid out all the materials on a small table in the centre of the room ahead of time, without any warning to the group. Two group members entered the room, took one look at the table, swore, and walked out again. I followed them both and persuaded them to come back into the room. It seemed that they were reacting to feeling patronised by the presence of the art materials: 'I'm not a f***ing kid' was the response from one. When we explored this further, both were able to connect their feelings to deep-seated struggles with play and playing. One spoke of feeling guilty that that they had not permitted their children to play or get messy, and both were able to link this further back to never feeling safe enough to play themselves. I learned a valuable lesson about 'landing' ideas on the group without space to explore what it meant.

The important message of this session relates to our brain having been designed *for us*, not *by us*, and therefore it is not our fault that we get caught in loops. The idea that it is 'not your fault' generally lands heavily for the group in those early stages, so, again, light touch metaphors and stories can support this:

> *'...coz I never ever ... knew that that was the case, that we have a new brain and an old brain ... and the old brain has certain ways of thinking and the new brain has and they clash ... and they clash basically and I had understanding and that helped me a lot that did. That helped me a lot... Instead of just going in... Oh I think this is wrong, oh I don't like this ... it gave me a greater understanding coz I understand some of my actions better, whereas before I didn't know why I was doing that ... why don't I want to hug my child why do I pull away ... but that helped me just get a better understanding of things and myself... It helped a lot really coz it was educational and how I was brought up.'*

Many people who have suffered abuse at the hands of those who are supposed to care for them will find some solace in self-blame. This can of course appear paradoxical, but it is in fact an understandable survival strategy. If I am to blame, then perhaps I can do something to change my situation. This belief is often learning from those adults who push the blame for their actions onto the child ('you made me do this'). Understanding that the adults were not actually in charge or were ruining the show rather than running it, can be deeply disturbing for a young mind, and so understandably we defend against it.

I always tell this story to invite the group to begin distinguishing between fault/blame and responsibility:

> *'I drive my car into the carpark and park in the designated spot. I come into work, and while I am at work, someone drives into the carpark, smashes into my car and drives off again. Is there any way that could be my fault? But my lights are smashed, it is getting dark and I need to drive home... Whose responsibility is it to fix the lights? Is that fair?'*

This story becomes another metaphor which the group can use to begin to approach and engage with how they have been shaped by their early experiences which they didn't choose. The innocuous language of smashed headlights is a gentle way into exploring early tragedy, intrusion and absence in a way that, for some, is more tolerable.

Session 3: The three circles and basic life tasks

This session is an opportunity to begin another process of formulating, sense-making and de-shaming their experiences. The group will be generally well-versed with the idea of a threat-focused survival system. I will sometimes offer a story or metaphor which resonates with the group experience: perhaps the first day of group, being the first in the waiting room, the letter from the Department of Work and Pensions reassessing your benefits. The information that you have gleaned from the check ins will be helpful at this stage. These examples will offer a way in that the group can connect with and contribute to. Knowing your group members is helpful here as you can invite them to bring their own experiences as below. The more we can invite the group to talk to each other and even draw on the flip chart, the more the learning will stick. These stories and metaphors are a helpful way in to introducing basic life task one: detect and avoid threats as a means of survival and reproduction, also known as the threat system.

Introducing the idea of shut down as a part of the threat detection and response system is often new to group members and can bring significant shifts and new ways of viewing their experiences – learning that disconnecting is an adaptive survival strategy that, while helpful in the moment, has unintended consequences in that the dissociation often becomes automatic. It can be helpful to use live examples of the response to the breathing practice, for example, to highlight that dissociation is normal and understandable, and this can create space to explore both the functions and the unintended consequences of a dissociative survival strategy. I will sometimes share the simplified idea that the hippocampus is a little like a road which takes all your memories where they need to go, but too much cortisol (threat hormone) can help with some things but tends to 'bomb' the road, creating big potholes. These potholes disrupt the movement of 'memory traffic' and mean that often our memory capacity is impacted negatively. Many have reported feeling reassured by this, that they are not broken because they struggle with their memory function. I am aware that some of these metaphors stretch the neuroscientific truth (as many of my colleagues tell me!), but the normalising and reassurance compensates for the truth stretching!

Basic life task two – the drive system is associated with acquiring and achieving which is linked to surviving but also to thriving and flourishing. For some, the drive reward system is very familiar, but for most, in my experience, it is threat-based drive: more striving than driving, and many confuse this with a healthy drive. The underlying motivation to acquire possessions can help the group distinguish between threat-based compulsive shopping and acquiring what is needed to promote health and well-being. I will often tell the story of the game of snakes and ladders – when you almost get 'there' to the top in the drive system, but then you hit a snake and are back to 2 again, not ever really feeling that sense of satisfaction and achievement. The visual image of Sisyphus pushing his boulder up the hill only for it to roll down the other side can also help here (the light touch stories can provide another less personally connected way into the material).[51] This is an opportunity for the group to share in activities that give them some satisfaction. We will see this in action when we begin to develop the Compassionate Kitbag a little later.

Basic life task three is to rest and digest, images of lions resting in the shade after catching the antelope will help here. This is also called the soothing system, which often presents a significant challenge to the group and needs to be approached carefully. I generally do not go straight in with the links between the development of the soothing system and early attachment relationships but working around the edges with the idea of resting and digesting as a basic life task which can come after the activation of the

---

51 Nb: a playful addition to the story of Sisyphus is to add that the reason for his eternal punishment was that he invited guests to his home for dinner and proceeded to eat them!

drive system. Supporting the group to begin to consider the ways they might need to develop this system, I often find that pets of varying kinds, from bearded dragons to mice, make an appearance in the soothing system for our group members.

> ### The swooshing scarfs of emotional regulation
>
> During the check in, Louie had been describing his experience of becoming overwhelmed with anger on the bus on the way to group. A woman sat next to him had been far too close, and to make it worse, she had a baby who was even closer. Louie was given time to describe how overwhelmed he had been and how much he had wanted to shout at her and jump off the bus, but he was coming to group so he couldn't. This was held by the facilitators until the end of the check in and the move to the psychoeducation phase.
>
> > **Facilitator:** *'Louie, can I use your experience on the bus to introduce an idea that I was hoping we could work on today?'*
> >
> > **Louie:** *'Yeah, sure, are we talking about how to throw agro women off the bus?'*
> >
> > **Facilitator:** *'Not quite, Louie, but thank you! So, Louie shared with us how angry he had got on the bus – we know what he wanted to do!'*
>
> This was a lead in to begin to explore the threat system, followed by drive and soothing. The group were then invited to use all the resources in the room to create the three systems. The group opted to work together and using coloured scarfs and corners of the room they created representations of the three systems. Together, the group 'visited' each corner of the room, stood in the scarf circle and took up the positions of the system. There was a great deal of laughter as the group mirrored each other's body postures – rage, terror, disgust. There were raised fists and some whoops of delight in the blue-scarf drive system, but when they got to soothing, no-on knew what to do and it seemed difficult to get in the green-scarf circle. Someone suggested that their cat was really good at soothing, so they played with ideas around cats and calming music. This brought things to life and started a rehearsal for noticing the three circles and how much time they spend in each. We then often return to the three circles as part of the check in: how big are your circles today? Not all groups can tolerate the scarfs, for some it will be pens and paper to draw out individual circles, how big they are in relation to each other and what keeps each system going. But it is worth persevering with the scarfs and props, as it is invariably fear that sits behind the resistance.

Session 4: The physiology of threat

Many group members come to therapy having very little understanding of and capacity to be connected with their physiology and their bodies in general. Having space to explore, through play, the physiology of the threat system offers a de-shaming experience by creating a better understanding of our physiology.

> *'It's like being afraid and ashamed of your own humanity. But the compassionate mind set... in a way, you are being realistic about human frailty and the kind of problems we all have... It really did address shame, you know.'*

This session is also designed to connect the group with the previous session, which introduced the three circles and exploring the need for balance.

The session is started in the usual way and then material from the check in is explored, reminding the group of the physical cues of threat activation. In my experience, the check in will always involve some kind of situation which has activated someone's threat system between the sessions. This leads to a Socratic discussion about the different symptoms of threat and the organs that are involved. It can be helpful to use pictures of the organs, but I often end up with a diagram on the flip chart, which shows the organs and the symptoms being connected (see Appendix 3.2). The group are then invited to use a random collection of objects to represent how the physiology of threat operates in our bodies. This random collection of objects can include old mobile phones, toys from Christmas crackers, wool, nut crackers, nuts, bolts... whatever you have to hand! The idea behind the random objects is that they can be used as props in a variety of different aspects of the work. We are introducing the idea that objects can be used to represent aspects of the self or others, moved around and related to in a different way. But most importantly, they can be played with and then put down, at the same time creating some emotional distance from the object and the associations with the self.

The group are then given some time to work together to create a visual representation of the threat system. This invariably gives rise to a great deal of laughter as the group members select objects to represent the different organs and pathways. The image represented here shows the playful approach that the group took to exploring the possibility of losing control of your bladder in the context of threat system activation.

I am often surprised by how little our group members have been taught through school or social learning about the basic physiology of the threat system. We come together at the end of the session to do some 'myth busting'. Again, back to the Socratic dialogue, I invite the group to consider the different symptomatic experience and what the function is of each symptom.

Here's a script to help guide this conversation:

> **Facilitator:** *'So, coming back to those symptoms we talked about at the beginning of the session, I wonder if we can have some time to consider what the purpose of these symptoms are. Can we shout out some of the symptoms you have just been discussing?'*
>
> **Group Member:** *'My heart pounds whenever I think about coming to group and sharing all my secrets with you.'*
>
> Other group members nod in agreement.
>
> **Facilitator:** *'So, looking at your body map on the floor, I can see that you have put the heart on, represented by the red playdough! Why does our heart pound when we are feeling anxious?'*
>
> **Group Member:** *'I don't know, but it makes me feel like I am going to die.'*
>
> Again others nod in agreement.
>
> **Facilitator:** *'It does, doesn't it? But actually, when your heart pounds it is because more blood is being pumped to your major muscle groups, arms and legs to enable you to either run away or fight.'*

Offering these simple but significantly affirming elements of the psychoeducation can offer group members another way to cultivate compassion for themselves and each other, through a shared understanding. Many group members have noticed that these sessions have enabled them to begin to change their relationship with their bodies. We might also describe this as a clever way to increase interoceptive awareness. This session is also a precursor to exploring how we can shift our bodies' threat response through Compassionate Mind Training practices.

Using Louie's example from the previous session, the group can be invited to work together and explore what Louie might be able to do when he notices that his heart has started pounding and his hands are sweaty. First, bringing his awareness (the first part of compassion) to the fact that his threat system is on, and secondly, that he will need to respond rather than wait for his body to react (developing the second part of compassion).

Session 5: Joining week

Session 5 is a joining week, when the structure is adapted to welcome new members with a recap of the Safe Space Agreement. There is also an opportunity for the existing group to return to the key elements of the past three weeks and share their learning with the new members. As previously discussed, there are many benefits to this, including rehearsing learning, filling in any missed sessions and preparing the newly formed group for the next stage of the work. The same structure is followed for Session 9 and Session 12.

Chapter 3.5:
Module Two – Compassion

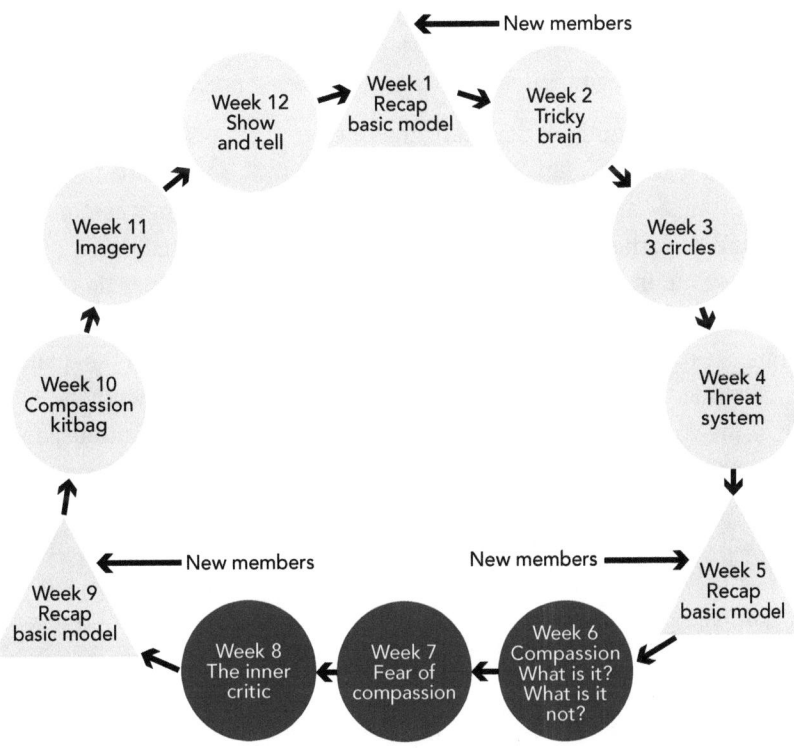

'Compassion was an alien concept ... scared the crap out of me... But feeling compassion for everybody, understanding that it was compassion for everybody, and that they were feeling compassion towards me without any other motives ... was very, very strange... You were with a group, you were asking for help, and they're asking for help, and you were helping each other... Asking for help in the beginning was hard.'

Session 6: Compassion – what it is, what it isn't, and why we might need it

This is the module where things often become more tricky for the group and the levels of understandable resistance increase. The important response here is to support the group to see what Paul Gilbert calls 'resistance as wisdom', in that, rather than correcting fears, blocks and resistances that emerge, we lean in and make space to explore and validate why they have emerged and the function they serve.

There is often much work to be done to dispel and correct misunderstandings about compassion, but my suggestion is to take this slowly. It is easy to tip our group into shame and defensive reactions when we begin to explore what the group think compassion is. So validation and pacing is key here. I invariably start with a flip chart exercise to get the group considering what compassion means to them. See Appendix 3.2 for an example.

Invite the group to shout out all the words that they connect with compassion and write them all on the left side of a flip chart. The alternative to this would be to give the group members Post-It notes and invite them to write down the words they associate with compassion and stick them on the flipchart. This may be more acceptable for those who struggle to speak out in the early stages of a group programme. If they do not come up, I would always add wisdom, courage, commitment and strength, and suggest that we will return to this. Next, ask the group who they think possesses all the of the qualities that have been identified. My experience is that the group will always say others, so write this on the top of the column. It is helpful to go lightly with this, to stay curious, and validate that this is always how people perceive compassion. It is helpful to add something about the societal context to this. Ask the group to think of the 'heroes' of compassion in history or fiction. Characters like Mother Teresa, Ghandi, Martin Luther King, Nelson Mandala are likely to come up. Hold these in your mind – they will be helpful later when we are exploring Compassionate Others and how they can help us. Ask the group what all these folk have in common and you will generally get answers such as giving selflessly to others and possibly self-sacrifice. This is another way to use the group's wisdom to validate why compassion is assumed to be something we do for others.

Then move to the second side of the flip chart and write 'Self-compassion' at the top, inviting the group to say, without censoring themselves, what comes up. I often use the idea of a truth serum to support the group to say what they really feel rather than what they think I or my co-facilitator wants to hear. What will always emerge are grimaces, 'urgh', blank faces, and a fair amount of disgust. Inviting the group to notice what happens in their bodies can help to bypass their cognitive defences, and get to the fears, blocks, resistances (FBRs) and contempt which are generally associated with the misunderstanding of compassion.

> *'While fears represent an unfamiliarity with compassion
> and blocks come from concerns about the processes involved,
> resistance can reveal internal critical processes.'*[52]

FBRs are understood in the context of CFT as cautions and precautions rather than interference. Fears are usually protective strategies that have developed in the belief that they keep us and others safe. Shame is known to be a threat response to a perceived social danger, linked back to our need for support from others to survive. Blocks are considered to flow from a misunderstanding or a different conceptualisation of compassion. In our modern environments, the distinction between these two motivational systems can become blurred as societal drives generate threat and apprehension. In threat-based drive, internal and external dialogue often includes 'shoulds' and 'musts', which results in a motivation to avoid or to manage threat, rather than a drive towards achievement. Resistance is commonly associated with concerns about our worthiness or the anticipation of aversive repercussions as a result of our compassion. Time spent exploring this becomes the bedrock of the work moving forward. The flip chart with the two very different columns can then go up on the wall in your group room reminding everyone that *this* is the work. The important thing to emphasise at this stage is that we are not going to be 'breaking down the barriers' or launching into battle with the FBRs! We are instead slowly and with respect turning back towards compassion and what makes it difficult and challenging to accept, as the quote above articulates very clearly.

This can be a very intense session, with group members beginning to connect with a dawning sense of the reality of compassion and that they may have been engaging in understandable complicity rather than a deep motivation towards the self and others. So, bringing some lightness towards the end can also be helpful. Compassion-Focused Pictionary is one of the games that we use to begin to playfully and with a light touch inure the group to the real meaning of compassion. All group members are invited to pick the words from the previous discussion about what compassion means and write them on a piece of paper, and then place the folded paper in a cup or bowl.[53] The group then work together, with each member picking up a piece of folder paper and then drawing an image which they feel represents the word. This is much harder than it sounds: have you ever tried drawing empathy?! One group member picked empathy

---

[52] (Lucre, K., Lacey, & Taylor, J. (2022). Compassion Focused Staff Support: An Antidote to Empathy Distress, In Psychological Staff Support in Healthcare: Thinking and Practice (pp. 204-223). Sequoia Books. In *Psychological Staff Support in Healthcare: Thinking and Practice* (pp. 204–223). Sequoia Books.

[53] Any activities that involve writing need to considered carefully with regard to literacy levels. Many of our group members may struggle with literacy, and so always have an alternative to writing for any exercise.

and, after a long sigh, drew an ear and a cup of tea. Of course, empathy sounds a little like cup of tea. From this time on, with the idea of developing a shared language in mind, empathy was often described as that 'cup of tea thing!'

Another game of this nature can also be used to demonstrate the rank system. You will observe the activation of the rank competing system in many different aspects of your group process. I often see an unconscious up-ranking in relation to difficult experiences presented in the check in. Check ins can grow in length exponentially as people try to ensure they get as much time as the last person to demonstrate how difficult their week has been. Sadly, down-ranking is commonplace in the group process; others feeling that their difficulties are less 'worthy' and therefore not deserving to be in the programme. We can of course talk about this understandable pull towards competing and withholding and the impact that this has on our ability to care and cooperate, but I am not sure this gets through the fog of shame and self-criticism. But a different version of Compassion-Focused Pictionary could. Invite your group members to split into two groups to play the game, so they are essentially playing against each other rather than collaborating together. After a few rounds of competing, bring them together in one group to cooperate. The important ending process for this game is to bring the group together to invite reflections on the two games. This is a platform to explore competing and withholding versus caring and cooperating with a focus on motivational switching, using your compassionate mind. There are many exercises and games which can explore the model using the felt experience in the group and the relationships between the group members.

Session 7: Working the with fears, blocks and resistances to compassion

This session returns to the right-hand side of the flip chart exercise from the previous week and various different exercises and games can be offered to support the group with the challenging work of further exploring compassion and what gets in the way for us all. At this stage, the group are invited to make some tentative links with what they didn't get from their early attachment relationships and how our capacity for compassion is shaped by this. But it is important to let these connections and discoveries form, rather than bringing it to the group before they are ready. Many group members remain locked in enmeshed relationships with early attachment figures or repeated attachment patterns. I have no desire to push group members to confront the reality of rupture and loss in the early stages of group, before any rudimentary capacity for compassion has been cultivated. The key here is to support gentle, validating experiences which enable group members to begin to make their own discoveries.

Pros and cons of the compassionate ideal

Invite the group to return to the flip chart from Session 6 and imagine that they had a person in their life who epitomised all these compassionate qualities. It can also be helpful to weave in some of the ideas of a compassionate hero, with characters, actual people, or something more imaginative. The group are then invited to draw up a list of the pros and cons of having such a person in their life. In one way, we are paving the way for later work on the Compassionate Other, but at the same time creating space for the FBRs to emerge through play (see Appendix 3.3 for an example). This will be one of the exercises where I will endeavour to leave the room and allow the discussions to unfold. Invariably, the group quickly get to the issues of trusting someone who 'appears to be too good to be true', and many will also bring the 'catch' or contingent care which they have often experienced in the context of kindness from others. Some group members will begin to make links with some of these ideas and the early experiences of care they experienced from others, and how it was coupled with abuse. Many will describe Jeremy Holmes' and Giovanni Loitti's ideas of the 'approach-avoidance conflict', in that a source of care is also a source of abuse, and this sets up an internal, unconscious conflict which often results in dissociation as a survival strategy.

The work here is to touch on these issues as they emerge and find a way to acknowledge and validate them, but also to keep the group on track with the Compassionate Mind Training and the light touch. We are not shutting down group members when they bring their early tragedy to the group, but we are supporting them to find a way to understand the ways that the past invades the present.

Working with Dalvinder's inner conflict

During the discussion about compassionate ideals, Dal brought their schoolteacher as an example of someone who had many of qualities of caring, understanding and wisdom. They went on to explain that this teacher had been the only person who had shown any interest, but that they had gone on to sexually abuse Dal for many years and they had not been able to tell anyone. Dal began to share many of the overwhelming details of the contingent care that was offered and the experience Dal had of being groomed by this teacher, who had then denied the abuse when it came to light years later. Dal was clearly grappling with the conflict between the fond memories of being this teacher's favourite pupil and all the advantages that this conferred, with the shame and turmoil of the abuse that accompanied this experience. We supported the group to acknowledge and help Dal name the conflict and highlighted this as a something to return to with a compassionate mind, putting a marker down for future work (we will return to this in Phase 4).

In the early stages of a group, I do not expect that group members will truly understand what compassion really is (i.e. a strong, courageous, committed motivation). But I do believe that this understanding will come in time. We are 'dropping pebbles', ideas that can be returned to, and it is my hope that, over time, the 'ripples' of understanding and connection do begin to make a difference:

> *'CFT gives you the tools to be able to understand yourself ... understand what's happened ... what's gone on, and gives you the tools to actually deal with it and move forward, you know ... the compassion you can feel for others you can actually start to feel for yourself.'*

The key message from this session is to normalise the fear of compassion, make some tentative connections to make sense of why that is and develop some new learning about what compassion really is. This work requires facilitators to be courageous and trust the process, this can end up being co-stimulatory, in that we are modelling the courage needed by the group.

Louie and the fluffy compassion

Here's a conversation that took place between Louie and the therapist:

Louie: *'I get what you are trying to say, that compassion can help you feel stuff and care more, but I need to be strong. This is not going to help me on the estate where I live. You don't get it, if people think I'm losing it my family will be at risk.'*

Therapist: *'This is a good point, Louie, but I wonder, how much strength does it take to hurt the person who has disrespected you?'*

Louie: *'Ha! Not much that is easy. I've been doing it long enough.'*

Therapist: *'Well exactly – this way of being is familiar to you, but how much strength does it take not to hurt this person and do something different, change how you are?'*

A long silence...

Louie: *'I think I know what you are getting at... it is harder to change so it takes more strength. But a different kind of strength.'*

This example is only the very beginning of the process, and we will follow Louie and the ways that he has grappled with learning to be different with himself and others.

Session 8: The inner critic

Here's another script:

> **Angela:** '...or the inner critic business; I never knew about that.'
>
> **Michelle:** 'No, well, I knew I had, like, the negative voice in my head, but I didn't know how to describe it properly or understand where it was coming from... It was very much, like, well, this is how my head is.'
>
> **Angela:** 'When I hear voices or I've got these thoughts running through my head, you automatically go to schizophrenia or something, or multiple personality or something, so to actually break that down and go, you know, that's an inner critic and my Compassionate Self-learning about that was another breakthrough moment for me and being present and breaking that dialogue apart, as it all becomes very squished together like I've got cotton wool in my head and I'm not thinking about anything.'
>
> **Michelle:** 'Or everything all at once.'
>
> **Angela:** 'And you've got the racing mind and you don't know how to switch off, so taking that five or even three minutes to be present and still helped; like I said, life changing.'
>
> **Michelle:** 'I agree.'

As Angela and Michelle have helpfully articulated, the explicit mention of an internal critic dialogue can come as a surprise for many, and can be something new which has not been encountered before. The misunderstanding of this can be something which presents barriers to introducing this idea. I recall one group session when I blithely began talking about the idea of an inner critic. This was met with a furious response from one group member, whose father had undiagnosed schizophrenia and was enraged that I was suggesting that she 'draw out' this in herself. Again, a slow approach is important here, with an invitation for the group to consider their own experiences in the context of understanding that we are made up of multiple parts. But that this is very different from the fragmentation associated with schizophrenia or similar psychotic illnesses.

Often, the group will have already made mention of an internal critical dialogue, and it can help if there has been some noticing of these moments when they occur prior to this session. We can then build on this shared understanding of the new brain and observing other's response to vulnerability. Again, I will draw on my own examples of internal critic processes and experiences, keeping Yalom's advice in mind to avoid overstepping into using the group to resolve my own difficulties. My group members are aware that being late tends to activate my internal critical dialogue and that, at times, this creates some stress. I have brought the stress as an unintended consequence of trying to avoid ever being late. My intention with this disclosure is to illustrate and normalise self-criticism. This can be a helpful way to support the group to be able to share their own experiences of self-criticism. The feedback from the breathing practice can also be an opportunity to explore the inevitable criticism which can emerge for us as facilitators.

There are many ways to work with the initial stages of differentiation and creating emotional distance, but one of my favourites is creating an image of the critic. Following some preliminary discussions to establish a shared understanding of the internal critical part of the self and some of the functions it serves, the group are invited to use art materials to create an image. The images are a varied and terrifying collection of dark and monstrous clay, playdough, plasticine, pen and ink, charcoal effigies, which speak to the darkness. This deathly part of the self, which silences, criticises, commentates and often suggests self-harm or death to the person, is a means of resolving relational and practical problems. These images are then shared and discussed with the group and this is often a key moment in the group which generates empathy and compassion, as the group members see and hear of each other's struggles with their inner critics. The images are then left in the therapy room as a means of beginning the process of separation and differentiation. I have ended up with a shelf in my office filled with hideous creatures of varying sizes and shapes.

> *'We were all struggling with the inner critic ... so they said give it a physical form... I went for plasticine and made this little gremlin thing... It was really useful, you could put your inner critic on the table over there and just separate from it for a second... And it wasn't about squashing it or anything... Over time, I could then explain it... My monster is being a pain in the butt today ... and over time not such a screaming voice in my head.'*

This example demonstrates how the process of differentiation enabled this group member to begin a slow process of creating and holding some emotional distance from their internal critic part, therefore getting some relief from its intensity and, over time, to soften the critic. It is also important to note this group member's understanding that this work is not about 'squashing' or destroying the inner critic, and is much more about bringing compassion to this part of the self. Like Socrates is said to have suggested, 'The secret of change is to focus all your energy, not on fighting the old, but on building the new'. The new in this case being the Compassionate Self.

It can also be helpful to bring these creatures back into the therapy space at a later stage of the programme to explore changes that may have occurred in the group member's experience of their images. I recall one such group where a group member had drawn a very large, dark stick figure that cast a long shadow over all aspects of her life. In the interim, she had created a Compassionate Other who took the form of a powerful fairy like creature.

She put the image of the critic in the chair and took the role of her Compassionate Other, whose presence and calming words resulted in the critic shrinking and transforming into a small, thin, scared stick man whose voice was barely audible. Phase Four will offer more on the process of transformation.

Another way into working with the critic is to explore the functions, but side-stepping any judgements. Invite the group to imagine that their inner critic has decided that they have had enough of the job of criticising and they have quit! The job of the inner critic is now vacant and the task is to write a job description for the new inner critic. Now, of course, we might wish our group members to decide not to recruit to this vacant post. But this is also an opportunity to name the universal reality of the inner critic and that it is unlikely that we can just banish or kill it off entirely, much as we may want to. Again, back to the language of transformation and working with, rather than the idea of having an adversary that needs to be quashed.

This exercise is a playful way into beginning to understand and explore the functions of the critic. The group work together on this task as a way of beginning to support the development of group cohesion and a shared language to describe their collective experience of the powerful and destructive survival strategy. See Appendix 3.5n for an example of the job description of the inner critic. The modification process often comes later as we develop the Compassionate Self to respond, rather than react to, the critic.

When the critic is not just a critic

At any point in this early work, turning back towards and beginning to make sense of the inner critic can reveal an internalised abuser. It can be tricky to identify and distinguish this from a vicious but protective inner critic. However, the years of working with my own and other's inner critics have taught me that there is a difference and it is important to make the distinction. My group members have coined the phrase 'abuser echoes', meaning that some internal critical dialogues carry the voice of internalised persecutors or abusers. This can be tricky for group members to identify as the voice may not be the familiar voice of the abuser and the words may also have changed. It is also a challenging task to separate the voice from the general experience of the self. People will often tell me, 'this is me, not a part, I am my critic'.

One of the ways into this, which fits well with our model of understanding compassion as a motivational system rather than an emotion, is to start by inviting curiosity about the motivation of the inner critic. What does this part of you want from you? Tuning into the nature of the critical dialogue can also give an indication of intent. For example, an inner critic who demands that the person avoids others as they are not to be trusted, might be encouraging a survival strategy linked to early traumatising relationships. This is slow work, and for many the real intention of the inner critic does not become clear until later in the programme, when we invite group members to take the role of their critic. I would not attempt this work in either a shorter programme or the early stages of the PEG.

In these early sessions, it is helpful for us to tune in to the nature of the critical dialogue, but I am not explicitly inviting the group to dive into exploring the dialogue in any depth or sharing it unless they do so spontaneously. We are focused here on differentiation and validation of the existence of an inner critic. The transformation work with the inner critic comes later in the programme, once your group members have begun to develop a compassionate identity and capacity.

Chapter 3.6: Module Three – The Compassionate Kitbag

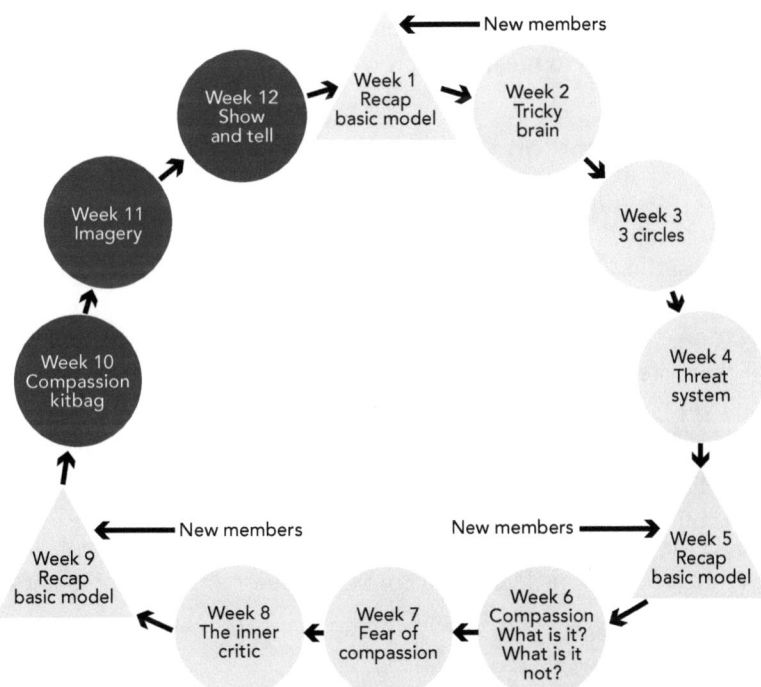

A key component of the preparation stage of the therapeutic work is the development of a 'Compassionate Kitbag'. This is a novel, multisensory based means of helping draw together the various elements of Compassionate Mind Training (CMT) and processes within the therapeutic work, to help participants to cultivate and facilitate their capacities for compassion.[54]

---
54   Lucre, K., & Clapton, N. (n.d.). The Compassionate Kitbag: A creative and integrative approach to compassion-focused therapy. *Psychology and Psychotherapy: Theory, Research and Practice*, e12291.

This is a more concrete example of how we can weave the wisdom of mountaineering into the psychotherapeutic process: before setting off to climb, time is spent preparing. This includes packing your kitbag with everything you need to nourish you on the journey. In the CFGP programme, this is a concrete practical collection of objects that patients are invited to gather together, share with each other and use in the explicit stimulation of the drive and soothing systems. Objects are also given by facilitators to support the psychotherapeutic work, and in such cases these objects can also become transitional objects. This concept focuses on the development of a compassionate motivation and Compassionate Self-identity, rather than just symptomatic relief, the latter being provided by toolkits, first aid kids and self soothe boxes, which are common in mental health and therapeutic settings. The Compassionate Kitbag is not something to be turned to only in times of distress of threat; this is what we take on the journey up the mountain to nourish and sustain through good times and bad. The work of Marcela Matos and other informs us clearly that the key to the development of compassionate capacity is regular daily practice, not just a panicked attempt to breathe when we are under threat.

> **Louie and the 'incident' on the bus**
>
> Louie came to group one day having had yet another 'incident' on the bus. He was flushed and breathless as he came in the room. Not being able to wait until the group had settled, he launched into a tirade about the bus driver and the man with the dog. He finished his monologue with a hard stare in my direction with an accusatory tone – stating that he had tried that 'breathing thing' I had suggested as he mimicked breathing in and out, fast and shallow. Unsurprisingly, he found that it didn't work… When we had settled into the group, with the breathe and check in, it was possible to return to Louie and explore why it didn't work and come to a shared realisation that trying to do something new for the first time while in threat is unlikely to be helpful, with only our old brain to support us. I often turn to Paul Gilbert's advice which also helps my group: 'you wouldn't wait until you have been thrown overboard in the storm before learning to swim' (I know I have said this twice, but I do believe it bears repeating).

Session 10: The Compassionate Kitbag

The Compassionate Kitbag's potential therapeutic value lies in offering numerous creative and tangible means of accessing compassion to a wide range of individuals who are typically fearful of, blocked and/or resistant to, compassion.[55]

---

55 Lucre, K., & Clapton, N. (n.d.). The Compassionate Kitbag: A creative and integrative approach to compassion-focused therapy. Psychology and Psychotherapy: Theory, Research and Practice, e12291.

> *'It's a virtual kitbag; you might keep the breathe exercise in there and for me it was the little stones... A picture... A smell... That calms and reminds you of the group'.*
>
> *'The idea of the kitbag having multiple resources to fall back on, I'm always trying to update it, it's a struggle but I am aware of it, that's it I can't unlearn what I've learned.'*

The kitbag is introduced during the early sessions in a more informal way, as group members are invited to consider what they might need on this journey towards compassion, which the group is at the beginning of. Gathering in ideas that are shared spontaneously paves the way for the third module, which focuses more explicitly on the Compassionate Mind Training.

It can initially be helpful to invite the group to gather in the multisensory elements that they may already be using. You may need to give some concrete examples (I always offer my love of reed diffusers and scented candles to shift my mood and as an act of compassionate for myself). It is also useful to remember the nuggets that may have been shared in the group previously: remember that piece of music you said you found helpful, the words of a poem, a beloved pet. This supports the group to see that they already have compassionate wisdom, which is the basis of this work. We introduce the idea of trash and treasure, acknowledging that celebrating our different passions is key to building a unique and personal collection. Some group members will easily trip into feeling ashamed of their choices. I recall one group where it took a considerable time to coax a group member into sharing that an important smell for them was Jeyes Fluid (a strong-smelling cleaning product), as it connected them to being at school and seeking solace with the janitor who was kind and understanding. In the same group, another member shared that the same smell triggered flashbacks of being abused in a school context. There is no right or wrong, only that our experiences influence what we find helpful or painfully restimulating. This group member eventually brought her Jeyes Fluid to the group and took the role of it, a session filled with messages of warmth, hope and strong smells!

Many group members will also tell you that they do not have anything. Jane definitely stayed fixed on the idea that she had 'nothing', and it was unhelpful and upsetting to force her to confront that she had nothing in her life that could possibly cultivate compassion. But gentle perseverance, creating a space where ideas can be shared and discussions can unfold in a slow-paced way, will invariably bring something for everyone.

Another way to begin the exploration of the things your group members may already have access to is the Compassionate Roles Map. This is an adaptation of Kate Hudgin's Intra

Psychic role atom, which is part of the Therapeutic Spiral Model, designed to support trauma survivors to prepare for trauma focused psychodrama.[56] This has been adapted to explore the internal and external elements of compassionate capacity. This is for some a more concrete and accessible map to begin to consider what compassion looks like in reality. The various elements are explained and the group are invited to create their own maps, using creative means, images, objects, words… whatever is acceptable to the individual:

> **Supportive Other –** Someone in the person's life who could support them, a positive relationship, not necessarily a human being. Many group members will not be able to associate people with supportiveness, so encouraging a more lateral approach can help.
>
> **Achievement –** This element of the map is to begin to consider what can stimulate the drive reward system. Encourage the group to start small, for example coming to group and sticking with the programme, volunteering to start the check in.
>
> **Source of support/strength –** Something to lean into to, for strength and reassurance. For some this might be faith or nature, for others it might be interests or hobbies.
>
> **Compassionate other –** This can again be human, animate or otherwise. The Compassionate Other can be tricky and we will explore this in the Session 11 below, but it can be helpful to invite a distinction between a Compassionate Other and a Supportive Other. The most important qualities of a Compassionate Other are a compassionate motivation and a voice to articulate this.
>
> **Quality of your Compassionate Self –** many of course will find this challenging, so the group are invited to support and offer ideas. Ideally, this quality of the self is recognised and acknowledged on some level.

(See Appendix 3.6 for an example of a compassionate roles map. Try creating one for yourself.)

> ### Jane's Compassionate roles map
>
> Jane had been reluctant to take part in the exercise, as outlined previously. She was angry with the facilitators for trying to 'force' her to engage in an exercise which she 'couldn't do'. But despite her complaints and protests, she did complete the exercise. Jane was reluctant for us to leave the room and kept telling us it didn't make sense. I have noticed over the years that I have a tendency to 'overexplain' and to keep

---

56 Hudgins, K. (2019). Psychodrama Revisited: Through the Lens of the Internal Role Map of the Therapeutic Spiral Model to Promote Post-traumatic Growth. *Zeitschrift Für Psychodrama Und Soziometrie*, **18**, 1–16. https://doi.org/10.1007/s11620-019-00483-7

confirming with the group that things makes sense. This leaves me vulnerable to being mildly exploited by the group, with some inevitably saying they don't understand. I can then get into ever more confusing explanations, which use up the time that the group would be working together. I have been supported by co-facilitators with this over the years, who have often ushered me out of the room as I am repeating explanations with the suggestion that someone in the group will help.

On this occasion with Jane, I was ushered from the room, leaving her to work through her struggle with the group, which is exactly what she did.

When we returned for the reflections and feedback, Jane was the first to announce that she had discovered a Compassionate Other and source of strength in one. It was clear to see that she had a sense of pride in this, which was attuned to and mirrored by the group response. Group members spoke of being really proud of how Jane had shifted from feeling hateful about the exercise to 'giving it a go', leading to Jane speaking of feeling proud of herself.

The discovery was her faith. She has been an active member of her local Christian church for many years, often offering support to others but struggling to take anything for herself. When she reflected on the different elements of the Compassionate Other, she realised that Jesus and what he represented to her was both a source of support and strength, and a way of accessing compassion. She also spoke of her experience of being held and cared for by the group as particularly important, as they had chosen to help and were not 'paid'. Jane had siblings who were much younger and had a vastly different experience of family life. Rather than receiving support from them, she had been the provider.

This is an example of how the group process can begin the reworking of the family constellation that Yalom and others have described, as well as demonstrating the power of the group to encourage change and growth.

The map then becomes part of the therapeutic process to be returned to and worked with, adding elements as new qualities are recognised and new achievements are made.

Session 11: Compassionate Mind Training

It may seem that week 11 is late in the group to be bringing CMT in formally. But the preceding sessions will always involve CMT through the introduction of practices at the beginning and sometimes end. It is also of note that the group will all experience the modules in a different order: for some, this is Session 3, so very early in the group programme.

This session is an opportunity to focus on imagery and embodied movement and practice collectively in the group as a basis to form personal practice:

> *'It's like the breathe we did once a week and everybody practised it at home ... and that just became natural... It formed a habit... It's like the critical part of me... It's building blocks, as long as I don't let things slip I can only improve on it.'*

It is different for each individual, however I find that starting with a practice called A Calming and Welcoming Place is often easier to tolerate than the Compassionate Self or Other.

A Calming and Welcoming Place

As with all imagery work, I will always start with discussions in the room involving the whole group to gather ideas. When introducing this, I generally steer away from using the term 'safe place', as I have found that many group members do not understand the concept and this can trigger shame and misunderstanding. Returning to the helpful distinction in CFT between safety and safeness, the former being part of the threat system and seeking a haven, and the latter being part of the soothing system.

With a light touch, we begin the process of gathering ideas around welcoming, calming places of belonging. This can start with sensory connections: do you prefer warmth or coolness, day or night, beach or forest, and from there we begin to build in other elements. The most important part of this process is to share ideas and the notion that the individual group member is the architect of their own image: they are in charge. This is an integral part of this process as many of our group members have spent a lifetime feeling unable to control anything, which is one of the reasons why so many of our patients resort to harming themselves. Invite the group to also incorporate magical or mythical elements: they are limited only by the extent of their own imagination. This is an important de-shaming, de-toxifying and reclamation process in working with and through FBRs and contempt. This reclaiming of the power of the new brain's imaginative capacities is needed to counteract the traumatic invalidation they may have experienced at the hands of abusive/neglectful caregivers, whose accusation was often that they had 'vivid imaginations'. So, you can put your sofa in the North pole, surrounded by icebergs and frozen mountains, or bring a cooling lake to the middle of a desert scene. These sessions can become quite animated as the group experiment with what could work. One group member created an image of the group therapy room filled with cats, a possibly terrifying thought for some, but for this group member the combination of the safe haven and secure base of the group room was enlivened by their presence.

The next steps involve taking these ideas into creative expression – pictures, sketches or maps, with objects to represent the various elements of their imagined scene. As someone with many ideas but very little artistic capacity, I am always motivated to support the group to create something helpful to them. I have been treated to a variety of beautiful colourful images and maps over the years, the following case study being one of my favourites. When we are engaging in such creative activities, if you stay in the room, it can be helpful for you to join in the exercise with the group – for me, this means modelling the limitations to my artistic capacity! This also reduces the feeling that some group members experience of being watched as they create, which many link to negative memories of school.

> ### A Calm Place
> My co-facilitator and I had left the room to give the group some time to create images of their individual Calm Places. When we returned, the group had spontaneously decided to co-create a map, which had each group member's Calm Place in a corner with bridges of varying descriptions connecting each place to the group room in the centre of the image. This was a deeply moving experience to see how the whole group had decided that they needed the group room to be part of their individual Calm Places, symbolising how they could join with each other but also withdraw to their own places of safeness. We were all amused by one group member's drawbridge, which she explained could be pulled up with a moat underneath, ensuring that none could enter without her permission. Again, this is rich with compassionate wisdom as the group begin to explore what is needed to enable connection. See the image below which is a representation of the original image.

Once the images have taken some form and been shared and discussed in the group, then we move into imagery to embed the images and put them to work. In my imagery practices, I will always remind the group that imagery is often not we expect it to be: wisps, fragments which come and go. My hope is to connect the group with their own compassionate intention, and the images can then be used to aid and stimulate. Without explicit guidance, I have concerns that imagery can push our group into threat-based drive, competing, self-criticism and often collapse into dissociation and shut down, overwhelmed by what they feel they cannot do.

Although I am offering a script (see Appendix 3.7),[57] I would generally avoid using them as they can interfere with communication of your compassionate intention. When offering workshops on this topic, I invite people to offer spontaneous practices to each other, with only their compassionate intention towards the process a guide. The results are a moving and deeply connected experience for everyone involved. It is often not what you say, it is the way that you say it!

---

57 For a recording, see https://soundcloud.com/kate-lucre/calming-place-imagery?in = kate-lucre/sets/practices&si = 5aeb8f25026548b9a0e83c1419e1a706&utm_source = clipboard&utm_medium = text&utm_campaign = social_sharing

Compassionate Other

This is often my next step into the more explicit Compassionate Mind Training process. As above, I think time spent exploring this in group helps with some of the inevitable self-consciousness that can emerge. The exercise with the Compassionate Roles Map will have begun to draw a distinction between Supportive Others and Compassionate Others and the need for both. For some group members, the idea of a Compassionate Other will land immediately, with strong compassionate characters with wise and supportive words which can be developed and practised. Others find this more complicated and will be a longer part of the journey. It is common that group members will wish to use real people as their Compassionate Others, often idealised parents, grandparents or family associates. This can run into difficulties as these idealised others may be associated with grief and loss, as well as the reality that they may have been complicit in, or at the very least turned a blind eye to, their suffering. As ever, we are treading carefully with these conversations to steer our group members towards the development of a Compassionate Other who can fully support and develop their wisdom, courage, strength and commitment. There will be times when we need to support experimentation with their chosen other, to see if they can 'do the job'. Many group members may still be stuck with enmeshed relationships that mirror the early abusive ones, which will take time in the therapeutic process to untangle and to gain perspective on. Confronting our group members with our perspective on the suitability of a particular family member for the role of Compassionate Other may repeat the intrusion of their early life and also lead to a breach of trust and possibly early drop out.

Adam and the PG Tips monkey

Adam had struggled with the idea of a Compassionate Other who could help and support him, but with some help from the group, he had landed on the idea of a someone who had protected him in his early days in prison. It seems that this person had been serving a much longer sentence and had a degree of respect, based on fear, from other prisoners. It felt important to acknowledge and respect Adam's choice, but there was an undertone of violence and aggression attached to this character. We worked with Adam to invite the creative opportunity to expand this image to include other characteristics, but this proved problematic for Adam ('But he wouldn't have said/done that'). As group facilitators, we can find ourselves invited into an adversarial debate with members about their choices. So in this situation, we stepped back to allow this work with Adam to unfold, in a sense attempting to model and invite discussion about the important qualities that a Compassionate Other should have, rather than directing. Some months later, Adam shared with the group that he had found a new Compassionate Other – the

> PG Tips monkey! Years ago, when Adam was a young child, there had been a TV advert for PG Tips tea bags with a talking monkey, which you could save coupons from tea boxes and send off for. Adam had remembered that he had as a child saved these coupons and sent off for the monkey, which he still had.
>
> He brought the monkey to session and shared with the group that he imagined that the monkey would read him sections of the Serenity prayer and support him to continue his journey in compassion. He gave examples of times when he had been angered by other people and, rather than following his usual pattern of withdrawing or becoming aggressive, he would imagine the monkey talking to him, calming and remind him of his compassionate intention towards himself.

During this exercise, we are also building on the material that emerges from the feedback and check in, where we draw attention to examples of self-compassion and compassion to others as they arise. This work is designed to build capacity and implicit exposure to the flows of compassion through the group process. There will be moments when we notice the compassion in action but, particularly in the early, more tentative stages, we do not comment but hold it to return to.

Session 12: Show and tell

This final session in the Compassionate Kitbag module is designed to bring together many elements of the Compassionate Mind Training process and deepen the connections that the group members have to each other and their kitbags. Group members are invited to bring the objects that are part of their kitbag to the session to be held and seen by the facilitator and fellow group members, who can take on the role of mentalising mother/father or siblings. These objects are then taken home to become part of the Compassionate Kitbag, thus having been imbibed with the approval and validation of the facilitator and/or group members. Some come with bags of 'stuff' and a barely concealed excitement at the prospect of sharing, while others are much more hesitant. We can match these responses to the early attachments patterns and bring our own compassionate wisdom and understanding to each member of the group.

Group members in this context often report an experience of feeling validated by the passing of objects to others, which can be linked to the value of haptic touch in deepening an emotional connection to the objects. One group member brought her singing bowl (a Chinese instrument often used to accompany chanting or meditation) to the group. In keeping with the group ritual and process, the bowl was passed around each group member who used the rotating mallet to produce a sound which reverberated. This was experienced as a deeply moving, shared and fundamentally affiliative experience in the group, which was specifically referred to as a moment of change and connection to the group process and their own journeys in self-compassion. This clinical example draws together the strands of the Compassionate Kitbag, sound, touch, shared experience in the service of cultivating, tolerating and developing the three flows of compassion. Within CFGP a further unique transitional object process is undertaken, in that group members are invited to take objects from the table which can connect them to the group.

In his writings on child developmental theory, Donald Winnicott developed the idea of transitional objects as the first 'not me' possessions that an infant makes a connection to. These objects are generally used by the child to soothe and placate when the primary attachment figure is absent. Despite the obvious significance of the transitional objects within the child development literature, there has been comparatively little literature detailing the function of transitional objects in adult psychotherapy. The transitional object can also serve the function of the secure base to mediate the impact of threat-based stimuli, which could be the material that the patient brings to the therapy space. As in early developmental stages of childhood, the transitional object supports the process of attaching to and managing absence from the primary attachment figure, in this case the therapy group (members and facilitators). Arthern and Madill also discuss the particular difficulty for patients with complex trauma who find it difficult to internalise the experience of the therapist as there is an absence of a secure internal attachment template.[58] Therefore, having a concrete symbol of the positive regard of the group can be helpful to mediate often overwhelming feelings. This process can occur with the objects that group members bring to share and also those that they take from the group:

> *'For me, it was the little stones... A picture... A smell...*
> *That calms and reminds you of the group.'*

All that said, others in the group may not be so keen to have their objects 'imbibed' with the approval from the group. I recall one group member bringing a tiny teddy bear in a cloth bag which they reluctantly took out to show the group. When I asked tentatively (as I already believe I knew the answer to the question) if she was OK to pass this around the group, she shook her head vigorously and pushed the tiny bear back into the bag. She was not ready to trust the group to take care of her most precious object, which had been gifted to her by one of the very few reliable adults in her early life.

---

[58] Arthern, J., & Madill, A. (2002). How do transitional objects work? The client's view. *Psychotherapy Research*, **12**(3), 369–388. https://doi.org/10.1093/ptr/12.3.369

This session is a place to introduce the use of music in the group to stimulate drive and soothing, and as another mechanism to develop cohesion in the group. Group members are invited to bring favourite or meaningful pieces of music to the group to be shared. Unsurprisingly, many group members find this invitation tricky and exposing, and it often may take many weeks or even months for group members to 'take the plunge'. I have sat in countless groups sharing with others a sense of collective appreciation for the courage of a group member to bring and share a precious and cherished piece of music. These pieces of music often move me to tears, and, as with the objects, can take on new meaning and significance having been imbibed with the group's collective appreciation. Some groups will co-produce a compassion playlist, which is developed and shred with the group, differentiating between soothing and drive innervation.

Compassionate Kitbag and transitional objects

Another function of some of the items in the kitbag is that they serve as transitional objects. There are many layers to this, some of which are linked to traditional literature and thinking in this area, and some which are more novel and which are specific to CFT.

In his writings on child developmental theory, Winnicott[59] developed the idea that transitional objects are the first 'not me' possessions that infants make a connection to. These objects are generally used by a child to soothe and placate when the primary attachment figure is absent. Over time and with the development of emotional maturity, this process is internalised and the need for the actual object therefore becomes less important. However, it is also important to de-shame the fact that, for some, this may never be fully internalised and that it can be helpful to still carry around and turn back towards those external objects.

For some groups, showing and telling about their objects and the significance fills the space, but we can take this exercise one step further to deepen connections through the medium of play.

Role-taking

A specific technique to develop the capacity for playing and playfulness while expanding the utility of the Compassionate Kitbag is 'role-taking'. This technique is derived and adapted from Jacob Moreno's concept of role theory, which he developed and articulated through the practice of psychodrama:

---

59 Winnicott, D. W. (1991). *Playing and Reality*. Psychology Press.

> *'Moreno's idea is that the concept of role is above all practical aimed at helping people to reflect on and change the beliefs they have about themselves.'*[60]

Therefore, this has great utility in the cultivation of compassion. The concept of role-taking within psychodrama was designed as a means of exploring, expanding and strengthening the more functioning aspects of self, via an explicit intentional process.

During the early stages of the PEG, this therapeutic technique is introduced as a means of deepening the emotional connections to the 'objects' from the kitbag, to explore meaning and significance. This technique also offers an opportunity to creatively stimulate the flow of compassion to self through imagery, gently exposing the group member(s) to the caregiving and care-receiving mentalities.

Indeed, one of the central therapeutic interventions in CFT is to help clients recognise how they can be caught in specific social mentalities, such as a competitive mentality, and how to switch into a care-focused and cooperative mentality. This technique has the explicit function using role engagement of supporting clients to switch into a caring mentality as they take the role of the treasured object.

Animating, relating to and interacting with a chosen object in this manner also serves to give the object a perceived sense of attuned and connected responsiveness, rather than just its mere presence, which are key features of attachment relationships. The group member is invited to consider how the object *feels* about them and what the object *wishes* for them. This is supported by research suggesting that the attentiveness and emotional responsiveness of an attachment object is key to establishing emotional security, over and above the mere presence of the object.

How this works in practice

After some initial discussion about the choice of object and what it represents, the group member is then playfully invited to step into/inhabit/become the object and be interviewed by the facilitator, as if they were getting to know each other. This involves both the group member and facilitator standing up, with the group member being invited to step into role as you sit down again together. Unlike more formal chairwork, there is no need to create a stage or shift the layout of the room, which we will explore in the next section. This can be done in the same chairs, or, if needed, the facilitator who is interviewing can ask to swap chairs with another group member so that they are sitting next to the member who is about to take the role.

---

60 Blatner, A. (1991). Role dynamics: A comprehensive theory of psychology. *Journal of Group Psychotherapy, Psychodrama & Sociometry,* **44**(1), 33-40. P.34

This technique facilitates a deeper understanding of, and more importantly, an *emotional connection* with, the nature of the relationship between the chosen object and the client. This often results in a process whereby the client is rapidly able to access a sense of compassion *from the inside* that they are typically fearful of or feel unable to self-generate. Consequently, the process can be powerfully evocative and simultaneously stimulate/exercise both the caregiving and care-seeking social mentalities that underpin the ability to be self-compassionate/self-reassuring.

Invite your group member in the role of their object to share a few practical elements to orientate into the process. This might be initial questions about how long the object has been in the person's life, where they live in the house, followed by specific questions to access the care-giving and care-receiving capacities.

At the end of the process, ask your group member, still in the role of their object, if there is anything else they wish to say, and, if not, wish them well. Then invite them again to stand with you and perhaps put down the object to aid the process of 'de-roling', before sitting again. Spend a few moments inviting some observations from the group member, checking they have de-roled and also gathering the learning and connections.

(See Appendix 3.8 for an example of role-taking, some suggested questions and a link to a video of this in action.)

A few important considerations with role-taking

The fundamental purpose of this exercise is to enable group members to play with ideas of object animation and personification, and also to begin to connect to their own capacity for resilience, which is initially via the object. This playfulness if modelled by the facilitator, in that the invitation to take the role is done in a light-hearted manner and the ensuing interview is also conducted in a playful, conversational style, while avoiding any deep exploration which one might usually undertake as a facilitator. This is important due to the vulnerability associated with taking on a different role, particularly for those whose sense of self is compromised. Stepping into another role often means that the person's usual defences are left behind, and caution must therefore be exercised. Instead, focus on interviewing in a manner that naturally and indirectly elicits roles, functions and meaning.

Another consideration for the depth of questioning in this work relates to the unconscious processes that are enacted in this exercise. As one therapist who had tried this exercise for herself once said, 'we are wading around in people's unconscious, so we really ought to be careful'.

Some group members have expressed a worry that stepping 'out' of themselves for a moment may bring a permanent disconnection. One group member, when I suggested taking the role of her dog, asked me where she would be while this was all taking place.

Those who generally experience themselves as completely fragmented and chaotic, may need support with practical and concrete measures. I invited her to select an object (she chose her ring), to represent herself while she took the role of her dog and we put the object on a chair so that she could see it. After she had completed the exercise, she put down the picture of her dog which she had used as the object and picked up the ring and reconnected to her sense of herself. This kind of addition will be very important for some group members who are prone to dissociation, which could be triggered by the care-giving and care-receiving social mentalities and the accompanying positive affect. As we have discussed previously, this can be as disruptive to your group members as negative emotional states and experiences.

Keep your group member in the third person i.e. 'So, Japanese box, how do you feel about Sherelle?', although it is important to avoid making the person feeling ashamed if they get it wrong and return to the first person. When this happens, I don't correct them, but instead repeat what they have said with the name.

Here's a script to help guide you with this:

> **Facilitator:** 'So, Japanese box, I am wondering if there are particular times when Sherelle uses you or turns to you?'
>
> **Sherelle:** 'Yes, I usually pick it up and look at the treasures inside when I am upset and angry.'
>
> **Facilitator:** 'I see, so it seems clear to you that Sherelle turns to you only when she upset.'
>
> **Sherelle:** 'Oh, yes, sorry… "she".'

Although the standing and sitting may feel a little superfluous, I think it is integral to ensure that your group member has a concrete way to step in and out of role. To avoid them feeling even more self-conscious then is necessary, always stand and sit with them, joining up with the activity.

People often ask me how this works in a time-limited group and if it works for the group to then practice together. I have never been keen on this idea as I cannot be sure what is happening with the exercise if I am not doing it. Given how easy it is to get plunged into uncharted waters and to get overwhelmed and dissociated, I would suggest not. Instead, invite the group with the person's permission to ask questions. These questions and reflections are often the most heartfelt and moving. As we will return to over the coming chapters, feedback and research from this programme over the years has been very clear that, when observing, others, we are also rehearsing our own answers to the questions. So, some will never 'take the role' of anything but still benefit in a meaningful way from the observing experience.

As a facilitator, I would also avoid demonstrating for the group. If we set this up with sensitivity, there will invariably be someone who will volunteer. If we demonstrate ourselves, it can place us in a vulnerable position and also allows your group to swerve taking the plunge! I recall an exercise in my action methods training when I took the role of my green stone pendant (Ponamu). I was completely taken by surprise and overwhelmed with emotion, tearful, shaking and speechless. Reflecting on this experience that occurred in the safeness of my own psychotherapeutic training, I became very aware that I could not predict how I would respond to this exercise and so would not take this potentially unprocessed material into the group.

For the reasons outlined above, and also because this exercise is always a joyful and moving experience, I would strongly suggest you try this before taking it to group. I have therefore woven this practice into every kind of workshop that I have offered in the last ten years and I continue to do so with heart-warming results. We have even offered a whole workshop on role-taking as a key element of personal practice and skills development.

'Play is the only way anything new can come about' – Piaget

> *'There was a great sense of humour... We all started being silly and the pressure is relieved... There was space to do that without it being, like, you know, no, this is serious therapy ... you can't laugh.'*

Central to CFGP and the successful facilitation of therapeutic processes and tasks is the ability of the facilitator to be playful and thus facilitate *playfulness* in the client. Play is essential to human learning and growth. Steven Porges has proposed that play is a neural exercise that engages evolved social engagement systems that allows us to cooperatively explore, experiment, learn and experience joyful connection to others.

Play can only truly occur when one feels safe enough to do so, which may be first achieved through the expression of compassion from the facilitator in the form of therapeutic presence. Jaak Panksepp reminded us that this can then skilfully be extended to the use of humour as a means of 'joining' and further promoting playful interactions that facilitate emotional learning and that are intrinsically rewarding.[61]

This of course creates a paradox for us all: we need to feel a sense of safeness to play and we often need to play in order to stimulate our capacity to feel safe. In the group, we are working to make a start on this process, and of course it is very different for each group member. Some will already have a capacity to play and be playful, but many, as in the case of the two group members from Session 2, demonstrate an aversion (likely based in fear) of anything remotely playful. So treading carefully but going boldly is perhaps the way forward. It requires therapeutic courage to turn back towards what we are being strongly encouraged to avoid and ignore. Dian Fosha reminds us that therapist risk-taking can enhance the sense of safeness, which I believe extends to the whole group:[62]

> *'Before I was pacing along the road looking out for dangers ... listening out for dangers causing issues... Now I'm looking around for fun... Looking to play up... Looking to have a laugh so I actually get to live life now, whereas before I couldn't do it.'*

It's still all about the chairs!

As we identified in the previous chapter, chairs hold significant meaning for the group and we will return to explore this as we move through the programme. I have often found myself walking round and round the therapy room checking the distance between the chairs and re-checking the circle. Although I would not recommend this, attention paid to the set-up of the room is an important way to create a sense of safeness for the group.

The decision about who sits where has always been a source of fascination. Some groups settle very early with their chosen seats and also the seats where the facilitators need to sit! I have on occasion been asked to move as I am in the 'wrong place'. For others, it is possible to play with the preoccupation with seating:

---

61 Panksepp, J. (2015). Give Play a Chance. *The Handbook of the Study of Play*, **2**, 477.
62 Fosha, D. (2001). The dyadic regulation of affect. *Journal of Clinical Psychology*, **57**(2), 227–242. https://doi.org/10.1002/1097-4679(200102)57:2 < 227::AID-JCLP8 > 3.0.CO;2-1

> *'We'd all mess around to begin to with ... just sort of walking in 'cos everybody has their set places to sit, so we'd either play each other up by jumping in their chair or moving the chairs just general... Tomfoolery.'*

If we can keep the actual setting of the room consistent, the meaning of where and how people use their chairs can become clearer and can be explored. I attempt to shift and change where I sit, as well as whether I enter the room first or last, and the responses to this can helpfully become part of the group material for discussion and exploration.

I recently noted in group that we had all been sitting in the same chairs for some time and invited comment. A few people opted to shift and one person asked if I could move to a different chair. There were some murmurs of dissent, and some others opted to move around in different seats. After the practice, a group member who had arrived late was invited in (remember the sign on the door from the previous section). This meant that I got up and let her in. She then sat in the chair I had just vacated, meaning I had to sit back in my old chair! The group were highly amused and we had to quickly explain why everyone was laughing to ensure she didn't think we were laughing at her.

Another way into shifting the chair dynamics is to play a game with the chairs. The game can be introduced at the beginning of the group after the initial breathe, feedback and check in, or at the end as a way of preparing the group to close.

I or my co-facilitator will invariably start off the game by saying, 'So I need to swap chairs with someone without speaking, so I need to use my body language and eye contact to alert the other to my intention'. This game has multiple functions, including to lighten the mood and get the group moving around, especially as I find that the check in can sometimes leave us all a bit sombre and lacking in energy. It is important to find a playful way into shifting people into different chairs, so experiment with using eye and body gestures to indicate our intention, and perhaps also maybe even touch. I recall one group member, Cherise, loved 'her chair' so much that she would often refuse to play this game at all. This was an occasion on which she had agreed to play, but warned the group not to try and move her! One group member was determinedly trying to get Cherise's attention to swap chairs with her and Cherise was of course just as determinedly avoiding him. So he got up and went over to Cherise, checking out with her first that it was OK before pulling her out her chair and sitting down. Cherise then spent the rest of the game waiting for someone to end up in her chair and when they did, she was up and out of her chair to try the same trick to get back to her chair!

Louie and the moving chair

In the early months of Louie's time in the group programme, he would come into the room, pull his chair into the middle of the floor next to the small table, bang his phone, keys and cigarettes down onto the table and sit back. This meant that my circle was disrupted and everyone else had to crane their necks to see each other, creating some tension in the room. Louie was immoveable and I wondered if he was silently pushing me to insist that he move his chair back so that the conflict he felt in being in group could be expressed. I also wondered (but not aloud at this point) if he was pushing me to exclude him from the group. From this place, he was well engaged with the group and responded well to others who said that they found it difficult to see around him.

I worked with this in supervision and with my co-facilitator and we decided to take a non-adversarial approach to the situation. We would note that it seemed difficult for Louie to be in the circle with everyone else, but that we wanted him in the group.

Over a relatively short period of time, we noticed that he moved his chair slightly less each week, until he was part of the group circle. This subtle shift seemed to coincide with Louie feeling more able to be part of the group, rather than separate from it. Our comments were made with a deliberately light touch, to show Louie our intention towards him and our wish for him to remain in the group. Observing Louie's interactions, there seems to have been a shift from a place of isolation symbolised by the moving of the chair to a place where he could begin to join up with what others shared. It reminds me of one of the first things Louie ever said in the group as he walked in on his first day: 'Don't think I'm ever going to give a sh*t about any of you'. This statement came as quite a shock to many in the group and represented the blockage in his capacity and flow of compassion to others (this sat alongside blockages in the other flows). Louie's fear of vulnerability meant that he was not able to put words to his fear of caring for himself or receiving care from others in those early groups.

I will return to Louie when we talk about endings and it will be helpful to have in mind his defences at the start of the programme.

Staying with the topic of chairs, much has been written in the group analytic literature about the significance of an empty chair, the chairs which represent those who are absent, planned or unexpected. So when setting out the room before the group, I set a chair for each group member, even if I know they are not coming. The presence of these empty chairs, with support from the facilitators, can invite the group to express their feelings towards those who have not attended. This of course can include the facilitators, and it remains as important to encourage the group to notice how this is felt:

> 'I suppose it was there from the beginning – you have that sort of the group is Kate and Graham, and then there's us, so when one of them is missing it's a bit like when your dad's away on business or your mum's out with her friends ... it just like ... someone's missing.'

This reflects the parental transference which is always present in the group, whether it is named explicitly or defended against (I will return later to how we work with this).

Checking out and warming-down

In the final stages of a group session, there is an explicit ending to the sharing aspect of the process-driven discursive work or the work in action, and the group are invited to join up together for a period of reflection. Group members are explicitly reminded that the group is coming to a close and space is given for a discussion about the experience of the work that has taken place. The sharing part comes first, where group members draw their associations and connections with each other and the collective work. These reflections are invited as the final stage of the closure of the group.

This explicit closing component of the group is an opportunity to process some of the emerging feelings, explicitly reinforce the examples of compassionate behaviours across all three flows, and strengthen a sense of affiliative connection between the group members by highlighting the shared experiences. If, however, the level of emotional arousal has been particularly high, there may be occasions when this closing section of the group requires more active interventions. In this context, the model offers the opportunity for spontaneous play-focused activities. These 'games' are contextualised to what is required by the group to either leave difficult unresolved feelings behind, increase the emotional energy in the room, or reduce tension in the room.

When a 'silly game' isn't just a silly game

> 'The togetherness, it's the whole group ... not feeling self-conscious about a playing a silly game... It was good.'

The group had been working with the inner critic and for the first time was beginning to turn back to recognise the powerful internal critical dialogue which for many was the soundtrack of their daily lives. As the group exercise completed and the group came back into the circle to a gather in reflections from the session, the atmosphere in the room was drawn and tense. The reflections on discoveries about the critic felt a little stilted and artificial. One group member spoke of feeling overwhelmed that they had spent nearly their whole life with this dialogue and was only now beginning to hear this as an echo of past abusers and not a truth. Others agreed and the mood was sombre. We were approaching the end of the group, and so I did not want to invite more discussion about the inner critic with no time to process what came up. So we agreed that a game was needed to 'shift gear'. These games can also demonstrate in a very real and embodied way that we can indeed shift from one social mentality/mind set to another. We played Zip Zap Boing, which is described just below.

I would like to offer you a brief summary of some of the games that we play, but this is not an exhaustive list, but just some of my favourites. My inspirations come from my training in action methods, my memories of childhood party games (updated by the recent joy of my children's party games), drinking games from my distant youth, my incredible psychodrama supervisors past and present, and Liz White. Liz was a truly inspirational psychodrama psychotherapist, who is sadly no longer with us, but her work lives on through many of the games of hers I have adapted, or 'compassionated'! Everything I will explain here is best practised before you reach the group. I only wish I could gather all those who read this book and we could play all this through.

Games to lift the mood and stimulate drive

There will be times in your group, perhaps towards the end, when the mood can feel heavy and there may be a lot of unprocessed sadness, grief and loss in the room. At such times, as the group is ending, there may not be space or capacity to address this explicitly. I will always try to give voice to what I am noticing and the invite the group to attune to themselves and each other.

The following game is designed to be a place to 'park' and let go of what cannot be addressed in the session. It is also to shift energy levels to support the group to manage the ending and navigate the space outside the group.

Zip, Zap, Boing

I have been told this game is like a drinking game, but I took it from a kid's party. Invite the group to stand in a circle facing in. The purpose is to pass 'it' around the circle. The facilitator starts and can either 'zip' the person to the left (usually with hands flat together held out in front), 'zap' the person to the right or 'boing' anyone. If you are the person who has been zip, zapped or boinged, then it is your turn to zip, zap or boing someone else.

Generally, people will forget whether zip is left or right, and if we set up it lightly, it can bring laughter, connection and experiments with eye contact (particularly if you are boinging someone!). The facilitators need to make sure that everyone is passed to at some point in the game and then, when it comes back to you, you can stop the game. Always invite reflections as you sit back down. Variations to this can include:

- Throwing a small beanbag to each other (not at each other, as sometimes happens!).
- Word associations (one person says potato, another tomato, and so on around the room).

Let's Walk Like…

As the name suggests, this involves inviting the group to walk around the room in no particular direction. The facilitator again starts the game with the instruction 'whoever holds the magic pen (or another object that you choose) decides how we walk, so let's walk like you have just won the lottery'. Then everyone follows the instruction and tries to simulate elation and excitement. The magic pen is passed to another group member as everyone continues to walk around the room. The person with the pen then issues a new instruction, 'Let's walk like someone is following you!' The game continues with the pen being passed around the group. Again, raising energy levels, developing skills in spontaneity and play.

Counting to ten as a group

As before, walk around the room, inviting the group to attempt to count to ten collectively. So, one person says 'one', another 'two' and so on. But the trick is that the group are not permitted to make eye contact with each other, and if two people speak at once, we have to start again. This offers the group an opportunity to practice and develop the idea of tuning into each other. You can replace counting with A-Z (alphabet), as some find the counting restimulating and upsetting.

Games to lower the energy and stimulate soothing

There will be some groups that can feel like there's too much energy in the room, which some may describe this as a manic defence. The pace of the group speeds up and it can feel like there is no space to think or even breathe in the room. Sometimes the developmental stage of the group can feel a little regressed and young, with jokes and banter that may not seem wholly appropriate. This often comes at the end of the session when there may not be enough time to make sense of the dynamic in the room. Naming this is important and supporting some curiosity about what the group might be responding to in the material that has emerged, coupled with games designed to settle.

The breathing practices with guided imagery connected to the Calm Place and Compassionate Other can be helpful in settling the group. One of my favourites, which also overlaps with supporting connections between group members, is an adaptation of a Loving Kindness meditation. Invite the group to join you in a soothing breathing rhythm practice, and once settled, invite the group to bring each member to mind in turn:

> *'Let's start with Sherelle and bring her to our minds, send her a wish of gratitude for all that she has shared with us today and all the humour that she brings to the group. We know she is struggling to be with us at the moment and hope that she can stick with the programme. We send her a wish of compassion and understanding.'*

The facilitator moves around the group, naming each member in turn (I find this particular practice quite stressful to guide, but deeply moving). The end of the practice is an invitation to take a breath and notice the flow of compassion going to each member of the group, coupled with an invitation to be open to receiving the flow of compassion from each member of the group. Finally, invite the group to send a flow back to themselves for turning up and being part of this. One group member at the end of this exercise leaned back in his chair, clearly very moved and said, 'I feel like a big fleshy f***ing aerial!' He followed this up by explaining that he could actually feel the flows coming towards him from the rest of the group and perhaps for the first time was able to allow himself to take in what was being given.

Postcards have a wide variety of possible uses in the group, but as part of the ending process, writing or drawing symbols on a postcard to represent what is being taken away can be both containing and concrete (see Appendix 3.4: A6 postcard sample). Group members will generally agree that compassion is hard to take on any level, and so the use of a postcard to remind them of an important discovery, sincere feedback from a group member, or a message to self, can also settle the group. Postcards are also used to mark the breaks in session and are often handwritten by the facilitators and sent to group members when there is a break to acknowledge that this might be difficult.

An alternative to the breathing practice which can be used for those who get stuck with the sitting and body focus is the 'Walking with Water' game. Each group member is invited to fill a cup with water and walk with it, noticing what happens. Is there an urge to spill it, not spill it, play with it etc? There has often been some eye rolling at this exercise, but one group member captured the purpose beautifully:

> *'I wasn't comfortable; it took me out of my comfort zone… The one where we had to walk around the garden holding a cup of water and seeing how the water moved with our movements… At first, I thought that was silly, but then that taught me a lot about control and calmness and stillness.'*

Games to help the group connect

As connections begin to form between the group members, it can be helpful to use games to make these connections more explicit. This can take the form of slowing down in the group to notice when group members share and relate to each other's experiences.

One of my favourite games to explore connections in the group is Mapping with Wool. Each member of the group is given a small ball of wool and invited to wrap it around the chair of the other group members, writing what the connection is on a Post-It note and attaching it to the wool with a miniature peg. This game involves movement and negotiating the space as the group work out how to do this without creating a disastrous trip hazard. The sharing of the nature of the connections after the mapping is often a moving experience, as words are put to the tentative and developing relationships.

I am always curious when I return to the room to see how the group have decided to create the connections. Some groups have sat together in their chairs holding the wool to create multiple coloured overlapping wool circles. Others have created a matrix of strands which fill the centre of the circle, as the image below depicts, although they are not always as neat as the image! As with all of these exercises and games, if you leave the room, be very clear on how long you will be and stick to it. I recall making an error with timing and I left the group for much longer than I had said or intended. I got distracted in a conversation with my co-facilitator about the group and lost track of time. When we returned, the group possibly misunderstood the instructions for the exercise and had bound themselves together with the wool, to the point where they were stuck. There are of course many layers to understanding what happened here, but what feels important is what happened in the room when they slipped from our minds.

Compassion Shop Game

Another game which can facilitate the group's connections with one another and is also designed to support and develop the development of the Compassionate Self is to open a compassion shop in your group. The shop is symbolised by the small table in the group being loaded with buttons, pebbles, cubes etc. The group are invited to enter the compassion shop, which trades only in qualities of compassion. Again, a light and playful touch with the introduction of this exercise can help some of the inevitable self-consciousness which can emerge.

The group members are invited to browse in the shop and notice which qualities of compassion they might need a little more of: wisdom, empathy, sympathy, commitment. They are then invited to step forward with their request, the rest of the group are then invited to notice if they have any of this to spare. Some encouragement is often needed – 'Oh, yes, Sherelle, you definitely have some courage, after what you did last week…'

– to support the group members to feel confident symbolically offering qualities to each other. The group member who is giving a gift is invited to pick up an object from the table and, by holding it, pass the chosen quality into the object, which is then given to another group member. Often, multiple group members will offer a little of their extra compassionate quality, meaning that the object is passed around the group before being returned to the original group member. This has some resonance with the earlier exercises where precious objects are passed around the group.

I am sure you imagine how convoluted this became during the Covid pandemic, with antibacterial wipes being used by each member as they passed it around the group, laughing through their masks!

The invitation to take objects from the therapy group as a gift has the additional and important function of becoming a transitional object, and of symbolising the developing sense of self which, in the early stages of group, members will often struggle to hold in mind. Within CFGP, this emerging sense of self can be linked with the cultivation of the Compassionate Mind (the capacity to engage with the flows of compassion to the self, to others, and to receive from others). In time, and in Phase Four, this compassion can be 'put to work' to turn back towards the suffering of early tragedy. Group members will also often report that the gift from the therapist/group represents the hope of change, being held in mind and the positive regard of others.

Always have a plan B

When you are working online or in a room, there will be occasions when your group will not be able to manage the activity or task that you have in mind to enliven the therapeutic process. This may be as simple as the group not wishing you to leave the room or that they are upset or conflicted about the nature of the exercise. I recall suggesting counting to ten as a group game, from the previous section, which resulted in a group member abruptly leaving the room. I followed her and discovered that the idea of counting was deeply restimulating of an early shame-based traumatic memory. So we changed the game to using the alphabet. Being prepared with an alternative version of the activity or game will help you to manage the inevitable dissent that can occur in group. Bringing creativity to the group process requires a level of flexibility that I am aware often disappears for me when my threat system is triggered. This of course makes sense, as our capacity to play is linked to our soothing and drive systems. So my metaphorical back pocket is filled with alternative games, as well as brief but reassuring responses to the group members who say they don't understand what is being suggested. As we discussed previously, there are many understandable reasons for this avoidance, linked to fears, blocks and resistance to the work being key to this.

Similarly, when planning a trip into the mountains, your pockets will quite literally need to be stuffed with extras: water, gear (boots in my case!), maps, torches etc. You'll also need alternative lines to follow if your route becomes impassable. Being prepared for all eventualities will enable you to relax and enjoy your slow progress up the mountain, stopping for moments to take in the view and see how far you have come.

Knowing when to back off

In rock climbing and mountaineering, you can plan a route, know your terrain, be ready, prepared and still you will need your compassionate wisdom in the moment to know when it is time to 'back off' a route and accept this is not going to happen. There are of course a myriad of reasons why this might occur, but how we use our compassionate wisdom to turn back to the reality of the situation you face may save your life.

In CFGP the stakes may not be so high, but the message is the same. Distinguishing between some avoidance to be worked with and a situation when your group 'cannot' do what you have suggested, will serve you well in this group process.

In one established group, we were working with some difficult material and an unplanned ending for one group member, which left the group a little fragmented and conflicted. I brought the connecting with wool game (see previous chapter) and fully expected the group to engage with the task as many groups had done in the past. As I got up to leave, having begun to pass the balls of wool to each group member, there was a ripple of discontent throughout the group. They all seemed to look at each other and then to me, with more than a hint of contempt. I gently enquired if they were all set and everyone shook their heads. One group member gave voice, having eyed the others to see if they were aligned: 'Naah... That sounds really stupid, I'm not passing a ball of wool around the chairs, I'll get tangled!' The others were in absolute agreement. It was clear to me in that moment that, anti-group or not, there was a mutiny and no room for persuasion!

I had nothing else in my back pocket on this occasion, having been so sure that they would manage this exercise. So I put it back to the group, asking them what they would rather do instead. The result was surprising, playful, and I think deepened the sense of group cohesion and connectedness, a winner all round. The group opted to write the connections they had to each other on Post-It notes and stick them to each other. This of course caused hilarity, which I think reduced the self-consciousness that many felt in pegging their inner feelings to a bit of wool in the middle of the room and the inevitable vulnerability that accompanied this. CFGP is a perpetual state of learning and adapting, exhausting at times but also rewarding.

The open, rather than revolving door approach

Managing attendance in a group psychotherapy programme will always be a challenge. How many groups missed is too many? What constitutes a good-enough excuse? The answers to these questions are of course very subjective, but developing a consistent system for managing attendance will support you. I feel that missing any more than two groups in a 12-session programme is likely to have a significant impact on the capacity of the individual to make sense of the material and also to feel part of the group. These repeated missed sessions can also have a negative impact on the group dynamic, stimulating envy and frustration, and can be part of an anti-group process. I will return to this in Phase Four.

As we have already established, there is a sadly high rate of attrition from therapy programmes for people with A&RT and this is part of what makes the prognosis for this group so poor. To add a further complication, many of these patients find themselves stuck in a cycle of being repeatedly offered inadequate and inappropriate short-term psychotherapeutic interventions. Patients either drop out, resulting in judgements about willingness to engage, or they keep returning to services, resulting in a new kind of revolving door. This cycle of perceived failure and rejection inevitably replicates the early rejecting and abandonment from significant care givers.

We have tried to address this with group members whose attendance causes concern or who are struggling at any stage of the process. They are given the opportunity to take a break from the therapy and either restart the programme or rejoin it at a later time:

> *'I really, really struggled, but luckily they understood that
> and I was given chances to return and this was the
> first time I've had second chances and now
> I've completed the 12 months as a whole.'*

This aspect of the programme was designed to foster engagement with and attachment to the group, through offering autonomy and choice. We try not to wait until someone has or is dropping out before we invite them to come and meet with us outside the group to explore what is happening for them and seek a helpful solution.

When we are concerned about someone for any reason, the first step is to bring it to group and invite a non-shaming conversation about what might be helpful. If this is not possible, the group member is invited to meet with the facilitators outside of the group. While this takes place, the place in the group is placed on 'hold', meaning that their chair remains in the group but they do not come to group, and meet with us instead. The group are consulted in such situations, but I always say that we hold 'veto rights', in that I am interested in a partially democratic process and wish the group to feel they have a say in how things are worked out. But I do not expect them to be responsible for important decisions about the fate of their fellow group members. I am also not always sure that, in the early days of therapy, the group's compassionate wisdom is sufficiently developed.

Adam's fresh start

Having worked through the assessment and formulation process, Adam opted not to attend the Waiting List Group, stating that he would rather wait for the 'proper therapy' to begin. He started the PEG group and at this time appeared to have retreated a little from the progress he had made in assessment. This was perhaps an understandable survival response to the shift from the individual sessions with the facilitator in Phase One, to dilution of the individual attention as the group forms.

Adam developed a pattern of addressing the small amount he did say to me only (it is of note here that he had met me for the assessment). It was as if he could not tolerate any of the other minds in the group. Any attempts to dilute this individual focus seemed to cause Adam to shut down and withdraw completely.

As time went on, it seemed that Adam was beginning to withdraw from the programme completely. He was often cancelling groups with excuses that ranged from childcare issues to floods in his home. We invited him to come and meet with us outside of group and try and work through what was happening before he reached a point of being discharged. The intention was to compassionately turn back towards the difficulty and support Adam to do the same and avoid repeating a similar pattern of withdrawal, disconnection and inevitable rejection. The message from this session was important: 'we seek to understand what is getting in the way of you engaging in group, but you cannot continue to dip in and out of therapy'.

Despite some initial misunderstandings and anger from Adam, it was possible to have an honest conversation about his capacity to be in the room with others. He quite simply could not tolerate the other minds and at that time I am not sure he wanted to. We invited him to put his place on hold, try using the Waiting List Group for a few months and see how he felt after that time. We maintained contact and he attended the Waiting List Group on a few occasions. After three months, he contacted us and asked to return to the group. He had been frustrated by the Waiting List Group and felt that he wanted to come back and 'get on with it'. He was given the option to restart or return to the cohort he had left. He opted to restart and although there were bumps along the way and a few 'breaks' in his attendance, he seemed to return with a renewed intention towards the group. He continued to communicate mostly with me, but with a possibility of exploring the other minds in the group as time passed. He spoke of the value of 'redoing' the PEG group to readjust to the group and allow connections with others to form.

The multiplicity of self

You will notice that we do not have an explicit session on the multiple selves. I have grappled with this over the years, and decided that introducing this idea is best done in a subtle and implicit way. Many group members have been scared off by my invitation to consider the(ir) multiple selves or multiple responses to a situation. Their fear has been linked to a misunderstanding about what I mean and an assumption that I am suggesting that they have schizophrenia or multiple personality disorder. Instead, we weave in the ideas of multiplicity of self into the discussion and teaching in the early sessions and through the programme. Janina Fisher invites therapists to begin gently using the language of parts, and I have found this advice very helpful. When group members present themselves as a totality of misery, rage or terror, we can gently introduce the idea that a part of them is this way, but also wonder if there is another part of the self which is able to notice and reflect on this. It does not always land… I have been sharply corrected many times that 'No, I am completely miserable, there is nothing else'. In such moments, we can accept what is being said and return to push gently at these ideas as we move on.

> ### Jane and the miserable part
>
> During one group session, Jane had been talking for a long time during check in, to let the group know just how bad things were for her and how overwhelming everything was. Characteristically, the group appeared to be shutting down, also overwhelmed. I tried to dilute some of the intensity with an invitation to reflect on this 'part' of Jane that was overwhelmed, but that also there were other parts which were able to be part of the group and to get herself here. Jane was furious:
>
> > *'I am not made up of other bits, that makes no sense, and in any case, you are not listening to me as usual and shutting me down.'*
>
> Although I could see how upset she was, I persisted (with hindsight, too much). I carried on trying to draw attention to all the important reflections and responses that she had offered to other group members. Essentially, I was confronting her with the 'evidence' that she was wrong and I was right. In that moment, I was caught up in a competing mind set and I needed her to see that she was made up of multiples. I have a worry that I may have been either reading something about multiple selves or responding to something from supervision with Paul about the importance of this. I also wonder if I was perhaps enacting something on behalf of the group, as a reaction to her taking a lot of time in check in. Either way, I was not attending to Jane and she withdrew and became silent and compliant. I realised later that I had pushed too far and reenacted something from her early life, where

she was told that her beliefs were wrong and didn't matter. I worked this through in supervision and returned to group and apologised to Jane, not for believing that she was made up of multiples, but for pushing my views onto her. It was the first rupture in the group that we repaired, but certainly not the last.

We will return to working with rupture in Phase Four.

Concluding comments

Congratulations for wading through this hefty section. Despite my advice to keep the content light, there does appear to be quite a significant amount to share about the modules! This is of course just a guide, and there will be a myriad of creative ideas that you will bring to this work. My intention is to offer some ideas to get started or to add to the ways you may already be introducing these ideas and concepts. My take-home message from this element of the work is to go slow and with a light touch, to 'drop pebbles', rather than drive home the key messages.

To finish, then, a quick reminder of the key messages that our group members will need to move on to Phase Four. Always bear in mind that there is ample time to recap and cover the material from the PEG.

> **Key messages:**
> - We have brains that are designed for survival not happiness.
> - It's not our fault, but it is our responsibility.
> - We have tricky brains with complex loops.
> - Life is short and often tragic.
> - We are shaped by the environment and social circumstances over which we have little control.
> - We don't choose this life but are subject to its vagaries.
> - We are the most affiliative of all species and need others.

To complete this preparatory Phase Three section, I would like to offer a few comments on additional adaptations that may need to be made to this model, in line with organisational requirements and the post-Covid landscape.

Chapter 3.7: Closed and Online Groups

Closed groups

Having spent a large portion of this section extolling the virtues of the slow, open rolling programme, this is not the only way to run the group. I will briefly turn my attention to the closed group.

When the time you have is more limited, a closed group can support the development of what Yalom describes as 'groupishness' or group cohesion, in that the group starts their journey together and do not have to tolerate the level of change and shifts to the group dynamics of a rolling programme. Managing the issue of dropout can be tricky. I find that allowing a bit of flex in the first few sessions, which is when the largest dropout rates occur, can offer an opportunity for new members to be added to the group. It can be tempting, in order to mitigate against dropout, to start with a much larger number of group members (10-13). I would avoid this, as I think that a large group may trigger people to drop out who might have managed in a smaller group.

The sense of settling in which can occur in a closed group can be deeply beneficial for all, us and them. Attending to the potential for group dynamics to become stuck is necessary and important. Some of the games involving swapping chairs and swapping roles can support this work.

I find myself wondering sometimes who decided that 12 sessions was the magic number for brief psychotherapy interventions. I think in the UK, the NICE (National Institute for Clinical Excellence) had something to do with this, with their recommendations in the past decade. However, in the UK, we also have clear guidance and governmental frameworks that are clear that treatment of people who would attract a diagnosis of personality disorder should be 18 months to two years, which offers plenty of scope for us to push to for longer interventions. If you need more evidence, check out Lucre *et al* (2024), and you can find more of the details of this study in the conclusion.[63]

But I think it can become a source of frustration for many clinicians I speak with, who are struggling to extend traditional group therapy programmes. As we discussed at the beginning of Phase Three, try to avoid getting caught in threat-based drive, trying to cram everything into a short programme.

With a 12-session closed group, you can extend each module with extra sessions. For example:

- Another session on the inner critic could allow you to role-take the critic and work more with its functions.
- More time with the three circles, focusing on what might be needed to change the shape, additions and subtractions.
- You can never have too many imagery sessions, moving into embodied work with the Compassionate Self.
- Extending the sessions on the Compassionate Kitbag, showing, telling and role-taking.

There is also room, if you have further sessions, to take your closed group into the Phase Four work, which we will be coming onto. I am aware that many 12-week CFT group programmes take people into chairwork. My hesitancy with this is really

---

[63] Lucre, K., Ashworth, F., Copello, A., Jones, C., & Gilbert, P. (2024). Compassion Focused Group Psychotherapy for attachment and relational trauma: Engaging people with a diagnosis of personality disorder. *Psychology and Psychotherapy* **97**(2).

linked closely to the group of patients I choose to work with and knowing that the Compassionate Mind Training needed to make this helpful and possible for many takes a long slow-paced group.

When chairs become boxes – working online

In our post-Covid era, many of us offer online groups. This has widened access to group psychotherapy, particularly in remote locations. Those of you who do this work will know well that it is not, however, straightforward to transition from chairs to boxes on a computer screen. Much has been written about this topic in recent years, and even within the CFT community, opinions are divided. Some will say that the variables online are just too great and the lack of neuroception (using our bodies to signal and create safeness in the room) make online working untenable. There are, equally, others who see the opportunity to reach those who would, for many good reasons, not be able to manage face-to-face group therapy.

In the early days of Covid, we moved our programme online. My group members had a mutiny after only a few months and refused to continue online, which gave me the push I needed to insist that we returned to our group room, with social distancing, face masks, hand gel and all the associated challenges! Much of what I will share with you came from that steep learning curve, coupled with supervising a myriad of online groups since then and running my own online psychotherapy programme for compassion-focused therapists. To be clear, I do believe that some Compassionate Mind Training groups can be run effectively online. I am not so sure about the CFT or CFGP, as I feel that we need to be in the room together to rework and rewire the attachment ruptures.

So, I would like to share some of the ways that we have adapted to meet the challenges of working online. First, the key components of the dynamic administration process which enabled therapists to maintain safeness in the room are no longer under the control of the therapist. Essentially, there are no chairs to set out, no room to heat, no door to keep shut. The result is that the whole concept of dynamic administration has had to shift in the mind of both therapist and group member. Some of the traditional therapist roles have needed to be shared, which requires a reworking of the traditional 'Safe Space Agreement'.

Pre-group planning sessions

This may already be standard practice for many of you, but having a session that follows the assessment process and is specifically designed to prepare the group to share an online space is essential. This would be shorter and more practical than the initial therapy session. The group would be invited to test their IT equipment and explore some of the following questions: can you see everyone? Is the signal enough to manage the whole group? Is the space confidential? (sitting next to grandma on the sofa is not a confidential space!). I was supervising a group, where one of the group members was indeed sitting next to their grandma on the sofa, and this did not become clear until the end of the session (their rationale was that their grandma was deaf).

Establishing these practical parameters will save time and potential conflict later. Regarding a confidential and protected space for the group, it will be helpful for you to consider the boundaries before this initial session. I would suggest that, if a group member is not well enough to be dressed and out of bed, then they are not well enough to be in group. I recall the first online session with my group in Covid times, when we all logged in together and everyone (apart from me) was in their pyjamas. I will never forget the look of horror on everyone's face as they all realised that this didn't work. One group member, peering out from under her dressing gown hood, said that felt like she had logged in without any clothes on at all. So we agreed from that time onwards that everyone would get dressed and ready as if they were coming to group before the sessions. This then became an essential ritual to prepare for group psychotherapy online and at home. One group member spoke of not realising how important the often long and boring bus ride was, until it was gone. She spoke of understanding that the bus ride to group gave her time to prepare herself, and the ride home to process what she had experienced.

This is also an opportunity to think with the group about how close they sit to the screen, as the more visible our bodies are to each other the better. I tend to sit slightly back for the screen so my hands and arms can be seen. I think this aids the unconscious assessments that are being made about our intentions towards each other. I am also aware that when I am very close to the screen, every twitch and facial gesture is visible, which can increase misperceptions. As much as possible, I want to give group members a similar experience to being in the room. When we sit together in chairs, we are not so close that we are exposed to every gesture and movement of each other's faces.

While I appreciate and acknowledge how challenging it can be to tolerate seeing our own faces on the screen, I have also sat in a group space where everyone has their cameras and mics off. My threat system quickly took a nosedive, 'no face' is of course far worse than the 'still face'. I quickly found myself quite shut down, unable to speak and wanting to log off. I have also supported facilitators trying valiantly to run CMT groups where everyone has, for good reasons, got their screens off. I would explore this in the planning session and perhaps invite the group to try it and see how it feels if we all switch off. My hope would be that the group discover that it is really unhelpful and not conducive to developing relationships and connections in the group.

Many groups use breakout spaces in the same way that I would leave the actual room to support the group to work together. Of course there are challenges with this, as you really have no idea what is happening in your breakout space. I have been known to listen at the door for a moment with a group I have concerns about, just to make sure that something is happening, and they haven't all lapsed into a shutdown, terrorised silence. I am thankful to report that this has never occurred. But with a breakout space, this isn't really possible. I would also suggest that if anyone needed me, they could return to the main room and invite me into the breakout space.

Rituals routines and safeness

So with this wisdom in mind, working online requires some attention to and development of rituals to enable us and them to prepare for and bring closure to sessions. This might be as simple as getting dressed, but also preparing the space you will inhabit in group. Invite your group to make changes to their usual room set up, perhaps a chair in a different place, or something extra – a plant or ornament to mark the different use of the room. Some group members have found it helpful to have a blanket which they cover the chair with and, after group, this is folded and put away with anything else used while in group. The preparing and packing away then becomes a ritual to demarcate the space. One group member would journal after group and then put away the book that she has used, another would use a candle which she would then blow out and put away with her blanket (this is a favourite of mine also), while another would walk around her garden with no shoes on as a way of grounding herself.

'Showing your working', as we discussed previously, becomes even more pertinent in this context. Sharing your thoughts more explicitly with your group members is key, as it is no longer possible to 'signal safeness' implicitly through the embodied presence in the room. Weinburg suggests that one way of working with disconnection is to offer a greater level of self-disclosure that may be needed to facilitate the transition to online check in. Within CFGP there is a level of self-disclosure implicit in the process which has perhaps made it easier to make the transition. The pace and tone of these online sessions needs to slow to allow extra time for the group members to settle with each other. We may also need to be more active in the therapeutic space, inviting group members to share their thoughts with you and each other. In this way, the containment offered by us may need to be more explicit. I had a session once where I think the pace had slowed a little too much, the pauses in the conversation had become quite long. One group member said, 'Have we paused or is my screen frozen?' This was a gentle and playful inquiry, which allowed space to think about what the silences meant online and how different they were to being in the room. But your group members may not be able to articulate this and so it will be important for you to inquire and name your own concerns if there is too much or too little space.

Blurred backgrounds are something to be thought about with the group. For us as group facilitators, I would suggest not using them as they can imply that there is something that the therapist wishes to hide, or that they do not wish to 'share' their space with the group. Instead, time spent creating a welcoming but neutral background which offers the patient a sense of being 'held in mind' is more conducive to safeness.

Online working does offer the benefit to group members to access things from their home environment, in particular when we are working with the Compassionate Kitbag. I will often give the group five minutes to go and find something that is part of their kitbag. This helps stimulate the drive system and also the soothing system, as they show and tell each other about what they brought. Pets have often made an appearance in and around the screen, which many associate with the Compassionate Others and stimulating soothing.

We can play games online and they are also integral part of the therapeutic process, but you will need to adapt and get creative. We use emojis with the stepping in and out game, as described in Chapter 3.2. So group members can use emojis to indicate feeling the same as the group members who have stepped in. The group can of course stand together and check in or stay sitting. Bringing embodied movement to your online group will help keep the flow. We may not be able to use wool, but we can make connections with each other using our hands, palms out on the edge of both sides of the screen to connect the whole group. When people check in with each other they will often say where the person is in relation to them, e.g. you are in the box next to me. Most online platforms sadly do not have everyone in the same place, which also means we are experimenting with being in different places in the online room. I have invited groups to get a scarf for the circle of strength exercise, which is stretched across their screen to create an unbroken visual link. The scarfs are then often draped on chairs or around people's necks for the remainder of the group.

To chat box or not, that is the question?

There are many issues with the chat box function on both Microsoft Teams and Zoom, and likely any other platform you might be using. I think one of the difficulties is the option to private message using it. I have likened this experience in a group to having someone whispering in my ear while I am trying to say something on a completely different topic. It is disconcerting and I worry that it can create tension in the group. Again, it is helpful to discuss this at the beginning and invite the group to have this as part of the Safe Space Agreement.

However, some groups I have supported attest to the value of the chat function as long as it is to the whole group. People will often offer heartfelt responses to each other which they may not have been able to articulate in the group. The point here is that every group is different and, whatever you decide, being clear and consistent will help you and group to navigate the inevitable pushes.

Concluding comments

As we draw this section on preparation and engagement to a close, it brings a smile that I thought this might be a single chapter! The time, attention and pacing at the beginning of this process is absolutely key to what is then possible as we move forward to the next phase. Like rock climbing, skip this bit, quite literally, at your peril.

Slowing down in our own minds and creating space to come together with your co-facilitator will support this process in your group. Letting go of all the content you imagine you have to agenda and cover will also give you space to attend to the group, remembering those little details really count. Bringing creativity, a light touch and our common humanity to the psychoeducation and practices has been identified as necessary to facilitate the group trying things at home. The basic components of the model are the foundation that we build this house of compassionate capacity on.

Central to the whole of CFGP and the successful co-facilitation of therapeutic processes and tasks is the ability of the therapists to be playful and thus facilitate *playfulness* in the client. As we have explored, play is essential to human learning and growth, a neural exercise that engages evolved social engagement systems that allows us to cooperatively explore, experiment, learn and experience joyful connection to others. But importantly, this can only occur when we feel a sense of safeness, so working together to bring both safeness and play in ourselves and our groups is a delicate balance.

> *'It was friendly banter with each other ... brother and sister stuff... It would make people feel comfortable and relate to things that had happened ... helped us know we were in a safe environment, you know?'*

Phase Four:
Compassion-Focused Trauma Group (CFTG)

Programme element	Format	Function
4. Compassion-Focused Trauma Group (CFTG). Compassion-Focused Group Psychotherapy.	■ 52 weekly sessions. ■ Two hours (no break). ■ 'Putting compassion to work.' ■ Facilitated by the same two highly trained compassion-focused psychotherapists.	■ Using the capacity for compassion developed in the PEG to turn back towards early ruptured attachment relationships. ■ Using the group as a secure base to begin to explore past and present relationships. ■ Bringing compassion to shame-based trauma memories. ■ Using the group process to develop new attachment relationships. ■ Working with conflict (internal and in the group). ■ Using the group process to explicitly and implicitly stimulate the care-giving and care-receiving social mentalities.

Chapter 4.1: Transitions and conflict

The main emphasis for this phase is to provide 'a corrective emotional experience for individuals to facilitate the development of adaptive ways of relating with others'.[64]

We are now moving on to the second part of the psychotherapy programme, where we support our group members to begin to use the capacities and competencies which they have been developing in Phase Three. This includes the ability to tolerate being in and part of a group with others. For many, the capacity for compassion remains at a very rudimentary level and there will be much work to be done to develop this further. But the intention of the CFTG is to support group members to put their Compassionate Self 'to work', to begin to turn back to and explore early traumatic experiences and how they continue to manifest in adult life. To ease this transition between the phases of the programme, it helps to be in the same room and on the same day. Phase Three (PEG) has always been 10-12pm and CFTG from 12.30-2.30pm. It makes for a very

---

[64] Capone, G., Schroder, T., Clarke, S., & Braham, L. (2016). Outcomes of therapeutic community treatment for personality disorder. *Therapeutic Communities: The International Journal of Therapeutic Communities*, **37**(2), 84–100. https://doi.org/10.1108/TC-12-2015-0025

intense day, but I always enjoyed how themes from the PEG make their way into the CFTG, no doubt carried in the unconscious material of the facilitators. It also helps to keep the programme as a whole, and it is easier logistically for the same facilitators to run both groups.

Although the whole programme has a slow, rolling format, because the PEG is only 12 weeks and the CFTG is much longer (between 40 weeks and 15 months), the CFTG will become full. At this point, the PEG stops and the CFTG becomes essentially a closed group for a period of time, usually at least four or five months. This enables sufficient group cohesion and safeness to develop to enable the intense exploratory work to take place.

The structure of the group also remains the same, with the breathing practice followed by feedback and check in. However, at this stage it is helpful to negotiate with the group to shorten this segment to allow more time for the emerging material to be worked with.

The group then move into what has over the years been playfully called 'the work', using the developing competencies in compassion to return to difficult early life experiences, current conflicts and challenging relationships. There is no particular plan for this aspect of the group and I am always listening carefully in check in for something that feels live and would be useful to return to. Sometimes the group will work together on an issue which resonates with the whole group and may span over a number of weeks, at other times we might focus on one group member's issue. At the end of the work, we return to the circle to reflect on the material that has been explored. I will return to this in detail as we move through the different ways of working in action and compassionate transformation, but an overview of the group at this stage feels important to have in mind. Many group members find the shift from the more structured and deliberately less-exposing components of the PEG, to the CFTG, quite challenging. Acknowledging this and working explicitly with the shift can be helpful but does not eliminate the risk of drop out at this point.

'Moving up to big school': Transitioning to CFTG

Many group members over the years have likened the transition from PEG to CFTG as the move from primary to high school, with the associated anxieties and trepidation. But many have also spoken of the experience of being welcomed and supported into CFTG by the existing 'senior' group members:

> 'The older ones showed us the ropes... Then you look after the newbies – you just take on that role and, I don't know, it naturally shifts.'

The slow-paced, lighter focus of the often-smaller PEG is designed to facilitate an easing in and preparing for the more exploratory aspect of the programme. Just like the steeper more challenging terrain of a multi-pitch climb requires time preparing on lower grade rock (or indeed indoors) to develop the capacity to manage the more demanding adventure ahead. Developing confidence, skill and capacity enables us to move onwards and upwards with courage and wisdom. There are also a number of explicit therapeutic techniques coupled with a general therapeutic style, which is slow-paced and supportive, designed to cultivate and then maintain a sense of safeness for group members undertaking compassion-focused trauma work. Much of this relates to the need to ensure that members feel in control of the process.

But CFGP is a whole programme with multiple components, and group members are therefore invited to join the 40-week CFTG immediately following completion of the PEG (i.e. finishing PEG week 12 and starting CFTG week 13). This transition into the CFTG is made ideally with the group member or members who commenced the programme at the same time, as described in Phase Three. This element of the programme is designed to aid the transition, providing group members with a supportive familiar face or 'therapy buddy'. The slow, open format is useful in that group members are invited to join a programme which is already 'running' and they therefore have access to support from existing members who can normalise anxieties about the group. The structure of the group is also maintained in both parts of the programme:

> *'It was difficult to be honest, because the 12 week group*
> *I'd settled in... Then all of sudden it was flipped on*
> *its head 'coz I was going to the afternoon group ... but*
> *then when you get in there that all changes because*
> *it was the same as the morning group.'*

However, before we get to this point, and despite the structure designed to create consistency and familiarity, the transition into the CFTG can be deeply unsettling for group members. They may have become accustomed to the membership of the 12-week PEG and disruption is frequently experienced when they join the new group. Over the years, we have noticed this can be expressed through attendance issues and dropouts. This can link with a sensitivity to instability and change common among group members who have experienced early A&RT. Yalom invites us to consider that the experience of emotional tension in group also has an interdependent connection with group cohesion in that each of these group processes supports the development of the other. Thereby, the difficulties associated with managing the move from the PEG to the CFTG, once navigated, can serve to deepen the bonds and connections between the group members in the programme. But navigating this is often very taxing on the group members individually and collectively, and there have been occasions when this has led to ruptures that have not been repaired. Members have then left or been asked to leave the programme.

There have been many occasions over the years that the programme has been running when a broadly even number of group members 'move up' from PEG to join the CFTG. This has often happened in the context of a low level of dropout from the PEG and a consequently high level of cohesion between the group members. Therefore, two groups are coming together who both have established identity and connections:

> 'A safety almost in that group identity ... and some people were just starting to open up and somebody new comes and they close up again, so then they have to sort of go through that process again.'

When two tribes go to war

Dal joined the CFTG in a small group of four who had been together from the beginning of the PEG. Although there had been ruptures in this group, there appeared to be a strong sense of cohesion, which seemed to solidify when they joined the existing four members in the CFTG. From the first session, there appeared to be unspoken tension which was expressed through complaints about parking, room temperature, new group timing. I invited the new group members to notice the complaints and wondered about what else did not feel quite right. The group were not ready to explore this and so I put it on ice to return to in time. The group increasingly sat with, passed the check in to and responded only to, their own subgroup. There were moments when the four would pass to each other and then almost leave the check in 'hanging', as if they could not bear to pass it to the others. Our attempts to bring this to the group and also to work around the edges were met with equal resistance on both sides. At one point, the new members suggested that perhaps they could return to the PEG as this group was 'not working'. There were many almost comical moments as the two groups dismissed my attempts to invite games and activities designed to find common ground. There have been many other cohorts who have been able to respond to such invitations. But in this case the group motivation felt competing and withholding rather than sharing and cooperating (as Paul Gilbert's 2020 paper on this topic explores[65]). I was left feeling at a bit of a loss and like a parent whose

---

65 Gilbert, P. (2021). Creating a Compassionate World: Addressing the Conflicts Between Sharing and Caring Versus Controlling and Holding Evolved Strategies. *Frontiers in Psychology,* **11**. https://doi.org/10.3389/fpsyg.2020.582090

children constantly 'bicker' despite being given lots of interesting activities to divert them! With help from our supervisor, we decided to turn towards and lean into the conflict, rather than trying to divert the group from the stuckness. After the check in, I invited the group to stand in a place in the room where they felt most comfortable to make contact with those they felt most connected to. Unsurprisingly, the two groups took up positions on either side of the room in a small group with their 'others'.

As a child, I recall a quite brutal school yard game where rival groups would line up at opposite ends of the playground and run at each other, with players from opposing sides trying to 'break the line'. This game came into my mind, along with the faint sound of 'Frankie Goes to Hollywood', bearing the title name. So I suggested an adaptation to the game, where the two groups lined up at opposite ends of the room and really looked at each other, noticing all the things that made them different. There was some uncomfortable shuffling and a few jokes as they got started. I then invited the group to walk towards each other keeping eye contact until they reached close proximity to each other. My motivation with this exercise was to support the group to acknowledge and bring compassion to their differences and the struggle to be connected. With the hope that, from this place, spontaneous connections could emerge. The responses to this exercise were very thoughtful and many were able to connect to a fear of losing their group that had kept them from allowing connections with the new people. Again, Paul's paper can help us understand that, when our rank social mentality is activated, we cannot simultaneously cooperate and share. The notion that when resources become scarce (as in the case of a bigger group), we will tend to withhold and compete. But as we explored in Phase Three, the medium of play offers an opportunity for compassionate wisdom to emerge and new relationships to form.

I would like to report that all the tension melted away and was replaced with newfound respect and appreciation. Maybe not so dramatic, but there was a shift which, in time and with a lot of work, enabled the two 'tribes' to come together and become one group. Leaning into Yalom's idea, in time there has been a strengthening of the bonds and mutual respect between the members of this and other cohorts, which seem to link to the initial conflict and discord.

The anti-group

> *'Creativity and growth [in the group] come from the recognition and transformation of destructive impulses.'*[66]

---

66 Nitsun, M. (2014). *The anti-group: Destructive forces in the group and their creative potential.* Routledge.

Not all groups are able to work through the transition, and some of these issues rumble on, impacting heavily on the whole-group process. For some, it is not just the change that presents significant challenges. For many, in particular those whose early attachments ruptures and trauma have led them to develop coping strategies or defences that can manifest in seeming contempt, disregard or even attacks on the group.

What Morris Nitsen called the 'anti-group' is helpful to have in mind at every stage of the programme, as these processes ebb and flow and vary in appearance from hardly at all to 'engulfing' of the whole group.[67] There are some occasions when the disturbance gets located in one individual, who may become a scapegoat, holding the obstruction and dissent for the whole group. It occurs at different levels; sometimes it is located in the individual and other times whole group. I recall a recent group where there appeared to be a split, like the one described above, but this time over 12 months into therapy. There were those who felt that the programme was a waste of time and there was 'no point in trying as it will be over soon', coupled with others who held the hope for the group and tried valiantly to encourage and cajole the others to join in.

Some examples of this may be consistent timekeeping issues, struggling with 'turn-taking', or altering the layout of the chairs. These can be understood and formulated in the context of understandable fears associated with the sense of connection and belonging to the group and the activation of the attachment system which inevitably accompanies this experience. Let's remind ourselves of the case of Louie and the moving chair from chapter 3.6, who insisted on moving his chair every week so that it was not in line with the others. He noted that his need to move the chair lessened as the weeks passed and he was more able to tolerate the sense of belonging to the group and compassion for fellow group members. This example demonstrates in a small way how the slow-paced consistency of the group programme is enabling patients to create new attachment relationships with peers and therapists.

Nitsen also reminds us, which I find helpful advice to hold in mind, that these processes are part of the developmental life of the group and can lead to increase in cohesion if made visible and worked with.[68] The important connection with Nitsen's idea and compassion is the need to turn towards and give voice to what is happening in the room. The 'positive' group members in the example above could not 'jolly' the group along; the situation required us to slow down and pay attention to what was happening in the room. In that situation, I invited the group members who were trying to bring positivity to name their feelings about what was happening in the room. This enabled there to be a voice for the anti-group process.

---

67 Ibid.
68 Ibid.

Here's a script to demonstrate this process:

> **Facilitator:** 'I am wondering how those of you who are able to talk today are feeling? I feel very aware that some of us are not able to speak at all today and have their heads in their hands.'
>
> **Group member 1:** 'I feel like there is a lot of tension between us and I want the others to know that there is hope.'
>
> **Group member 2:** I feel guilty that I feel OK and that I am looking forward to what comes next.'
>
> **Facilitator:** 'Perhaps all we can do today is notice and acknowledge that we are not all in the same place today and carry on the work that we planned, even though some are not able to be part of this?'

We continued as planned, with some of the anti-group members deciding to opt out, these were the same members who had been giving feedback that the group was pointless as the facilitators would be 'kicking them out soon'. Given the stage of the group, I decided not to spend too much time trying to 'persuade' the others to take part. Two members of the anti-group decided to leave, and we agreed that if they choose to leave, we would not follow. Another anti-group member opted to stay and work with the ambivalent parts of the self. This gave rise to a useful exercise, exploring and bringing compassion to ending loss and understandable ambivalence about change, which also links with the creative and transformative potential of the group process.

The anti-group continued: working with conflict

> *'[In therapy,] early familial conflicts are relived,
> but they are relived correctively.'*[69]

As we have described, the structure of the programme can lead to difficulties as group members adjust to what is often a larger group. Also, as the intensity of the group process increases, there can be more conflict between the group members and difficulties arise in the transference with the therapists. Much has been written about the importance of understanding the 'enactments' in the room and finding ways to work

---

69   Yalom, I. D. (n.d.). With Leszcz, M.(2005) *The Theory and Practice of Group Psychotherapy.* New York: Basic Books.

with the material that is emerging in the room, but also attending to the links with past relationships which may be unresolved. As Yalom and Lesczc invite us to consider in the quote above, there is an opportunity for early familial relationships to be reworked through the lens of compassion and for new attachment relationships developed. Rupture and repair in the group process has also been much documented with a clear understanding that this process is not only necessary but also linked clearly with improved outcomes. Within the CFTG programme, conflicts represent opportunities for group members to experience rupture-repair and reaffiliation processes that have often been starkly absent from their attachment relationships. Much of the CFTG structure and process is geared around having created sufficient safeness in the room to allow for disagreements, challenging of authority and protesting at feeling treated unfairly/misunderstood to occur and be compassionately worked through. Such in-session safeness (i.e. attachment security) is associated with higher levels of rupture resolution.

> *'...he [group member] said something to me which I found offensive... Previously, I would have sat there and boiled or I've would've lost my temper ... but I made eye contact with him and said your behaviour made me feel uncomfortable... He apologised ... It was a turning point.'*

This example highlights how the CFTG can shed light on the change process that may be running in the background and underneath conscious awareness. The programme addresses the inevitable difficulties with rupture at this stage by the explicit cultivation of the Compassionate Self, which is then accessed and used to provide an alternative perspective and way of moving forward from difficult interactions.

Clara, Dalvinder and the need for a boundary

Leading on from the difficult experience with the introduction of a new facilitator, described in PEG, Clara had continued to be caught in an anti-group process. This often involved attacking the group facilitators, dominating the group and making unfavourable comparisons with previous, 'better', therapy and therapists. Other group members would attempt to provide an alternative perspective to Clara, which felt as if they were trying to protect the facilitators from her. For many, this was a toxic repeat of their early attachment relationships, feeling responsible for the protection of parents and or siblings.

Dal joined the group with another three group members from the PEG and almost immediately became locked in a transferential tangle with Clara. For Dal, it seemed that Clara's attacks and demands connected them with unprocessed rage towards their dependent and demanding mother. For Clara, Dal's assertiveness and willingness to get involved in conflict seemed to ignite her sense of injustice as the 'elder' group member who should be respected.

The conflict between the two group members rumbled on and despite many attempts to explore the underlying transferential issues, Clara insisted that the root of the issue was Dal. Dal became increasingly angered by Clara's provocation, which included comments about their transgender identity. During one session, Dal became angry and upset and walked out of group and the facilitator followed. While they were both out of the room, Clara had pushed other group members to reject Dal and suggested that '*she*' should not be in the group. When the facilitator and Dal returned, another group member advised them of the conversation and that they felt uncomfortable. Dal exploded, swearing at Clara in a threatening way, pushing their chair over and damaging the door as they stormed out of the building. During the ensuing discussion, where group members were invited to share their feelings about the incident, the group members were clear that, although they had been scared, they wanted Dal to be given a chance to return. At Dal's instigation, they did return, having first come to a session to make reparations with the group.

Clara could not accept this group decision and continued to speak about feeling unsafe around Dal. This transferred to another new group member who joined CFTG and for whom it began to look and feel like bullying. This signalled the end of the group's capacity to support and work with Clara and she was discharged from the programme. Disentangling projective scapegoating processes from a realisation that some group members are not ready or able to be part of the group is challenging work.

Tuning into the group and supportive supervisory space were key components of the work with Clara and Dal. The setting and holding of the boundary with both group members was also fundamental to working reparatively with the rupture. The group process is partially democratic, in that all decisions about the group are discussed

and explored, and space is made for everyone's opinions. But I hold what I playfully call 'veto rights', which means in essence that I do not expect the group to be able to make all the important decisions about membership of the group, how we manage ruptures or respond to prolonged absences or persistent lateness. My intention is to ensure that everyone has a voice and is heard, but that they do not carry (which is sometimes experienced as) the onerous duty that sits alongside fully democratic therapeutic communities.

It is challenging for many to tolerate disagreements, and I often feel a spoken and unspoken pressure to smooth over any such disagreements. But the work in the group is to tolerate the tension and cultivate a compassionate strong, wise, committed response.

> *'There was a big who ha ... doors were slammed ... then she came back and said I felt like and you made me feel like this and, you know, people apologise and actually she became quite a part of the group... I guess again it's a testimony to the effectiveness if, you know, for those people who kept at it... it bears fruit.'*

This is another example of the deep understanding that group members gained of the benefits of sticking with the programme. This links in with the previous comments about the value of repaired ruptures which can in time deepen bonds.

But for the times when this is not able to cut through well-worn survival strategies, I would like to share another perhaps more controversial idea with you. This works well if you have two group members who have fallen out and have not been able to repair the rupture in the ways described above. This exercise can only really be used in a well-established group where there is some trust and compassionate capacity. I have tried, when there is not so much groupness present, and it has failed dramatically! As you can imagine, suggesting this with Clara and Dal could have resulted in a storm.

Aisha, Louie and case of reversing roles

The conflict between Aisha and Louie had been rumbling along for many months and there had been various attempts to work with this, but both had remained adamant that there was not an issue. It was an interesting situation, as Louie had previously spoken very fondly of Aisha and felt that she had been a catalyst for a big change in him. He had said that Aisha reminded him of his partner, whom he later disclosed to the group he had been violent and controlling towards for many years. Aisha's disclosure of her own abusive partners had opened his eyes to his own behaviour and the impact.

This revelation had led to Louie making a commitment to change his way of being with his partner, which had likely been the catalyst for her leaving him. The result was that Louie ended up in a homeless hostel for the rest of his time in group and I wondered if this sat underneath the barb that seemed to emerge in his relationship with Aisha. Aisha, on the other hand, had used her work with Louie to bring courage, strength and commitment to herself, but would often undermine Louie in subtle ways. I wondered if she was still finding the compassionate place, which was neither passive or aggressive.

I asked them both if they would like to play a game to try and make sense of each other's positions. Both agreed, as they had often expressed a fondness for each other despite the triggers and connections they shared. So we invited them to swap chairs and role reverse, so Louie became Aisha and Aisha became Louie. There were, of course, particular sensitivities in this case to be considered. We checked out carefully that Aisha was comfortable with the role reversal before starting. We then invited them to have a conversation about their week. This exercise is designed to train and develop the capacity for mentalising, holding other's minds in mind, within a playful medium. These techniques and processes are all opportunities to exercise the vagal brake that down-regulates the intensity of threat-based defensive reactions to remain socially engaged long enough to repair/resolve ruptures.

In this instance, Aisha and Louie played their roles with a light touch, while we also asked them a few questions about the other. This was illuminating and helpful as some of the connections above came to light. To be clear, such exercises are never an 'instant hit' or trigger for change, but there was a shift in the stuckness which made space for further explorations into the underlying causes of the rupture.

I have focused a lot of the attention in this section on the conflicts and ruptures, as they will often need to be addressed in the early stages after a transition before the group can get down to the transformative work. As I have already said, the ruptures will of course bubble up again, but the hope is that this initial work will lay a foundation for how tension can be resolved.

Circle of strength

There needs to be an equal emphasis during this phase on inviting the group to come together with a shared compassionate intention and notice what they can bring to each other and the work. One of my favourites is again an adaptation of a Liz White exercise. You can introduce this game anytime, at the beginning of the PEG group, and as part of the early work in CFTG.

Put a pile of scarfs in the middle of the floor and ask the group to stand in a circle together. Invite each group member to pick a scarf that they like the look of and place the scarfs on the floor behind the group, so that each overlaps to create a circle. Once this is completed, let the group know that the scarf they selected actually represents a quality of their Compassionate Self. (If you tell the group this at the beginning of the exercise it is likely that no one will pick a scarf at all!)

Go around the group and invite each group member to say the quality that is associated with the scarf they chose. Be clear that the scarf and the quality do not have to be connected i.e. the green of the scarf is linked to my love of nature. The scarf is merely a symbol. We will then leave the scarfs on the floor for the reminder of the session as a reminder of what we all bring and share with the group. These qualities can then be called on to support the group process and we can remind the group about how much compassion is present in the room. I will always join in this exercise.

Concluding comments

This section has focused on the important work of managing the transition into the CFTG. Expect some bumps along this road. There will be conflict as the group quite literally sit in each other's chairs and metaphorically bump up against each other.

But that said, I am always reminded of Yalom's message of hope that the ruptures, if attended to and repaired, give way to greater experience of cohesion and connectedness. This cohesion then allows the group members to experience the sense of safeness which lays the foundation for the exploratory work.

So let us turn our attention to how we prepare practically and emotionally for the exploratory trauma focused group work.

Chapter 4.2: Getting ready

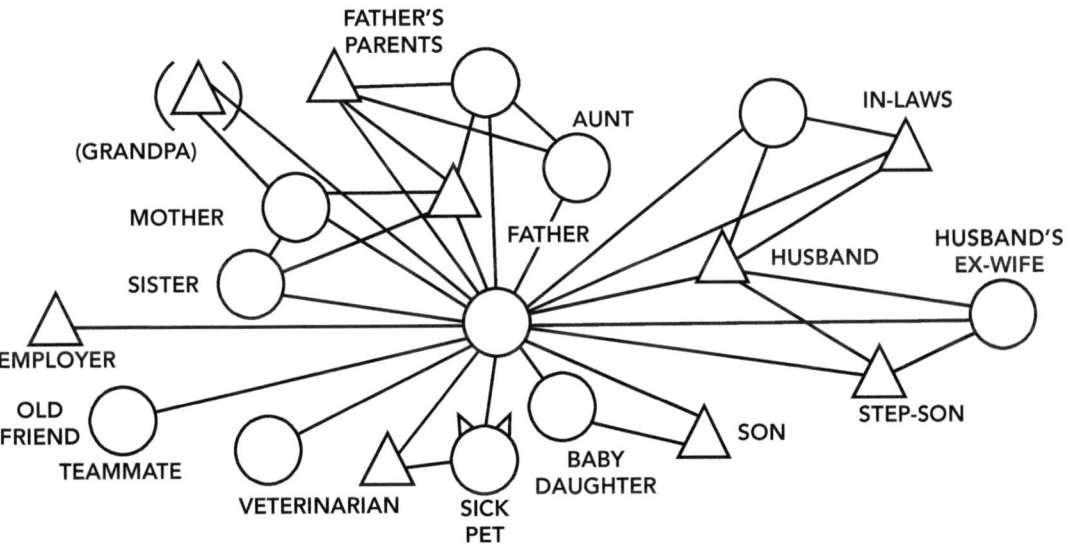

Preparation stage

I find it hard to know where to start with the CFTG, given that it is a continuous, rolling group. The conflicts seem to bubble up when new members transition into the group. However, the transference material can often emerge again through the course of the active trauma work, which we will explore this later in the chapter.

This section will attempt to offer the general sequence of work and how the initial mapping and formulating in group can provide a foundation for more intense exploratory work as time goes on.

The rolling programme format also enables new group members joining the CFTG to observe some of the in-depth work before being invited to take part themselves. When new members join, there will often be a few weeks where the group focus on welcoming new people and some focus on the Compassionate Kitbag and what is needed to turn back towards the difficult material.

In the weeks following new members joining from the PEG, work is undertaken to support the group to come together, find common ground and develop some rudimentary sense of cohesion. As we have already established, this is not an easy task. One of the exercises that can support the group to orientate to where everyone is on their therapeutic journey is to invite them to use the room to map out where they are in their journey. In practice, this will often involve the group creating a continuum, with each end of the room representing the beginning and end of the programme. In our group room there is a door at one end that goes out to the garden, which creates a visually symbolic ending point. Group members are invited to stand on the continuum to demonstrate where they are in the programme, thus orientating the whole group to each other's journey. Group members are also invited to mark where they feel in relation to starting and ending, which offers an opportunity for ambivalence or fear of ending to be acknowledged. Some have stood by the door to demonstrate that they are almost at the end of the programme and thrown a beanbag back down the other end of the room to indicate not feeling ready to end. Others have opened the doors and stepped into the garden, indicating their readiness to end and move on. This exercise gives space for a nonverbal representation of the journey in CFGP, a subtle reminder of the ending, space to consider work to be done, and for the group to orientate themselves in relation to others.

In the CFTG, however, there is a change of pace in the membership. In the PEG, there are new people joining the group every four weeks and people leaving to move on to the CFTG. Once the group is full, then the PEG stops running and CFTG essentially becomes a closed group for a period of time, usually between six and nine months. This will depend on dropout from the CFTG which might warrant more people needing to come in through the PEG or the length of CFTG that you are offering. Either way, the group closes, enabling the group cohesion to settle and a 'tribe' or cohort to form. It is within this closed group that the intense exploratory psychotherapy can take place. Trust is formed, bonds are made,

> *'You bond in a certain way, I spent a year with these people and I felt like I knew them all really well but a lot of them, I couldn't tell you what they did for a job or even their surnames, because it wasn't focused on that superficial stuff... We bonded over things that were very intimate and personal. It made this bond which feels unbreakable at this point because it's very deep seated.'*

Moving from safety to safeness

In the early stages of therapy, most of our group members will only be familiar with the safety seeking system, and the green soothing system can be not only a source of confusion but also irritation. People will often say that they just 'don't get it' and cannot understand why we 'go on about it so much'. We can make sense of this through the lens of attachment theory and the work of John Bowlby. Our systems are primed by our experiences and our internal working model or template is developed accordingly. As we explored in Phase Three, even the idea of 'safe' is often a source of irritation and confusion to our group members. But slowly, over time, we are developing the capacity to feel social safeness with each other in the therapy room and with themselves through the continued Compassionate Mind Training practices. This can helpfully involve the use of transitional objects, which we discussed in Phase Three:

> *'I've still got my stone, it's got a little nick in it ...*
> *and every now and then if I feel stressed*
> *I'll pick it up and do a breathe with it.'*

Over the decades of running these groups, the necessity of cultivating the conditions for safeness has become increasingly clear. This is from the anecdotal narratives from the group, as well as the repeated references to this in the qualitative study which we undertook.[70] I would also like to invite you to cast your eye over the word cloud which we created, in which the size of the words represent how often they were used in the transcripts of the interviews (see Appendix 4.1: Word Cloud).

> **Sherelle's shift from the table to the library**
>
> In the early stages of the PEG, Sherelle had developed a Calm Place image which she used to settle herself. This place was under the table in her kitchen of her family home. This had been the place that she had hidden when her parents had become intoxicated and violent, during the times she had been allowed to return to their care. Despite this, Sherelle continued to idealise her parents, believing that services had been wrong to remove her from their care and she held a strong and unshakeable belief that she would have been OK had she stayed with them.
>
> Over the months in group, we explored this with Sherelle and invited her to be curious about what she experienced when she used the image. She remained resolute that

---

[70] Lucre, K., Ashworth, F., Copello, A., Jones, C., & Gilbert, P. (2024). Compassion Focused Group Psychotherapy for attachment and relational trauma: Engaging people with a diagnosis of personality disorder. *Psychology and Psychotherapy* **97**(2).

this was as good as she could envisage and that hiding was all she could make sense of. This was understandable safety seeking, a functional and important aspect of the threat system, and indeed, it was all Sherelle knew how to access. As time passed and with the discussions and connections with living in threat and developing the soothing system, Sherelle seemed more able to be curious about what she needed.

During a preparation session for 'the work', as many describe the work in action, we started with a Calm Place imagery exercise. During the feedback, Sherelle shared that she had a new place, which had just emerged in her mind spontaneously during the exercise. This new place was a comfortable room filled with cushions and beanbags, with large windows and a little ladder on wheels which rolled around the room. As she described it, it was clear that this was a place of safeness, and accessing an image of this kind could not be forced and had taken many months of work in group. On exploration, there appeared to have been a subtle shift connected to her experience of in-session safeness that she was able to translate to her imaginal world. Shifting the group from safety to safeness and supporting the process of distinguishing between the two states starts with the PEG and continues more explicitly in the CFTG.

The next section explores some of the ways that we turn back to the difficulty and collaboratively plan for the exploratory work.

Formulating, mapping and planning

The Compassionate Mind Training work sits alongside time spent mapping, planning and formulating. The intention behind this work is to quite literally map out life patterns and experiences to identify those which will need to be turned back towards and worked with in the group. We might return to the CFT formulation, explored in Phase One. There are many ways to work with the formulation as a group. We can work together with one person's difficulties, mapping out using the flip chart. It is a great opportunity for the group to take charge of the process, writing on the flip chart, following the process to create the connections between the different elements of the model. Emphasis is on slowing this process to facilitate the group making connections to what is being presented and their own life narratives. We are building on the work started in Phase One and, for many, this will be deeply challenging and stimulating work, beginning to make connections between the understandable survival strategies they have developed, their key fears, and, most significantly, early life events. As has been discussed previously, it is common for group members to be deeply defended against the impact on their adult lives of ruptured attachments. Self-blame is often the way that they can make sense of their experiences without risking psychological collapse. Coming to a realisation that those who were to care for us were actually the source of our suffering can be very painful, and so needs to be approached with caution.

An alternative to this is to work with the issues that the group are presenting with. Group members will often bring the survival strategies that have become stuck patterns of relating to the self and others. The group can then be invited to make a list of all these understandable survival strategies and to identify the unintended consequences which are not planned but which create further issues. Even just this exercise can generate material to be worked with in terms of trying on different ways of responding to key fears. This exercise is also designed to explicitly de-shame the ways of reacting to and surviving early tragic life events. We replace familiar narratives of dysfunction and disorder with the idea of understandable strategies designed to enable survival but which have unintended consequences (as we discussed in detail in Phase One).

Sherelle's risky sex

During check in, a number of group members had shared a sense of frustration with impulsive 'behaviours' they often engaged in, knowing how destructive they were. This included problematic alcohol use, illicit drugs, compulsive shopping, cutting, taking overdoses and seeking risky sexual encounters. All had been catalogued previously by mental professionals as evidence of their 'Borderline Personality Disorder'. Many spoke of feeling stupid and ashamed of these behaviours, as well as feeling judged by professionals involved in their care.

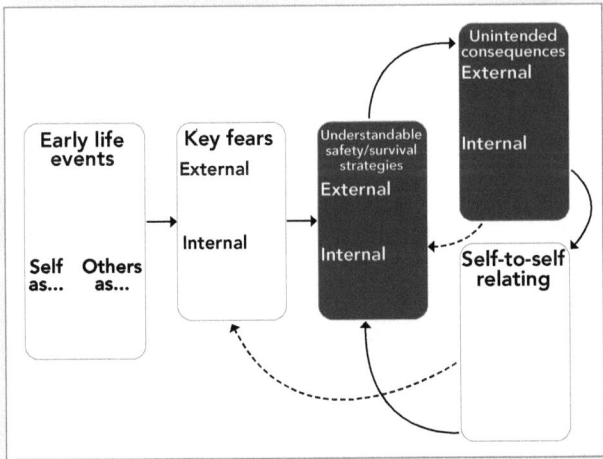

After some initial reluctance to share, Sherelle disclosed to the group that she would regularly offer herself for sex with men she had only just met, the most recent example of which had been a gas engineer who had come to fix a problem with her boiler. He had become violent, leaving her injured and fearful for her safety, warning her that he would return with other men.

We began the formulation session with a discussion of all the survival strategies that group members had observed in themselves and others. This sharing seemed to detoxify the shame felt by many. A feeling of relief was shared by many as they heard each other's stories. We used the flip chart to map these 'survival strategies' with the next column in the formulation 'unintended Consequences' (see the highlighted sections of the formulation diagram. We asked Sherelle if we could return to the situation she had described the next week and work through the whole formulation. She had not previously been able to tolerate any connections between her early life and her current difficulties. This was a preliminary session, and the following week, Sherelle agreed that she was ready to try to understand why she puts herself in these situations.

So as a group we returned to the formulation diagram and began to work together to support Sherelle to make sense of her experiences. Initially, we needed to offer some guidance to the group to keep suggestions tentative and also to link their ideas to their own experiences. I recall previous groups when slightly over enthusiastic group members have gone 'all in' with interpretations which the person in the 'spotlight' was not ready to hear: 'Oh, this is all because your dad abused you and so you think that all men will behave like this.' Tony Bateman's good advice about interpretations being experienced as 'hand grenades' for those who have not made the connections yet themselves is very relevant here. Instead, invite the group to connect this with their own experience: 'I feel that my problems with compulsive shopping come from the need to feel in control of something; I didn't have any control over what was happening to me when I was little.' I think this approach reduces some of the intensity of having the whole group's attention on one person, and therefore increases the potential for significant connections to be made with the past and present.

Sherelle worked with the group, moving back and forth through the formulation diagram, using the shared wisdom of the group to consider the key fears that were driving the survival strategies. With encouragement from the group and shared connections, Sherelle began to consider why she felt compelled to seek risky sexual encounters. She had previously assumed that this was another example of why she is 'broken' and cannot manage meaningful relationships. But she shifted in this session to consider the sexual, physical and emotional abuse that she had suffered at the hands of all the men she had known. She began to wonder if perhaps she had come to expect this kind of treatment from all men and at an unconscious level had created the conditions for this to happen. As facilitators, we nudged gently at various points of this discussion and invited other group members to share their own discoveries, but tried to stay in the background. I am minded again here of the conductor analogy from Phase Two (see Appendix 4.2 for the full formulation).

Mapping out the Compassionate Roles in Phase Three helps the group identify what they already have in their Compassionate Kitbags. Further maps can facilitate a greater understanding of emotional landscape that they will be exploring with the work of turning back towards early tragedy.

Social Role Atom exercise

This form of mapping exercise is one of many options:

> 'We had one where we had to draw out on a piece of paper. We had to put a dot at the centre which was us and it was kind of like a solar system as I remember it, and I might have got this wrong because it was a long time ago ... and around the dot we had to put all the people who were in our lives represented as other dots, and we had to use the distance and the colours to represent how we felt about those people, so if you didn't have a great relationship with your family like I didn't ... my family was way over here and they were done in little red dots, whereas as my friends and my yoga groups were little green dots and they were much closer and that was a really valuable activity and that's one I took away with me and thought about for days afterwards and ... it caused me to re-evaluate some relationships that I had and the roles that people played in my life and that was great ... And all that needed was a pen and paper so that was fantastic.'

As this quote describes, this exercise offers another opportunity for some emotional distance and exploration. The map enables group members to visualise their relationships as an atom, and then bring compassion and curiosity to the dynamics at play. This exercise does not require any kind of literacy capacity as group members will generally use symbols to present the people in their atom.

Knowing a little of the social context and circumstances of your group will be important in planning this exercise. I recall many years ago launching into this full of enthusiasm, having tried it myself in my training. The results were pretty disastrous, as a number of group members had almost completely empty atoms and were filled with shame as a result. This works best for groups with recurring themes of troublesome or stuck relationships in familial and social groups. Additionally, some time spent exploring the reason for creating a map of this kind will enable reactions to be noted and worked with.

Creating the map is the first step, followed by an opportunity to observe where people have been placed or how the connections have been symbolised. The next step is to bring a compassionate perspective to the map, as described in the quote above, which is a springboard for possible change. This is most effective and meaningful when the group members develop their own realisations and consequent plans for action. I recall Jane working with this exercise and struggling with how small her map was, I could see her being pulled into a competitive mind set. The group supported her to consider what she wished to see on her map and she was able to identify a number of people from her church who often invited her to join them for a coffee. With some encouragement, she put them on the map with a dotted line to represent a work in progress. A week later, Jane returned to group exuberant having made contact with one of these people and had been out for coffee with her, leading to her filling in the dotted line on her map.

This is an important example of how these exercises can tap into the intuitive wisdom of the group members and invite them to take compassionate challenges that feel very different to homework directed by the therapist. The importance of keeping the work undertaken in group 'alive', in that the maps can be returned to and adjusted, with subtractions and additions, is again a source of empowerment for your group.

Know your terrain

Of course, in mountaineering, an actual map is essential. Knowing the terrain we are likely to encounter will help us to plan accordingly, as we introduced in the previous chapter. But this phase of planning takes us to a deeper level and creates the compassionate commitment. The question I try to explore before packing my bags is why? What do I want and need from this adventure? As it is with this element of the group, matching the commitment and capacity of the group is very important.

Inviting your group to be honest about what they need and expect from the exploratory work will help them and you decide if this is a good idea. I recall a near-disaster climbing experience recently when I attempted to push myself and my climbing partner up a mountain without the right equipment. My motivation, if I am honest, was to compete with others in our climbing party who were waiting back at camp to see how we got on. I didn't want to go back saying that we didn't do it. This motivation bubbled up from my rank competing system and was doomed to failure.

Your group members may not be driven to compete with each other (although some are, of course) but many will have unrealistic expectations about what this 'work' will look like and require. So exploring this through the mapping, planning and formulating can support everyone to start on solid ground.

One final metaphor which I find useful in preparing for intense exploratory work is to ensure that you plan for the way back. In therapeutic work, this will involve the Compassionate Kitbag, to access in times of struggle. Many group members have spoken over the years of needing multisensory resources to support the work. In mountaineering, it is more literal; I remember being stuck abseiling down a mountain, having not read the advice to take your trainers and walk off the top!

Ways of working with multiple selves

As we discussed in Phase Three, the idea of the multiplicity of self is woven into the group-based discussion from Session 1. It is fundamental for our group members to begin to understand that they are made of multiple parts which will be activated depending on the situation they find themselves in. As we move into this phase of the programme, I would tend to be more explicit about the multiplicity of self and invite the group to use the language of parts.

There might be more than one part!

In this intensive, more exploratory phase of the group programme, we are inviting the group to develop curiosity about their inner and outer family. The Social Role Atom exercise may support with the mapping of the social system and people in it. We also move into mapping out the inner family or multiple selves. Throughout the PEG, the idea of the multiplicity of self is introduced and worked with implicitly. As has been described, many group members struggle with the idea of the multiplicity of self. I have had angry and fearful reactions to introducing this idea. Misunderstanding around the idea of schizophrenia and 'multiple personality disorder' are often associated with my introduction of multiple selves. I have adapted what I offer over the years and in true CFT style developed self-disclosure examples, metaphors and stories, which are designed to demystify and normalise our multiple selves or parts. The Disney film *Inside Out* has been hugely helpful to this end. I will often share with my group that when I get behind the wheel of a car in Birmingham, a different part of me gets into the driving seat! An angrier, easily frustrated competitive part, and if I do not bring my Compassionate Self along too, things can get tricky. Group members have spoken of valuing this normalising and also some 'inside information' about facilitator imperfections!

Multiple Selves map

We can follow the same principles as the Social Role Atom, but without the 'me' in the middle, as many of your group will not have a sense of self which exists separate to the parts. The map can be created with all the multiple parts of the self-represented in whatever way is helpful for the individual, with lines to represent the relationship (or lack thereof) between the different parts of the self. The questions might be, 'So, now you've got the parts, what is the relationship between angry self and stuck self? Do they know about each other, are they mates?' Again, a light touch is needed and recommended here to begin to map out the emotional landscape of the multiple parts (see Appendix 4.3: Multiple selves map).

I am always in awe of the creative and interesting ways that the group will represent the aspects of the self. But I have often found myself a little stuck and anxious when faced with such tasks myself. I have felt the pressure to make it very 'clever' and entertaining for others. This takes me away from the meaning of the task and the wisdom which I carry into how I set out these exercises for my group. As has been discussed before, I would recommend against trying anything in a group which you haven't tried yourself. How can you invite others to engage with something you have never tried? As part of the exercise, I will sometimes share with the group some of my own struggles with it, as I am demonstrating my understanding, ensuring they know I've tried it and pre-empting some of the stuck points, all in one!

This work can span multiple sessions or be touched on as a starting point.

This map can then guide the work that may need to develop with chairs, props and definitely action.

> *'Does it help that angry self cannot tolerate sad or anxious parts? Maybe we can move this into the chairs and see what your Compassionate Self or Other can bring.'*

Archetype cards

I was introduced to these cards during my action methods training and went out and bought some immediately. I use them in groups of all kinds, therapy, workshops and any opportunity I can. These cards have brought laughter, revelations and moments of real shift. I am thinking that I should be on some kind of commission!

The cards can form part of the work developing awareness and understanding of the multiple parts of the self and can also pave the way for chair work. They are called Archetype Cards and each card has a name, coupled with light and shadow attributes. I spread the cards all over the floor and invite the group to pick two cards, one is their Compassionate Best Self (wished for) and the other is the part of themselves they fear they might be (Hated or Hateful self). The interesting twist to this exercise is that the names on the cards can be create assumptions (for example, 'God' or 'Prostitute') which require a closer inspection to reveal the layers of meaning. This exercise can be a helpful way to get some of our more reticent group members out of their chairs and crawling around together on the floor. The playful activation and experimentation with our rank system, which comes with the potential for competing for a card, can also be a helpful way into discussions about how normal it is to compete, particularly when the resources are scarce.

Over developed, underdeveloped and emerging roles

This game can be a gentle introduction to work with chairs and takes the work with parts of the self, roles and mapping into action. Building on the ideas introduced previously, I will often introduce this exercise as part of a series of sessions where we explore the multiplicity of self from a variety of different angles. Initially, I will set out three chairs, two are back-to-back and one is off to the side. I then invite the group to work together to consider the roles or parts of themselves which are over developed, usually linked to threat activation: 'What part of you always ends up running the show, even if you don't want it to?' The group are then invited to write what these roles are or use symbols to represent them and put them on the chairs. I do love a Post-It note for such exercises, so they can be stuck all over the chairs, which aids the visual nature of the work.

We can link this with the formulation work on survival strategies, understandable but often associated with unintended consequences. The underdeveloped role, which is the chair behind the overdeveloped role chair, is placed there to represent the part of the self or the role that may be trapped by the overdeveloped role (there is not a judgement about positive or negative). This role is usually obscured from the group member's conscious awareness and can be tricky to put into words. The group can be helpful to each other with this as they will generally have mirror opposites in their over and underdeveloped roles, in that some will tend towards aggressive ways of reacting while others may tend towards more passive ways of reacting.

The emerging role is linked to the Compassionate Mind Training work and the development of compassionate capacity. This is the chair slightly off to the side, with the aim that the Compassionate Role or part can provide a supportive observing other function for the over and underdeveloped roles.

Louie and the mirror

In this session, Louie was really clear that his overdeveloped role was furious rage, which he even had a name for – 'big D' (D stood for Destroyer). It was more challenging for Louie to consider his underdeveloped role, which is the part of himself that does not get any airtime. He spoke of feeling confused about the chair behind and was initially insistent that there wasn't any other part.

The group members worked together, sticking Post-It notes on the chairs with all the different overdeveloped roles. Louie looked at the overdeveloped chair and noticed that Leonie had put 'appeasing' as her overdeveloped role and 'angry' as her underdeveloped role. This sparked a discussion about how she knew, and led to Louie begin to connect with a split-off very vulnerable part of himself which had been part of

> his very young life. Survival in his instrumentally violent family had made it necessary for Louie to disown this vulnerable, care-seeking part of himself. Louie was able to connect this discovery with a picture he had drawn during an earlier image-making session:
>
> > '...and it was a sudden understanding ... shit, that's me I've drawn me and wanting comfort ... comfort and strength it just like ... shit... because that is something that I never received.'
>
> Louie had drawn an adult hand covering the hand of a child, which he had believed was his hand covering the hand of his son. But the quote above indicates the discovery that he was the child in the image. Louie's emerging role was assertiveness, strong, wise and capable of keeping Big D in check!

Rolling a role

This is one of my favourite games, which I have adapted from the inspirational work of Liz White, whose *Action Manual* is now sadly out of print but has provided so much inspiration. This is related to working with the multiplicity of self, differentiating and bringing compassion to all aspects of the self.

This is a whole-group exercise. Invite the group to write down the numbers one to six on a piece of paper. Again, being mindful about literacy and people may need some help with this. Numbers one and two are for overdeveloped roles or parts of the self, we will have already begun to explore this and the idea will not be new to the group.

Three and four are underdeveloped roles – we describe these as roles which may be stuck underneath or behind the overdeveloped, so no judgement about good or bad. Finally, five and six are the emerging roles, these can best be understood as your Compassionate Self which is currently 'under construction'.[71]

Once the roles have been set out, we set out the stage as usual and bring two folding chairs to the front, asking for two volunteers to play the game. The 'game' involves each of the two group members taking the large foam dice which I have for the purpose and rolling it. Whatever number it lands on, this is the role that they will take up. When both have rolled the dice and identified their roles, the group decide on a scenario which the two will have to improvise with. One of my favourites was, you are double-booked at the dentists.

The two then interact with each other for a few minutes in their adopted roles and the rest of the group have to guess what the roles are. The results are generally hilarious! There are multiple elements to this – on one level, this is beginning to bring awareness

---

[71] I generally find that my group members are quite clear about these role distinctions. But, interestingly, when I am doing workshops with therapists, it gets much more tricky!

and a lightness to the different parts of us that might be stuck or under construction. This is also an experiment with motivational switching, so in the feedback I am always curious about what they noticed switching into these roles.

It is also a rehearsal for those who get the emerging roles to try on the Compassionate Self and play it out, hopefully seeing the possible positive results.

Concluding comments

This element of the programme builds on the initial work undertaken in the PEG and begins the explicit preparation for exploratory compassion-focused trauma work. Many of the group will have observed the work in action at the outset of their time in CFTG, as the senior groups members finish up their work and prepare for ending.

Time spent planning, mapping and formulating, supports the group to really know what they are turning back to, beginning to unpack and explore. The tone remains light, but there is a need to acknowledge that the more intensive work is coming.

Although action methods, chair work and exploratory work are separated into the three following chapters, the exploratory work in the group will move between these different modalities with some fluidity. My hope and intention is that it will be easier to work through the concepts with a separate space for each.

Chapter 4.3: Compassionate transformation in action Part 1 – Action methods

This part of the programme draws on key elements of action methods, whereby group members are invited to work through early traumatic memories, often with the use of objects or props (e.g. chairs, buttons, pebbles, scarfs and cubes) to represent people and places. This process of symbolising can enable group members to achieve emotional distance from a particular memory or experience which reduces the risk of the memory triggering post-traumatic stress symptoms of reliving, overwhelming feelings and dissociation. The memory is then transformed or, put simply, the ending is changed, thus offering an opportunity for reattribution or new understanding to be made of the experience. The compassionate transformation will often involve the group member coming to a realisation that what happened to them was not their fault and this can follow hearing the views of the other group members. These techniques and principles have been adapted and 'compassionised' from the work of incredible psychodrama psychotherapists, Liz White, Daniel Tomasulo, Tian Dayton and Dr Kate Hudgins, all of whom have explored and shared the transformative impact of embodied work in action to shift stuck trauma material.

The unique and explicit focus on bringing the Compassionate Self or Compassionate Other to the situation is designed to build on the CMT training from the PEG phase of the group programme. This addition is designed to enable group members to engage in 'motivational switching', which involves the explicit movement from a competitive threat-focused orientation into a caring orientation. In other words, if we can help individuals shift from a competitive and potentially persecuting view of the world to a more caring and cooperative one, this will have a range of impacts on physiological systems. Over time, this work is also designed to offer the opportunity for a new internal perspective about the early trauma memory to be developed. It also enables emotional processing and the resolution of trauma memories with the introduction of the compassionate perspective.

Setting the stage

Liz White compared group workers to aspiring gourmet cooks, always looking for a new technique. This can bring creativity and inspiration to the work but we must all be mindful that, as one of my group members reminded me, 'once we are out of our chairs everything changes'. Moving the group into action has a process that we follow to ensure that we create a space of safeness – for this work, safety is not enough. The preparation for this phase of the group is best made explicit as well as woven into the group process. The Compassionate Mind Training in session and the invitation and encouragement to practice between sessions is to cultivate a compassionate capacity. This is used as the basis for exploration of the early trauma and tragedy and how this manifests in the present.

It is also important to be clear with the group, who may not have observed or taken part in the work in action, what they can expect and how it might impact them:

> *'The impact on other people in the room, it changed things for them it wasn't just the person at the front in the chairs, it was everybody.'*

This is a positive example of how one person working in the group can have a helpful impact on the rest of the group. It can of course work the other way, and people can be deeply activated by what they are bearing witness to.

People often ask how you decide who will use the group in any particular session; there is no hard and fast rule for this. There are times when something emerges in the check in, which I then suggest we could return to and work with this situation or memory. It is particularly pleasing when another group member makes this suggestion, as then the rhythm of the group is owned not just by us. We will sometimes 'put a marker down' when something has been raised but the person is not ready, or we are engaged in a different piece of work. This can involve the use of a box which is used to hold the objects or markers that represent the identified memories or material to be returned to. A recent conversation with a supervisee running a CFGP programme shared the experience of taking the lid off the box that held the markers. It seemed to shift something in the group and encourage them to begin to take things out of the box to indicate a wish to use the space.

When working with slightly more reticent or avoidant group members, we may need to be a little more direct in our approach. I have found over the years that you can end up with a box full of 'markers' that have been placed but never returned to. During a recent group, where we were feeling the struggle to get started with the work in action, I wrote the dates of the next five groups on the board (which was the number of groups that we had in succession until there was a break). I then left the group with the task of nominating themselves or each other to the sessions and identifying something that they would like to work on. There was much dissent initially, and concerns about fairness and parity, but they engaged in the task, and this provided a much-needed prompt to get the momentum going.

The preparation starts before you enter the room, being clear with your co-facilitator who is going to lead the work in session. One of you will lead the work and the other will be with the rest of the group, tuning in to what else is arising in the room. Once in session the preparation of the room is also important, when we are working in action, we first create a stage. This involves moving the chairs into a slightly squashed horseshoe to create a space at the front where you and the group member or members will work. There is then an invisible line which separates the work in action on the stage from the rest of the group in the 'audience'. Your group member's chair, and indeed yours, must stay in the 'audience' so that they can return to their chair at any time and step away from the work in action. This is designed to support group members to use their own agency and compassionate wisdom in the work:

> *'...coz you were kind of on a stage ... there was a separate bit, you were separated you come out of your normal chair in the group and you come to front and there like a few chairs there ... so you got the whole group there with you ... but kind of watching but being supported... At first, it is quite nerve racking for people to do that ... but once you are in the chair something else happens you kind of really ... tune in to that side of you and it just kind of, like, natural for me to once I got into that thing.'*

This quote also reminds me of the important of setting out the horseshoe and being clear on the rationale for this. I recall one of the early groups when I was perhaps a little 'gung ho' with my approach to work in action. We decided to try some chairwork (I have a feeling that this may have followed attendance at a workshop on using chairs in therapy...). I invited the group member using the session to bring their chair into the middle and we pulled some other chairs in also.

The result was quite disastrous. I could see the group member, in the middle of the room, scanning around the room and seeing a sea of faces all around him. We had to abandon the work and I apologised the next session for setting up the room in a way that lacked safeness. We used the horseshoe from that time onwards.

The language that we use is also important, and I have often struggled with the stage and audience because of the performative connotations. I invited a group member onto the 'stage' to engage in some chair-based dialogue with her young self. But the word triggered a significant flashback to an unprocessed buried memory of being on a 'stage' at school as a small child and wetting herself in fear. She was then forced to sit on this stage for the duration of the assembly. She had no conscious memory of this incident until my use of the word stage activated it in her. She became very shut down, withdrawn and initially could not speak, no doubt transported back to that moment. I guided her off the stage and back to her chair, inviting her to make connections with other group members and the room around her. Once she had reconnected, she decided to work with memory, with the help of her Compassionate Other. They came onto the stage she had set and took the young child from the situation, reminding the adults that they should have taken better care of her. This experience taught me a great deal about how mindful I needed to be with my use of language and reminds me of the advice from Phase Three about always having a plan B. This situation ended with a positive outcome for the group member. This also reaffirmed the need to separate the 'stage' from the group, so members can step back into their chair if needed. As you can imagine, this piece of work in group took a lot more time than I had previously imagined. But this work was deepened by the group experience, as the previous quote identifies, there is something powerful about the group bearing witness to and being with the person at the front.

Take your time

This brings me to another helpful message for this work – you can never be sure how long this work will take and what will emerge. As the previous example highlights, we need to have sufficient time for a change of direction and a return to place of co-regulation. I think in the early days post training, I was full of ideas of pieces of work that processed entire memories and were wrapped up neatly with the evocation of compassion. I have had to adjust these ideals and perhaps come to a more realistic understanding of the individual and group's capacity to engage in long pieces of work of this nature.

The timing is a fundamentally important issue to be considered here. We need at least 50 to 60 minutes to engage in some work in action. Following this, we need at least 15 minutes to pack up the room, return the horseshoe to a circle, gather in reflections and bring a containing ending to the group. This will often be games or chatter to enable people to let go of some of the material before they leave.

At any step of this process, we can get pulled off course or distracted by other pieces of work. This can leave the group feeling uncontained, confused and overwhelmed. If you are considering embarking on a piece of work in action and you do not have this amount of time available to you, I would suggest that you do not start – back to plan B again! Overrunning the time boundary of the group may in some circumstances feel intuitive, attuned and perhaps compassionate, but I would avoid it as I think it is a slippery slope away from safeness. I have had many groups, where the work has not been anywhere near completed as we have had to attend to unexpected twists and turns. In such circumstances we may need some rituals, like the games we spoke about in Phase Three, to move away from unfinished work, with some markers to ensure that it is held by the group to return to the next week. In such situations, I have often found that people return the next week with a fresh perspective and the processing has indeed continued in a helpful way during the intervening week.

There have also been a few groups where someone has become so distressed that they have needed to stay behind for a few moments with us to regulate themselves. Caution about the continuation of the processing work is important here and being clear what you are offering and for how long.

Although the need for members to stay behind after group is rare. It has got me thinking about the need for space to decompress after the group. A non-therapy, mindful movement or chair-based yoga space to 'come up for air' after the group has finished. This is still under construction. We have been met with appreciation at the thought but a fair amount of resistance, so we haven't got started yet.

The compromise has been that, particularly in the summer months, we have made it possible for group members to stay on for up to half an hour after group and use the garden space. This is not a supervised space, although I am always in the building. This idea came from group members requesting gardening materials to grow plants and flowers. We had a lovely crop of courgettes, which fed the slugs and snails and some tomatoes that refused to turn red! Many have spoken of finding this unstructured post-group space helpful with an emphasis on growing something and all the rich symbolism and resonance with the growth of compassion. But others find the idea abhorrent!

Where to stand and what to do with your hands

Moving out of our seats and into action is challenging for us all in different ways. In the early days of developing action methods in CFGP, I often felt very aware of myself, how I stand, what I am wearing, what I am doing with my hands. Essentially, I can find myself increasingly self-conscious and, at times, a little anxious. There have been moments when I have been transported back in time to those early days on the actual stage, where forgetting my lines felt like the least of my worries, my seemingly awkward, ill-fitting body felt much more pressing. It has been helpful to remind myself that it is not about me and that my most important task is to engender safeness in the group member by my side. I am thankful to my body that these days I rarely feel this awkwardness as I get up to move the group into action. I firmly believe that I have my yoga practice and climbing to thank for this, ensuring that I keep listening to the messages from my body and learning how to create safeness in myself. My message is one of hope for those who may stay sitting for fear of exposure and humiliation.

Whatever we are feeling with the performative associations of this work, be sure that your group member's experience will be much more intense and unsettling. They are preparing to turn back to powerful, painful and buried memories from early life. So we need to regulate ourselves to provide a container, source of safeness and regulation to the group member we are working with. At the outset, it is important to be clear that whatever work you are undertaking can be halted at any time, the scarfs packed away and we return to the circle. I also suggest that my group members may want to use the stop sign if it is hard to find their voice in such moments. This is common when we are working with early attachment and relational trauma, as group members will at times regress back to those moments in early life when the tragedy occurred.

I generally ask my group member explicitly where they would like me to be. Generally, the response is next to them, but of course not always. A group member who was working with his avoided and buried rage, had spoken of believing that if he connected with his anger, the homicidal fury which would erupt could destroy him and everything around him. When he agreed to take the role of his angry self for the first time, he asked me to stand on the other side of the room, fearful that he might hurt me. Of course, I agreed to this, but during the work, with his permission, I moved a little closer to demonstrate that he could manage and tolerate his anger more than he had imagined.

Whether we are working with chairs or without, group members will often sit in the space they have created for the work. Again, I will always ask, but instinctively I would kneel or crouch beside the person doing chairwork and sit down with my group member in the scene. This work is intimidating enough; I figure that the last thing they need is me standing over them! Particularly with action methods work and setting scenes, I will always invite the group member to consider whether they want me in the scene with them or outside holding the space for them. This might seem unimportant in the grand scheme of the work, but actually it is paramount for each individual member to be considered.

Easing out of our chairs

There is a great deal of helpful advice in the psychodrama literature about the benefits of warming up the group before moving into action. Tian Dayton suggests an Emotional Floor Check, and I have adapted this for CFTG.[72] Take lots of individual pieces of paper and write down different emotions – angry, sad, scared, excited etc – and scatter them across the floor. The group are then invited to wander around and stand on the paper that they are feeling at that moment. This exercise is designed to orientate the group members into the present moment and shift the dynamic of facilitators asking questions.

The group members move around the room and try out the different areas. This can be extended to inviting the group to stand on the emotions that they are not comfortable with, or avoid, or one that they do not like in others, or one which was overrepresented in their family. Tian Dayton describes this as a gentle easing into work in action where there is an emphasis on cohesion and the shared experience of the group. The group will often be able to see how they are similar and different from others, 'Ah! You find anger uncomfortable as well'.

---

[72] Dayton, T. (2015). *Neuropsychodrama in the Treatment of Relational Trauma: A Model Using Experiential Group Processes for Healing PTSD*. Health Communications, Inc.

The importance of props

The use of objects – scarfs, beads, buttons, beanbags, pebbles, marbles, wool, cards, chairs and such like – has been the subject of much discussion in group over many years. Some are dismissive, irritated by the inference of play, and speak of feeling patronised, while others are very interested in the objects and keen to 'get stuck in', and everything in between. Everyone has a response or reaction of some sort, even if it is indifference and normalising, validating and giving space for dissent is key. We (staff) are not immune from these reactions. I was offering a staff support session in a Category A prison recently and I decided to face my own fear of being humiliated and brought the scarfs, beads and beanbags. I wish I could have recorded the expressions on the faces of the prison officers and healthcare staff as they entered the room. What stayed with me was the courage and willingness of this group of staff to give all this 'weird stuff' a go and step out of what feels comfortable. Introducing the use of props in Phase Three will support a process whereby group members become inured to this over the months, and then more ready to be able to make use of props for the work in action. Working gently with prejudgements and giving space for this to be voiced can make space for play, with the freedom and change that this can bring. But as the previous examples have illustrated, this is slow work and the group will often need to be encouraged to voice their contemptuous reactions!

Objects offer a great deal of therapeutic utility, in that they can be picked up and, most importantly, put down again. They can be 'anthropomorphised', given life (a beanbag can become a person or beloved pet) and new roles (a scarf can become a wall and a pebble, a table). They can serve to set out a scene to be stepped into and worked with, but then, at the end, de-roled and put away. I have found this concrete way of working very helpful in working with complex attachment trauma, which is more tricky with imagery alone.

I recall doing some imagery rescripting work many years ago with an early abuse memory and inviting my patient to bring a Compassionate Other into the scene. Some time passed and I asked what was happening now. 'He's dead,' he said, and I assumed that the Compassionate Other had killed the perpetrator and felt that, while not ideal, it was a step in the right direction. It turned out a little later when I invited my patient to connect again with his child self, that I discovered that the Compassionate Other had in fact killed the child. I felt that the imaginal nature of this work meant that I could not really get a hold of what was happening.

The practicalities of props

If the work involves returning to an early memory, after the stage has been set, invite your group member to select the scarfs that they will use to create the scene. The invitation to choose and then lay out the scarfs themselves is important. We want our group members to have as much control and autonomy as possible, to begin to counter what was taken from them. That is, of course, until they cannot, and we may need to ask to step in and take a more active role, but I will return to this. The scarfs will need to mark out a solid boundary around the scene, the room, or the house, or the playground – wherever the original experience took place. The solid boundary can then be stepped into and stepped out of, offering another opportunity to step away from the intensity of the work if needed. The marking out of the space also serves to begin to connect with the memory, inviting the actual layout of a room or place. Next, the invitation is given to select objects to represent the people and things that were present, so perhaps the bed or a parent. Again, slowly stepping into and deepening the connection with the memory to be worked with.

Once the scene has been set, there will always be options for how to proceed. Some group members will already be intimately connected with the experience of the (usually) young self, while others might need to step into the scene and take the role of the child. Many group members, for understandable reasons linked to survival, will have disconnected from or disowned their child self. You can then ask a few questions to orientate your group member with the young self and their experience.[73] 'So, you are Louie and you are eight years old, have I got that right? Thank you for agreeing to talk to me about how things are for you at the moment. Can I ask you a few questions about what is going on?' After the initial orientation and connection, the key question here is always, 'what do you need?' I will always be guided by the group member and where they need me to be, and this could change. I have started many scenes outside the scarfs and then been invited in or noticed a shift and asked if they needed me closer. Often, the child does not know, which then gives rise to the same question being asked of your group member once they have been invited to step out of the role and the scene.

There will be times when the group member will spontaneously connect with what is needed, and other times this discovery will be made through the evocation of the Compassionate Other or self. (I have explained this in more detail at the end of this segment.) Often, I will invite my group member through the breathe and embodied movement to make a connection with compassion and respond to the question from this place. I am always deeply moved by the attuned, intuitive responses that come. As a general principle, the response is usually for either rescue and or intervention from a strong, wise other. This can take the form of the adult self, Compassionate Other, or sometimes a group member or members.

The next step is to change the ending of the scene, to compassionately transform it. Group members have used objects to represent Compassionate Others or their own

---

[73] Please note, I am not offering scripts or a step-by-step guide for this work as I would not suggest engaging in this type of intense compassion-focused action without training, which can be gained from my workshops.

adult self who have entered the scene to rescue, support and challenge the abuser. Some group members will opt to take the role of the Compassionate Other and enter the scene, while others will request support from the group. Generally, there is a rescue coupled with a compassionate challenge to the abuser. I have witnessed auxiliaries hold the place of a policemen, Gandalf (Lord of the Rings), and an animated teddy bear, to name a few! These others have been invited in to put things straight. A magic wand was employed on one occasion to open a barricaded door and release the child from captivity, before sealing the door with the abuser still inside. Magic and myth can be deeply helpful to this work, as we are supporting people with very early developmental trauma. It is important to bear in mind that we are responding to the needs of a child, which is likely to be aided by magic and mystery. These moments can often bring something light and playful in the midst of the catharsis.

The use of auxiliaries

One way of explicitly inviting group members to support each other in the trauma work is through the request for members of the group to hold the place of the different aspects of the self or others who are being worked through and act as an auxiliary. This work is designed explicitly and implicitly to support group members to cultivate their capacity for giving compassion to others, which is a key component of the therapy work. As in the previous segment, group members can be invited to step into a compassionate transformation scene as their adult selves.

One group member was working through a memory of being beaten and humiliated in the street by her father. She knew immediately what she needed and she invited the whole group to form a human barrier between the object representing her child self and the object representing her father. This was a powerful moment of catharsis and group connection as they huddled together in an act of compassionate defiance. The group member then took the role of her child self and was then surrounded by the group who all made a connection with her with a mixture of solidarity and reassurance. This exercise is, for many group members, also a gentle exposure and experimentation with touch. Many group members really struggle with touch, and for us as therapists, the advice is often conflicting. But I have witnessed over and over group members using touch to support each other in the work, in a way I think they would struggle with in everyday life.

Another alternative to this is for a number of auxiliaries to hold the place of all the different roles in the scene (with the exception of the abuser). This function offers the group member who is engaging in compassion-focused trauma work to quite literally step out and observe the scene they are working with a degree of emotional distance. There are benefits for the auxiliaries and observing members as it offers an opportunity for identification with the group member or vicarious modelling. Again, the idea of motivational switching is relevant here to develop the capacity of group members to move from one motivational state or orientation to another. These concepts are particularly pertinent for CFTG as members of the group will often have a strong tendency towards self-criticism and the experience of shame-based trauma.

A very touching ending to a piece of compassionate transformation work, involved the group member entering the scene as his adult self to rescue the child. He opted to step out of the scene and observe the two group members who held the place of his adult and child selves. In practice this means that the group member will with you step off the 'stage' and back to where the chairs and the rest of the group are sitting to see the scene more clearly. Under his guidance, a message of hope and encouragement was given to the child by the adult self and the scene ended with an embrace with both auxiliaries agreed to. I definitely had tears in my eyes, as did others, to witness this moment of connection and resolution on so many different levels.

The use of auxiliaries, however, needs to be managed carefully. This work can of course only be attempted in a settled group programme, with a level of trust, understanding and explicit compassionate motivation established between the group members. With the explicit agreement of the member who is working, auxiliaries are invited to volunteer to come and be part of the work; all parties must agree. The instructions for the auxiliary are also important – they are invited to come and 'hold the place', not take the role of the part self or other. Making this distinction before the work and reinforcing at the time the auxiliary volunteers will support the auxiliary to be clear about what is expected of them. Despite this, I have still had experiences of auxiliaries being 'left' with feelings that do not belong to them. So there needs to be an active process of de-roling and 'putting down' any feelings associated with holding the place for another group member.

The auxiliary role will also be supported by the rest of the group when holding a place and repeating the message. Many group members will be hesitant to take up the auxiliary role as they are fearful of 'getting it wrong'. So reassurance that the group will support the remembering of what has been said and to make adjustments as needed. Also, when repeating a message or statement, we must always check out with the group member working in action that this is accurate. There is also room for body postures, facial expressions etc to be adjusted to ensure that this fits. With good intentions, sometimes your auxiliaries will 'ad lib' the message and may need some help to ensure that there is a good fit.

Some work in action will be planned in advance, with group members placing markers as described previously, but there are also opportunities to use the material that emerges spontaneously in the check in. This allows some flexibility within the structure of the exploratory phase of the work and also for group members to make choices.

Compassionate transformation

Sherelle's compassionate transformation

Sherelle had chosen to use the group to work on an early abuse memory that had taken place within the children's home where she had been placed. Sherelle had been sexually assaulted by another child in the home and forced to keep it secret. She had blamed herself for this. The aim of this piece of work was compassionate transformation to allow Sherelle to see the scene from a different angle. She had placed a marker down for this work and with encouragement from the group returned to it.

Sherelle was invited to use objects from the room and props to represent the different people who had been present during the abuse, and this scene was clearly marked out using scarfs, ensuring that the scene was contained. Sherelle talked through her choices of objects to present the different characters and placed them within the boundary marked by the scarfs. During this time, the therapist stayed close to and matched the actions of Sherelle to provide an experience of affiliative safeness during the exercise.

At the point where the scene had been set, Sherelle was invited to use an object to represent her young self. She chose a pebble, which had been a gift from the group and as such was imbibed with the group's feeling of compassion and care for her. The pace and tone of the process was slowed at this point to allow for some space for Sherelle to observe the scene and settle with the emotional connection. Sherelle was then invited to take the role of her child self, by holding the pebble. The facilitator asked her questions about the situation and her experience and how she was feeling, aimed at deepening the connection with the younger, wounded self (as traumatised group members will often be fragmented and disavow the younger parts as a means of survival). She was invited to focus on the soothing rhythm of the breath and bring her Compassionate Self to this scene. Some time was spent using a standing guided imagery practice to support Sherelle to connect with and embody the qualities of strength, wisdom and courage.

The facilitator then invited Sherelle to turn back to the scene and consider what this very young Sherelle needed, and her response was to be rescued from the scene by her Compassionate Self. A request was made for volunteers to hold the place of Sherelle's child self, holding the object that had represented her in the scene and also another to hold the place of Sherelle's Compassionate Self.

Sherelle was then invited to gently direct her fellow group members, who had volunteered to ensure that body postures, words, emotional meaning and actions fitted for her. She then stepped out of the scene, to enable an experience of emotional distance, and allowed the scene to be replayed by the volunteer group members with the compassionately transformed ending. Once it had been established that Sherelle was satisfied with the scene, time was taken to ensure that the group members who had held the place in Sherelle's scene had 'de-roled' and were not left holding any of the trauma material worked through in the scene. Sherelle was guided to 're-role' the objects and put away the props that had been used.

The group then returned to the circle to reflect on their personal responses to the experience. This was an opportunity for validation and reinforcement of the courage and connection for all group members. Group members spoke of being deeply affected by the experience and a strong sense of connection with their own experience of early abuse and intrusion. Time was taken for this to be discussed, explored with a commitment from others to use the group in a similar way. As the group drew to a close, some group members continued to describe strong feelings coupled with concerns about the end of the group. A discussion about this was invited by one of the facilitators, with an invitation to engage in a game focused on bringing lightness to the ending of the group, with the explicit function of allowing difficult feelings to be left in the room. These are the games that we discussed in Phase Three.

Group members will often focus on experiences and specific memories of victimisation from their early life in compassionate transformation work, understanding that the experience of shame-based trauma is generally more intense if the abuser was also a primary attachment figure. But this segment of the programme can also be used to support group members with shame-based trauma memories related to actual or perceived harms to others. The focus in this work can be supporting the group to distinguish between shame and guilt. It is a complex area, but I find that we can get mixed up and use the word 'guilt' when we mean 'shame' – I wonder if shame is a word that is often too difficult to say out loud.[74] Supporting the group to understand the difference will help prepare for the work in action. I draw on the incredible work of Dr June Tangney who makes the distinction between constructive guilt and crippling shame. For us in CFT, shame sits in the rank system, an evolved mechanism to keep us 'in group' and is a mindset that gives rise to an array of emotional responses. So many of our group members are stuck in a rank-motivated shame cycle of self-hatred. Guilt, however, is part of our care-giving and care-receiving system, and as such can support a 'constructive' motivation towards making reparation and moving forward. As Paul Gilbert puts it:

---

[74] This short film was based on the narratives and experiences of group members from CFGP and was designed to explore and understand shame: www.youtube.com/watch?v=b2ZCedVuB0g

> *'The evolutionary root of* **shame** *is in a self-focused, threat system related to competitive behaviour and the need prove oneself acceptable/desirable to others.* **Guilt,** *however, evolved from a care-giving and 'avoiding doing harm to others' system.'* [75]

In essence, guilt might be characterised by a statement such as, 'I have done bad and I wish to make reparation', while shame might be summed up as, 'I am bad and there is no hope for reparation'. It is understood that it is that desire to make reparation that can bring healing. All this focus on language can be a bit opaque to your group members, so I will generally offer a scenario, presented through a Socratic medium.

The supermarket

I am running late and I need something to eat, so I dash into a nearby shop and grab some crisps and go to the check out. I see there is a woman in front of me and she is bent down and not looking. I see the opportunity and sneak in front of her. I turn back and see that she is helping a small child who is crying and she has also dropped her shopping. What might I feel in this moment? Generally, your group will identify guilt: you have wronged her and you feel bad about it. In this moment there is a choice to help her pick up the shopping let her back in front and wait my turn. I would then encourage an exploration about how that might be experienced, and often people describe relief. Then I present plan B, where I turn pay for my crisps and leave the shop, I invite the group to consider what I might be feeling as I walk away. This gives rise to some discussion about shame as connected to how I might then live in the mind of the shop assistant as well as the woman. This distinction can help the group turn back and shift from the stuckness of shame to creative possibilities of guilt. We need to be mindful here to distinguish between perceptions of wrongdoing, i.e. allowing someone to hurt another, and actually hurting others.

Guilt, like everything in CFT, is all about balance. Some of the work with your group will be to notice and work with feeling overly responsible and guilty. Some may need some help to adjust and rebalance their feelings of guilt, which may mean putting down or giving back some of the responsibility that may have been projected and introjected into them in early childhood. We will return to ways of working with this in action later in the section.

---

75 Gilbert, P. (2003). Evolution, social roles, and the differences in shame and guilt. *Social Research,* **70**(4), 1205–1230.

Adam's revelation

Adam had raised a number of times that there was a part of him that was 'evil' and he had done things that were unforgiveable. It seemed that Adam was stuck in a down-ranking shame cycle. Despite encouragement from the group, Adam had been reluctant to share any details of the things he had done. He had shared that there are times when he will pull out his hair and starve himself, and this had been increasingly apparent in his appearance in group. He came to session one week looking particularly gaunt and frail and had clearly pulled hair from his face and head.

During the check in, a member of the group asked him directly why he did this to himself and that it made her sad to see to him obviously suffering and unable to share or take the support. Adam pushed this back a little and the group member persisted. I stayed in the background allowing the conversation to unfold. Adam began to become angry, which quickly turned to sadness and he turned to the group member and addressed her directly, one of the first times he had spoken directly to anyone other than me. He said in a flat and small voice that he had tried to kill his partner many years earlier because she had cheated on him and he had never known why and had tortured himself ever since. The rest of the story was that he had then tried to take his own life and had been discovered by his then very young daughter, which served to deepen his shame and humiliation. He had left the family home and never returned. Adam spoke of ruining the only chance he had been given for happiness and connection. This was one of the many acts of 'evil' which he believed made him a source of contamination for others, at times making it almost impossible for him to take anything from the group. I asked Adam if we could return to this when we had completed the check in, to which he shrugged.

We did return to this and with some gentle persuasion from the group, Adam agreed that it would be helpful to return to the memory of this event and rework it. As we got started, it seemed that there were two unresolved aspects to this memory: firstly, the attack on his wife, and secondly, his daughter discovering him trying to hang himself. He also spoke of feeling tortured that he never knew why his partner had cheated on him. He first took the role of his pebble and received some encouragement and reassurance, according to the 'bookending' protocol which is described below.

The chairs were moved into a horseshoe, with Adam's chair remaining in the circle, so that he could return to this at any point. Adam was invited to create the scene with scarfs to mark out the room where the incident had taken place and select objects to represent his partner and himself. Adam had identified that his wish was to talk again to his partner and find out why she had cheated on him and then change the ending. He took the role of his partner and she had nothing to say, no answer to this question, which was a repeat the situation which had led to the assault. I invited him to take up the role of the part of his partner which he had not heard from, the chair behind. While in this role, I asked Adam as his partner to say why she had cheated on him, and with tears, he responded instinctively, 'I'm lonely'.

This statement was a moment of catharsis for Adam. He had not considered this at all, having focused on all attention on providing for her and their daughter, albeit by illegal means. This shifted his perspective at a deep emotional level. He returned to his own role to say things to his partner that he had never been able to say, because of the new compassionate wisdom about what might have been happening for her. It was in this scene that he was able to say a genuine sorry for what he did to her. Of course, we can never be certain that the 'discoveries' made when we take the role of another are completely accurate. The insights gained, however, are always helpful, support the therapeutic process and can bring some healing to ruptured relationships.

Adam took the invitation to step out of the scene into 'mirror' to observe two auxiliaries who had agreed to step in to hold the place of he and his partner. Stepping out into mirror meant that Adam stepped off the 'stage' and the auxiliaries played out the scene, allowing Adam to observe from another angle and hopefully inviting a different perspective. He was able to witness the conversation where Adam asked his partner why she had cheated and she explained that she had been lonely and isolated. From his stance in mirror, we evoked his Compassionate Self with a standing breathing and embodiment practice. I stood beside Adam and guided the practice, and from this place he was able to see how much they had both suffered . This final stage is designed to allow the new perspectives to be integrated before closing the piece of work.

Forgiveness

This piece of work with Adam was the beginning of an ongoing compassionate transformation, which paved the way for Adam to allow himself to turn back to and acknowledge his early deprivation and sexual abuse. This work had to take place before he could tolerate his own suffering and allow himself to be held in the mind of the group. I wonder if he had to first forgive himself for what he did to his ex-partner, to feel guilty for this, before he could allow himself to turn back to what had been done to him and work with the anger that emerged.

It is interesting to me that it is not always that way round. Sherelle had been abused in the care system, which was unacknowledged. Subsequently, her own children were removed from her care, with all the accompanying judgements and shame. I think Sherelle had to first return to the injustice in her own early life and have this responded to before she could take up the mantel of her responsibility for the damage she has caused her children.

This brings me to the sticky, highly charged and often misunderstood concept of forgiveness. As the child of very rigid Catholic family, I carried an aversion even to the word 'forgiveness', and therefore avoided considering this part of the therapeutic work. My experience of Catholicism as punitive, judgemental and requiring me to let others off the hook despite how much they hurt me, led me to misunderstand forgiveness. I was mostly unaware of my aversion until my own personal therapy, when I had the fortune to stumble across Desmond and Mpho Tutu's *The Book of Forgiving*.[76] I listened to this book read in a lilting African accent and it moved me beyond words and corrected a long-held misunderstanding.

I learned that forgiveness and the four-fold path explained in the book was actually deeply compassionate and gave a frame to some of the work I already leaned into with the group. For many, this will already be an intuitive part of your psychotherapeutic practice and understanding that our group members must first have a space to tell their story. This means that the group, including us, must need to be able to tolerate this story. This brings me back to ensuring our group members do not pass the tissues too quickly and shut down these difficult and painful disclosures. It took Adam and many others I have worked with, months to summon the courage to say out loud what had happened to them. The second step in the path, which often comes with the first, but not always, is the opportunity to name the hurt. For Adam, he needed a great deal of support to tolerate his vulnerability and accept the impact that this abuse continued to have on his life. Adam spoke with feeling about being unable to touch and cuddle his daughter no matter how distressed she had been. He was making links for the first time with being groomed and sexually abused, and his subsequent fear of any form of intimacy. Adam had also spent decades starving himself and pulling out the hair of his beard to punish himself, directing the rage inwardly.

Here is where it gets controversial, or maybe not. Forgiving is not condoning, letting anyone off the hook, allowing or making excuses for. This step is all about letting go of the hurt and accepting what we suffered. Adam has disowned the young, hurt part of himself and defended against feeling the pain for most of this life. This had given rise to Skull, who we will hear about in Chapter 4.4. Adam's work to map his inner family in the earlier part of the group gave him some sense of the buried and disowned parts which he returned to. He then made an active choice to acknowledge and the let go of the rage and betrayal he felt by the man who abused him, and also his mother who let it happen. Some of this work happened in the discursive parts of the group as members shared their stories and then began to support each other to disentangle the projections of blame and responsibility.

The final step of the path is to release or renew the relationship, and again the focus is on the active choice. For Adam, his choice was to put both his mother and his abuser in the chair and read the letter he had composed, with support from the group and his Compassionate Self. Adam chose a letter as he felt he needed some time to put together everything he needed to say. When he tried to respond with spontaneity, Skull (his inner critic) got in the way and shut the whole process down. Essentially, this was a statement of commitment to continue his journey in compassion without either of them,

---

76 Tutu, D. M. & Abrams, D. C. (2014) *The Book of Forgiving: The fourfold path for healing ourselves and our world.* Harperone.

the abuser who lived in his mind and his mother who often intruded into this life. This work of course spanned many months and combined work in action with sharing and reflecting in the group space. Not all your group members will reach this point by the end of their time in CFGP, but I remain ever hopeful that something can shift. But I have found it helpful and challenging to hold the four-fold path in my mind as we turn back to and face the terror of hurt and avoidance.

Grief and grieving

This process can make way and allow for what Paul Gilbert describes as the one of the most important aspects of our compassion-focused work: developing the compassionate competencies and capacity to tolerate grief and yearning for what was missing. The explicit and implicit building of the group cohesion and connectedness through experiments with touch and play develops the care-giving and care-seeking system. This has, for understandable reasons, been shut down for many of our group members in the context of early emotional deprivation.

The idea that you don't miss what you have never had is deeply relevant here, as we actually do miss the secure attachment relationships even if they are absent, but this yearning is buried. This care-seeking and receiving system can be activated by the group process and the exploration of early losses, which can give rise to a process of realisation and grieving for the loving parents they didn't have. I have recently had the pleasure of listening to Darcy Harris on the subject of facilitating the grieving for absent attachments.[77] The work is long and slow and needs to be trodden carefully with space for discoveries to be made and managed.

Remember Louie drawing the picture of the child's hand and realising that it was his child hand needing the comfort of his father? This, of course, gave way to sadness:

> '…because it is the first time that I was upset without being angry and part of that was because I felt safe … because I wouldn't have been able to do it otherwise, but it was the suddenness of it and the understanding afterwards, it was a revelation and it does still bring up emotion – that's the moment and it's a scary bloody moment it really is a scary moment. But I thank them for it.'

---

77 Harris, D. L. (2019). Non-death loss and grief: Laying the foundation. In *Non-death Loss and Grief* (pp. 7–16). Routledge. www.taylorfrancis.com/chapters/edit/10.4324/9780429446054-2/non-death-loss-grief-laying-foundation-darcy-harris

This quote also demonstrates the importance of the group who are supporting and enabling the grieving process.

Once identified, there are many ways that we can work implicitly in the group process and explicitly with grief, individually or as a group. Sometimes, this might be an extended check in, with the invitation for group members to make connections with their own narratives and experiences.

An action-based group exercise which can be helpful when grief, loss and sadness are emerging is based on The Whirlpool of Grief. Here, the group are invited to work together and recreate The Whirlpool of Grief (see Appendix 4.4 for the image that I will often draw on the flip chart). The group can create their own individual images, but it can be helpful to develop their capabilities in cooperation to invite them to create a group based sculpt. In practice this means that the group will be invited to use objects and images to recreate, in this case, the whirlpool of grief using the whole room. So, initially, they set out the room to represent the different stages in the process and then place themselves either in the sculpt or they are represented by an object to illustrate where they feel they are in this process.

The invitation to turn the whole room into the group sculpt can be met with some initial trepidation, followed by enjoyment in being able to what might be perceived as 'making a mess'. Rather than people being sculpted or arranged to demonstrate the dynamics or feelings at play, the group uses the room to recreate the diagram as it relates to them collectively. In my groups, chairs have been upturned to create the jagged rocks of pain and despair, scarfs have been used to recreate the 'washed up beach of denial', coloured paper has been scrunched and bunched to make the whirlpool of processing grief. This creative sensory exercise usually gets everyone out of their chairs, shouting instructions to each other and working together to develop the scene. The work of placing themselves in the scene is often more sombre and reflective, with connections made to each other and the shared losses.

Much of this chapter has focused on individual pieces of work in action. This will always need to be interspersed with group-based pieces, which may stem from an individual issue or something which seems to resonant for the whole group. I think that these whole-group sessions can offer some relief and respite from the intensity of the chair and work in action. This is for everyone, us and them!

Jane and triangle of compassionate

Our group members with A&RT often struggle with social skills, and this stems from adverse childhood experiences and the lack of secure, reassuring and supportive adults to guide and develop situation-appropriate ways of communicating. Jane was no exception, having also had very few adult relationships which could have helped her to develop her social skills and capabilities. Jane during her check ins would frequently make quite cutting remarks about other group member's appearance and things they said. Over time, it was becoming more apparent that the group were pulling away from Jane, and they had stopped passing the 'check in' to her.

During one such check in, Jane noticed that she had again 'gone last'. The rest of the group looked at their feet and said nothing. After a long silence, one group member, still looking at the floor, asked Jane why she kept commenting on Kate's trousers. Jane seemed surprised and said that it was a joke. The same group members looked up again and said it felt quite passive aggressive, like Jane was 'getting at' Kate for often wearing the same trousers. Jane again was surprised and replied that she did not know what passive aggression was. It is of note that Jane was also regularly looking at the floor and therefore not 'reading the room' or seeing the discomfort in others.

We decided to take this into action, to explore the differences between passivity, aggression, passive aggression and compassionate assertiveness. What followed was primarily role playing the different parts what is often described as "The assertiveness Triangle"[78]. We laid out the room with passive at one end and aggressive at the other, and invited some spontaneous, role-played conversations, with group members invited to 'act out' the different ends of the spectrum. At the passive end, one group member agreed to paint the house of another despite being allergic to paint, and at the aggressive end, there was a threat to throw someone out of a window for bumping into them! Many were confused by passive aggression, so a group member took an aggressive stance and walked towards someone in a passive stance and they met in the middle and created a tight-lipped barely concealed raging appeasing response. It was as if a light went on in Jane and she stepped into the passive aggressive place on the continuum with her own acidic comments about my trousers and 'and how nice that you are wearing those trousers *again*'. In practice the room was then laid out with a continuum Passive at one end of the room, aggressive at the other and passive aggressive as the third in the middle between the two extremes.

We then used the room, to create a fourth place, which in practice makes the whole scene become a triangle and explored compassionate assertiveness, using examples from the material the group members (Appendix 4.0 Compassionate assertiveness

---

[78] Paterson, R. J. (2022). *The assertiveness workbook: How to express your ideas and stand up for yourself at work and in relationships*. New Harbinger Publications. https://books.google.co.uk/books?hl=en&lr=&id=_P9bEAAAQBAJ&oi=fnd&pg=PT12&dq=the+assertiveness+workbook+randy+paterson&ots=49e031D-h5&sig=Wng4R0nwE6BFhlHQFer_eCRwYMw

Triangle). I was prompting this aspect with reminders of moments of courageous, assertive and wise action, saying no and holding boundaries. We then had another strand of shared language to return to in the group process – *'Oh, were you having a throw-them-out-the-window moment?'*

This example demonstrates that we are also working around the edges with social skills acquisition and development, competencies that were robbed from our group members through the trauma in their attachment relationships.

When things get stuck

There will be times in this work of compassionate transformation where a group member gets stuck, with fixed beliefs based on old messages about fault and responsibility: 'I can lay out all these scarfs and look at it again, but it *was* my fault, I made it happen'.

This is an understandable defence, which of course enabled the group member to survive their experiences and is often tied with important messages that were given to them by others. It is important to first validate the experience and acknowledge the stuckness.

It will sometimes be too early to expect your group members to be able to bring the compassionate perspective to this scene. We will need to be cautious in inviting the compassionate perspective if we feel that it is unlikely that they can connect with this in a meaningful way. The Compassionate Self or Compassionate Other may still be in the embryonic stages of development and so not ready to work effectively with the stuckness. We have the auxiliaries as we described earlier, but sometimes even they cannot shift fixed perspectives.

There are also ways that we can work with this in action, to move the process onwards and support the group member to quite literally see the whole scene from a different perspective. This is another place where role-taking can offer a way of shifting the perspective of a situation. This is particularly helpful when working with a memory of a past event. I have had many moments when the question 'what do you need?' is met with a blank expression or self-blame: 'I needed to have been stronger, better'. In such moments, I have invited the group member to take the role of an inanimate objects in the room or scene that we are working with, with the intention of viewing the scene through a fresh and objective lens.

One group member had been stuck with overwhelming guilt that she had not stopped the abuse from her father towards her younger siblings and herself. While working with a memory of her dad coming home drunk and becoming violent, she had become stuck with the sense that she should have stopped it and could not allow anyone else in. At this point, an invitation to view this cognitively was not making any difference. So I invited her to take the role of the lamp that sat in the corner of the room – she had represented this lamp in her scene as she had liked it. I also felt that there was a deeper symbolic meaning to her affiliation with the lamp. This lamp had brought light and illumination to the darkness and terror of her unpredictable and violent father. Something that the person has a positive connection too can be helpful but it is not a requirement.

As the lamp, she was invited to share what she saw and what she knew. As the lamp, she saw everything that took place, but without the burden of old, toxic messages. I gently guided the group member, still in the role of the lamp, to offer a different message – that she was a child and could not have stopped her father and was definitely not to blame. This was enough to create some room to consider an alternative understanding and therefore to change the ending of this scene.

When you need to take the wheel

There will also be times when the member you are working with may become stuck, frozen and overwhelmed, and you may need to offer more concrete support. We can anticipate this and conceptualise it as a functional, dissociative process. As discussed in Phase Three, we can normalise dissociation as a something that happens to us all, in moderation, but in particular those who have been exposed to traumatising situations from which they needed to escape in their minds. The unintended consequence of this is that this way of surviving becomes fixed, automatic and unconscious, leaving the individual confused, disorientated and inevitably self-critical. The education and normalising in Phase Three will generally need to be returned to in Phase Four and reinforced.

In situations where group members get stuck and dissociated, your group will sometimes be able to offer this spontaneous support:

> *'We was doing an exercise with light and dark in ourselves and one person we had to bring out because they had gone into that dark space and they couldn't get their selves out, we went and got her hand and took her out, it was good.'*

I find that group members are often very adept at noticing disconnection and dissociation in others, but perhaps not in themselves. The invitation to use the objects on the table or their own multisensory kitbag can provide much-needed grounding. Neil

Clapton and I wrote about the significant body of evidence supporting the efficacy of haptic touch, sensory soothing and the provision of transitional objects for managing dissociation in our 2020 paper on the Compassionate Kitbag.[79]

There will be other times when it is necessary to step into our own authority to support the group member you are working with if it seems that they are no longer able to manage. I have noticed that this situation often emerges in the context of work in action, where your group member becomes dissociated. As the quote above suggests, sometimes touch is needed, which is a controversial issue in psychotherapy. I have grappled with this throughout my career, from social work to psychotherapy, and I have read papers and asked supervisors and trusted colleagues. But, ultimately, the best advice I have been given is to trust my own instincts and find a way to ask… without it sounding creepy! I often suggest that there may be times when it might be helpful to have a hand on your arm to guide you, and this lays the groundwork for spontaneous reaching out or making yourself available to be reached out to.

There will also be times when your authority is needed to regulate and provide the safeness in the group. It is therefore imperative that we do not give up our authority while attending to the group's need for us to be benevolent and understanding. This is of course the foundation of compassion – the capacity for strength and gentleness combined with honesty and clarity. This includes working with lateness and other boundary breaches in the group, as we discussed in Chapter 3.2: How it works.

I had a particularly difficult group in the early days of the programme. I had invited a new group member, who I was not sure about. This is one of the examples of my desire to prove how great the programme was overshadowing my judgement. I should have listened to my reservations because it turned out that this member was really not ready for group work and behaved in a racist and offensive manner. My co-facilitator and I were so stunned by his behaviour that we froze and did not respond to his behaviour or hold the boundary. After the session, it was as if we 'woke up' and realised what had happened. We took this to supervision to explore the projective process that my co-facilitator and I had become caught in, which was linked to the group member's disowned sense of responsibility. Unusually, we took the decision to close his place without discussing with the group, and we let everyone know by phone and also apologised to the group for our failure to act. This was generally well received and a few members had said that they not planned to return to the group the next week.

I learned something really important about holding my authority as the convenor of the group and why we absolutely must say sorry when we get it wrong. The concept of a

---

[79] Lucre, K., & Clapton, N. (2020). The Compassionate Kitbag: A creative and integrative approach to compassion-focused therapy. *Psychology and Psychotherapy: Theory, Research and Practice*, e12291.

'concertina hierarchy', which comes from therapeutic community theory and practice, is deeply helpful here as we need to be able to expand and contract, a little like an old-fashioned accordion or 'squeeze box'. Stepping in and out of our explicit authority role as needed. We did not maintain our authority, and as a result, the group did not feel safe.

Concluding comments

My intention has been to offer an overview with some concrete examples of ways that we can mobilise compassion and invite the group to step out of their chairs and out of their heads to turn back to explore the past. This chapter could have been a whole book as there are so many ways into this work, but I hope this has offered a flavour of the courageous and cathartic work that is possible in this group process. Endings can be changed, scripts rewritten and compassion mobilised, and made into something concrete and tangible.

Again, to emphasise, I believe strongly that this work requires experiential training in action methods and sociometry. In short, I would suggest that you try this yourselves in the context of recognised training programmes before launching this method into a group programme.

So onwards to the 'folding chairs of doom', another medium for change and enlivening your group.

Chapter 4.4: Compassionate transformation in action Part 2 – Chairwork

When getting started with chairwork, it is important to acknowledge that chairwork in psychotherapy, like action methods, has a long and rich history, which stems from Jacob Moreno's development of psychodrama, followed by Fritz Perls, who developed Gestalt Therapy, and more recently, Dr Tobyn Bell, who has adapted chairwork specifically for compassion-focused therapy. This chapter will explore the practical considerations and of course the stories of chairwork in groups.

'The folding chairs of doom!'

So-named playfully by many group members over the years… It is important that the chairs that we use for chairwork are different from the usual therapy chairs and that we can move them easily and pack them away at the end of a piece of work. In the UK, a set of Argos' finest folding chairs have become part of the group room furniture, leaning in the corner of the room, waiting to be called on. On the days where we have agreed to use them, I will pull them out of the corner to the side. As the group enter the room, there have often been calls of 'Oh no… the chairs of doom are out' to the members coming behind. Despite some of the understandable trepidation which accompanies this work, it is generally welcomed and understood to be a key part of CFTG.

In this chapter, we will explore some of the infinite uses of chairs in the exploratory therapeutic groupwork, drawing on ideas from psychodrama and Gestalt Therapy. This is not meant to be exhaustive, and within the confines of this text, I have chosen a few of my favourites to explore in detail.

In essence, chairwork supports the process of differentiation, creating an emotional distance between parts of the self and illuminating relationships with others. Chairwork supports the work of transformation, changing meaning and stuck association with aspects of the self and others. Finally, you guessed it, chairwork can support the process of integration of the multiple selves with the Compassionate Self in charge. Chairs are also used as props to support working with the multiplicity of self, turning back to unspoken conversations and to further develop compassionate capacity. Chairwork, as with all work in action, has the opportunity to give group members agency over their memories and enables them to be in charge of how long they stay with the experience before moving. Tobyn Bell's research identified how the therapist seeing the person's inner world could generate shame, but the group process can be used to work this through. As Gillian Rathbone's work reminds us, the group can be 'an arena for the resolution of shame'.[80]

People in training have often expressed concern for those who are observing from the 'audience' and how they cope with seemingly all the attention being on them. In over 15 years of this work, I can recall one incident where a group member left the room while someone was engaged in chairwork. They were clear that they could not tolerate the intensity of the work or the focus on another member of the group. This was sadly a catalyst for them leaving the programme. But for the majority of group members, the experience of bearing witness to and often being an active part of someone's work is a deeply moving experience:

> *'The impact on other people in the room, it changed things for them it wasn't just the person at the front in the chairs, it was everybody.'*

I have repeated this quote as a reminder of the group's experience of observing.

> *'Things come up which I wasn't expecting, it wasn't like I could think about it cognitively ... like I am gonna talk about this when I am sitting there... It's just things really emotional came from a different part of me... Quite challenging and important as well.'*

---

80 Rathbone, G. (2012). The Analytic Group as an Arena for the Resolution of Shame. *Group Analysis*, **45**(2), 139-153. https://doi.org/10.1177/0533316411436142

This highlights how chairwork and work in action generally enables group members to bypass cognitive defences and work at a deep emotional level. Group members have also often reported that, in chairwork, other people 'speak your truth', and that this can be helpful to experience from the observer's stance in the audience. This has certainly been a catalyst for group members deciding to engage in chairwork after witnessing it. This supports the incredible work of Dr Tobyn Bell who has been practising, researching and writing about the benefits of CFT chairwork for well over a decade.

Meeting angry, sad and frightened

Many will be familiar with the traditional ideas of CFT chairwork to explore the multiple aspects of self (angry, sad and frightened). The chairs are placed by the group member to denote the relationship between the different parts of the self. When working with multiple selves, I will invite the person to sit in the chair and allow that part to come to front. I have found that inviting your group member to role-take each part of self can be overwhelming and it then becomes difficult to separate and take up another chair. This links to the idea that the immersion for some, at times, can become too overwhelming. The distinction is subtle, but rather than inviting the person to be the part, I invited them to allow this part to come to the front. In dialogue, I am asking 'so how would it be if *this part* of you ran the show?', whereas in role-taking I am asking, 'so, angry self, how would it be if *you* ran the show?' If I am using the role-taking technique, I would take more time de-roling between parts of the self and may also work with fewer parts in one session.

This work has multiple elements and phases which could take place over several sessions. This work leads on well from the work in Chapter 4.2 using pen and paper exercises to map out the multiples. The starting point is the multiples and perhaps something of the message from each part or what the part would wish for: 'if nothing stood in your way, what would you do? What would you wish for?' Accessing the motivation which sits within the part of the self is a helpful starting point to begin to bring compassion to all the parts.

The next step may be to invite the conversation with the parts of the self: 'What does angry self think of sad self?' Maybe invite your group member to use the chairs to represent the relationships, to turn towards or away from one chair or another, or even place one chair behind the other. The symbolic movement of the chairs can help the group member to connect with how this experience of their multiple selves looks and feels.

When engaging in chairwork, it is helpful to have in mind the potential for 'leakage' between different parts of the self. As it is for us all, there will be certain overdeveloped and therefore more comfortable parts of the self. These parts will be more accessible and at times more difficult to move away from.

> *'They called it chairwork. You sit in all different chairs and it was different parts of you – one could be your anger another could be your, erm, sadness, and when you sat in that chair you kind of experienced it. Kate would ask questions … while you are in that chair and you respond from that position… That was really powerful and helped me to see myself more clearly.'*

Louie and the leaky parts!

Louie had agreed to do some chairwork as he had become increasingly aware of how much his threat system had become overrun with anger over the years, which left no room for sadness or fear to be tolerated. He had begun to make some tentative connections with the instrumental violence within his family and in particular his father's tendency to react to any suggestion of vulnerability with immediate brutality. He shared with the group a memory of returning from school bruised and bloodied having been jumped by boys in an alley near his home. His father's response was to beat Louie, demanding that he went back and found them and 'finished the fight'.

At this point, he was not ready to return to this memory (later in the programme, he returned to it and compassionately transformed the ending with help from his auxiliaries and his Compassionate Other, 'Buffy the Vampire Slayer', who brought strength wisdom and some 'kick ass' to the situation). But he volunteered to use the chairs to lay out the multiple aspects of his threat survival system. We set out the room in the usual way, creating the horseshoe with the chairs and marking out the space for the 'stage'. Louie first set out the chair for his angry self, and smiling, he sat straight down in the chair and remarked that it felt comfortable. We explored a little of the angry self's motivation and wishes. 'Being in charge always!' was the essence of this dialogue. I asked him to stand and take a step from the angry chair to see what else showed up in his threat system. He spoke in quiet voice of feeling something that might be a bit like fear. I invited him to take a chair to represent this part, but he flatly refused to sit in the chair, which we understood. Instead, he stood holding the back of the chair and, with some gentle questions, began to make some tentative connection with how young this part of him was. Things quickly shifted and his voice became louder and more aggressive, much more like the anger part. Unbeknownst to me, and underneath Louie's awareness, he had hooked his leg around the 'angry chair' and had connected back with this part of himself. My co-facilitator who was sat in the audience noticed this and pointed it out, treading carefully to avoid embarrassing Louie. He had also been unaware and this was the catalyst for a helpful and fruitful discussion about leaky parts, which others could also engage with.

This case example demonstrates in a visual way how challenging the process of differentiation can be. The use of chairs enables group members to make the separation of the parts of the self-concrete and visible. The group can also be invited to hold the place of the different parts of the self, thus enabling the person to see and hear the dialogue before bringing the perspective of the Compassionate Self or Other, as described above.

The empty chair: Anyone you want to talk to?

This aspect of chairwork, which is a mainstay of Gestalt Therapy, might be the most familiar to people, with the idea that we can put anyone in the chair and say all the things that it was not possible to name previously. This can also be used to work with the transference material once it has been identified, and the feelings can then be directed through the empty chair, usually to the adult who hurt them.

The previous section on forgiveness illustrated the importance of allowing and facilitating appropriate anger towards those who failed to care and protect, which can be part of naming the hurt. This is unlikely to be easily accessible for many group members who have internalised anger to avoid punishment from powerful others. In such situations, there may a need from some compassionate coaching, ideally from the group who can be recruited to provide support and ideas. I recall many occasions on which group members got stuck and an auxiliary would be invited to offer some suggestions or take over and double for the group member, often stepping up on the stage and sitting beside or placing a reassuring arm on the group member's shoulder to accompany an alternative, assertive and boundaried response. Many group members have stepped up with perhaps an overdeveloped angry part to share some of their rage with someone who struggles. This can have benefits for all, diluting anger for some and activating it for others.

Jane had been working with the shame that she had carried for her entire life, which had led to her avoiding any intimate relationships or even friendships. She was beginning to connect her aversion to closeness with her father's contempt, which coloured all memories of him and in particular his reaction to her overdose. She described that he had found her and dragged her into a cold shower and the next day arranged for her admission to a local psychiatric unit where she remained for four years. She had internalised the shame and feeling of being unacceptable. The group suggested that she give it back to him, as it didn't belong to her. She found a dark-coloured stone to pour the shame into, pulled out the empty chair and leaned over to give the stone back to her father.

Just as she leaned forward, she paused, looked back at the group with some sadness, and said that she didn't want him to have the shame either. Although he had hurt her deeply, she knew that he was also hurt and wounded by his relationship with his mother who had been abusive and cold. So she took the stone and buried it in the garden, symbolising her wish for no one to have this shame, especially not her. There was a shift in Jane after this session, there a little less prickle in her way of being in the group, warmer and less critical. I think she started a process that enabled her to turn back to other relationships and let go of more painful material. This is also a powerful example of the healing power of forgiveness.

Many empty chairs

Working with abusive, absent and critical attachment figures can become particularly tricky and stuck when there is a continuing relationship with the attachment figure, often a parent. I have worked with many people over the years who have spoken of feeling anger towards the attachment figure who mistreated them in early life, but who were unable to reconcile this with the empathy they felt towards the frail and elderly person in their adult life. So many of our traumatised patients have been unable to extricate themselves from the coercive relationships with their attachment figures, perhaps still waiting and yearning for the love to be offered. This was most definitely the case for Dal, and as their mother's carer, they spoke of often feeling conflicted about the rage which seemingly had nowhere to be directed to, and which, of course, then got transferred onto others.

It is possible in such situations to have multiple empty chairs representing the different aspects of an attachment figure or other. Dal put out a chair for the sick and vulnerable part of their mother, as well as one for the cruel and hurtful part. The ensuring dialogue was different for each part and enabled Dal to reconcile the conflict. Dal was working with the idea that they could be both angry with and empathic towards their mother who had failed to care and protect.

The empty chair and the chair behind

When working with difficult or stuck relationships where there is a motivation to resolve, understand or repair, we can use an adaptation of the Gestalt empty chair technique to support a mentalising compassionate dialogue. As much as possible, be clear at the beginning with the group member about what they are hoping for, as this will help guide the work in action. We will want to be clear about the nature of the relationship to the person. If the relationship is or has been abusive towards your group member, then I would not use this technique, as role-taking an abuser can be extremely re-traumatising and generally is not helpful.

The group member is invited to set out two chairs in whatever way feels right for them; often they are placed facing each other. First, the member is invited to sit in their chair and say what they would like to say to the other. The invitation is then to switch into the other chair, as they sit taking the role of the other person and hear the message, taking time in this process to allow the person to settle into the role. I will often offer some initial questions to support this process; again, we are orientating Jane into the role of her of sister, before moving to the next stage.

Here's a script of Jane's conversation with her sister:

> **Therapist:** 'So, welcome, Joanne. Jane has invited you here as she has some things she really needs you to hear, is this OK?'
>
> **Jane (as Joanne):** 'Yes, that is OK.'
>
> **Therapist:** 'So Joanne, I just wanted to check with you that you heard what Jane (your sister) has asked you? Or do you need a reminder?'

If the message has become lost, you can invite, with Jane's permission, an auxiliary to come and repeat the message with help from the group, bearing in mind the advice from the previous section. Once the message has been received, a response is invited from the member, in role as the other. Sometimes this brings new material and insights, but equally it can give rise to a familiar and often stuck dialogue. In such circumstances, it can be helpful to invite the member in role as the other to put a chair behind (back-to-back) and take the role of the part that does not show up. This is invariably the voice of the unconscious.

> **Therapist:** 'Thank you, Joanne, for responding to Jane. I wonder if I could invite you to move to chair behind yours and speak from the part of you that Jane does not see or hear?'
>
> **Jane (as Joanne):** 'OK.'
>
> **Therapist:** 'Welcome. You are the part of Joanne that Jane does not ever hear from. I wonder if you can respond to Jane's question from this place?'
>
> **Jane (as Joanne's unconscious):** 'I just can't give her what she needs… It is not that I don't want to or I don't care… I can't be the sister she needs me to be… I love her, but I can't care for her… I just don't know how to…'

Jane was the invited to de-role her sister Joanne and move back to her chair to hear the message. She was asked if she wanted to hear the message again through an auxiliary, but Jane opted not to. She spoke of feeling that, when she sat in the chair behind, she felt completely connected with Joanne's sadness about what she cannot do, and the anger that she felt in the front chair was absent. This powerful experience for Jane was a precursor to making an important decision to stop angrily 'pursuing' her sister for not being available to her.

Jane's response to this work was a spontaneous bringing of compassion to the situation and an understanding which guided her decision. Therefore, the evocation of the Compassionate Self or Other as a response to the work was not needed. But in such situations, I would notice that the Compassionate Self is already present, to reinforce and validate the group member's progress. There will, however, be occasions when this needs to be made more explicit, and we will return to this in more detail in the next chapter.

Talking with the critic

Many group members over the years have questioned why we would want to open up a dialogue with the inner critic. In Phase Three, we support the work of differentiating and creating emotional distance from the inner critic. Some would say that dialoguing or talking to the critic might contradict this. This, of course, makes good sense against a backdrop of understandable avoidance, denial and attempts to disown the critic as a means of survival. When introducing the idea of a conversation with the critic, we start with an exploration – usually in the formulation stage – about how their current strategies are working out. The language of unintended consequences is useful here. Most will be able to acknowledge that the current strategy has little utility and has been unsuccessful in silencing the voice of the critic. We can also invite the group to consider what happens when they attempt to 'fight' with the inner critic. This often leads to an honest realisation that the critic generally feels more powerful than the Compassionate Self or Other. We can then remind our group member that the critic has the 'advantage' of coming from our overdeveloped threat protection system and stimulated by the natural bias that it is 'better to be safe than sorry'. This reminds me of the Native American parable of the two wolves that are fighting inside us, one good, one bad, and the idea that the wolf who will win is the one that we feed. Often our Compassionate Self has only been fed and developed more recently, so may not be as developed.

These kinds of group-based discussions introduce the idea of dialogues with the inner critic. We can build on the work in Phase Three with image making around the critic and exploration of where the critic came from, usually vulnerability in early life.

I will often use role-taking as a precursor to chairwork in group. We can spontaneously invite our group members to take on the role of the inner critic as part of the preparation for chairwork and compassionate transformation. I think of these exercises as a 'fact finding mission', to understand more about the roles and functions. One of the many great possibilities with role-taking is that it can be used as a functional analysis of a part the self, which bypasses cognitive processes. This process can also help to establish whether the critic is a protective survival strategy or an internalised abuser, as referred to later in this chapter.

We follow the same protocol for this exercise as we do for role-taking for the kitbag, but the difference is in the steer of the interview questions:

> **Facilitator:** 'So, you have been with Dal for nearly all their life. Actually, you cannot remember not being in their life. I wonder when you think you are needed most?'
>
> **Dal, in role as critic:** 'They always need me because people always want something from them and they are not strong enough to say no. I help them see how bad people are and how weak they are for not saying no.'
>
> **Facilitator:** 'What is your wish for, Dal?'
>
> **Dal, in role as critic:** 'They need to listen to me more – I know what's best. I am always having to shout. They try and ignore me, but it is not going to work.'
>
> **Facilitator:** 'I wonder how it is being here to today and being heard by us all here?'
>
> **Critic:** 'Actually, I feel a bit better getting to have my say.'
>
> **Facilitator:** 'I see... So when you get an opportunity to speak, what then? Is there room to have a conversation?'
>
> **Critic:** 'Maybe I won't have to shout so loud.'
>
> **Facilitator:** 'That is really interesting and helpful to know. So a conversation might help everyone? I was wondering if I could ask another question. I am curious about what you fear most? I know nothing really scares you, but maybe what worries you most?'
>
> **Critic:** 'I have to shout loud so that they don't forget me or get rid of me.'

> **Facilitator:** 'That makes so much sense, but what if there is no plan to get rid of you? I don't think anyone wants to get rid of you, and I don't think we could! But maybe there might be an opportunity to work a little more together?'
>
> **Critic:** 'Maybe...'
>
> **Facilitator:** 'So one last thing – I wonder if you have a sense of what you need?'
>
> **Critic:** 'Well, a bit of help might be good. I'm here on my own doing all the work. Keeping an eye out for all the dangers. To be honest, it is pretty exhausting.'
>
> **Facilitator:** 'Well, I definitely think that we can help with that. It has been so good to hear from you and I hope to chat with you again soon.'

Once we have differentiated the critic from other parts of the self and understood the function or strategy that this part serves, we are ready to begin to develop a new compassionate relationship with the critic. This often comes from the last question from the segment above, asking what the critic needs. My experience is that the response can sometimes relate to being heard: 'I have something to say and she/he doesn't listen, so I have to shout louder and remind them more forcefully about what happened in the past.'

This scripted piece paves the way for more dialogues with the critic and the introduction of the Compassionate Self or Other, moving into transforming meaning and creating a new relationship with the critic.

Climbing, like working with the critic, is not a battle

We live in a world where the language of conflict is all around us. We are 'battling cancer', 'waging war on crime', 'beating mental ill health', and then driving our points home with bullet points in PowerPoint presentations. It all starts to feel exhaustingly adversarial. We can get caught in the same trap with our group members working with the inner critic. It can be tempting to wage war on the inner critic, but remember that the critic is a part of the self and so needs to be treated with the same compassion as the other parts.

Working with the inner critic, like climbing, is not a battle to be fought and won, it is a conversation to be engaged in. You can bring the words of compassion but the work is in your mind. The cultivation of a compassionate mind is key here, to know the words and the compassionate intention that sits behind them.

It is the same with climbing. I have thrown myself at many cliffs in my time, full of anger, frustration and a need to 'nail it'. Every time, mother nature has unceremoniously spat me out. We can have all the strength and technique, but it is the intention to be with rather than to conquer which will allow us to make slow and steady progress up the mountain. The moments I cherish are those when I stop to take in the view, allow myself to be present with my threat system and meet my critic who tells me I shouldn't try this, then calmly do it anyway.

As I write this, I am full of moments when my group members have slowed down and pulled up a chair with the motivation to understand rather than conquer. It is these conditions which allow change to occur.

Adam meets Skull

For many months, Adam had alluded to a part of himself that had done really bad things and that he could not hope to ever overcome or make amends for. We had never seen this part of Adam in the group as he was often withdrawn and quiet. Adam called this part of himself Skull, and it connected him with the times when his food restriction had reached a dangerous and risky point.

Adam was reluctant to bring this part of himself to the session as he was fearful that the group would see him differently and judge him as harshly as he judged himself. But, just as he had worked to take off his gloves and hat and even to take a pebble, with encouragement, he agreed to put Skull in the chair.

He set out two chairs, one for himself and one for Skull. He first sat in the chair and tried to speak to Skull, which quickly got stuck and became quite fearful and withdrawn. With some support he managed to say that felt that Skull was unhelpful to his life. He then switched to the Skull chair and immediately his whole demeanour shifted – he sat upright, shoulders back, staring straight ahead. His voice was louder, demanding, insistent. He told Adam that he could not manage without him, that he was weak, but that it was OK because he (Skull) was strong. Skull went on to launch a tirade of verbal abuse towards Adam and that he was weak and pathetic for coming to therapy. Adam shifted back to his original chair at hearing this and quickly slumped down appearing small and quite young. I stopped the exercise and asked Adam what he noticed. He spoke of a part of Skull reminding him of the teacher at school who had told him he deserved the bruises inflicted on him by his mother.

At this point, it became clear that part of Skull was an internalised abuser, and we needed to work differently with this. As I have mentioned, it is very important to make a distinction between the protective inner critic who has emerged often as part of surviving a hostile early rearing environment, and the internalised abuser. The internalised abuser can be difficult to spot, but as we discussed previously, will often emerge when we explore intention. The internalised abuser invariably does not wish the person to thrive or even stay safe, and usually it will give instructions or reminders to cause harm, and offer no advice or guidance.

We stopped the exercise and brought Adam out of chair, and invited him to observe the two chairs, Adam and Skull. Adam, now with some distance, began to see the connections between part of Skull and the many people who had abused and hurt him in his childhood. It seemed that Skull held not only the narrative of these experiences but also the clear message from his abusers that he was to blame. So we put another chair in for the internalised abuser, or 'abuse echo' as the group often name it, and agreed that we would work differently with this part. Tobyn Bell's research can support a greater understanding of the distinctions to be made between self-hatred, which sits alongside contempt, and self-criticism, which has a protective albeit harsh tone.

The ensuing dialogue was with the part of Skull who wished to protect him from those who had hurt him, and invited the idea that Skull could do with some support i.e. a Compassionate Other. I often find in this work that the greatest fear of the inner critic is that they will be killed off. We can give some resolute reassurance that death to the critic is not the plan, but perhaps turning the volume down is an acceptable goal. Skull, in this sense, had a protective and corrective function, and as such could be supported to be calmed and, over time integrated, into the self.

Working with internalised abusers

Once identified, we will need to work with the internalised abuser with greater caution and a different approach than we do with a protective critical part. The instinct might be to put the echo in the chair and invite a tirade, but I would avoid this – as we said before, this is a part of the self. To do so generally increases the strength of the part you are fighting with.

We need to work around the edges to cultivate and develop the Compassionate Self to turn back with wisdom, courage and strength to distinguish between what belongs to the group member and what doesn't. This quote illustrates the understanding that this group member developed about his internalised abuser, which came through the group process:

> *'For me, having spent so much time beating myself up and then understanding that the verbal beating was just echoes of things said by an overly expectant … impatient … father … and that it was a denial of legitimacy your feelings are … wrong or you have no right to feel them … kind of thing and that's … it's a terrible thing to say to a child.'*

This discovery then lays the foundation, with support from the group, to begin to develop a different lens to view the experience. For some, beginning to identify the internalised abuser is the precursor to developing a compassionate response, while for others the compassionate response comes first from the group. The process is repeated and slowly internalised.

Once distinguished, the work of putting down or letting go of what no longer serves or belongs to the member can be helpful. You will recall the work on the four-fold path in the previous chapter. Group members have used scarfs and coats to represent the layers of internalised abusive others and these can be taken off to illustrate the externalising of the abuse echoes. Objects holding the toxic messages have been symbolically buried and letters have been read to the abuser in the chair. Tobyn Bell describes the need to make the memory 'molten' and therefore more fluid and malleable. For some, this will involve accessing the memories which accompany the echo and these can be worked with explicitly using the compassionate transformation work described in the previous chapter.

Bringing compassion

The final stage in all work in action, which may not always be in the same session, is the evocation of the Compassionate Self or Other to bring a new perspective to the scene. As with other exercises, I would not bring a chair for compassion because part of the function of the chairs for aspects of the self is that the person can stand up and walk away from them. My hope is for compassion to become embodied and not allocated to a chair. So I will generally invite a standing embodiment and breathing practice to support the group member to 'feel' compassion and where it resides in the body.

'Bookending' the compassion-focused trauma work

I am sure it is already clear that this work is painful and a source of considerable terror for most of our group members – whether this is shared or not is another issue! I think we have to assume that there is much work to be undertaken to co-create the necessary safeness. The idea of using the Compassionate Kitbag and the support of the group explicitly in the context of this exploratory work has always been in my mind. But there have been times when it did not seem to be enough to encourage members out of their chairs and onto the stage. An arched brow of scepticism seemed to be the main response to group member's words of support or encouragement: 'you are not the one about to throw yourself into this'.

In response to this, we came up with the idea of 'bookending' the work in group with activities to promote safeness and connection. This bookending is designed to stimulate an internal supportive and reassuring response from the group member, because external reassurance is easily dismissed. This can sometimes involve games, but we will explore this in more depth in the next chapter.

So we return to role-taking, discussed in Chapter 3.5. As I have suggested before, the utility of this exercise is endless and it is powerful in its simplicity and accessibility. Suffice to say I am a big fan, and usually, once the initial reticence has been addressed, most group members will feel the same.

Group members are invited to select something from their Compassionate Kitbag and bring this to the session when they are planning to use the group. We can also work more spontaneously as needed and objects from the table can be used to represent the symbol of compassionate identity. The group member is invited to take the role of the object before the work commences, and the questions centre on the work to be undertaken and a perspective and advice is sought from the object that has become the compassionate symbol.

Sherelle and the Daisy lip balm

During the check in, Sherelle brought a situation where she had taken up her authority when confronted with a taxi driver ridiculing her Daisy Duck paraphernalia. Sherelle had worked hard in group to develop her Compassionate Kitbag with many objects connected to Daisy Duck, who had become her Compassionate Other. Sherelle had been able to gather objects around her to build her ego strength and she had used these objects to begin to turn back to the reality of her early trauma. Sherelle connected the altercation with the taxi driver to memories of her father, who would not allow toys or playing. This disclosure signalled a shift for Sherrelle from a defended position in relation to her parents, to beginning to confront the reality of deprivation, intrusion and neglect. She was able to notice how angry she had been about the comments from the taxi driver. We did not explore this in any depth at this time, but it seemed that Sherelle was noticing the transference of unresolved anger towards her father to the taxi driver.

After the check in, with some encouragement from the group, Sherelle shared a specific memory that had emerged when the taxi driver had derided her. She recalled her father putting cockroaches into her bed as a punishment and then being forced to get into the bed. Since then, her bed had never been a place a place of sanctuary and she spoke of wishing to reclaim this space.

She decided to work with this but felt fearful that this would be disrespecting her father's memory and that he would somehow 'know' what she had done. This gave us an indication of the power that Sherelle's father had exerted over her, which made sense given the narrative of omnipotence that Sherelle had shared. There had never before been an opportunity for other minds to inform her thinking. The shock of the other group members about what he had done to Sherelle as a seven-year-old, I believe, was part of what made this work possible. We slowed down this part of the work to ensure there was space for Sherelle to notice and respond to the other group members.

Sherelle was invited to consider how she would like to work with this memory and she opted to put her father in the chair and tell him the impact that this had on her life. I invited her to consider what she might need to do this, she smiled and nodded to her Daisy Duck lip balm that she carried with her. This was a symbol of her Compassionate Other, which she had used to respond with assertiveness and anger during the week, so it had already proved to be helpful. I invited her to take the role of the lip balm and asked her lip balm what thoughts she had about what Sherelle was planning. The lip balm was of course supportive and encouraging, and said that she was proud of Sherelle turning back to this memory.

Sherelle stayed in the circle for this exercise and moved to the stage when she was ready. We set the stage with a chair to represent her father and with her lip balm in her pocket as a concrete representation of her compassionate capacity, she spoke to the empty chair and finished the exercise, turning back to her space in the group. This act symbolised for the first time Sherelle feeling able to take charge of the relationship with her father and turn her back on him and the terror he instilled in her. We also witnessed, over time, a loosening of the idealised place that he occupied in her mind.

Concluding comments

Chairwork in the context of CFGP can offer a slightly more structured approach to reworking old attachment relationships, adaptively connecting with the multiplicity of self and ultimately bringing compassionate conversations, but perhaps not all in one session!

I hope this chapter has offered some ideas for chairwork and how this can be offered in the context of safeness in a group. As has been discussed previously, I would not attempt this kind of chair work in a shorter group as we need to be able to take the time to prepare and close the sessions. In shorter programmes, there is great utility in role-taking to work with critical dialogues and develop the Compassionate Self.

The preparatory work is key to maintaining safeness in the room and we need to be able to change track and respond to the needs of the group. This all takes more time in the room and in the programme.

On to compassionate transformation part three, the final more discursive aspect of the exploratory work that I would like to share with you.

Chapter 4.5: Compassionate transformation in action Part 3 – Sharing, talking and gathering

In this final section on compassionate transformation, we will focus on the more discursive elements of the programme and the value of blending these with the action. Exploring in more detail the transferential and projective processes can be helpful, as these are necessarily part of this work. This chapter concludes with the importance of gathering in the group and closing the session.

Sometimes we just talk, and try to play

> 'Wow, that's quite difficult to answer what was best ...
> it was being a group and running for a long time and
> getting off my chest some things... The best bit was that
> I was waiting for 30 years to get that off my chest.'

Not every session involves action and explicit trauma transformation work. We also need to create space for coming together in a more discursive way, to let some of the intense sessions settle and to continue to work with and attend to the dynamics in the room. Over the years, group members have at times complained that we are not 'doing' anything in group, unless the folding chairs and scarfs are out. This often makes me smile, as there have also been complaints that we spend too *much* time out of our chairs in action and not enough time together sharing and being connected. I suppose the message here is that we will not be able to please everyone in the group every session, and perhaps we should not try to, instead maintaining attunement to ourselves and the group as a whole:

> 'The stuff that happened that was good, happened in the round
> the room stuff... Sort of open honest interaction between two
> people. Sometimes people could say stuff that you weren't
> expecting and it gets all the way through the armour and it
> was insightful positive things that can make an enormous
> difference because you don't have the time normally.'

Foukes' ideas about the role of the conductor are deeply relevant here. At the outset of such sessions, I am aware of letting the check in run longer than usual, especially after a few sessions of work in action. I might offer the group something like, 'I wonder if we need some time to talk to each other today and see where our shared connections take us?'

I will endeavour to follow Fouke's advice and support the orchestra to play as independently as possible. I will be trying to nudge the group along a little and shine a light on some of the symbolic images that the group represent. A group member recently shared that her kitchen had been 'demolished' by workers from the city council, but no one could come to install the new one. This had left her in chaos. This sharing was in the context of a strong anti-group process, with some group members feeling and acting aggressively towards the group. I summarised her story and invited the group to be curious about other situations that might feel demolished or broken. This gave rise to discussions about the connections with the struggle in the group. I added another nudge that perhaps I was the builder who hadn't come to sort out the mess. These tentative interpretations can be offered to the group to see if there is capacity to think symbolically and dissolve some of the transference. Where there is therapeutic opportunity, the group can then be invited to explore their own associations with the metaphor.

Another aspect of the discursive elements of the programme returns me to the incredible work of Wilfred Bion. At times, we will need to just listen, absorb the projections from the group, digest them and, likely at a later stage, offer back to the group something more processed and manageable. This is of course Bion's ideas of the need for containment in groups and we are also modelling to the group that difficult material can be tolerated and not ejected back into the room or ignored. I think we also need Donald's Winnicott's idea of holding, whereby the group at times may provide a shield and insulate each other from stress. This is through the offering of encouragement, positive regard and a titration of the challenges.[81] This must be adapted according to the individual needs and capacity of the group members. As the group develop their compassionate courage, strength and wisdom, more can be tolerated. This will inevitably involve ruptures when we get it wrong. But thank goodness for only needing to be 'good enough'! In these moments, we can trust the group to do the work, share the connections with each other, even in the moments when you feel like some are not connected or sharing:

> *'The thing with the group is that you think you are just going to shrink back and you are not gonna share, but it wasn't set up like that. Even the days when you found it difficult, someone else spoke your truth, somebody spoke as if it was you. That is where you got the sense of belonging when you don't feel like you've got the words but your words come out of somebody else's mouth and that is when you think oh my god we are in the same boat different circumstances, but god, yeah, I get that ... I feel that and that is when you couldn't hide behind anything even if you didn't speak or you didn't want to share.'*

---

81 Winnicott, D. W. (1991). *Playing and Reality*. Psychology Press.

The magic of compassion

This is another example of the how the group process facilitates an integral aim of the CFGP. I recall many examples of group members having what we might be called an epiphany, where they would begin to realise that they shared early traumatic experiences which had shaped them and blocked their capacity for compassion:

> *'I started feeling it* [compassion] *with them I'd get upset for other people and what had happened to them and I realised ... well, hang on, they've just said something that is really identical to you.'*

This experience of hearing the stories of others shared in the check in forms the basis of the compassionate understanding, which can gradually challenge some of the fears, blocks, resistances and contempt of compassion across all three flows:

> *'Then that is how it works, because you build compassion for the people around you because you are natural to that but that you are mirroring each other so then you end up having to develop compassion for yourself too, because you are all doing it together, very much a sense of camaraderie for us all together, joined in, and it bonded us in a way ... like I say, life-changing bond.'*

I think what is being articulated here is the flow of compassion for others, which builds gradually alongside the safeness and trust, becoming a 'vehicle' for self-compassion.

> *'You are so hyper focused on everyone else in the group instead of yourself you end up looking up direct mirrors of myself and that is how it works because you can flow compassion to the people around you because you are natural to that but then you are mirroring each other and you end up having to develop compassion for yourself.'*

This can also be reflected in the way that the group functions and communicates with each other, such as the firm but gentle challenge when a group member offers compassion to another but cannot take it back. I recall one group member stating clearly that they would not accept the offer of compassionate care if it was not accompanied by compassionate care for the self, fearlessly strong compassion in action.

Bring out the kitbag

Throughout the programme, we return regularly to the psycho-educative elements of Phase Three, subtly weaving the key messages into the material that emerges in the group process: reminding the group of their collective 'tricky brains', their overdeveloped threat systems and so on. The big posters on the wall can also be used as an aide memoire. There will also be occasions when it is helpful to be more explicit and invite the group to return to the Compassionate Mind Training to update with new learning, perhaps noticing the softening of defences.

The kitbag is a way to make this concrete, as we illustrated earlier with Sherelle's new place of belonging which had shifted from safety to safeness as the group programme unfolded. The defensive reactions to the idea of a Compassionate Other have been explored a little in Phase Three and many will dismiss this idea as childish or 'not for them'. Returning to this can allow for shifts to be made and new opportunities for exploration of the utility of a Compassionate Other. You will recall Adam's shift from the prison inmate to the PG Tips monkey!

There will have been many group-based discussions about the Compassionate Other, coupled with imagery practices, which highlight the diverse opinions and ideas within the group. Drawing on these, I will often introduce an exercise around Compassionate Heroes. This is a shift away from the cognitive conversations which can get stuck and a little binary.

I will invite someone who already has an idea of a Compassionate Other to step forward and take the role of their Compassionate Other or hero. This will by now be familiar to your group. Settle the group member into their role, paying attention to tone of voice, stance and enquire about clothing and general appearance. Ask the hero to say what is really important to them about the group member and what message they would like to give to the group member.

Then invite an auxiliary to volunteer to take the role of the hero, again taking care to replicate the posture (with guidance from the group member). The group member, in role as themselves, is invited to ask the hero for the message, which the auxiliary then delivers.

There is then an opportunity to switch roles so the group member takes the role of the hero and the auxiliary takes the role of the group member and asks for the message. As you can probably see, explaining this can become confusing, scripting it is even more so! But the point of this exercise is motivational switching from care-giving to care-receiving and back again. It also serves as a rehearsal and stimulation of the discussion for the rest for the group about the capacity to give and receive compassion that resides in us all with a little practice!

'Once upon a time...': stories and storytelling

This way of working links closely with the influence from nature-based cultures and my own English oral tradition of using stories to make sense of our experiences, as well as imparting wisdom from the past, thus offering a medium for transmission of hope and change. You may recall the reference to this in the introduction.

Storytelling is another circle-based way into making links and meaning. This has the dual function of creating and offering some emotional distance from the material, bypassing cognitive reasoning and therefore appealing to 'new brain' imaginative processes. There is also the reclaiming of a key attachment process of being read to, which will have been missing for many group members. Storytelling also offers a way into developing Compassionate Others, by drawing on ancestral history. I recently told my group the story of Boudica, the Briton queen who raised a rebellion against the Romans and, despite brutal treatment, fought for justice. This was in the context of group members feeling ashamed of their ancestry and struggling to find a 'real' Compassionate Other who they could feel connected to. An interesting discussion ensued about the nature of cruelty, the need to control and how this has shaped us. We were able to use this to draw links with their own experiences of callousness and cruelty at the hands of others and how this has shaped them. Paul Gilbert makes a helpful distinction between callousness as insensitivity to the suffering of others and cruelty as a deliberate act of harm to others. Tragically, our group members will often have experienced both within their family or close social network. Dal said with a laugh that she knew how Boudica felt, always on a mission! The story in this situation offered an opportunity to view the situation from a different perspective, bringing curiosity and openness.

We have also engaged in collective storytelling, an adaptation of the old childhood game of writing a line of a story, folding the paper and passing it on. One group member then volunteers to read the whole story out loud. The results are generally hilarious and often offer some fascinating insights into the collective unconscious material, grappling with heroes and villains, nihilism and hope. I endeavour to avoid too much interpretation with these kinds of games and playful exercises, but instead invite the group to associate with the material when we are gathering in and closing off the session.

There have been other occasions when we have taken the stories into action to explore the different roles. In response to a resounding theme in the group about powerlessness and subjugation, I told the story of Cinderella. We created a group sculpt, offering opportunities to take the role of the different characters and speak from that place.

With this exercise, we did move into action with the stage set and the whole group using the stage to take roles and play them out. For those familiar with the language and practice of dramatic art, it may look a little like an improvisation. This is another opportunity to explore under- and overdeveloped roles. Group members suggested characters for each other based on their experience of them. Dal was invited to take the role of Cinderella. The light and playful touch from the group enabled Dal to see this as a possibly overdeveloped role, stuck caring for others. Having taken up this role and played the downtrodden Cinderella, they spoke of being able to connect with the rage they felt at being forced to care for their mother. This was the first time they had been able to say any of this out loud. Dal then opted to take the role of the fairy godmother and cast some spells. We then wondered how Dal could channel their own inner fairy godmother rather than waiting for 'prince charming'. This shone a gentle light on their tendency to insist that services meet all their needs and complain when this did not happen. But this was not made explicit by us, instead nudging a little and letting the group make the links, which they did.

Love Island

There is much work and focus in the group on cultivating, maintaining cohesion and connections between the group members. We understand that the experience of safeness in the room is an essential foundation for building a new trusting attachment relationship. It is from this secure base that group members can begin to trust each other to turn back to early trauma and tragedy. This can lead to strong bonds being made between the group members.

But there is also a need to balance this with the boundaries of the group psychotherapy programme. The intensity of the psychotherapeutic process can create intimacy and positive and as well as negative transference in the group, which also needs to be managed.

In Phase Three, I introduced the rupture in the Safe Space Agreement, when Louie tried to initiate a relationship with another member of the group. During the setting of the Safe Space Agreement, it had been agreed that it would not be helpful to see each other outside of group, as members were concerned about breaches of confidentiality. I have also had concerns about the inevitable rupture to the trust in the group, coupled with the possibility of a repeat experience of untold and unexplained secrets. These toxic secrets of abuse and intrusion have been part of the attachment history for so many of our group members.

> Alana was coming towards her ending in the group and, although time and space had been given for her to consider what she might need to work on, we had felt a little pushed back. My co-facilitator and I took this to supervision and explored, by role reversing, what might be happening for Alana. On one level, beginning to withdraw and shut down in the run up to an ending felt very familiar, but there was something about this situation which we intuitively felt was different.
>
> We decided to bring it to the group and invite Alana to consider her ending and what she needed for the group. She became very tearful and told the group that she had messed up and so probably needed to leave now. The group made space for this, although Louie initially tried to interrupt, Alana was able to share with the group that she had seen Louie on several occasions outside the group. The group were invited to first bear witness to Alana's disclosure, and although some tried to interrupt and reassure her. It felt imperative for Alana to be able to say sorry to the group for what she felt was a breach of trust. A little like supporting the group to allow people to cry and be upset rather than quickly passing the tissues to avoid sitting with the distress.
>
> This was not designed to be punitive, instead understanding that guilt and the wish to make a reparation sits in our care-giving and care-receiving system. Being given an opportunity to feel this and work with the group towards a repair, was also a deeply healing experience for Alana in the context of previously unresolved ruptures. The group were invited to share their own observations and associations with the disclosure, which brought themes of secrets and lies from early life. The quote from Chapter 3.2 also demonstrates that this rupture was not fully repaired and impacted on her ending of the programme. I have had to learn this lesson over and over: the ending of the group is rarely the ending of the work. We will return to how we manage allowing and inviting the ending ruptures.

The mid-point review

Halfway through the CFTG, each group member is invited to identify a date and put it in the group diary to reflect on their journey in therapy:

> *'I spoke about it as an epiphany and it is one of those*
> *moments when you realise you've changed from that to*
> *... this, and you don't know where the middle has gone*
> *but you know it was a sudden understanding.'*

In mountaineering, we have a 'bivvy spot', which is a stopping place on the way up the mountain where we take in the view, consider the journey so far and plan for the next stage. This has usually involved an overnight stay on the mountain, where we check our gear, share anecdotes with our climbing partner about the moment you nearly dropped your shoe, or that piece of gear that wouldn't come out. This is also a space where we might share our observations of our climbing partner – 'I can't believe you managed to get a gear placement in that crack, your footwork was ace, please take up the slack on the rope a bit when I'm following you…'

These reflections and observations of the day's highlights are an essential part of the preparation for the next day's challenges. Knowing what you did well and what you narrowly missed provides the foundation to build on.

Similarly, we pause halfway through the CFTG and invite each group member to take some space to reflect on their journey so far, using the metaphor of a 'bivvy spot' and the reasoning behind it. The group members are reminded when they are halfway through and invited to put a date in the diary for their mid-point review, or mid-point reflections as we have renamed it. This never fails to instil some terror into the group. It is designed to be helpful and support a process of reflecting on the journey so far and planning for the next stage. But it is also a reminder that time is passing and there will be an ending.

The group starts in the usual way with the practice and check in. After the check in, the group member who is 'reflecting' is invited to share something of their journey so far. Some will write something, others have made images or just shared their thoughts. The group are then invited to comment and share their own thoughts and experiences of the person's journey through their eyes. This is always very moving as significant effort is put into this by all concerned. During one review session, a group member noticed that their therapy buddy, who was doing his review, had actually changed completely in appearance. They recalled how in the early days of therapy, he would sit with his head down and his arms wrapped tightly around himself, as if trying to protect himself from the others in the group. But now he sat up, looking around, engaging with the group and had much to say, and he was observably taller! This was undeniable, but to be noticed in that way seemed to bring about a further shift in his recovery.

Following this, the group member is invited to express what they need help with from the group moving forward. With some gentle encouragement, words are often put for the first time to the nature of the early tragedy, abuse and intrusion, with a commitment to return. This compassionate commitment can then be held in the mind of the group and the member is held to the work, gently but with strength.

There is only transference

I have referred to the concept of transference throughout this text to illustrate how often this will emerge in your group work and require your attention. But the topic is vast and opinions divided. I will not even attempt to offer a treatise on this topic, but instead offer some examples and ways of working. We can get tangled when the past intrudes into the present, and it will for us all. I find this concept deeply useful, but at times the way it has been described and discussed is less helpful and a little impenetrable. This may be a little controversial but I find it better to think just of transference, which can flow any way in the group, quite like compassion in that sense.

As a starting point, we all have strong feelings about people from our past that may not have been resolved or processed. This is particularly so in group psychotherapy where we are all in different ways plunged back into early familial dynamics by the nature of being a group. This deep unconscious pull is likely to be particularly strong for those who have had significant ruptured and traumatised early attachment relationships. The other important consideration is that working with transference, positive or negative, is a very normal part of the psychotherapeutic process and can bring growth and discoveries. The following case example is an illustration of the ways we can recognise and work with transferential material with the group as the catalyst for change.

Dalvinder on being triggered or connected

One of the group, Saaran, had engaged in a particularly harrowing piece of work, connected to a very early memory of sadistic abuse she had suffered at the hands of her mother. Many group members had been particularly upset by that fact that the abuse was perpetrated by her mother. Generally, it had been difficult for the group to acknowledge that mothers could be the source of trauma. This felt linked to my as yet unnamed role in the group as a mother or maternal object.

We returned to the circle to reflect on the work that Saaran had undertaken. She was visibly distressed and shaken, looking around the room for a response. Dal, who did not see any of this as their eyes were fixed on the floor, stated in a flat voice that they felt very triggered by what they had witnessed. I think they were about to say more, but my male co-facilitator jumped in uncharacteristically quickly with the suggestion that maybe they were connected to rather than triggered by what they had witnessed.

Dal looked down and then straight at Graham. They were furious, their whole body shaking. They launched into a tirade of accusations, demanding to know why Graham thought it was OK to tell them what to do and how to feel. They were *not* connected, they were triggered and they were absolutely sick of Graham imposing himself on everyone in the group and everyone was sick of it too. The strength of this reaction was completely at odds with the situation.

Dal then got up shouted a little more at Graham and left the room. This was all at the very end of the session with almost no time to close the session. Dal had left by the time I went out and there was clearly some work to be done to settle the group, and Saaran, before closing the session.

So back to supervision, and some ideas that this may have been a transference reaction, Dal's unresolved fury towards her father which they had never been permitted to express. The little that they had shared about him indicated that he was authoritarian, overbearing and often absent, not allowing any space for Dal or their needs. So we returned the next week with the idea of creating space for the rupture to be worked through. Dal also returned, unrelenting in their fury and determination to ensure that this situation was not 'brushed under the carpet'. They experienced everything Graham said as provocative, irritating and unacceptable. Graham opted to apologise for how they had experienced him, but this seemed to inflame the situation.

The resolution of this rupture was long and slow and, in the end, came from the group, who tentatively and then more assertively suggested that Graham was not really the problem. This message would not have been possible from either Graham or I… remember Bateman's idea of the interpretative hand grenade?

In the end, another group member came to Graham's aid and helpfully named how the tirade against Graham made them feel. He spoke of recalling how his mother would attack his father, bullying him into submission. The parallels with how others were experiencing Dal and how Dal had experienced Graham, made it possible to see beyond the rupture to Dal's relationship with their father.

Dal made some courageous steps into what lay behind their fury at Graham and was then able to connect with some guilty feelings. The guilt, of course, sitting in the care-giving and care-receiving system, and so brought some healing possibility for Dal. They needed to be allowed to say sorry to Graham and begin to work towards directing the anger where it belongs – at the empty chair with their dad in it.

I hope this case example illustrates how much time is needed for processing traumatic material to manage the inevitable ruptures. This was not an isolated incident and group members will often be deeply affected by the work on the 'stage'. Disentangling and reattributing the transference material is an integral but time-consuming process. The sad reality is that there is not always time or sufficient motivation to do this painful aspect of the work. I find it particularly difficult to accept that some may finish the programme still carrying around unprocessed feelings towards early attachment figures.

Who is putting what into whom?

Cynthia Rogers, whose ideas on group analysis have influenced much of my thinking, offers a playful description of projection and projective processes.[82] She suggested that projections are disowned or intolerable feelings that we all have. But within group psychotherapy, these are metaphorically thrown up in the air, unconsciously of course (rather like a tennis ball). Someone who has a valency for this particular feeling will likely end up with it, in that the disowned feeling gets introjected by the other person:

*'If split-off, disowned feelings are bouncing around
in a group someone will pick them up.'*

Those who are empathic are more susceptible to taking on those denied feelings, like those who had to internalise and identify parent's feelings in order to manage chaotic and disorganised attachment relationships. This is not something to be avoided, but if we can bring this into the language and conversation of the group, disowned feelings can be re-owned and projective processes resolved. How and when we approach transferential material and suspected projections can be tricky to navigate, and our group must be ready to receive what we have to offer.

Timing is all

Following a planned break in therapy due to my summer holiday, there had been a lively and animated discussion about mothers who had generally been abandoning, feckless and unavailable. This had been followed by some ideas that a bonfire could be created and these 'mothers' thrown onto the fire. The group concurred that this was a good way to proceed. I wondered with the group if there was any connection between the feckless mothers and my recent holiday. I was met with a startled response from the group – 'Of course not, you are the therapist'. This was followed with some fantasies about my holiday destination as a yoga retreat in Thailand (sadly, this was far from the truth).

It was clear in the response from the group that they were not yet ready to explore the maternal transference and projective processes that were likely alive in the room and the resentment they might hold towards me for leaving them. I therefore decided, as group analyst Geogory Van de Kliej suggests, to 'put it on ice', hold this idea to return to when the group were ready to explore it.[83] This occurred some

---

82 Rogers, C. (2017). 'Just don't get involved': Countertransference and the group – Engaging with the projective processes in groups. In *Introduction to Countertransference in Therapeutic Practice*. Routledge.
83 Kleij, G. V. D. (1983). *The Setting of the Group. Group Analysis*, **16**(1), 75-80. https://doi.org/10.1177/053331648301600108

months later when a group member recalled that I had suggested that I might be their mother, and on this occasion there was an agreement with the idea and that I wasn't a very good one either! It was also of note that this situation occurred in group at a time when I was facilitating alone and I found myself wondering if part of the defence related to being a sole facilitator and the precariousness of this for the group. If I go, there will be no one to hold and contain them.

The group's developing capacity to find me wanting or inadequate and to be able to express this, is an important illustration of the maturation process, although it is less than comfortable to be confronted with the disapproval, contempt and denigration of seven or eight group members. I recall a recent group in which there had been a complaint about the breathing practice being boring and repetitive. I responded with a light-hearted story about a single mum who often found herself making beans on toast for tea. The group took this up with some glee and connected up their own stories of early maternal deprivation. This brings me to the other important aspect of this: we must be able to tolerate the negative transference and remain constant. Graham Music offered me some helpful advice on this: 'Unless we can tolerate it (the pain, distress, homicidal fury), our group members cannot process and work through it'. This takes us back to Wilfred Bion, and his inspirational work on containment, that we must be able to digest what is pushed on or into us in order to support the group.

With this example and the projective processes in mind, when solo facilitate, I often feel very responsible for the group and very inadequate. With the support of supervision in action, it has been possible to identify what elements of this belong to me and what have been landed in me by the group, who will of course struggle to take up ownership of their own recovery. I would like to be sharing with you that this supervisory exploration always takes place before I have enacted the projection, but this is not the case. I have found myself on many occasions working very hard to keep the group 'happy', worrying about the idea that the therapy is failing and that it is my job to 'fix it'. With this in mind, Paul Gilbert shared an idea that has stayed with me over a decade later. I think I was likely rushing my way through supervision with lots of talk about all the 'things' I was doing. He described a dynamic whereby we have our metaphorical 'therapy toolkit' under our chairs and, when things aren't working, we assume we need to offer something else. This image stayed with me, of saying, 'Hang on, I've got something else...', rummaging under the chair for a metaphorical something, and when this is dismissed roundly by the group, we rummage again, 'I've got it this time...'. So it goes on, with the group being invited into a place of unhealthy omnipotence while we feel wretched and inadequate. This is a big part of our work, to slow down and turn back to these dynamics, with the help of supervision and personal therapy.

Managing risk

Although I am raising this issue for discussion at the end of the programme, this thread will weave through all phases and stages of this work. Your capacity to tolerate risky group members will, for some, be dictated by your organisational structure, but also pay attention to your own capacity.

As an ex-forensic social worker, I have aways been aware of having a high threshold for tolerating risk. At times too high – back to the tightrope between belligerence and tolerance. There have been many occasions when I have needed some support from supervisors and helpful colleagues in order to see that putting someone in the group who has an extremely low capacity to tolerate frustration may be dangerous.

That said, we have worked well with people who present with significant risk to themselves as well as to others. The key here is always motivation. We can support someone who is suicidal who wishes to be supported by the group. Sherelle made an attempt on her life toward the end of the programme, in response to the court decision to permanently place two of her children with her ex-partner. She was consequently admitted informally to inpatient services. The group sent letters of support and her care team arranged for her to be brought to group to maintain the contact and connection.

This was a difficult time for Sherelle, but the consistency of the programme seemed to provide a holding and containing function to enable her to grieve for and bring compassion to her loss. I am not sure this would have been possible, had the therapy stopped while she was an inpatient.

Gathering in and closing the exploratory work

Managing the impact on group members of this challenging and demanding psychotherapeutic work has required specific interventions to be made a part of the group protocol to offer a source of containment. To conclude the work in action, or when the group has been more discussive, it is important to return to the circle, as described previously, to mark the ending of the session.

Liz White offers helpful advice about having a distinction in your mind between sharing and reflecting. During the work in action, there will be an explicit invitation for sharing experiences, connections and associations. The closing of this work needs to be explicit, and we invite the group to 'gather in' for at least 15 minutes before the end of group to ensure there is sufficient time to hear from everyone. Recall the repeated message and invitation to slow down and take the time necessary to maintain safeness. This closing component of the group is an opportunity to process some of the emerging feelings, explicitly reinforce the examples of compassionate behaviours across all three flows and create a sense of affiliative connection between the group members by highlighting their shared experiences.

This will also be a space for reflections on the session and an invitation to notice what group members might still be holding. Group members often make connections with their own unresolved early tragedy and what they observed or took part in as auxiliaries. Remember the quote from earlier in this segment, that it has an impact on everyone. At this stage there will not be time to focus on this emerging material and so we will often need to explicitly 'park' what comes up, with an agreement to return to it the next week. This can be difficult, as many of the group will have little or no external sources of support available to them.

We will often invite the group to either find an object or write down anything that they have been left and are struggling with. We then have a bowl that these objects are left in. We will let the group know that we will hold what we need to return to, as another way of demonstrating that we will be holding them in mind during the week. The bowl will be left on the table and will then be on the table at the beginning of the next week to ensure that we do not lose what has been left.

Often, coming back into the room the next week, there will be a groan – 'Oh, great, the bowl is still on the table'. Understandably, many might wish that the bowl and its contents were forgotten, but it is important that we are not complicit in a survival strategy of avoidance and denial.

Many have expressed scepticism about how this could possibly make people feel any better or have any impact. But there are often surprised conversations the next week when group members report that, in a small way, they were able to leave something behind to enable them to manage. At the end of one group I was working with, which was the last session before a planned break, the group symbolically left behind something that no longer served them. One group member, who was full of arched brows and scepticism, returned after the break to share that he had put cutting his arms into the bowl and had managed not to hurt himself. He came back to this again six months later and, with some surprise, told us that he had not cut himself since that time. I wonder if there was something about the act of naming the survival strategy that he was struggling with, allowed this to stop being a secret and released him in some way, thus enabling him to enact his compassionate intention towards himself.

If, however, the level of emotional arousal has been particularly high, there may be occasions when this closing section of the group requires more active interventions. In this context, the model offers the opportunity for spontaneous play-focused activities. These games are contextualised to what is required by the group to either leave difficult unresolved feelings behind, increase the emotional energy in the room, or reduce tension in the room: 'to promote spontaneity in a culture of play and to promote trust and communication between group members'.[84]

We introduced many of these games in Phase Three, but it is important to be clear about your intention before inviting your group to embark on a game with you. A game without a clear reason or intention, and lacking a plan B, can be destabilising for everyone. Having a range of games and ending activities can then be owned by the group, and it is always a source of joy when someone requests a particular game or suggests that we might need one.

Another function of the games, as described previously, is to invite connection and cohesion in the group as a way of mitigating the loneliness and isolation of re-emerging shame-based trauma memories.

Concluding comments

Your group will sometimes need a break from all the action in and out of chairs and will need to sit, share and be together. This chapter has offered a few of the ways we can invite the discursive elements of the group process. Within this part of the programme, the extra space often allows for more transferential and projective processes to emerge and be worked with. We can explore the stories, metaphors and free association in the group. These moments can feel very precious, yet also very tense, as the group will not always be in the same place and on the same page. The extra space can also give room for old ruptures and conflicts to emerge and be worked with. At such times, the pull to smooth away and problem solve will always be strong (well, it is in me!).

Remember the ideas from Phase Three about showing your working. We can offer the group some help with this work by being clear in this phase about our intentions and inner working, for example explaining that you have decided not to go after a group member who has stormed out because you feel that running after them will not help and that sometimes we need to sit with our anger and frustration.

The final chapter in Phase Four explores the necessary attention and care that needs to be paid to the ending of the group psychotherapy programme.

---

84   Kipper, D. A. (1986). *Psychotherapy through clinical role playing*. Brunner/Mazel.

Chapter 4.6: Integration, endings and homemade brownies

Managing and working with endings in the context of group psychotherapy has been an important focus in clinical research and commentary; everyone is talking about it and for good reason. I find Yalom's words helpful in understanding how much the ending is part of the change process:

> *'Termination is more than an act signifying the end of therapy; it is an integral part of the process of therapy and, if properly understood and managed, may be an important factor in the instigation of change.'*[85]

---

85 Yalom, I., Brown, S., & Bloch, S. (1975). The written summary as a group psychotherapy technique. *Archives of General Psychiatry*, **32**(5), 605–613.

A specific protocol has therefore been developed to consolidate the Compassionate Mind Training work, integrate the affiliative experience of the group, and provide new learning about early traumatic attachment relationships, saying goodbye and allowing for a process of grieving. This final stage of the programme has a lot going on! Reminds me of the final pitches on the mountain, when you are tired, dehydrated, the light is failing, and you cannot remember why you wanted to do it in the first place! A similar sentiment is definitely present in the group as we move towards ending: 'You are kicking me out, why should I bother doing anything?'

We have explored all the phases and stages of this developmental work in some detail, and the need for a slow-paced and attuned approach is, I hope, clear. The ending is no different. We must plan for this from the outset of the programme, providing containment through clarity. Over the years, I have experimented a little with duration in response to group feedback. We started with 12 months and, following the qualitative analysis, this was extended to 18 months. For some, it will never be enough, which is likely to linked to early deprivation and is of course something to be worked with.

Over the years, I have found it helpful to offer some flexibility to end dates, in the context of unplanned group cancellations. This might seem to contradict the need for a consistency and clarity, but being responsive also feels important. Ideally, your co-facilitator will cover for you when you need to be absent, but when this is not possible, I will always offer to add extra sessions on to the end. But there will always need to be a clear plan about how these extra sessions will be used.

The diary that sits in the middle of the table holds the review and end dates. Unsurprisingly, the group will generally avoid looking at it, so we have to offer gentle and playful reminders to keep the ending live in the minds of the group. I think there is a tendency to ignore the book and therefore also ignore the prospect of ending. Reminds me of a young child who might hide from you by covering their face with their hands, 'You can't see me'.

Endings for some group members can be a reminder of the repeated experience of being let down, abandoned and forgotten by others. But like the projective processes which are triggered by planned absence we looked at in the previous chapter, these associations and connections are rarely conscious. It is, therefore, our job to hold these understandable unconscious associations with the ending and abandonment in our minds and support a process of discovery, not interpretation.

The rolling nature of the programme offers people the opportunity to witness the ending for other group members before their own. The observations of the work in action allow connections to be made and unconscious material to bubble up into conscious awareness. By the time we get to this point, many group members will have embraced the ideas of parental transference and acknowledged that they are angry, sad and frightened by the idea of ending. We will come to the value of the moving group in Phase Five, but it is important to ensure that the ending of the programme is not avoided by us, with the offer of this follow-up group space. Group members are also invited to gather their Compassionate Kitbags for the onward journey in compassion.

Jane had begun to share more of her struggle with binge eating and had expressed a commitment to treat her body with more compassion. She brought her kitbag to group and shared something new that she had added. It was a single piece of chocolate wrapped in tin foil, tied with a bow, which represented her compassionate wish to be able to enjoy a single piece of chocolate without needing to eat the whole bar and then purge. The kitbag can be used to symbolise and make concrete the compassionate commitments group members are making to themselves following the end of the group.

As some group members begin to prepare for their ending, there are a number of exercises which I feel are an important preparation to finish the programme and explicitly support the work of integration. Anyone who has attended one of my group workshops will have experienced versions of these. But there is no particular ordering for them, and it will depend on the capacity in your group.

Janus Gate

Ending wouldn't be ending, for me, without Janus Gate. This is yet another adaptation from the inspirational Liz White. This exercise is introduced with an explanation of Janus, the Roman god with two heads who represents January. One of the heads faces back, into the past, and the other forward, into the future, as January is the gateway from the old year to the new. This introductory explanation of why we call this exercise 'Janus Gate' is important, as the group need to understand where these concepts derive from. Like all work in action, an explanation of why it might be helpful to look back in the past and then forward into the future is necessary before we invite people out of their chairs. If possible, I am keen for everyone to have the opportunity to complete their own individual Janus Gate.

We need the whole room for this exercise, so instead of moving the chairs into a horseshoe, we move them all to the side. We are not deep diving into complex trauma material with this exercise, so the need for a defined stage is not so great. Two of the folding chairs are placed in the middle of the room, back-to-back, and the group member working with you is invited to step up and create their own Janus Gate. The language is, as ever, important – there is first an opportunity to look back over your time in the group and consider what you would like to leave behind, and then to move into the other chair and consider what you are taking with you, on the next stage of your journey in compassion.

There are a number of different ways that we can complete this exercise and the decision will be your individual group members. First, invite your group member to sit in the chair, look back, ask them far back they go when they sit in the chair. The answer to this question is always intuitive and different for everyone. Some will go back to early life, others will go to the beginning of the programme. Next, invite them to name three 'things' that they would like to leave behind. Encourage your group member to identify aspects of the self or unhelpful others if they get stuck (e.g. harming myself, my dad voice, despair). Being really clear that this is not an exercise in avoidance but is intended to allow the member to let go of what might be still holding them back. As your group member will be sitting on a chair, I find it best to kneel down beside them, as described previously, so that I do not stand over the group members.

They can either use objects or people to represent these three things, or a mix of both. Generally, I find that the group members who have observed others previously will opt for people. The auxiliary role is again to hold the place of the part of self or other. The member then sculpts the auxiliary so that they represent the object or person in question, either by demonstrating the body posture and words, or by telling. Then they move on to the next of the three, being mindful that our auxiliaries are not stuck holding an uncomfortable body posture while we go through the process. Invite the auxiliary to relax and then return to the posture when everyone is ready. Then the member who is still sitting in their chair looking back identifies each element and the auxiliary holds the posture and says the words. Invite the group member to have a last look at what they are leaving and take a few steps away, symbolically, to sit in the chair facing forwards. The auxiliaries can again relax.

The invitation here is to look into the future, again choosing how far to look forward, and then name three things that they are taking with them, noting the emphasis, 'What are you taking with you?' Group members will often choose to look a few months beyond the end of therapy and will identify various qualities of compassion that they know they will need on the next 'leg' of the journey. Invariably, the group feature as well. During one such exercise, a group member insisted on taking everyone with them. It got pretty crowded with seven people huddled together trying to make contact with the member who was taking a few symbolic steps forward with everyone!

As before the group member either selects objects or people to represent what they are taking with them. Objects that are selected, usually from the table, are placed on the floor in front of the member. After the selection, the member is invited to notice which aspect of self or other they are most drawn to, and then we complete a role-taking exercise to strengthen the associations with quality. The final stage of this process will be asking for a message from the compassionate quality.

If the member selects people rather than objects, then, as before, they are sculpted and given messages, usually of hope. One of my favourite memories of this exercise was on a hot sunny afternoon as Louie was coming towards the end of his time in the group. He had been reluctant to even consider Janus Gate as he had 'nothing' to leave behind or take with him. The group challenged him on this, and almost insisted. He grudgingly agreed to do Janus Gate as long as we could do it outside in the garden of the therapy space. So we moved all our chairs our into the garden and recreated the therapeutic space on the lawn (this was not the first time, nor will it be the last, that group members have requested to decamp outside).

Louie unsurprisingly left behind the haunting memory of his father's violence but took the young Louie who had needed more care than he had been given. When we moved forward to what he was taking with him, he got a bit stuck and uncharacteristically awkward. We slowed things down and he was able to say that one older male group member had been instrumental in his journey towards accepting himself and seeing the value in caring and being cared for. This group member volunteered to come and hold the place of himself and was joined by two other male group members who represented courage and wisdom. At the final stage of the exercise, where Louie took a few symbolic steps into the future, he opted to walk making a connection with each of the three members. So the four of them walked down the garden holding hands. Louie had started the programme trapped with only aggression in his threat system and no capacity to give or receive care. The memory of this stays with me nearly ten years later. This is indeed the affiliative 'super' power of the group, to dissolve old transference wounds and allow for new ways of relating to develop with the self and others.

The exercise is also very useful for shorter, closed groups. The exercise can be offered in the ways described above, but when the whole group are completing together, it is possible to do a whole group Janus Gate. The group will work together, taking up the standing space looking back and then forward and deciding on three things they are leaving and taking. These are helpfully represented with objects as everyone is in the action and there no auxiliaries to support!

On the one hand, this exercise offers much therapeutic opportunity for movement, as well as beginning to play with the idea that troubling experiences and survival strategies can be put down and we can 'switch' into a different mindset or mentality. I think it also makes explicit the journey that has been travelled and the changes that may at times be obscured from the individual group member:

> 'A big change was being able to look at people in the group, yeah, and being able to talk to people, and I could see these changes in others as well seeing people change. I could see that and that gives you a lot of hope.'

Back to the chairs!

Many group members will return to the chair work from earlier sessions, sometimes following the realisations that change has occurred. This can come with the group process, with moments of connection and a new understanding coming from the review process.

> 'It bears fruit ... you know, if you are prepared to keep turning up and keep being honest there is a good chance of getting something ... noticeable out of it... Almost all of the people who stuck it out ... who were there and started when I started, they all changed a lot ... some of them perhaps didn't realise ... that they had changed as much as they had but we see them from outside ... see the ways that they talk and behave each week and then they concede that there's a progression.'

This offers an opportunity to bring the strengthened compassionate perspective and to notice changes. At this stage, group members often are more able to complete a dialogue with the critic.

> ### Jane's final chat with the critic
>
> Jane had struggled to turn back towards her critic, always feeling that 'it' was too powerful and she has nothing to offer. She had been able to put her critic in the chair and, with some help from the group, invite this part of her to see the changes she was trying to make. The critic would often tell her that she was lonely and sad, and that nothing would ever change as she was not strong enough.
>
> A few sessions before the end of the programme, she asked to put her critic in the chair again as she felt a little more ready to dialogue. I wonder if 18 months in a group of caring and Supportive Others enabled the internal switching from critical to compassionate as part of a mirroring process.
>
> She set out the chairs, this time next to each other, and she smiled at herself and noticed it was different from before, when the chairs had been distanced and opposite

each other. She sat first in the chair of the critic and noticed immediately the sinking feeling and dread about the end of the programme. The critic (through Jane) said that she wouldn't manage and would shrink back to who she was before. It was pointless to hope for anything better than this. The final message was to 'accept the reality, it is easier this way'.

Jane stepped out of the chair and immediately shook her head. She stood up straight and instinctively I offered no direction or guidance, I didn't need to. She pulled up the chair even closer to the chair of the critic and sat down, leaning in conspiratorially. Her voice was much clearer than I had heard before, and she smiled at her critic and said:

> 'Look here, it is time to take off the training wheels. I know you think you are helping me and there was a time in my life when you did. I wouldn't have survived without you. But I have grown and changed and the world you are trying to protect me from doesn't exist. I want to have a turn at running things. I am not going to get rid of you... Just give me a go!'

She turned back towards the group who had burst into spontaneous applause. I had to hold the urge to do the same myself. We were all moved to tears, it was so unexpected, but she found herself exactly where she needed to be. The scene was light and playful, her manner as if trying to coax a sulky child. She decided to switch back into the critic chair and hear the message from her auxiliary, the response from the critic was quiet and young but she had not bullied her critic into submission, she had coaxed her critic to join the team! Later, in the reflecting part of the session, Jane said with a smile that one of the first jobs for her newly appointed compassionate leader was to 'have a bit of a tidy up'. This was one of the first times that Jane was able to share that she struggles with hoarding but could see how her Compassionate Self might be able to make some changes.

With the notion of creating a team in mind, I hold a hope that group members can begin to integrate their multiple selves, as Jane was attempting to with her critic, with the Compassionate Self in charge. Dal had understandably really struggled with the idea that a battle for supremacy with your multiple selves is ill-advised. We described earlier the importance of developing an understanding of the critic and not domination. Dal had survived by starting fights with everyone, vexatious complaints to housing, social care, mental health and any providers they perceived was falling short. In group, we had also been accused of disrespected their gender identity and not meeting their needs. They would often step in and light small fires of antagonism in the group, with the expressed intention of supporting others in the only way they knew how. It was a long and carefully trodden road to support Dal to turn back to the anguish of having no one having their corner in childhood, and the perpetual fighting actually kept this pain alive as well as transferring the angst to others.

So we all worked hard with Dal to invite them down from their 'high horse' and stop 'riding off into battle'. We created a light-hearted metaphor about fighting injustice, which served as one of those shortcuts I have mentioned to bring the group together in their thinking. Someone would say, 'Dal are up on that high horse again, riding off to battle?' On a good day, this would raise a smile of acknowledgement and change of tack. On a not-so-good day, when their capacity to feel the intention of the group was diminished, there would be a scathing reaction and accusation of 'Shutting me down… again'.

Dal had worked hard in the group, with ruptures and repair with facilitators and group members, and this seems to have one of Dal's mediums for beginning to tolerate the unbearable feelings of loss and grief. They worked with the overdeveloped 'fighter' and the emerging 'feeler'.

This was another spontaneous moment in group which had not been part of a planned piece of work. Dal was recounting a dream about themself as a small child surrounded by all these people they didn't really know. The group were curious with Dal and they began to connect the dream with the experience of their multiple selves. They then described an image that they had been working on which involved a large table with a white tablecloth. Dal has imagined their Compassionate Self sitting at the head of the table with their multiple selves sat around, their Compassionate Self was pouring the tea and generally keeping everyone in check. Their intention was to ensure that everyone at the table had their say but that no one could dominate or bully the others.

This is, I think, a great example of integration, which had arisen spontaneously from the months of differentiation and transformation work to enable Dal to develop their Compassionate Self to stop the fight and not incite it!

There are so many ways to capture the change and integration process in action, but the value of letter writing is a way of creating permanent and undeniable 'evidence'. I have often struggled to support groups to engage in letter writing. One of the issues that I think can emerge is the impact that a blank sheet of A4 can have on a person's threat system. So we started with A5 postcards, hoping that members would run out of space and need more paper, which is often what happens.

It is generally helpful to offer some guidance with the letters and to begin the exercise with a compassionate evocation imagery practice. Some group members might get started by taking the role of something from their Compassionate Kitbag or their Compassionate Other. The interview process, as described in Phase Three and earlier in this phase, is designed to elicit a compassionate perspective at the outset.

Sherelle's letter to her young self

Sherelle had struggled with her literacy throughout her life, having not completed her schooling, and had over time been able to share this with the group. She had generally avoided any activities where there was an opportunity to use written words to describe her experience. Towards the end of her time in the group, she asked for some help from the group to write a letter from her Compassionate Self to her young self to acknowledge her suffering. Again, this was part of a long process of conversations with her young self and compassionate transformation of early toxic messages from her parents and staff in the care system.

Sherelle had reached a point in her journey where she had moments of connection with the terror of her early life and some sympathy for her young self. This was, of course, fleeting.

She worked with the group to write the letter, asking how to spell the words she wanted to use and checking the meaning of other words. What emerged was a deeply thoughtful, compassionate and courageous letter to her young self, telling her that she would be there for her always and that none of it was her fault. She opted to read this letter out loud to the group and, of course, to herself. She took the letter away with a commitment to continue with her journey in learning to read and write.

Others will put the young self in the chair to read the letter and perhaps then shift into the chair and hear the letter. Auxiliaries can help to read the letter and hold the place of the adult self and child self as needed.

The ending process can also have all three aspects of differentiation, transformation and integration in one place, where group members are noticing the multiplicity of self and able to make spontaneous changes.

Dalvinder and the transformed glass

We invited the group to wander in the garden and in the therapy room to find something that resonated and connected with their Compassionate Self. Dal found the exercise quite confusing and was initially reluctant to take part, asking why an object would help. With some support from the group, they returned to the sharing space with a dirty piece of broken glass and stated that this was them. I have to admit that I had an inner sigh, as there were many times that I felt Dal's antagonism in the group could disrupt the other's willingness to be vulnerable.

We tried to make some space to explore this further but Dal was resolute and insistent that they would be taking the glass home. I worried about this and invited them to leave it with us. But they returned the next week with the same piece of glass polished with a little smiley face etched into it. Unbeknownst to us, Dal

> polished glass as a hobby! They told us that they had felt dirty, broken and discarded like the glass, but they transformed the glass just like they had been transformed by their time in therapy. Sometimes we need to trust our group members' wisdom and support them to be in the driving seat. I have to tell myself this very often! Cynthia Rogers speaks of trying not to get 'lost in the control' of the group.

With other ways of transforming meaning in mind, we work a lot with metaphor and stories as a way of shifting stuck perspectives. Over and over in group, members will casually describe themselves as broken. These are old messages that are reinforced by being diagnosed with various 'disorders' but invariably not being offered treatment, by repeated 'failed' relationships, and by the pervasive experience of being judged and categorised. We can tell people that we see them through a different lens and the group works really hard to offer new affirming messages to each other. But maybe we need to listen to the subjective experience, tolerate the discomfort and meet our group members where they are.

A metaphor I often turn to and share with the group is the Japanese art of Kinsugi. Broken Japanese pottery is repaired with liquid gold, which serves two functions. Rather than attempting to hide and disguise the damage, the liquid gold emphasises and turns the damage into something of beauty. Secondly, the new pots being imbued with gold are now stronger than the original pots would have been. This is such a good fit for those who feel defective and less than others. We can think of the group process as like the art of Kinsugi – we repair the experience of brokenness and create new and stronger attachment relationships.

I have offered a few of the individually orientated ending exercises but would like to turn to one of my all-time favourites which is the Compassion Shop Game. You may recall this was referenced in Phase Three.

Opening the compassion shop

We return and reopen the shop at various points in the programme, which supports the group to see what has changed for them. As part of the ending, we support the group to take what they need to move forward towards individuation.

The process of stepping forward with what is needed and inviting others to invest objects with compassionate qualities continues until everyone has requested and received what they need from the group, and gifted the extra qualities. This exercise is always filled with laughter and a deep sense of connection and cohesion:

> *'Instead of being in a situation where no one understands, you know the experiences we went though weren't everyday experiences. Other people will try and understand and be compassionate but they don't really get it. It's no fault of theirs but they haven't experienced it, but you are put in a therapy group with people who have experience it. It is life changing – before, you are on your own taking the whole world on, then here's a group with people who are the same. I went from feeling like I was all on my own to we were all like a bunch of warriors – we have been through it and come out the other side.'*

That said, the ending of a group is not always joyful and full of hope, and there are many who, for reasons too many to list, stop coming and drop out of therapy.

Those who cannot manage goodbyes

Over the ten years of running CFGP, our dropout rate has remained reassuringly low, at 20%. As I described previously, most dropout during the PEG and some cannot manage the transition into CFTG. But there will be occasions when unresolved ruptures, the intensity of the work and other unpredictable life events lead to people dropping out. I have always tried to be proactive in such situations and meet with the person as soon as possible and see if there is a solution to be found. Often, being held in mind, some individual attention and some flexibility is sufficient to support a return. For those who cannot return even to say goodbye, there is always work to be done with the group to support an ending and closure.

Once it is clear that someone has left the programme, we will take the chair out, but there have been times when I have used a folding chair to invite the responses and reactions to the loss of a group member or facilitator. Post-It notes can be used to give voice to anger, sadness, shame, doubt, grief and anything else that may be holding up the group's capacity to move on from the unplanned ending, giving the group permission and maybe a nudge here and there to express strong feelings about someone who has left.

There are also those who check out before the end but keep coming back. The journey in compassion-focused group psychotherapy has been set in a slightly arbitrary manner and there will be those who complete the programme but do not reach the point of integration as illustrated above. I have not yet worked out whether it is better to invite someone to say goodbye at the point that this becomes clear, or to 'ride it out' and hope. It is of course not a precise science, and I recall situations when my desire to keep everyone in the group has overshadowed intuitive wisdom that it was time for someone to acknowledge that they had come as far as they could and to leave. Equally, I recall grappling with my own wish, which was part mine and part group projection, to keep someone in the programme. But I invited this person to give herself permission to stop coming and she did, and I know it was the right decision. Honestly, though, I missed her even though I knew she had been showing up for us and not herself. Leaning in and tolerating the resentment of group members who are not where they wish to be, will never sit easily with me, but it is a work in progress.

The leaver's book

When I think about the big, brown ring-bound book that sits on the table, surrounded by pebbles, buttons and beanbags, the idea of cave paintings comes to mind. Being held in mind, preserving history and learning for the future.

The pictures, messages, song lyrics and affirmations that have filled this book over the last ten years have served all of these functions and more. The presence of the book reminds the group that the end will come, but that there is help and advice along the way. There are stories of struggle, humour, transformation and integration contained in the pages. There is so much wisdom in one book that has been looked at, written in, avoided for over ten years. From the very beginning of the programme, I have wanted departing group members to be able to leave something behind to be remembered by, and for those left behind to take comfort and hope from the offering. This is one of my many favourites:

> *'Maybe the journey isn't about becoming anything. Maybe it is about unbecoming everything that isn't you so you can be who you were meant to be in the first place'*

The idea of the book reminds me of El Potrero Chico, a mountain range in Northern Mexico where there are books at the top of the mountains for everyone to write in. These books are wrapped in plastic to protect them from the elements, and when I first saw one of these I immediately thought it was a like a flag to stick in the rock, to exclaim 'I've done it'. The book contains messages of hope and exhilaration in so many different languages, and writing in the book means that your journey will be remembered in some way. Only, often when you get there, you are so dehydrated and exhausted with the gruelling descent ahead of you, there may be little inspiration. This is another reason all the good stuff happens while you are doing the climbing or the compassion!

The final group

The ending group process involves the integration of the therapy experience and tolerating the internalising of the care and understanding from the other members of the group, acknowledging and practising compassion for the self as the movement towards ending and individuation from the group. This involves a process of grieving for the loss, acknowledging the impact of the therapeutic process, and planning for the future. It is anticipated that this therapeutic intervention will redress the experience of shame-based trauma and self-criticism, and improve general symptoms and activities of daily living.

Over time, a group-based ritual has emerged that most group members have opted to take part in, which can create a sense of safeness and predictability around the ending stage of the group. The group member who is leaving chooses a cake or sweet treat that is then prepared by the facilitator. This is intended to provide an experience that will repair the marking significant events, in that many group members will have had the experience of birthdays and special occasions either being ignored or marred by trauma. I started this up by chance one Christmas, when I mentioned how much I love baking. This prompted a challenge from the group to bring them cakes on the last session before the Christmas break. The Christmas brownies were a hit, and we decided collectively to shift this ritual to the ending.

The group starts in the usual way, with the breathe and check in, maintaining consistency for the group. We facilitators will then take the orders and go and prepare drinks for everyone, which offers a further opportunity for an explicit change of role linked to individuation. My hope is that this, while inviting a parental transference on one level and providing tea and cakes on another level, invites the process of individuating. We are celebrating the 'graduation' from the programme and inviting the members who are leaving to begin to connect with us in a different way, hopefully dissolving some transference.

I have made gluten-free rainbow layer cakes, Oreo cookies, vegan red velvet cakes and many more, and the importance and significance of this has never been lost on me. It always raises a smile for me that the request for drinks and sweet treats will always be present, but as I said in Phase Three, we have to wait until the end for this. Then we all sit together and write the postcards, and look over the book, sharing quotes or affirmations from its pages. The room gets pretty messy, with cake and tea bags strewn over the little table, people sitting on the floor resting postcards and cups of tea precariously on their knees. In such moments, I am conscious of sharing a little more of myself, again to dissolve the transference and to bring some lightness to the ending. This stance can then invite more questions – do you have children? Why do you do this work? How old are you actually? And on it goes. We will have to choose judiciously how many of these questions we answer, but, turning back to Yalom, if it is in the service of the group and comfortable with us, then it can help with this ending. A group member recalled recently that I had shared that I hosted a BBQ and everyone had dumped their children with me and left! She brought this in response to another group member's fantasy about my perfect life.

> **Adam's gloves are finally off!**
>
> From the beginning, Adam struggled with the fear of contamination, often coming in wearing gloves, hat, scarf and a large coat, which he kept on throughout the session. This was accepted by the group, and over time he worked to relax some of his defences against belonging and true membership of the group. He was also suffering with a deep-seated self-hatred that resulted in starving himself and pulling out the hair in his beard. As someone who had restarted the group and essentially ended up having a longer group experience, he had witnessed many endings. He had always refused drinks or cake graciously but with deep conviction.
>
> Adam's ending felt very mixed. It had been such a journey for him to complete and although the changes were visible and clear, there remained much work to be done. I had assumed that he would refuse, as before, and prior to the ending group he had opted not to choose a cake. But when we began taking drinks orders, Adam asked if he could have a cup of tea – two teabags, four sugars, and please could I rinse the cup in boiling water first. I nearly fell over as he took off his coat, hat, scarf and gloves and took a piece of cake that was offered.
>
>> 'I realised after the group … that's how I know it was helping because it wasn't me forcing myself to do that it was just happening … something was just happening I'd just decided to take my gloves off one day and it was just that simple… I decided to start looking at people when they were looking at me.'
>
> The ending for Adam marked a shift in his capacity to tolerate and acknowledge his membership of the group. I wondered about Adam beginning to tolerate being seen in the group, having worked so much with the self-hating image of himself that he had been stuck with so long. This was part of a gradual shift in sharing more and talking to other members of the group.

The giving of gifts

A gift-giving exercise follows, in that the members who are leaving write a message for the group which is contained in a book and each remaining member will write to the person leaving with a message of encouragement and compassion for the next stage of their journey. These cards are given to the member leaving, who is invited to either read them, have them read by the group members or to take them away from the group. As facilitators, we also write a message for the members who are leaving.

These rituals have so many layers of significance for the group and seemingly no one is immune, despite the protestations and derision. During our recent seven-year follow-up study, a few graduates shared with me that they still have their postcards and transitional objects gifted by the group during the programme.

Many group members over the years have bought gifts for everyone. I have a beautiful array of hand-crafted cards, moulded statutes, books and so much more. I believe it is imperative that we accept these tokens and allow the group members to say thank you and express gratitude.

Louie and the gift of Rosa

Louie arrived for his final group session with a large and ominous looking bundle of tissues, which he carefully placed on the table in the middle of the room, and, with a smile, took his chair in the circle. During his check in, he spoke with some emotion of his recollection of the earlier need to pull his chair into the middle of the room and how hard it had been to tolerate being part of the group. He put his head down and, in a quiet voice, said what he had always needed was a family. He then stormed out into the garden and the group continued, allowing him space to calm down. He rejoined the group and was acknowledged with a nod from a few group members. Over the long months during which the group had been closed (where no new members join or leave), the members had developed an intimate understanding of each other and how and when to bring compassion to each other.

Towards the end of the check in, another group member asked Louie what he had in the tissues and whether we were going to get to see it. Louie leaned forward and unwrapped the tissues to reveal a tarantula spider skin, completely intact (Appendix 4.5, for anyone who wants to see it!). This was the skin of Rosa, Louie's tarantula who had recently shed. Louie gifted the skin to us, as it was a metaphor for his experience in the group. He spoke of having slowly over time shed his skin, just like Rosa, and like Rosa, after shedding he had been raw, exposed and vulnerable.

For some weeks after Rosa had shed, she would hide in her log and hiss if anyone came near. As tarantula shed everything and are completely raw. Louie spoke of 'shedding' his old skin, which had been keeping others away with violence and intimidation. But once he had begun to turn back and understand himself, he could not reverse back into the old skin. The vulnerability for Louie came from the new skin of compassion, which took some time to grow and develop. He ended his time in the programme with a simple gift for the group and a demonstration of what was possible with a new compassionate skin: 'it was the first time I have ever felt sad without being angry and that was because I felt safe'.

At the end of this final session, which must end on time, there is often a lot of shuffling chairs and slow packing of coats and bags. Many seem reluctant to leave the space, which of course is understandable. Others will take their postcards and be gone before we have said goodbye! For those who linger, over the years I have tried to work out a way to make myself available if people want to make a physical connection with me, usually a hug. I would never offer it, so there have been many awkward moments where a graduate steps forward and then back and I might open my hands to signal that it is OK to approach. This must be a personal choice and something that we feel comfortable with.

Concluding comments

Time spent planning, preparing and supporting the group with the ending is an integral part of the psychotherapeutic process, and it can become the springboard for the next stage of the journey in compassion. We sit and talk about everyone's feelings about the ending, the associations that this brings, and we take the work into action to create meaning from symbols. The group members are key to this, as the work of Judith Herman clearly articulates:

> *'Recovery can take place only within the context of relationships; it cannot occur in isolation.'*[86]

The group bears witness to and supports the capacity to grieve and feel sorry for the loss of what is deeply valued. I will often remind the group that the sadness is linked to how important this has been:

> *'I lost a lot of hope with the ending... It ended... That was worst for me ... (tearful) that's it really, sometimes I could say it was the worst but that's only because it was emotionally difficult so it wasn't the worst it was just that I was in a bad place.'*

In this programme, there is an explicit invitation for grief, sadness, anger, joy and celebration. It is noteworthy that this next quote is from the same group member who expressed the previous sentiment. The group needs to be able to hold both the sorrow and the joy:

---

[86] Herman, J. L. (1998). Recovery from psychological trauma. *Psychiatry and Clinical Neurosciences*, **52**(S1), S98–S103. https://doi.org/10.1046/j.1440-1819.1998.0520s5S145.x

> *'It's changed my life really, even though its small,*
> *it's still changed my life... I'm a different person*
> *now for the good... So I think it's essential ...*
> *it's the best thing I've ever done in that sense.'*

I wonder if the length and intensity of the programme can support group members to internalise the safe haven, secure base and proximity seeking capacity and move forward towards individuation. It always makes me smile when I hear someone say, 'I imagined what the group would say and it helped'. I feel that this quote articulates this process well:

> *'I still have bad days, but they are not as bad as they used*
> *to be because still in the back of my head there is a thought,*
> *what would the group say? it's a constant thing then because*
> *you do bond in a way that, you know, I spent a year with*
> *[them]. I felt like I knew them really well but I couldn't tell*
> *you what they did for a job or their names because it wasn't*
> *focused on that superficial stuff. Well, I know that person*
> *because we bonded over things that were very intimate and*
> *personal and it made a bond that is unbreakable and lives in*
> *my mind and it is very deep seated.'*

This seems to sum up the shift from a position of defence and being closed off to others, like Adam, with his gloves, hat and scarf, to being able to allow others to support the process of differentiation, transformation and integration:

> *'You think you are strong for keeping up all the barriers. I used*
> *to think I was strong for keeping up the barriers, but then you*
> *go through this and you realise how strong I was for taking the*
> *barriers down and then do what you needed to do... Oh yes, it*
> *takes true strength to let the barriers down, it really does.'*

Phase Five:
The Moving On Group

Programme element	Format	Function
5. The Moving On Group Individuation	■ 12 monthly one-hour drop-in sessions ■ Patients not discharged if they do not attend ■ Facilitated by Lived Experience Practitioner (a service user who has completed the CFGP) and a psychotherapist ■ Slow-paced group that is member led	■ Supporting the gradual process of individuation ■ Enabling the grieving process to be resolved ■ Providing a platform for patients to engage in peer led support

Chapter 5.1: Moving on

'The maintenance group is to help us strengthen what we have learned in the group and to help each other.'

We are nearly there in so many different ways. The original programme ends after 12 months with a post-therapy, six-week follow-up session with one of the facilitators, and then discharge either back to GP or secondary care team if they were still involved. This never sat quite right with me; we spent months encouraging a healthy dependence and attachment to the group and at the end say goodbye and discharge them. This felt like a severing of the connections we had spent a long time developing. Our early graduates from the programme let us know that they felt that same way:

> *'I lost a lot of hope with the ending... It ended...
> That's what was worst for me... (tearful) That's it, really,
> sometimes I could say it was the worst but that's only
> because it was emotionally difficult so it wasn't the
> worst it was just that I was in a bad place.'*

> *'...because even if you feel ready to finish, even if you feel
> ready to leave... those first couple of weeks after the end of
> the programme when your family has been taken away...
> really painful... I was in pieces the first week after, and
> I hadn't expected to be ... because I was excited ...
> yes, I've done it I've finished ... I was really proud, and
> I could feel the benefits ... but that first Friday when I
> didn't have that group I felt left... I felt lost...'*

These quotes are representative of much of the anecdotal and formal feedback that we received from the programme graduates. They told us that the ending was too abrupt, like having a door shut behind you as you leave. This was in spite of the extensive work that had gone into planning the ending, supporting future planning and marking the ending with rituals and play.

So we listened carefully to the feedback from the group, also taking into account that many will never feel ready to let go whatever is offered.

One of our graduates went on to make some suggestions about what sort of support could be offered:

> *'Something less formal, not necessarily run by the therapists ...
> something slightly structured, perhaps you turned up at a rented
> space rather than having to meet in a coffee shop where we can't
> always talk privately ... erm, and sometimes people do wanna
> share private stuff that's going on. I think some kind of informal
> group maybe once a fortnight or once a month, where people feel
> like they can go and connect and perhaps meditate for a short
> time... I think it would be a huge advantage.'*

This advice, coupled with the seeming keenness many folks seem to have about maintaining contact with members of their group got me thinking about what might be possible. Having worked in a therapeutic community for a number of years, I was reminded of the post-therapy support group that was made available to those who had completed the programme. I did a bit of reading around and found very little research evaluating the efficacy of such offers. It was therefore a leap of faith for all concerned to get started. But start we did.

When I reflect on the journey that we have had with the Moving On Group (or MOG), my mind goes to the 'Matrix' trilogy, particularly the last film. For those not familiar with the film, 'The Matrix' takes place in a digital world generated by Artificial Intelligence who use humans as glorified batteries (this bit is not so relevant!). Over time, multiple versions of the matrix were created and failed. One version exerted too much control, another not enough control, and so on.

So, we started with the Three Circles Group, an FB page and a room in a local community centre. Our service funded the room, and the rest was left to the group. This may have been the version which left people a little directionless and lost. Group members were given the contact details for one of the graduates who would add people if they made contact. But this left all the responsibility with one person. At first it seemed ideal, a fully service-user-led initiative, where we supported silently from the sidelines. We were occasionally invited to attend the group as guests, which felt like a positive dissolving of the transference and a testimony to the group moving on.

But over time, the weight on one person holding the group proved too much. Sadly, I think that they found themselves on the receiving end of paternal transferences and the group projected all their grown up authority into this one person. Consequently, they struggled, feeling overly responsible while also burdened and resentful.

So, we ushered in version two, a slight downgrade from the first group, and the meetings took place in a less formal setting. The group remained independent and arranged to meet and chat in a coffee shop. I understand that this group was no longer coordinated and chaired as it had been in the past. The coffee shop meetings migrated to the pub and things may have taken a turn for the worse at this point. This group soon folded, and we were left thinking again about what might be needed.

The Moving On Group

All this learning led us to develop a new post-programme support group. We wondered if the group needed more containment in the early stages and our graduates, who we consulted, agreed. You will remember in Phase Two that I shared the journey and thinking behind the role of Lived Experience Practitioners in CFGP. Sarah has been instrumental in the set up and holding of MOG. She meets group members 'on the other side' who will have been in the Waiting List Group with her two years earlier. Seeing Sarah often offers the opportunity to reflect on the journey and process of change. Sarah can also notice the differences, which can be deeply helpful after a long absence.

Sarah again takes a front seat with this group, and I am in the back... We have worked together for a number of years now, holding the space and navigating the pull on me to get back into the therapist's chair! I described my hard work in the Phase Two Waiting List Group to avoid the pull to start the therapeutic work before the group members had joined CFGP. But this was nothing compared to working with graduates who are making a transition from healthy dependency and significant maternal transference into life after CFGP. As always, it is a mixed bag; many are ready to move towards individuation and are very interested in conversing with Sarah about how she has managed various aspects of the ending.

For understandable reasons, there are others who can not even tolerate eye contact with Sarah and would only communicate with me. You will recall in the last chapter that some group members do not feel ready to graduate from CFGP and so the MOG can feel like a negation of their grief, although we work hard to dissolve the transference and keep the focus light and informal. For those wishing to get a little more therapy, I think the change is a little jarring and perhaps Sarah can end up on the receiving end of some of the envious projections. Of course, all deeply unconscious, but Sarah often picks up a sense that some group members are angry about the shift but cannot express this with me, so Sarah gets it. It is of course indisputable that we convene the group together, invite the graduates into our space and, at the end of the group, they must leave us.

Observing this dynamic, a memory from early childhood comes into my mind. My brother, as the older sibling in a single parent family, was often invited to help my mother with the financial matters and other 'grown up stuff'. I recall boiling with rage at the feeling of exclusion. I wonder if something of this can get enacted for some in the MOG. Sarah is a co-facilitator but also someone who has previously been a group member, so she has inhabited both camps. There is always much work to be done in our joint supervision sessions, to untangle the projections and find ways to respond with courage, wisdom and gentleness. We keep our supportive and containing supervisor very busy!

The structure of the group

We are learning as we go along about how to manage the boundaries of this group. We have always found it more helpful to be in a different building, or at least a different room from the group room. The pull back into therapeutic work is so much stronger in the familiar setting.

The group is offered face to face, for an hour a month. Deliberately offering a sub-therapeutic dose, i.e. much shorter in duration and frequency. The tea and biscuits are again designed to create an informal, social atmosphere. Interestingly, I cannot recall a single occasion when a graduate has accepted a drink or a biscuit in this group. I could fill pages with ideas about what this means, but I do wonder about the links with the previous section about how hard it is to individuate and take up a different space. Sarah wonders if we have successfully inured the group about not having food or drinks in the therapeutic space, so shifting this boundary is tricky.

Sarah and I were in those early sessions very excited to support the group to move on and had this great idea that we could all set out the chairs together. I am recalling this with a smile because of what an epic failure it was! It was perhaps too soon to insist on this much individuation. So, holding the space for this group means boiling the kettle, setting out the chairs, sending out the reminders with the same attention to detail that we have discussed previously in the section on dynamic administration.

We have remained steadfast on the structure – or lack of structure – of the group. We are not leading from the front, and I am definitely trying to blend into the wallpaper! We make it clear at the outset that we are holding the space and how they choose to fill it is for the group to decide. This has of course been challenging, graduating from a programme with a clearly defined and containing structure. But this is the point of this group, to allow the graduates, with Sarah's guidance, to take the reins of what comes next.

I am very conscious of developing the role, and I start with the ending session from CFGP, making tea and cake. I am attempting to dissolve more of the maternal transference but give a bit more 'behind the scenes' information. Carefully, I might share something of a low-level error that I made with the group planning or, more generally, I share a little more of myself. I am still following Yalom's advice that it needs to be in the service of the group.

There have been many MOG sessions where the graduates have picked up the mantle of their collective authority and supported each other with difficult decisions, losses, triumphs and joy. I recall one group in which everyone opted to sit outside as the weather was very warm. Sarah and I followed the group outside and put the chairs in a circle in the garden space, smiling at their autonomy and growth.

Covid

I think I might have said that I wouldn't mention Covid, but Covid changed our Moving On Group for quite some time. A number of group members completed the programme the day before lockdown. I was deeply worried for them and even considered inviting them back to our online CFGP but was persuaded by my supervisor that this may not be wise. So we started an online MOG. My hope was that it offered a lifeline, and there were many deeply emotional moments in that group as we all grappled with the not-so-brave new world. As lockdown rolled on, we decided to make the MOG open ended to respect the unique challenges facing graduates of CFGP. My inner jury are still out deliberating whether this was a good idea, but it seemed like the right thing to do at the time. Covid restrictions receded a little and we moved back into the room, but with masks and social distancing. It somehow didn't feel like the right time. In retrospect, I think I got caught up in something of an omnipotent projective process – it felt really pleasing to be able to offer the group indefinitely and honestly, and I enjoyed the favourable comparisons with other services. I think this may have blinded me to the need to review this open-ended offer. I believe that this may have exacerbated the struggle that some graduates have experienced in letting go of the group. The group has reduced to one member a few times over the years, and we have had to take the decision to close the group, which has caused ruptures and disappointment. On to version three, which is still a work in progress.

Version 3

This is a very new iteration of the MOG and it is currently under construction. I am mindful of not imagining that this is going to be the golden ticket. This may be helpful for some, while others may understandably struggle. We have often wondered whether Sarah taking a more explicitly active role could support with some of the individuation difficulties we encounter. Sarah has developed the idea of a group which is explicitly focused on mapping compassionate resources for the next stage of the journey. She might start with some sharing of her own to invite the group to begin to bring their own resources to show and tell with the group. This will of course be reminiscent of the early stages in the group programme, but with a different flavour.

We have had some great MOG sessions at which graduates have brought and shared their compassionate kitbags, with recent updates as they move away from therapy.

I am hoping in the future to be able to withdraw from this group and for Sarah and another LEP to hold this space. I think my presence with all that has been discussed in this section can complicate the task of moving on. Our intention and hope is that the graduates will use this space to explore what is needed, plan a new route, get some guidance, and head off up a new line. I had a message from someone recently who told me with a smiling emoji that they were ready to move on from the Moving On Group. This made me smile as this is what we hope for.

Concluding comments

Perhaps the most important message from this final phase in this programme is that there is no magic formula. It may be more helpful to consider that these groups will evolve and change over time according to our capacity and that of our graduates. Expect tangles and tricky group dynamics to manage, so robust supervision will be needed to help you navigate this.

Over time, co-facilitation of the group with Lived Experience Practitioners has been an integral part of what makes MOG work. The bi-directional flows of compassion that are at play in the MOG process can bring growth and healing for all. In Sarah, the graduates see their progress reflected through the eyes of someone who really gets it and Sarah gets to see the value she brings to their journey in compassion and to keep her own journey on track – while I pour the tea.

This final quote from one of the group members clearly articulates what we hope that the MOG can offer:

> *'You don't have to face all that loss because you know that there is something else, but there is also people that you've met through the group… and because it's people that you respect and trust and all the rest of it, and because the ground rules stay the ground rules, and it's ground rules that we came up with ourselves … all that trust and shared history is still there … and because of what you've been through and because of the therapy groups that you've been through, the respect is there as well and … it's like meeting old friends – you may have only know them for 12 months, or even less with some, but it's like meeting old friends because you've been so deep and been through so much with them.'*

The final words

Drawing this book to a close, I think Judith Herman puts the essence of group psychotherapy in such simple and powerful words and offers a succinct summary of much which my group members have been reporting:

> *'Traumatic events destroy the sustaining bonds between individual and community. Those who have survived learn that their sense of self, of worth, of humanity, depends upon a feeling of connection with others. The solidarity of a group provides the strongest protection against terror and despair, and the strongest antidote to traumatic experience. Trauma isolates; the group re-creates a sense of belonging. Trauma shames and stigmatizes; the group bears witness and affirms. Trauma degrades the victim; the group exalts her. Trauma dehumanizes the victim; the group restores her humanity.'*[87]

Some data

I hope that the voices of the group have illustrated the ways that they have been supported through the psychotherapeutic process. But for those who are keen to see the data from the seven-year research study, it is now in out in the world.[88] But for everyone else, here are the headlines.

---

[87] Herman, J. L. (1998). Recovery from psychological trauma. *Psychiatry and Clinical Neurosciences*, **52**(S1), S98–S103. https://doi.org/10.1046/j.1440-1819.1998.0520s5S145.x

[88] Lucre, K., Ashworth, F., Copello, A., Jones, C., & Gilbert, P. (2024). *Compassion Focused Group Psychotherapy for Attachment and Relational Trauma: Engaging people with a diagnosis of personality disorder.*

The study, which took place over seven years, evaluated the qualitative and quantitative experience of 40 patients who were referred to the tertiary psychotherapy service. As you will already know, these are patients who could attract a diagnosis of personality disorder but are more helpfully described as being 'at the edge of therapeutic opportunity' because of their attachment and relational trauma (A&RT). This redefining aims to offer a more robust understanding of the causes of their difficulties, i.e. early attachment ruptures, rather than a categorisation of the behaviour which often accompanies these early experiences. The reworking of this diagnosis through an evolutionary lens aims to offer a de-shaming perspective on this cluster of interpersonal, emotional, cognitive and neurobiological difficulties, which often attract stigma, denigration and exclusion from therapeutic provision.

We gave self-report measures pertaining to a variety of symptom, process and adjustment variables to the whole group at different points in therapeutic process – crucially, at the point of assessment, the start of the programme, the end of the programme, and after one year of treatment as usual (TAU). These data showed significant change, across all measures, when analysed with a robust package of statistical measures, included individual change scores and Intention to Treat. My supervisor said we threw the kitchen sink at it and the data remained significant all the way to the one year follow up!

The headline for those commissioning services is that, at the conclusion of the evaluation, 50% (n: 15) had been discharged by mental health services and many of this subgroup had returned to work or education.

At the conclusion of my PhD viva, the external examiner asked me if I had one message for commissioners of services for people who could attract a diagnosis of personality disorder. I was so full of nervous energy, without pausing for breath I said: 'Don't be cheap!'

(By this, I meant give psychotherapy services the opportunity to provide programmes of longer duration, slower paced with greater flexibility within a structured model to manage the inevitable ruptures associated with this work. Our study also identified a therapeutic process of establishing group-based safeness as a necessary precursor to cultivating compassion and reworking early shame-based trauma memories.)[89]

Seven-year follow-up study

In the last two years, we have embarked on a follow-up study. We made contact with all 30 of those who completed CFGP and had agreed to be part of the original study. Of

---

[89] I didn't say any of the clever stuff in brackets, but I definitely thought it!

those, six people agreed to be interviewed about their recollections and learning from the programme. This group had completed the therapy between four and seven years earlier. These data were analysed according to an Interpretative Phenological Analysis protocol. I can offer a brief overview of the themes, but the paper detailing these data will be out in 2025, so keep an eye out.

The main message of this study is again about internalising and integrating the compassion-focused group psychotherapy process. Graduates spoke of the importance of personal practice in compassion, which started in the programme and supported discoveries about self and old stuck patterns. The transformative power of compassion in relation to self and others and how much this way of being changes life choices moving forward was also a common theme. It was deeply moving to read.

In addition, 11 of the original 31 completers agreed to redo the self-report measures. The early analysis of these data appears to show a significant change from one year to second follow up (four to seven years after the programme). This means that the process of change and improvement has not only been maintained, but for those who completed the forms, accelerated over the intervening years. These are very exciting findings and I believe that they support what our group members have reported throughout this book.

There are now new CFGP programmes being developed and producing similar findings in various corners of the UK and beyond.

My concluding thoughts

This has been I hope a story of courage and hope, which is based on the inspirational work of so many in the field of psychotherapy. But my final words are of gratitude for all those who have stepped into this work and taken the risk to turn back to, and not away from, the suffering that has shaped them:

> *'There's two things: one, for me, is meeting people along the way who do care and who you can think about from time to time and they do sort of come into your mind if you are in a low mood or you are experiencing something bad. For me, well, I can think I've got this group of people who I went through the therapy with, who have gone through similar things, and that is something there for me that I use. Another thing that I use is that there are lots of parts to me, not just the self-critic who used to take over before, it is just one part that isn't going to go away, I know that. The critic just isn't as loud as it used to be.'*

I realise now as I draw this book to a close, that we have only just got started with this. There is so much more to explore, share and make sense of. I want to be really clear that this book is not a manual to follow, but a guide to support you alongside the considerable training that is required to undertake this kind of work safely. I am deeply grateful for this process which has shed light on my gaps and blind spots as well as helped me to see my own intentions more clearly.

I would like to give the last and most poignant words to Sarah, Lived Experience Practitioner and Compassionate Mind Trainer. The inspirational journey she and others like her have taken makes this book and this work worthwhile.

Sarah's last word

Seven years ago, I was spending almost all of my time alone in my flat, trying to avoid contact with the world as much as possible. My nervous system was shattered and I was living in a state of such high anxiety that a ringing phone or doorbell would cause me to dissolve into panic and tears. I was literally and metaphorically stuck, unable to make the simplest decision. Afraid of everything. I couldn't find a place where I felt mentally or physically safe. I was exhausted, tired and wired from decades of white-knuckling my way through the constant vibration of anxiety which sporadically flared up into panic attacks so intense I would feel wrung out and numb, bruised for days afterwards. I realised I needed to ask for help, and because I couldn't trust anyone and was coming from a place of rigid self/reliance, this was pretty terrifying.

At this point, I was a long way from recognising the trauma I had experienced, let alone understanding that it was rumbling round and round my nervous system like a storm trapped in the hills. After reaching out to mental health services and being assessed, I was offered what was to be a life-changing experience – a place on the compassion-focused group therapy programme in Birmingham.

I had tried various forms of therapy before and at the time I couldn't have imagined anything more frightening than a group. But I was told that this was the programme on offer and, if I could commit to one session per week for a year, I would be offered a place to join. And something about that initial assessment, where I was so nervous and agitated, and the therapist was so regulated and understanding, something actually shifted for me right in that moment, before the therapy even began. I didn't know at the time but the assessing therapist I met that day was one of the group therapists who would walk alongside me through the following year, every week, one step at a time, on one of the most important journeys I've taken.

With the benefit of hindsight, I know that, in that moment, something in me sensed and connected with compassion – as I sat there, realising that not only was I not going to be criticised for being activated and afraid, but I was actually made to feel that it was ok to feel exactly as I did in that moment, and that I wasn't going to be rejected or cast aside for having these big, difficult-to-manage feelings, but rather encouraged, silently but with a shared and gentle understanding, to sit with and through the experience.

After having lost my job to my illness some months before, and spending a great deal of time alone because I just couldn't trust the company of many other people, one of the most vulnerable days of my life was the day I attended the first session of CFT. I remember walking into that room like a blinkered horse, eyes down, defences up, not knowing what was going to happen and having absolutely no control of the situation or my level of exposure. Having to trust that a small group of strangers was going to treat me kindly was almost more than I could bear... But I had got to the point where staying stuck was more painful than attempting change, and I knew that I had to give the process my best shot. I had previously met both of the group therapists at this point and just tried to hold onto the memory of their kindness and warmth at those initial meetings.

A group of us slowly filed into a small room and were guided to sit in a circle with the therapists amongst us. Once we sat down, we were invited to take part in a short breathing practice to start the session. I had already started experimenting with mindfulness meditation about a month earlier at home as a potential way of managing my experiences, but had found it was only able to hold me steady for the duration of the practice, after which I was deep in the grip of anxiety again within minutes. I certainly hadn't expected to sit in a circle of strangers and begin a group therapy session by being guided to connect with the breath.

But there was something about those few minutes of quiet, of feeling the energy and effort of the group working to focus our attention, that felt supportive and connecting in a way that I couldn't understand in anything more than an abstract way. And as, one at a time, the group shared a few words of feedback about how they had struggled with the challenge of the breathing practice in their own unique but recognisable ways, I felt a fragile web begin to form in the room, as experience connected with empathy and courage connected with vulnerability and other people's truths. Over time, as we began to trust, some of these truths were more welcome and palatable than others... And yet space was made for it all. We were implicitly encouraged to share our truth, ugly or beautiful, in a space where whatever we were bringing would be honoured.

For the rest of that first group session, I listened to seven other people share a snapshot of what they were bringing with them that day, their lives, their struggles and fears, frustrations, pain and truth. People who, under any other circumstances, may never have met, from many different worlds and with many stories to share, on the surface having no particular thing in common, and yet connected by disconnection and suffering. Some of the stories felt familiar in a way, not so much in detail but in tone, and some felt alien and strange. Some people's concerns were easier to connect with, to feel empathy for, than others. but there was something about the willing vulnerability of everyone in the space that gave me the courage to speak when invited.

To this day, I have no idea what I shared with the group. I have no memory of my words. but I do remember, as I finished speaking, being asked to hand the share space on to another person. I looked up for the first time during the session and made eye contact with a beautiful young woman sat opposite me in the circle and she gave me a small, warm, encouraging smile.

That moment of connection helped me to commit myself to this weekly gathering. Not just because I was exhausted, not just because I was out of options, but because I was so grateful to that woman and it occurred to me that there may be a time when she too might look at me across that circle and need gentle encouragement to be brave, and so began what I think of as my most life-changing year.

I was 43 years old, unable to work and spending most of my time alone stuck in a cycle of feeling anxious for no discernible reason and not knowing how to ground myself. But once a week, I got up, took a deep breath, clamped on headphones and sunglasses to brave the journey to group therapy, time after time having to convince myself to lean into an experience over which I had no control, sensing that I just had to trust the unfolding process, whatever it might bring. There was something about the group as an entity which felt, quite soon into the process, like a safety net. It was as though, even if I screwed it up, got it wrong, said or did the wrong thing, it was going to be acknowledged and accepted and I wouldn't be shamed for making mistakes. Don't get me wrong, as relationships developed there were experiences of tension and conflict as well as experiences of warmth and understanding, but all of these interactions shared this element of connection... I see you... I hear you... your truth is valid.

And so I began to lean into and trust this weekly gathering, this tribe with a common goal, this recognition of the fact that we all suffer, suffering is a part of life, and we were there to learn how to be kind to ourselves in our suffering and how this kindness to self is the starting point for healthy interactions within a world that we cannot control.

Feeling my emotional responses to other group members' stories was somehow easier than feeling my own pain initially... but it was a turning point for me to recognise that I couldn't think my way out of my illness. I had to feel the feelings (and throw a couple of Wobblies along the way, that turned out to be real breakthroughs). And once I understood that this was not a cognitive process, this was when real change began to happen for me. As I began to feel more space between thoughts and reactions, I began to feel more grounded, calmer, and could even occasionally hear my inner wisdom gently guiding me... a clear calm voice, one to be trusted when I left space for her to be heard. Over time, I could feel her responding to the stories of others as well as my own experience, showing me how we all suffer, and that if we can gently engage with this reality, we can create enough space to respond to life from a place of love rather than react from a place of fear.

The year went by so quickly and I began to feel a pull of sorrow as I realised my journey on the programme was drawing to a close. The thought of losing my Friday tribe, my safe place, there was a feeling of grief present, but it was tempered by the compassionate skills and techniques I had learned as well as the recognition that I was now allowing myself to have feelings... which was a pretty novel experience. Knowing that to suffer is to be open to the world and that this new openness would allow me to continue exploring life and give me an opportunity to become my best self. I was about to ride off towards an unknown but now vaguely exciting future.

I left my final therapy session knowing that my work was to begin sharing my lived experience in some way that could be useful to others. I had always suspected I had a skill for communicating ideas and that perhaps I would be a teacher or a guide, and now I had something useful to share. Very soon after completing therapy, I began training as a mindfulness meditation teacher at central England college and then almost immediately went on to train as a yoga teacher at the contemporary school of yoga in Birmingham. Armed with new qualifications and opportunities, a sense of curiosity and the mentorship of my former therapist Kate Lucre, I took step after step into unknown territory, beginning by teaching meditation, yoga and mindful movement and then being invited to rejoin the NHS as a peer mentor. This then evolved to Kate inviting me to deliver compassion-focused staff support across the mental health trust as co-facilitator and Lived Experience Practitioner. None of these choices or opportunities would have been possible for me had I not experienced the strength that is to be found in community, in allowing the group to hold you and to make the medicine sweeter, and being willing to be vulnerable with others is perhaps one of the most profound things I learned during my time on the programme, allowing myself to be afraid but doing it anyway, whatever it may be, knowing that there is no shame in failing, and in some ways, as innately creative humans, that this is at the very heart of what we do. Get up every day and fail, and do so joyfully. Knowing that we will do better the next day.

And so to today.....

The hypervigilance of childhood, the ability to sense the emotional weather of a room, has softened from sharp watchfulness to gentle atonement (on my good days!), allowing me to feel the weight and shape and shifts within a group, letting me teach who is in front of me in that moment, and be of the very best service to others that I can be.

The fear of not being able to control the future that haunted me my whole life has morphed into a courageous and slightly playful curiosity, allowing me to be bold and innovative in my groupwork and teaching, leaving space for intuitive connection with students and what they are bringing to the space and also being willing to gently challenge them as well as myself to get embodied and have a non-judgemental, felt experience during their practice,

I am open in my recovery and healing so that those around me can choose to heal in private if they wish, knowing that there is no shame in making a different choice if they ever choose to do so. My yoga teacher recently said to me that the more real we are willing to be with the world, the more we shine, and these days I'm OK with things not working out. This still surprises me on a daily basis… and gives me the freedom to try new things, to take risks, and to share this with you today, which would have been inconceivable five years ago.

What I hoped for from CFT was to feel safe. I thought I could get there by understanding what had happened to me. But CFT taught me that I couldn't think my way out of the trauma. I had to feel my way out and that it is not only OK to ask for help but integral to our experience as affiliative creatures. That there are times when we don't feel safe and that this too is OK. We acknowledge it, allow it to be what it is, feel it, and then choose love over fear. This is my process. Choose to practice regulation. Choose to be kind, or as kind as I can. And on those days where this work is hard, treating myself kindly as I recognise that most of us, myself included, are doing the very best we can. So this year finds me exploring new ways to hold space, both for myself and for others, with that particular balance of softness and strength that feels like absolute flow when you are in it, in my newest role as Compassionate Mind Trainer and Lived Experience Practitioner for our trust.

Continuing to stay open to the feeling of uncertainty as I embrace new challenges and opportunities to work with both staff and clients is exhilarating, at times terrifying, sometimes sad, other times hilarious and always rewarding in a way that nourishes my courage and curiosity.

I find a creative magic in groupwork which fascinates me and, I suspect, will continue to be at the heart of my exploration as my role develops. Our ability to come together around the campfire to gently hold, examine and pass around the precious artefacts of our experience in a place that, even if just for now, feels like home, is a privilege and a gift to everyone brave enough to step into the circle.'

The end.

Appendices

Appendix 1.1: Example Assessment Summary

Date

Dear Eleni,

Firstly I am sorry about the delay in getting this summary to you. Thank you for coming to the three assessment session with me on 1st and 17th February and 3rd March 2023. This is summary of those meetings and what we agreed would be the plan going forward. When we met for the first time you gave me letter which it felt important that I read as our first introduction. In this there was a description of the multiple parts and how much of what one of part of you knows is not known to the other parts. It also seemed important for me to know that other parts may emerge during the course of the assessment who are not connected or joined with each other.

I wonder if this first communication was motivated by an understandable need for me to know how complex and intricate your experience of your selves is. I also wondered with you early on if we might get 'lost' just trying to map out and explore all the split off parts of you. We agreed in beginning our conversation that we would instead spend time with the story of the events of your life. We moved around a little in our discussions, so if there are any elements of my recollection which are not accurate, please let me know.

Early Life

When we first began talking about your early life, you let me know that you had been seen by over 25 therapists since childhood, many of whom had been deeply disturbed by the story of your early life. I wondered if you were asking me at this stage if I could manage to bear your story without becoming tearful or overwhelmed. I also wonder if you were pushing to see if I could hear your story and also be a container for the pain and anguish that historically you have managed alone.

At times it was hard to piece together the narrative of your early years, which of course is connected to how fragmented things have become for you over the years. There are gaps in your memories of your very early life, but it was clear that your life before the age of ten was spent in conditions of severe deprivation and neglect, which led to being taken into foster care.

Following this, it seems there was little time to make sense of these early experiences as there was no stable base for you. You spoke of becoming involved in gangs from the age of 16 years when you left the care system. This seems to have been a survival strategy to be independent with a clear role for yourself which resulted in others relying on you to resolve problems. Mostly it seems involving violence as a means of retribution, earning yourself the nickname "the punisher ". I wonder if this role that you created for yourself was a way of trying to put right the trauma and abuse from your early life, whilst at the same time ensuring that those around you did not turn on you.

This lifestyle also resulted in a serious drug addiction which you spoke of fearing would result in your death. Prompted by this fear you left, despite the sense of loss and grief. You made contact with your mother and moved to live near to her and it seems care for her. Despite it being clear to you that your mother was not able to provide any form of care to you in your early life, it seems that you still yearned to be close to her and this motivated your decision to live with her. You spoke of feeling aware that the situation was something of a repeat from your early life, where you felt that you had to either tolerate abusive behaviour from others or give a great deal of yourself to get your basic needs met.

You left and moved again in 2020, it seems as a spontaneous decision to move away from the trapped situation you found yourself in.

Survival Strategies

Over the course of the three sessions, we spoke about the how the different parts of you have developed. Having agreed not to spend all our time with this, it feels important to acknowledge your experience of being fragmented. It seems that you learned very early in life that the adults in your life were not only unable to protect you but that they were the source of threat and terror. There was no safe space to make sense of yourself and your experiences.

To survive there was a process of fragmenting which meant that the hurt and suffering from your early life was 'locked away' in the young parts of you which you spoke of as being located in the 'nursery'. These parts hold all the unbearable feelings of loss and pain that you do not ever connect with. It seems that over time you have learned to keep these split off parts of you separate, at times quite deliberately by denying their importance or even their existence. But the grief has not resolved and as we spoke you described moments between the sessions where some of these feelings have emerged.

Formulation

We spent a little time at the end of assessment process, trying to draw together some of the strands of our discussions about your experiences. We agreed that it was understandable that your inner world had become fragmented as a way of surviving the terrifying and unpredictable conditions that you grew up in. From the deprivation of your family life to the multiple chaotic foster placements.

The gang and drug addiction perhaps offered something predictable, albeit equally disturbing. Keeping people away with violence and intimidation has kept you safe but has not allowed you to flourish and grow. But despite the stories of horror, I have noticed a shift in the way you have been with me in the sessions and how much more you of yourself you have allowed me to see. I have much appreciated this.

Conclusion

When we met for the last session, it was possible to think together about ambivalence towards therapy which at times perhaps you communicated by missing parts of the assessment sessions. But the final session we were able to take the whole time to consider the best way forward, which felt like a statement of commitment to yourself.

During this final session I shared with you that I had not been sure if you were looking for therapy when we first met and you agreed that you had not been sure. But it seems that over the course of the sessions you shifted from feeling that you needed to keep all the fragmented parts of yourself separate to an openness to beginning to understand how the different parts have protected you from painful memories but also kept you stuck.

We agreed that the group programme could offer an opportunity to have a different kind of 'crew' to begin to make sense of and turn back to the early suffering and deprivation. The next step will be an invitation to the waiting list group were you can find out more about the programme and have a monthly space to meet with others while you wait for the programme to start.

If there is anything in this letter which I have got wrong or we need to discuss, please let me know. I look forward to welcoming you to the group programme.

Warm wishes

Appendix 3.1: Example Safe Space Agreement

What we say here stays here.

If the facilitators are really worried about anyone, they might take it outside the group without sharing the concern first (but this generally doesn't happen).

If we are going to be late or can't make it, to let the group because they will be worried about you.

If we bump into each other outside of group, let's be careful in our greetings – not everyone will be want to explain how they know you!

If you miss too many groups, we will pause your place in the group and meet with you to make a plan.

If it is too much you can always restart.

The escape pod! You can use these chairs if being in the circle is too much – we will understand and support you.

Let's keep all our contact in the group and wait until we have finished before catching up outside of group – we share things here which are deeply personal and not for chatter outside.

Let's keep our phones off or on silent if we have to take a call.

Let's try and get involved and try new things in this group.

Problem solving might seem to be the kind option but may not help, let's sit with each other's difficulties first.

Appendices

Appendix 3.2:
How the body responds to threat

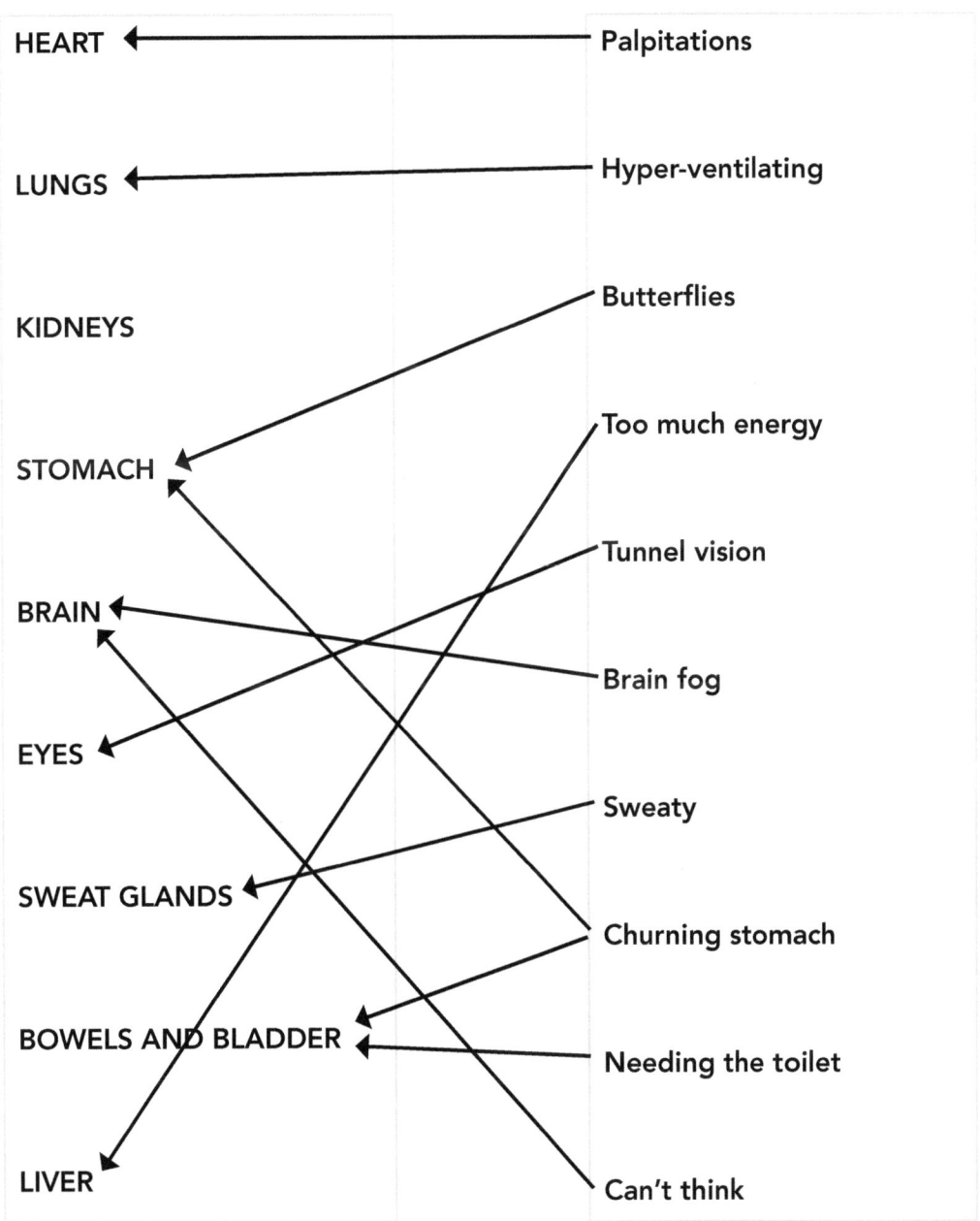

Appendix 3.3:
Pros and cons of a compassionate being

A being with all the qualities of compassion that have been explored.

Pros	Cons
Helpful	Don't trust it
Supportive	It will make me weak
Not so alone (maybe!)	Let my guard down
	Not realistic
	It doesn't make sense
	What is the point?
	There will be a catch
	It doesn't exist
	I don't want it
	Urghhhh!

Appendix 3.4: Compassion Postcard

Appendix 3.5: Job description of the inner critic

Job overview

- To observe for mistakes and be ready to shout demands.
- Remind how weak and unprepared they are.
- Don't let them get close to or trust anyone.

Essential criteria

- Good sarcasm skills.
- Very observant.
- Ready to launch into action at any moment.
- Must be loud.
- Must be persistent.
- Sees the bad in EVERYTHING.

Desirable qualities

- Swearing is an advantage.
- Short tempered.
- Prone to angry outbursts.

Appendix 3.6: Compassionate roles map

Quality of your compassionate self
- I'm determined and committed to my therapy
- The group tell me that I am funny and warm, I am starting to feel a little of this

Supportive other
- My dog Felix – who is always there to meet me when I come home. He knows when I am struggling and helps me by making sure I get out of the house everyday to walk him and my friend Clare

Compassionate other
- Sheriff Woody from Toy Story – he is calm, gentle, warm and wise. I imagine him talking to me when I feel desperate. He congratulates me on the things I don't notice I have done well too!

Achievement
- I came to group every week for the last month!

Source of Support / Strength
- The tree outside the window in the group room. I take it with me in my mind and it helps me to cope

Appendix 3.7: Calm Place Imagery Script and link

Calm Place Imagery Script

https://soundcloud.com/kate-lucre/calming-place-imagery?in=kate-lucre/sets/practices

OK, so let's get started. Let's settle into this Soothing, calming, welcoming place Imagery Practise.

Let's start with making a connection with the stable, permanent ground beneath your feet. So you might want to wiggle your toes. But really notice that connection with the ground underneath your feet. Taking a moment to really feel that sense of being grounded, that sense of permanence.

Being connected to something permanent and immovable.

And then beginning with a few slow breaths.

Gently drawing the breath in through your nose. Tracking the air down into your lungs and your diaphragm. And then continuing all the way down. To your feet. And then connecting the breath with the ground underneath your feet. So we're breathing in through the nose. All the way down to the feet. So you're connecting the breath. With the ground underneath you. Creating a steady flow of breath. And we're also checking in with ourselves. Bringing awareness. Awareness to the body. Our bodies that hold us and carry us around. I think we often don't pay attention to our bodies until they're malfunctioning, and then we might be shaking a fist at them.

But let's just notice our bodies in the chair this morning. Sending it gentle acknowledgement. And maybe even a nod of gratitude. Maybe bringing movement to your body in the chair, maybe walking gently to bring balance to the weight over both hips. Creating the gentle curve at the base of your spine. Allowing your shoulders to drop. Letting your head be balanced evenly over in between your shoulder blades. Maybe releasing any tension by bringing movement to your hands. And then something playful to mind. Maybe just a small thing that's made you smile over the last few days, or you might need to stretch back longer. Maybe something you saw something you read. Maybe something that you heard from somebody? Something that made you smile. And let your body remember this. Really allow yourself to feel the memory of that smile, that playful something. And then settling in with the soothing rhythm of breath.

Finding your own soothing rhythm. You might find that you speed up and slow down your breath to connect with the rhythm that feels, settling and calming. You might find that your mind wanders or there are distractions. There might well be in these current times. If there are just tip a nod to them. Notice. Acknowledge them. And then gently tiptoe back to the breath. Sometimes it could be helpful to have something to hold as a way of transitioning our tension back. To the breath. So taking a few breaths. To settle into this still space. Allowing things to be as they are. And then I'd like to invite you to take a journey. To step into your own calming, welcoming place. Now with imagery. We might just get a fragment or a sense. Doesn't have to be a fully formed image with colour and sound, so we're just stepping into this place. This could be a place that you visited before, or this could be a place that's brand new today. But often this is a work in progress. So let's just take this steady step by step. Step in and justice take in your surroundings. Notice what you see around you. What scenery do you need in this place? And remember, you're the architect. So you can paint in whatever it is that you need. To notice what you see and what you need in this place. Take a look around you. Allow yourself to soak it up. The important aspects of this place. Notice the colours. You can change the hue. That is the temperature. Again, you have a volume switch. Notice the textures and sensations. Allowing yourself to connect in this practise with what you really need. So taking in your calming, welcoming place. And allowing yourself to feel that sense of being deeply welcomed by this place. This place is grateful to you for having chosen it. Allow yourself to feel that sense of gratitude. This place knows you inside out. Doesn't judge you. Accepts you. And celebrates. Your choice. Allow yourself to feel that sense of being deeply welcomed by this, which is your place, this place that is here just for you. To support, to encourage, to nurture and nourish you. So take a breath. Take a moment. Settle into this, your calming, welcoming place. Feel welcomed. And then find a spot in this place. This could be a familiar spot, or this could be a spot just for today. A place where you feel most settled, most at ease. And settle yourself into this spot, this place. Take in your surroundings. Really soak them up. Take a breath. Take a moment. Noticed that sense of being gathered and being held in this place. And then, if there is one, allow yourself to receive a message from this place. This could be something that you really need to hear today. There may not be a message, but if there is one, allow yourself space to hear it. Could be some encouragement with something you're struggling with. Could be reassurance. Could be just a message of acceptance. Just allow yourself to take a breath. Take this in. And then gently bring this practise to a close. If you have a message or just a sense from this place, then imagine that you're putting this in your pocket, holding on to it, and then gently letting the image fade. Bringing attention back to your feet and closing your practise.

When you're ready, you might decide you want to stretch and bring movement. To signal to your body that you've completed your practise. And this concludes our calming, welcoming place imagery practise.

Appendix 3.8: Role-taking

Adam was a member of a compassion-focused group psychotherapy programme and had been invited to bring objects from home which had significant meaning and could become part of his Compassionate Kitbag. Adam had been reluctant to engage in this aspect of the work and had stated that he did not have anything that helped him feel calm or courageous.

In this context, he had shared with the group that, as a child, there had been an abundance of toys around the home but they remained in their boxes and were not allowed to be played with. He described a feeling of terror associated with the idea of playing and resisted exercises that involved playing such as using art materials and compassion-focused games.

Adam quite unexpectedly came to group with a bag that he said contained something that 'might do as a compassionate object'. Very tentatively, he shared a brightly coloured elephant that had been a gift from his teacher early in his education. He had kept the elephant in a box in a cupboard, which he rarely looked at. As it was passed around the group, he spoke of feeling very fearful and anxious that that the elephant would be damaged.

Adam agreed to take the role of the elephant which he called 'Bruce', but only with the agreement that he could stop the exercise if it became too much. He was invited to hold the elephant and stand up and then, as he sat down, he took on the role of Bruce. After an initial introduction, he was asked how long he had been in Adam's life and the sort of situations which Adam might think of him. He (as Bruce) described with tears in his eyes that Adam would often think of him when he felt alone and despairing. Bruce reminded Adam that the teacher who had made the gift had cared very much for him and had seen his strengths and ability. When asked, Bruce (through Adam) spoke of feeling very warm towards Adam, coupled with a motivation to help him see the things that he struggles to hold in mind, that people have cared about him and that he is strong (like Bruce). At the end of the process, Bruce was invited to give a message to Adam: 'You are stronger than you know and you need to take me out of the box because I am an elephant and I can remember this for you.' He stood up to step out of role and sat again to step back into being Adam.

The following sharing session enabled Adam to settle with the things that he had learned from being Bruce, he resolved to take him out of the box and place him by his bed so he could be reminded more often. This exercise enabled Adam to connect with the unconscious meaning associated with the elephant and the connections with his early life, which he was repeating by denying himself access to opportunities for soothing.

Role-taking suggested questions

These are to serve as a guide only and not designed to be a script. You may want to make some adaptations to these, but keep in mind that the purpose of the exercise is to deepen and bring understanding of the meaning of the object from the kitbag.

How long have you been in (group member's name) life?

Where do you live in their home? In a drawer on the shelf…?

What is your role/what do you do for……/when do they turn to you?

When are you needed? Under what circumstances?

What do you mean to….? (activating care-giving/receiving mentalities)

How do you feel about …..? (motivational systems)

What is the message to ….?

Appendix 4.1: Word cloud

Appendix 4.2:
Compassion-Focused Therapy Threat Formulation – 'this is how I survived...'

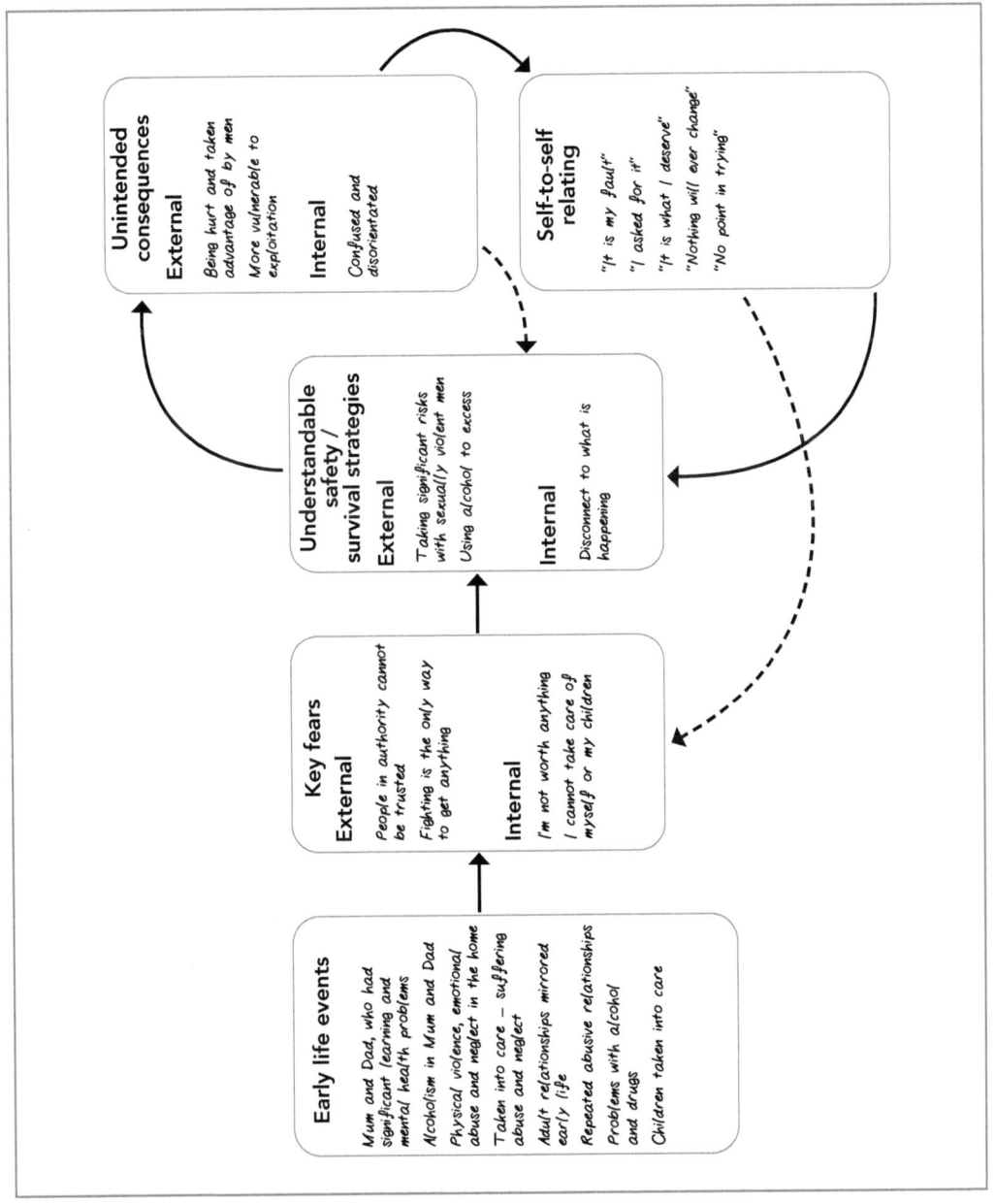

Appendix 4.3: Multiple selves map

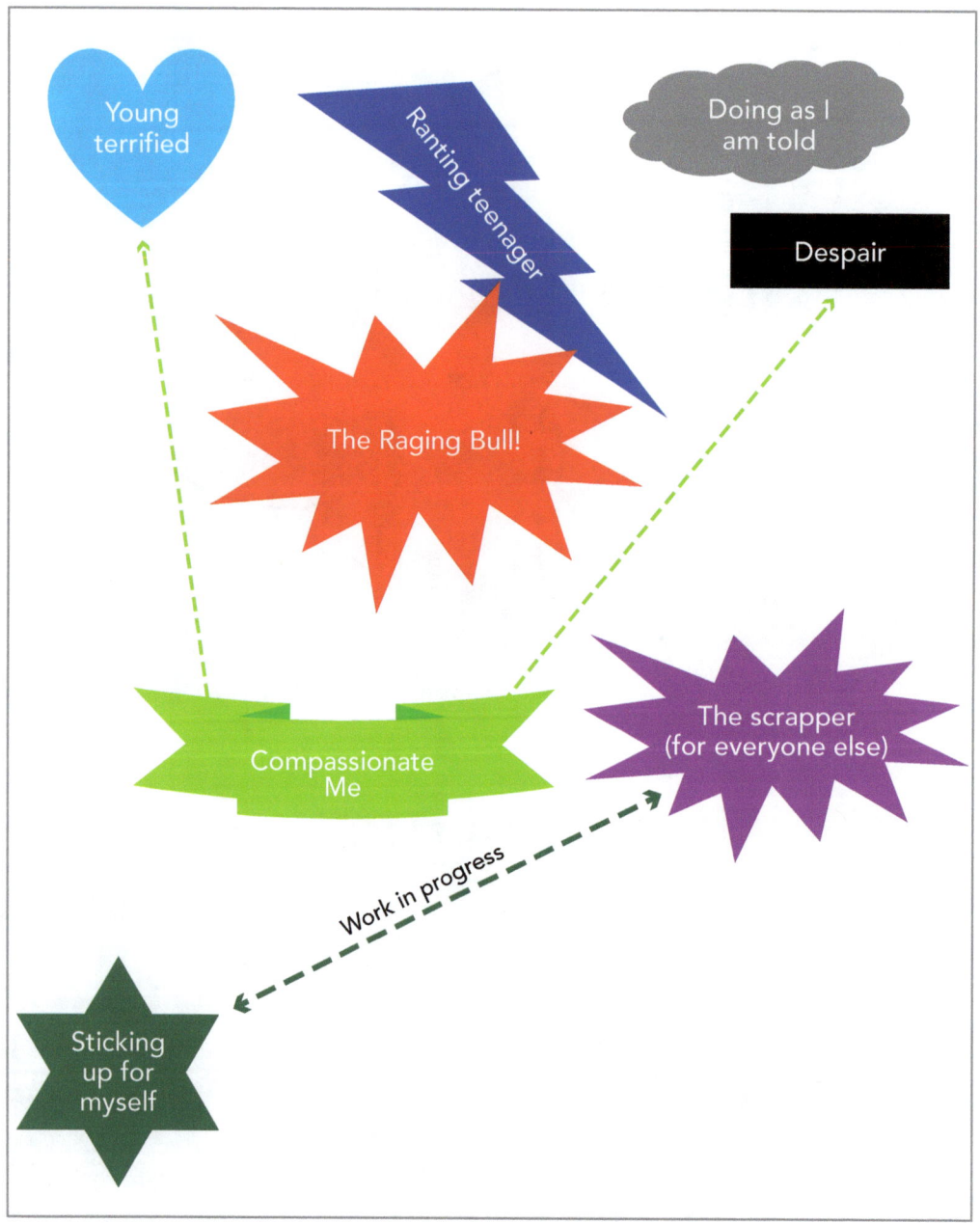

Appendix 4.4: Whirlpool of Grief

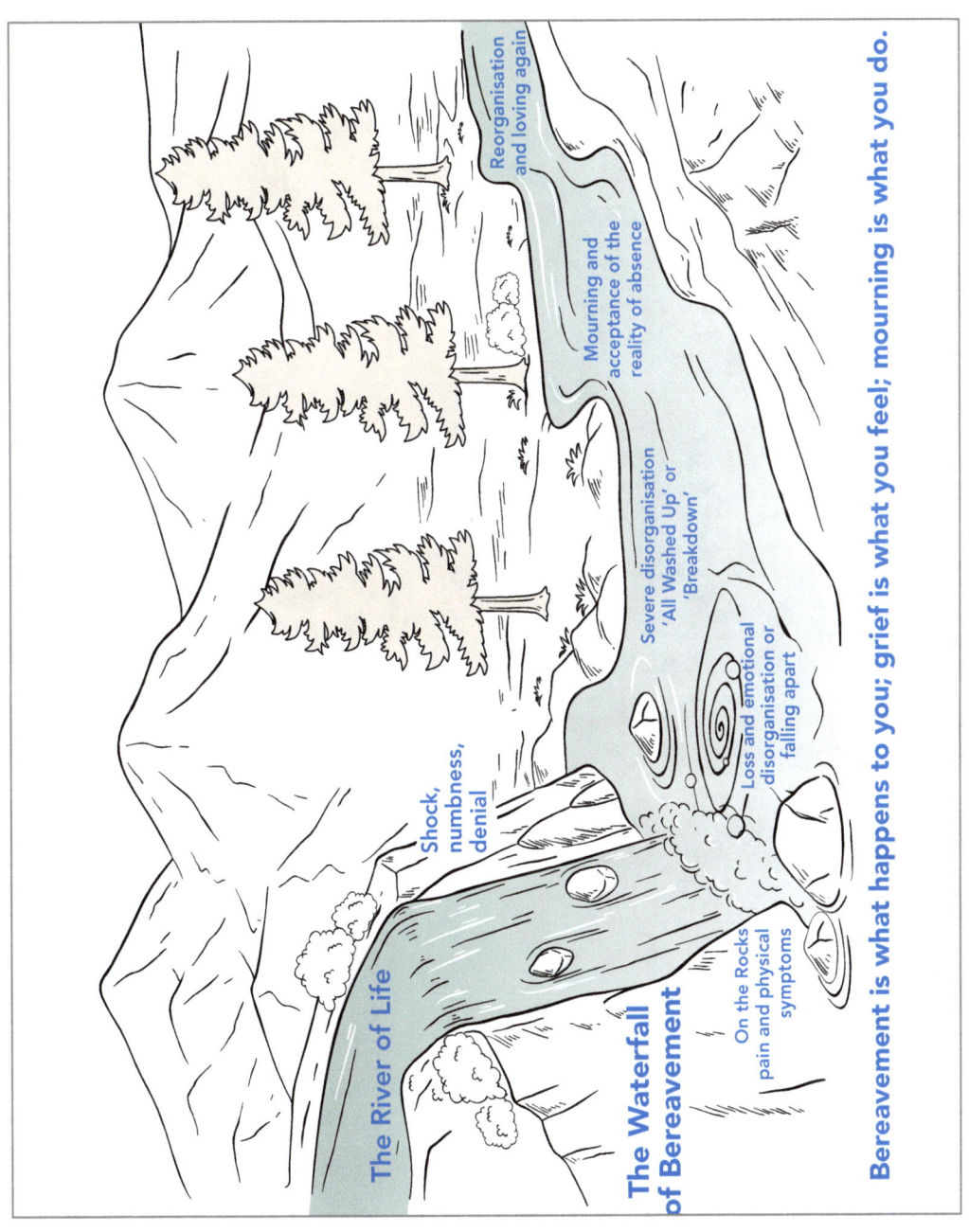

Appendices

Appendix 4.5: Rosa!

References

Adil, J. (2010). Ancient origins of the term patient. *The Psychiatrist*, **34**(3), 117–118. https://doi.org/10.1192/pb.34.3.117b

Adshead, G. (1998a). Psychiatric staff as attachment figures. *British Journal of Psychiatry*, **172**(01), 64–69. https://doi.org/10.1192/bjp.172.1.64

Adshead, G. (1998b). Psychiatric staff as attachment figures: Understanding management problems in psychiatric services in the light of attachment theory. *The British Journal of Psychiatry*, **172**(1), 64–69.

Agnello, C. (2019). Necessary and Sufficient: Examining the Role of Attachment Trauma and Psychological Maltreatment as Primary Etiological Factors in the Development of Borderline Personality Disorder. *Dissertations*. https://digitalcommons.nl.edu/diss/375

Allan, S., & Gilbert, P. (1995). A social comparison scale: Psychometric properties and relationship to psychopathology. *Personality and Individual Differences*, **19**(3), 293–299.

Allan, S., & Gilbert, P. (1997). Submissive behaviour and psychopathology. *British Journal of Clinical Psychology*, **36**(4), 467–488.

Allan, S., Gilbert, P., & Goss, K. (1994). An exploration of shame measures—II: Psychopathology. *Personality and Individual Differences*, **17**(5), 719–722. https://doi.org/10.1016/0191-8869(94)90150-3

Allen, B. (2008). An analysis of the impact of diverse forms of childhood psychological maltreatment on emotional adjustment in early adulthood. *Child Maltreatment*, **13**(3), 307–312.

Allen, J. G., Fonagy, P., & Bateman, A. W. (2008). *Mentalizing in clinical practice*. American Psychiatric Pub.

Alshurafa, M., Briel, M., Akl, E. A., Haines, T., Moayyedi, P., Gentles, S. J., Rios, L., Tran, C., Bhatnagar, N., & Lamontagne, F. (2012). Inconsistent definitions for intention-to-treat in relation to missing outcome data: Systematic review of the methods literature. *PLoS One*, **7**(11), e49163.

Andersen, B., & Rasmussen, P. H. (2017). Transdiagnostic group therapy for people with self- critic and low self esteem, based on compassion focused therapy principles. *Journal of Compassionate Health Care*, **4**(1). https://doi.org/10.1186/s40639-017-0043-1

Andrews, B. (1998). Shame and childhood abuse. In Shame: *Interpersonal behavior, psychopathology, and culture* (pp. 176–190). Oxford University Press.

Ansell, E. B., Sanislow, C. A., McGlashan, T. H., & Grilo, C. M. (2007). Psychosocial impairment and treatment utilization by patients with borderline personality disorder, other personality disorders, mood and anxiety disorders, and a healthy comparison group. *Comprehensive Psychiatry*, **48**(4), 329–336. https://doi.org/10.1016/j.comppsych.2007.02.001

Antony, M. M., Bieling, P. J., Cox, B. J., Enns, M. W., & Swinson, R. P. (1998). Psychometric properties of the 42-item and 21-item versions of the Depression Anxiety Stress Scales in clinical groups and a community sample. *Psychological Assessment*, **10**(2), 176.

Arlo, C. (2019). Integrated Group Psychotherapy Program [IGPP] for Multi-Diagnosed Clients. *International Journal of Group Psychotherapy*, **69**(2), 149–171.

Arntz, A. (2015). Imagery rescripting for personality disorders: Healing early maladaptive schemas. *Working with Emotion in Cognitive-Behavioral Therapy: Techniques for Clinical Practice*, 175–202.

Arntz, A., Mensink, K., Cox, W. R., Verhoef, R. E. J., Emmerik, A. A. P. van, Rameckers, S. A., Badenbach, T., & Grasman, R. P. P. P. (2023). Dropout from psychological treatment for borderline personality disorder: A multilevel survival meta-analysis. *Psychological Medicine*, **53**(3), 668–686. https://doi.org/10.1017/S0033291722003634

Arthern, J., & Madill, A. (1999). How do transitional objects work?: The therapist's view. *British Journal of Medical Psychology*, **72**(1), 1–21. https://doi.org/10.1348/000711299159754

Arthern, J., & Madill, A. (2002). How Do Transitional Objects Work? The Client's View. *Psychotherapy Research*, **12**(3), 369–388. https://doi.org/10.1093/ptr/12.3.369

Ashfield, E., Chan, C., & Lee, D. (n.d.). Building 'a compassionate armour': The journey to develop strength and self-compassion in a group treatment for complex post-traumatic stress disorder. *Psychology and Psychotherapy: Theory, Research and Practice*, n/a(n/a). https://doi.org/10.1111/papt.12275

Ashworth, F., Clarke, A., Jones, L., Jennings, C., & Longworth, C. (2015). An exploration of compassion focused therapy following acquired brain injury. *Psychology and Psychotherapy: Theory, Research and Practice*, **88**(2), 143–162. https://doi.org/10.1111/papt.12037

Banerjee, P. J., Gibbon, S. D., & Huband, N. (2012). Assessment of personality disorder. *Clinical Topics in Personality Disorder*, 139.

Barnes, B., Ernst, S., & Hyde, K. (2017). *An introduction to groupwork: A group-analytic perspective*. Macmillan International Higher Education.

Barnicot, K., Katsakou, C., Bhatti, N., Savill, M., Fearns, N., & Priebe, S. (2012). Factors predicting the outcome of psychotherapy for borderline personality disorder: A systematic review. *Clinical Psychology Review*, **32**(5), 400–412.

Barnicot, K., Katsakou, C., Marougka, S., & Priebe, S. (2011). Treatment completion in psychotherapy for borderline personality disorder – a systematic review and meta-analysis. *Acta Psychiatrica Scandinavica*, **123**(5), 327–338. https://doi.org/10.1111/j.1600-0447.2010.01652.x

Bartels-Velthuis, A. A., Schroevers, M. J., Ploeg, K. van der, Koster, F., Fleer, J., & Brink, E. van den. (2016). A Mindfulness-Based Compassionate Living Training in a Heterogeneous Sample of Psychiatric Outpatients: A Feasibility Study. *Mindfulness*, **7**(4), 809–818. https://doi.org/10.1007/s12671-016-0518-8

Bateman, A., & Fonagy, P. (2003). Health service utilization costs for borderline personality disorder patients treated with psychoanalytically oriented partial hospitalization versus general psychiatric care. *American Journal of Psychiatry*, **160**(1), 169–171.

Bateman, A., & Fonagy, P. (2006). *Mentalization-based Treatment for Borderline Personality Disorder: A Practical Guide*. OUP Oxford.

Bateman, A., & Fonagy, P. (2010). Mentalization based treatment for borderline personality disorder. *World Psychiatry*, **9**(1), 11.

Bateman, A., & Fonagy, P. (2016). *Mentalization-Based Treatment for Personality Disorders: A Practical Guide*. Oxford University Press.

Bateman, A. W., & Fonagy, P. (2000). Effectiveness of psychotherapeutic treatment of personality disorder. *The British Journal of Psychiatry*, **177**(2), 138–143. https://doi.org/10.1192/bjp.177.2.138

Bateman, A. W., Gunderson, J., & Mulder, R. (2015). Treatment of personality disorder. *The Lancet*, **385**(9969), 735–743. https://doi.org/10.1016/S0140-6736(14)61394-5

Beaumont, E., Durkin, M., McAndrew, S., & Martin, C. R. (2016). Using Compassion Focused Therapy as an adjunct to Trauma-Focused CBT for Fire Service personnel suffering with trauma-related symptoms. *The Cognitive Behaviour Therapist*, 9. https://doi.org/10.1017/S1754470X16000209

Becker, D. (2000). When she was bad: Borderline personality disorder in a posttraumatic age. *American Journal of Orthopsychiatry*, **70**(4), 422–432.

Behr, H., & Hearst, L. (2008). *Group-analytic psychotherapy: A meeting of minds*. John Wiley & Sons.

Bell, T., Dixon, A., & Kolts, R. (2017). Developing a Compassionate Internal Supervisor: Compassion-Focused Therapy for Trainee Therapists. *Clinical Psychology & Psychotherapy*, **24**(3), 632–648. https://doi.org/10.1002/cpp.2031

Bell, T., Montague, J., Elander, J., & Gilbert, P. (2020). "A definite feel-it moment": Embodiment, externalisation and emotion during chair-work in compassion-focused therapy. *Counselling and Psychotherapy Research*, **20**(1), 143–153. https://doi.org/10.1002/capr.12248

Bender, D. S., Dolan, R. T., Skodol, A. E., Sanislow, C. A., Dyck, I. R., McGlashan, T. H., Shea, M. T., Zanarini, M. C., Oldham, J. M., & Gunderson, J. G. (2001). Treatment Utilization by Patients With Personality Disorders. *American Journal of Psychiatry*, **158**(2), 295–302. https://doi.org/10.1176/appi.ajp.158.2.295

Berke, J., Birtle, J., Bloom, S., Bradley, C., Briggs, D., Broemer, H., Catala, B., Clarke, A., Coletti, M., Devlin, C., Kressel, D., Lees, J., Loat, M., Lombardo, A., Manning, N., McNeilly, G., Moos, R., Norton, K., Paget, S., ... Ziegenfuss, J. (n.d.). *International Editorial Advisory Group*. 132.

Bernard, H., Burlingame, G., Flores, P., Greene, L., Joyce, A., Kobos, J. C., Leszcz, M., MacNair-Semands, R. R., Piper, W. E., McEneaney, A. M. S., & Feirman, D. (2008). Clinical Practice Guidelines for Group Psychotherapy. *International Journal of Group Psychotherapy*, **58**(4), 455–542. https://doi.org/10.1521/ijgp.2008.58.4.455

Bernstein, R. F. (1998). Reconceptualizing personality disorder diagnosis in the DSM-V: The discriminant validity challenge. *Clinical Psychology: Science and Practice*, **5**(3), 333–343.

BHP. (2021, May 17). *What happens in Group Therapy: Mirroring*. Brighton and Hove Psychotherapy. https://www.brightonandhovepsychotherapy.com/blog/what-happens-in-group-therapy-mirroring/

Blatner, A. (1991). Role dynamics: A comprehensive theory of psychology. *Journal of Group Psychotherapy, Psychodrama & Sociometry*, **44**(1), 33–40.

Blizard, R. A. (1997). *Dissociation: Volume 10, No. 4, p. 246-254: Therapeutic alliance with abuser alters in DID: the paradox of attachment to the abuser*. http://scholarsbank.uoregon.edu/xmlui/handle/1794/1812

Bornstein, R. F. (1998). Implicit and self-attributed dependency needs in dependent and histrionic personality disorders. *Journal of Personality Assessment*, **71**(1), 1–14.

Bowen, M. (2019). Stigma: A linguistic analysis of personality disorder in the UK popular press, 2008–2017. *Journal of Psychiatric and Mental Health Nursing*, **26**(7–8), 244–253. https://doi.org/10.1111/jpm.12541

Bowlby, J. (1980a). *Attachment and loss: Vol. III. Loss*. New York: Basic Books.

Bowlby, J. (1980b). *Attachment andLoss, vol. 3: Loss, Sadness, and Depression*. London: Hogarth Press.

Bowlby, J. (1982). Attachment and loss: Retrospect and prospect. *American Journal of Orthopsychiatry*, **52**(4), 664–678. https://doi.org/10.1111/j.1939-0025.1982.tb01456.x

Braehler, C., Gumley, A., Harper, J., Wallace, S., Norrie, J., & Gilbert, P. (2013). Exploring change processes in compassion focused therapy in psychosis: Results of a feasibility randomized controlled trial. *British Journal of Clinical Psychology*, **52**(2), 199–214. https://doi.org/10.1111/bjc.12009

Braun, V., & Clarke, V. (2006). Using thematic analysis in psychology. *Qualitative Research in Psychology*, **3**(2), 77–101. https://doi.org/10.1191/1478088706qp063oa

Braun, V., & Clarke, V. (2016). (Mis) conceptualising themes, thematic analysis, and other problems with Fugard and Potts'(2015) sample-size tool for thematic analysis. *International Journal of Social Research Methodology*, **19**(6), 739–743.

Brown, D. (n.d.). 8t L. Zinkin,(1994). *The Psyche and the Social World: Development of a Group Analytic Theory*. New York: Routledge.

Brown, T. A., Chorpita, B. F., Korotitsch, W., & Barlow, D. H. (1997). Psychometric properties of the Depression Anxiety Stress Scales (DASS) in clinical samples. *Behaviour Research and Therapy*, **35**(1), 79–89. https://doi.org/10.1016/S0005-7967(96)00068-X

Brüne, M. (2016). Borderline Personality DisorderWhy 'fast and furious'? *Evolution, Medicine, and Public Health*, 2016(1), 52–66.

Buchheim, A., & Diamond, D. (2018). Attachment and Borderline Personality Disorder. *Psychiatric Clinics*, **41**(4), 651–668. https://doi.org/10.1016/j.psc.2018.07.010

Burlingame, G. M., Fuhriman, A., & Johnson, J. E. (2001). Cohesion in group psychotherapy. *Psychotherapy: Theory, Research, Practice, Training*, **38**(4), 373–379. https://doi.org/10.1037/0033-3204.38.4.373

Burlingame, G. M., McClendon, D. T., & Alonso, J. (2011). *Cohesion in group therapy. Psychotherapy*, **48**(1), 34.

Burlingame, G. M., Seebeck, J. D., Janis, R. A., Whitcomb, K. E., Barkowski, S., Rosendahl, J., & Strauss, B. (2016). Outcome differences between individual and group formats when identical and nonidentical treatments, patients, and doses are compared: A 25-year meta-analytic perspective. *Psychotherapy*, **53**(4), 446.

Buss, D. M., & Penke, L. (2015). *Evolutionary personality psychology*. https://psycnet.apa.org/record/2013-35883-001

Byrne, L., Happell, B., & Reid-Searl, K. (2016). Lived experience practitioners and the medical model: World's colliding? *Journal of Mental Health*, **25**(3), 217–223. https://doi.org/10.3109/09638237.2015.1101428

Capinha, M., Matos, M., Pereira, M., Matos, M., & Rijo, D. (2020). The Early Memories of Warmth and Safeness Scale: Dimensionality and Measurement Invariance. *Journal of Affective Disorders*.

Capone, G., Schroder, T., Clarke, S., & Braham, L. (2016). Outcomes of therapeutic community treatment for personality disorder. *Therapeutic Communities: The International Journal of Therapeutic Communities*, **37**(2), 84–100. https://doi.org/10.1108/TC-12-2015-0025

Carlyle, M., Rockliff, H., Edwards, R., Ene, C., Karl, A., Marsh, B., Hartley, L., & Morgan, C. J. (2019). Investigating the Feasibility of Brief Compassion Focused Therapy in Individuals in Treatment for Opioid Use Disorder. *Substance Abuse: Research and Treatment*, **13**, 1178221819836726. https://doi.org/10.1177/1178221819836726

Casement, P. (2013). *On learning from the patient*. Routledge. https://www.taylorfrancis.com/books/mono/10.4324/9781315879468/learning-patient-patrick-casement

Castonguay, L. G., Castonguay, L. G., & Beutler, L. E. (2006). *Principles of Therapeutic Change that Work*. Oxford University Press.

Chartonas, D., Kyratsous, M., Dracass, S., Lee, T., & Bhui, K. (2017). Personality disorder: Still the patients psychiatrists dislike? *BJPsych Bulletin*, **41**(1), 12–17. https://doi.org/10.1192/pb.bp.115.052456

Chiesa, M., Fonagy, P., Holmes, J., Drahorad, C., & Harrison-Hall, A. (2002). Health Service Use Costs by Personality Disorder Following Specialist and Nonspecialist Treatment: A Comparative Study. *Journal of Personality Disorders*, **16**(2), 160–173. https://doi.org/10.1521/pedi.16.2.160.22552

Chiesa, M., Lacoponi, E., & Morris, M. (1996). Changes in Health Service Utilization by Patients with Severe Personality Disorders before and after Inpatient Psychosocial Treatment. *British Journal of Psychotherapy*, **12**(4), 501–512. https://doi.org/10.1111/j.1752-0118.1996.tb00845.x

Chodron, P. (2018). Becoming Bodhisattvas: A Guidebook for Compassionate Action. Shambhala Publications. https://books.google.co.uk/books?hl=en&lr=&id=dQBlDwAAQBAJ&oi=fnd&pg=PT7&dq=pema+choden+buddhism&ots=zDmlD_0gVh&sig=sG5_g1LxHGX2V6jAsq5Ujz9s6Ks

Clapton, N. E., & Hiskey, S. (2023). The Way is in Training: Martial Arts-informed Compassionate Mind Training to enhance CFT Therapists' Compassionate Competencies. OBM Integrative and Complementary Medicine, 08(01), 001. https://doi.org/10.21926/obm.icm.2301001

Cleary, R., & Armour, C. (2022). Exploring the role of practitioner lived experience of mental health issues in counselling and psychotherapy. *Counselling and Psychotherapy Research*, **22**(4), 1100–1111. https://doi.org/10.1002/capr.12569

Clerkin, E. M., Teachman, B. A., & Smith-Janik, S. B. (2008). Sudden gains in group cognitive-behavioral therapy for panic disorder. *Behaviour Research and Therapy*, **46**(11), 1244–1250. https://doi.org/10.1016/j.brat.2008.08.002

Coan, J. (2008). Toward a Neuroscience of Attachment. In *Handbook of attachment: Theory, research, and clinical applications* (pp. 241–268).

Cohen, J. (1988). *Statistical power analysis for the behavioural sciences, 2nd edn*.(Hillsdale, NJ: L. Erlbaum Associates).

Collins, R. N., Gilligan, L. J., & Poz, R. (2018). The Evaluation of a Compassion-Focused Therapy Group for Couples Experiencing a Dementia Diagnosis. *Clinical Gerontologist*, **41**(5), 474–486. https://doi.org/10.1080/07317115.2017.1397830

Cooley, C. H. (1902). The looking-glass self. *The Production of Reality: Essays and Readings on Social Interaction*, **6**(1902), 126–128.

Cooper, A. A., Kline, A. C., Baier, A. L., & Feeny, N. C. (2023). Rethinking Research on Prediction and Prevention of Psychotherapy Dropout: A Mechanism-Oriented Approach. *Behavior Modification*, **47**(6), 1195–1218. https://doi.org/10.1177/0145445518792251

Corrigan, F. M., & Hull, A. M. (2015a). Neglect of the complex: Why psychotherapy for post-traumatic clinical presentations is often ineffective. *BJPsych Bulletin*, **39**(2), 86–89. https://doi.org/10.1192/pb.bp.114.046995

Corrigan, F. M., & Hull, A. M. (2015b). Recognition of the neurobiological insults impo sed by complex trauma and the implications for psychotherapeutic interventions. *BJPsych Bulletin*, **39**(2), 79–86. https://doi.org/10.1192/pb.bp.114.047134

Cozolino, L. (2014). *The Neuroscience of Human Relationships: Attachment and the Developing Social Brain (Second Edition) (Norton Series on Interpersonal Neurobiology)*. W. W. Norton & Company.

Cozolino, L. J. (2008). *The healthy aging brain: Sustaining attachment, attaining wisdom*. WW Norton & Company.

Craig, C., Hiskey, S., & Spector, A. (2020). Compassion focused therapy: A systematic review of its effectiveness and acceptability in clinical populations. *Expert Review of Neurotherapeutics*, **20**(4), 385–400. https://doi.org/10.1080/14737175.2020.1746184

Crawford, M. J., Price, K., Gordon, F., Josson, M., Taylor, B., Bateman, A., Fonagy, P., Tyrer, P., & Moran, P. (2009). Engagement and retention in specialist services for people with personality disorder. *Acta Psychiatrica Scandinavica*, **119**(4), 304–311. https://doi.org/10.1111/j.1600-0447.2008.01306.x

Crawford, M. J., Price, K., Rutter, D., Moran, P., Tyrer, P., Bateman, A., Fonagy, P., Gibson, S., & Weaver, T. (2008). Dedicated community-based services for adults with personality disorder: Delphi study. *The British Journal of Psychiatry*, **193**(4), 342–343.

Critchfield, K. L., & Benjamin, L. S. (2006). Principles for psychosocial treatment of personality disorder: Summary of the APA Division 12 Task Force/NASPR review. *Journal of Clinical Psychology*, **62**(6), 661–674. https://doi.org/10.1002/jclp.20255

Crowe, T. P., & Grenyer, B. F. S. (2008). Is therapist alliance or whole group cohesion more influential in group psychotherapy outcomes? *Clinical Psychology & Psychotherapy*, **15**(4), 239–246. https://doi.org/10.1002/cpp.583

Cuppage, J., Baird, K., Gibson, J., Booth, R., & Hevey, D. (2018). Compassion focused therapy: Exploring the effectiveness with a transdiagnostic group and potential processes of change. *British Journal of Clinical Psychology*, **57**(2), 240–254. https://doi.org/10.1111/bjc.12162

Dalal, F. (1998). *Taking the Group Seriously: Towards a Post-Foulkesian Group Analytic Theory*. Jessica Kingsley Publishers.

Davies, S., & Campling, P. (2003). Therapeutic community treatment of personality disorder: Service use and mortality over 3 years' follow-up. *The British Journal of Psychiatry*, **182**(S44), s24–s27.

Dayton, T. (2015). *Neuropsychodrama in the Treatment of Relational Trauma: A Model Using Experiential Group Processes for Healing PTSD*. Health Communications, Inc.

De Leon, G. (2010). Is the therapeutic community an evidence-based treatment? What the evidence says. *Therapeutic Communities*, **31**(2), 104.

De Saeger, H., Kamphuis, J. H., Finn, S. E., Smith, J. D., Verheul, R., van Busschbach, J. J., Feenstra, D. J., & Horn, E. K. (2014). Therapeutic assessment promotes treatment readiness but does not affect symptom change in patients with personality disorders: Findings from a randomized clinical trial. *Psychological Assessment*, **26**(2), 474–483. https://doi.org/10.1037/a0035667

Depue, R. A., & Morrone-Strupinsky, J. V. (2005). A neurobehavioral model of affiliative bonding: Implications for conceptualizing a human trait of affiliation. *Behavioral and Brain Sciences*, **28**(3), 313–349.

Dobson, K. S. (2009). *Handbook of Cognitive-Behavioral Therapies, Third Edition*. Guilford Press.

Dolan, B. M., Warren, F. M., Menzies, D., & Norton, K. (1996). Cost-offset following specialist treatment of severe personality disorders. *Psychiatric Bulletin*, **20**(7), 413–417. https://doi.org/10.1192/pb.20.7.413

Donald, F., Lawrence, K. A., Broadbear, J. H., & Rao, S. (2019). An exploration of self-compassion and self-criticism in the context of personal recovery from borderline personality disorder. *Australasian Psychiatry*, **27**(1), 56–59. https://doi.org/10.1177/1039856218797418

Downs, S. H., & Black, N. (1998). The feasibility of creating a checklist for the assessment of the methodological quality both of randomised and non-randomised studies of health care interventions. *Journal of Epidemiology & Community Health*, **52**(6), 377–384. https://doi.org/10.1136/jech.52.6.377

Drew, J. (2019). Sapiens: A Brief History of Humankind. *Comparative Civilizations Review*, **80**, 142–148.

Durand, S., & Schank, J. C. (2015). The evolution of social play by learning to cooperate. *Adaptive Behavior*, **23**(6), 340–353. https://doi.org/10.1177/1059712315608243

Evans, C., Connell, J., Barkham, M., Margison, F., McGrath, G., Mellor-Clark, J., & Audin, K. (2002). Towards a standardised brief outcome measure: Psychometric properties and utility of the CORE-OM. *British Journal of Psychiatry*, **180**(1), 51–60. https://doi.org/10.1192/bjp.180.1.51

Evans, John Mellor-Clark, Frank Mar, C. (2000). CORE: Clinical Outcomes in Routine Evaluation. *Journal of Mental Health*, **9**(3), 247–255. https://doi.org/10.1080/jmh.9.3.247.255

Fanaian, M., Lewis, K. L., & Grenyer, B. F. S. (2013). Improving services for people with personality disorders: Views of experienced clinicians. *International Journal of Mental Health Nursing*, **22**(5), 465–471. https://doi.org/10.1111/inm.12009

Farina, B., Liotti, M., & Imperatori, C. (2019). The role of attachment trauma and disintegrative pathogenic processes in the traumatic-dissociative dimension. *Frontiers in Psychology*, **10**, 933.

Fay, D. (2007). *Becoming Safely Embodied: A skills-based approach to working with trauma and dissociation*. Somerville, MA: Heart for Life Publishing.

Fay, D. (2017). *Attachment-Based Yoga & Meditation for Trauma Recovery: Simple, Safe, and Effective Practices for Therapy*. W. W. Norton & Company.

Feiring, C., & Taska, L. S. (2005). The persistence of shame following sexual abuse: A longitudinal look at risk and recovery. *Child Maltreatment*, **10**(4), 337–349.

Feliu-Soler, A., Pascual, J. C., Elices, M., Martín-Blanco, A., Carmona, C., Cebolla, A., Simón, V., & Soler, J. (2017). Fostering self-compassion and loving-kindness in patients with borderline personality disorder: A randomized pilot study. *Clinical Psychology & Psychotherapy*, **24**(1), 278–286.

Field, A. (2000). *Discovering statistics using SPSS:(and sex, drugs and rock'n'roll)* (Vol. 497). Sage.

Flores, P. J., & Porges, S. W. (2017). Group Psychotherapy as a Neural Exercise: Bridging Polyvagal Theory and Attachment Theory. *International Journal of Group Psychotherapy*, **67**(2), 202–222. https://doi.org/10.1080/00207284.2016.1263544

Fonagy, P., & Bateman, A. (2006). Progress in the treatment of borderline personality disorder. *The British Journal of Psychiatry*, **188**(1), 1–3.

Fonagy, P., Campbell, C., & Bateman, A. (2017). Mentalizing, attachment, and epistemic trust in group therapy. *International Journal of Group Psychotherapy*, **67**(2), 176–201.

Fonagy, P., Campbell, C., & Luyten, P. (2018). It's all in the eye of the beholder: Personality and personality disorder as interpersonal phenomena. *European Journal of Personality*, **32**(5), Article 5.

Fonagy, P., Target, M., & Gergely, G. (2000). ATTACHMENT AND BORDERLINE PERSONALITY DISORDER: A Theory and Some Evidence. *Psychiatric Clinics*, **23**(1), 103–122. https://doi.org/10.1016/S0193-953X(05)70146-5

Ford, D. C., Merrick, M. T., Parks, S. E., Breiding, M. J., Gilbert, L. K., Edwards, V. J., Dhingra, S. S., Barile, J. P., & Thompson, W. W. (2014). Examination of the factorial structure of adverse childhood experiences and recommendations for three subscale scores. *Psychology of Violence*, **4**(4), 432.

Fosha, D. (2000). Meta-Therapeutic Processes and the Affects of Transformation: Affirmation and the Healing Affects. *Journal of Psychotherapy Integration*, **10**(1), 71–97. https://doi.org/10.1023/A:1009422511959

Fosha, D. (2001). The dyadic regulation of affect. *Journal of Clinical Psychology*, **57**(2), 227–242. https://doi.org/10.1002/1097-4679(200102)57:2<227::AID-JCLP8>3.0.CO;2-1

Foulkes, S. H. (2018). *Therapeutic group analysis*. Routledge.

Fox, J., Cattani, K., & Burlingame, G. M. (2020). Compassion focused therapy in a university counseling and psychological services center: A feasibility trial of a new standardized group manual. *Psychotherapy Research*, **0**(0), 1–13. https://doi.org/10.1080/10503307.2020.1783708

Frick, W. B. (1999). Flight into Health: A New Interpretation. *Journal of Humanistic Psychology*, **39**(4), 58–81. https://doi.org/10.1177/0022167899394004

Gale, C., Gilbert, P., Read, N., & Goss, K. (2014). An evaluation of the impact of introducing compassion focused therapy to a standard treatment programme for people with eating disorders. *Clinical Psychology & Psychotherapy*, **21**(1), 1–12.

Gallop, R. (2002). Failure of the capacity for self-soothing in women who have a history of abuse and self-harm. *Journal of the American Psychiatric Nurses Association*, **8**(1), 20–26.

Genes on the Couch: Explorations in Evolutionary Psychotherapy. (2014). United Kingdom: Taylor & Francis. (n.d.).

Gilbert, P. (2003). Evolution, Social Roles, and the Differences in Shame and Guilt. *Social Research*, **70**(4), 1205–1230.

Gilbert, P. (2005). *Compassion: Conceptualisations, Research and Use in Psychotherapy*. Routledge.

Gilbert, P. (2009). Introducing compassion-focused therapy. *Advances in Psychiatric Treatment*, **15**(3), 199–208. https://doi.org/10.1192/apt.bp.107.005264

Gilbert, P. (2010). An introduction to compassion focused therapy in cognitive behavior therapy. *International Journal of Cognitive Therapy*, **3**(2), 97–112.

Gilbert, P. (2011). Shame in psychotherapy and the role of compassion focused therapy. In *Shame in the therapy hour* (pp. 325–354). American Psychological Association. https://doi.org/10.1037/12326-014

Gilbert, P. (2015). A biopsychosocial and evolutionary approach to formulation. In *Case Formulation in Cognitive Behaviour Therapy* (2nd ed.). Routledge.

Gilbert, P. (2017a). *Compassion: Concepts, Research and Applications*. Taylor & Francis.

Gilbert, P. (2017b). Compassion: Definitions and controversies. In *Compassion: Concepts, research and applications* (pp. 3–15). Routledge/Taylor & Francis Group. https://doi.org/10.4324/9781315564296-1

Gilbert, P. (2019). Psychotherapy for the 21st century: An integrative, evolutionary, contextual, biopsychosocial approach. *Psychology and Psychotherapy: Theory, Research and Practice*, **92**(2), 164–189. https://doi.org/10.1111/papt.12226

Gilbert, P. (2021). Creating a Compassionate World: Addressing the Conflicts Between Sharing and Caring Versus Controlling and Holding Evolved Strategies. *Frontiers in Psychology*, **11**. https://doi.org/10.3389/fpsyg.2020.582090

Gilbert, P. (2022). An Evolutionary and Compassion-Based Approach to Yearning and Grief. In *Compassion-Based Approaches in Loss and Grief*. Routledge.

Gilbert, P., & Andrews, B. (1998). *Shame: Interpersonal behavior, psychopathology, and culture*. Oxford University Press on Demand.

Gilbert, P., & Bailey, K. G. (2014). *Genes on the Couch: Explorations in Evolutionary Psychotherapy*. Routledge.

Gilbert, P., Catarino, F., Duarte, C., Matos, M., Kolts, R., Stubbs, J., Ceresatto, L., Duarte, J., Pinto-Gouveia, J., & Basran, J. (2017). The development of compassionate engagement and action scales for self and others. *Journal of Compassionate Health Care*, **4**(1), 4. https://doi.org/10.1186/s40639-017-0033-3

Gilbert, P., & Irons, C. (2004). A pilot exploration of the use of compassionate images in a group of self-critical people. *Memory*, **12**(4), 507–516.

Gilbert, P., McEwan, K., Catarino, F., & Baião, R. (2014). *Fears of compassion in a depressed population: Implication for psychotherapy*. https://derby.openrepository.com//handle/10545/621735

Gilbert, P., McEwan, K., Mitra, R., Richter, A., Franks, L., Mills, A., Bellew, R., & Gale, C. (2009). *An exploration of different types of positive affect in students and patients with bipolar disorder*.

Gilbert, P., & Procter, S. (2006). Compassionate mind training for people with high shame and self-criticism: Overview and pilot study of a group therapy approach. *Clinical Psychology & Psychotherapy*, **13**(6), 353–379. https://doi.org/10.1002/cpp.507

Gilbert, P., & Simos, G. (2022). *Compassion focused therapy: Clinical practice and applications*. Routledge. https://books.google.co.uk/books?hl=en&lr=&id=m99aEAAAQBAJ&oi=fnd&pg=PT14&dq=gilbert+and+grigoris+compassion+focused+therapy&ots=sDSOX7s6Bi&sig=skmX0VafHkuIRHDe713FgOEkg00

Goodman, M., & Weiss, D. (2000). Initiating, screening, and maintaining psychotherapy groups for traumatized patients. In *Group psychotherapy for psychological trauma* (pp. 47–63). Guilford Press.

Granås, J., Strand, J., & Sand, P. (2023). A patient perspective on non-attendance for psychotherapy in psychiatric outpatient care for patients with affective disorders. *Nordic Psychology*, **75**(4), 313–327. https://doi.org/10.1080/19012276.2022.2093777

Graser, J., Höfling, V., Weßlau, C., Mendes, A., & Stangier, U. (2016). Effects of a 12-Week Mindfulness, Compassion, and Loving Kindness Program on Chronic Depression: A Pilot Within-Subjects Wait-List Controlled Trial. *Journal of Cognitive Psychotherapy*, **30**(1), 35–49. https://doi.org/10.1891/0889-8391.30.1.35

Grodin, J., Clark, J. L., Kolts, R., & Lovejoy, T. I. (2019). Compassion focused therapy for anger: A pilot study of a group intervention for veterans with PTSD. *Journal of Contextual Behavioral Science*, **13**, 27–33. https://doi.org/10.1016/j.jcbs.2019.06.004

Gunderson, J. G., Stout, R. L., Shea, M. T., Grilo, C. M., Markowitz, J. C., Morey, L. C., Sanislow, C. A., Yen, S., Zanarini, M. C., & Keuroghlian, A. S. (2014). Interactions of borderline personality disorder and mood disorders over ten years. *Journal of Clinical Psychiatry*, **75**(8), 829.

References

Haas, E., Hill, R. D., Lambert, M. J., & Morrell, B. (2002). Do early responders to psychotherapy maintain treatment gains? *Journal of Clinical Psychology*, **58**(9), 1157–1172. https://doi.org/10.1002/jclp.10044

Haigh, R. (2013). The quintessence of a therapeutic environment. *Therapeutic Communities: The International Journal of Therapeutic Communities*, **34**(1), 6–15. https://doi.org/10.1108/09641861311330464

Hansen, N. B., Lambert, M. J., & Forman, E. M. (2002). The Psychotherapy Dose-Response Effect and Its Implications for Treatment Delivery Services. *Clinical Psychology: Science and Practice*, **9**(3), 329–343. https://doi.org/10.1093/clipsy.9.3.329

Harari, Y. N. (2014). Sapiens: A brief history of humankind. *Harvill Secker*. https://books.google.co.uk/books?hl=en&lr=&id=B4ARBAAAQBAJ&oi=fnd&pg=PP9&dq=sapiens+a+brief+history+of+humankind&ots=tQgtmgHsBK&sig=LUvVbPluJxS_tVYPKJQGNlJsTzM

Harris, D. L. (2019). Non-death loss and grief: Laying the foundation. In *Non-death loss and grief* (pp. 7–16). Routledge. https://www.taylorfrancis.com/chapters/edit/10.4324/9780429446054-2/non-death-loss-grief-laying-foundation-darcy-harris

Harris, D. L., & Hiskey, S. (2015). Homework in therapy: A case of it ain't what you do, it's the way that you do it? *The Cognitive Behaviour Therapist*, **8**, e20. https://doi.org/10.1017/S1754470X15000549

Harrison, T. (2000). *Bion, Rickman, Foulkes, and the Northfield experiments: Advancing on a different front* (Vol. 5). Jessica Kingsley Publishers. https://books.google.co.uk/books?hl=en&lr=&id=7GSxUyST-xoC&oi=fnd&pg=IA3&dq=tom+harrison+advancing+&ots=i5vN4i8WMw&sig=YNWJ9GfCQxaAc1yH0vqdYyfNqaI

Heriot-Maitland, C., Knight, M., & Peters, E. (2012). A qualitative comparison of psychotic-like phenomena in clinical and non-clinical populations. *British Journal of Clinical Psychology*, **51**(1), 37–53. https://doi.org/10.1111/j.2044-8260.2011.02011.x

Herman, J. L. (1992). Complex PTSD: A syndrome in survivors of prolonged and repeated trauma. *Journal of Traumatic Stress*, **5**(3), 377–391.

Herman, J. L. (1998). Recovery from psychological trauma. *Psychiatry and Clinical Neurosciences*, **52**(S1), S98–S103. https://doi.org/10.1046/j.1440-1819.1998.0520s5S145.x

Herman, J. L. (2002). Peace on earth begins at home: Reflections from the women's liberation movement. *Breaking the Cycles of Hatred: Memory, Law, and Repair*, 188–199.

Herman, J. L., Perry, J. C., & Van der Kolk, B. A. (1989). Childhood trauma in borderline personality disorder. *The American Journal of Psychiatry*, **146**(4), 490–495. https://doi.org/10.1176/ajp.146.4.490

Hobson, N. M., Schroeder, J., Risen, J. L., Xygalatas, D., & Inzlicht, M. (2018). The Psychology of Rituals: An Integrative Review and Process-Based Framework. *Personality and Social Psychology Review*, **22**(3), 260–284. https://doi.org/10.1177/1088868317734944

Hobson, R. F. (2013). *Forms of feeling: The heart of psychotherapy*. Routledge.

Holmes, J. (2001). *The search for the secure base: Attachment theory and psychotherapy*. Psychology Press.

Holmes, J. (2004). Disorganized attachment and Borderline Personality Disorder: A clinical perspective. *Attachment & Human Development*, **6**(2), 181–190. https://doi.org/10.1080/14616730410001688202

HOPWOOD, C. J., KOTOV, R., KRUEGER, R. F., WATSON, D., WIDIGER, T. A., ALTHOFF, R. R., ANSELL, E. B., BACH, B., BAGBY, R. M., BLAIS, M. A., BORNOVALOVA, M. A., CHMIELEWSKI, M., CICERO, D. C., CONWAY, C., DE CLERQ, B., DE FRUYT, F., DOCHERTY, A. R., EATON, N. R., EDENS, J. F., … ZIMMERMANN, J. (2018). The time has come for dimensional personality disorder diagnosis. *Personality and Mental Health*, **12**(1), 82–86. https://doi.org/10.1002/pmh.1408

Hudgins, K. (2019). Psychodrama Revisited: Through the Lens of the Internal Role Map of the Therapeutic Spiral Model to Promote Post-traumatic Growth. *Zeitschrift Für Psychodrama Und Soziometrie*, **18**, 1–16. https://doi.org/10.1007/s11620-019-00483-7

Iliakis, E. A., Ilagan, G. S., & Choi-Kain, L. W. (2021). Dropout rates from psychotherapy trials for borderline personality disorder: A meta-analysis. *Personality Disorders: Theory, Research, and Treatment*, **12**(3), 193–206. https://doi.org/10.1037/per0000453

Jacobson, N. S., Roberts, L. J., Berns, S. B., & McGlinchey, J. B. (1999). Methods for defining and determining the clinical significance of treatment effects: Description, application, and alternatives. *Journal of Consulting and Clinical Psychology*, **67**(3), 300.

Jinpa, T. (2015). *A Fearless Heart: Why Compassion is the Key to Greater Wellbeing*. Hachette UK.

Johnstone, L. (2013). Controversies and debates about formulation. In *Formulation in Psychology and Psychotherapy* (2nd ed.). Routledge.

Jones, B., Juett, G., & Hill, N. (2013). Initial outcomes of a therapeutic community-based outpatient programme in the management of personality disorder. *Therapeutic Communities: The International Journal of Therapeutic Communities*.

Judge, L., Cleghorn, A., McEwan, K., & Gilbert, P. (2012). An exploration of group-based compassion focused therapy for a heterogeneous range of clients presenting to a community mental health team. *International Journal of Cognitive Therapy*, **5**(4), 420–429.

Kabat-Zinn, J., & Salzberg, S. (2004). *Lovingkindness: The revolutionary art of happiness*. Shambhala Publications.

Kalleklev, J., & Karterud, S. (2018). A comparative study of a mentalization-based versus a psychodynamic group therapy session. *Group Analysis*, **51**(1), 44–60.

Kamphuis, J. H., & Finn, S. E. (2019). Therapeutic Assessment in Personality Disorders: Toward the Restoration of Epistemic Trust. *Journal of Personality Assessment*, **101**(6), 662–674. https://doi.org/10.1080/00223891.2018.1476360

Kaufman, J., Plotsky, P. M., Nemeroff, C. B., & Charney, D. S. (2000). Effects of early adverse experiences on brain structure and function: Clinical implications. *Biological Psychiatry*, **48**(8), 778–790. https://doi.org/10.1016/S0006-3223(00)00998-7

Kellogg, S., & Garcia Torres, A. (2021). Toward a chairwork psychotherapy: Using the four dialogues for healing and transformation. *Practice Innovations*, **6**(3), 171–180. https://doi.org/10.1037/pri0000149

Kelly, A. C., & Dupasquier, J. (2016). Social safeness mediates the relationship between recalled parental warmth and the capacity for self-compassion and receiving compassion. *Personality and Individual Differences*, **89**, 157–161.

Kelly, A. C., Vimalakanthan, K., & Carter, J. C. (2014). Understanding the roles of self-esteem, self-compassion, and fear of self-compassion in eating disorder pathology: An examination of female students and eating disorder patients. *Eating Behaviors*, **15**(3), 388–391. https://doi.org/10.1016/j.eatbeh.2014.04.008

Kelly, A. C., Wisniewski, L., Martin-Wagar, C., & Hoffman, E. (n.d.). Group-Based Compassion-Focused Therapy as an Adjunct to Outpatient Treatment for Eating Disorders: A Pilot Randomized Controlled Trial. *Clinical Psychology & Psychotherapy*, **24**(2), 475–487. https://doi.org/10.1002/cpp.2018

Kelly, A. C., Zuroff, D. C., Leybman, M. J., & Gilbert, P. (2012). Social safeness, received social support, and maladjustment: Testing a tripartite model of affect regulation. *Cognitive Therapy and Research*, **36**(6), 815–826.

Kinderman, P., Read, J., Moncrieff, J., & Bentall, R. P. (2013). *Drop the language of disorder*. Royal College of Psychiatrists.

Kipper, D. A. (1986). *Psychotherapy through clinical role playing*. Brunner/Mazel.

Kirby, J. N., Tellegen, C. L., & Steindl, S. R. (2017). A Meta-Analysis of Compassion-Based Interventions: Current State of Knowledge and Future Directions. *Behavior Therapy*, **48**(6), 778–792. https://doi.org/10.1016/j.beth.2017.06.003

Kleij, G. V. D. (2016). *The Setting of the Group: Group Analysis*. https://doi.org/10.1177/053331648301600108

Kling, R. (2014). Borderline Personality Disorder, Language, and Stigma. *Ethical Human Psychology and Psychiatry*, **16**(2), 114–119. https://doi.org/10.1891/1559-4343.16.2.114

Knights, D., & McCabe, D. (1998). 'What Happens when the Phone goes Wild?': Staff, Stress and Spaces for Escape in a BPR Telephone Banking Work Regime. *Journal of Management Studies*, **35**(2), 163–194. https://doi.org/10.1111/1467-6486.00089

Kolk, B. A. V. der. (2003). *Psychological Trauma*. American Psychiatric Pub.

Kolts, R. L. (2016). *CFT Made Simple: A Clinician's Guide to Practicing Compassion-Focused Therapy*. New Harbinger Publications.

Kolts, R. L., Bell, T., Bennett-Levy, J., & Irons, C. (2018). *Experiencing compassion-focused therapy from the inside out: A self-practice/self-reflection workbook for therapists*. Guilford Publications.

Lahousen, T., Unterrainer, H. F., & Kapfhammer, H.-P. (2019). Psychobiology of attachment and trauma—Some general remarks from a clinical perspective. *Frontiers in Psychiatry*, **10**, 914.

Laithwaite, H., O'Hanlon, M., Collins, P., Doyle, P., Abraham, L., Porter, S., & Gumley, A. (2009). Recovery after psychosis (RAP): A compassion focused programme for individuals residing in high security settings. *Behavioural and Cognitive Psychotherapy*, **37**(5), 511.

Lama, D. (2009). *For the benefit of all beings: A commentary on The Way of the Bodhisattva*. Shambhala Publications.

Lawrence, V. A., & Lee, D. (2014). An Exploration of People's Experiences of Compassion-focused Therapy for Trauma, Using Interpretative Phenomenological Analysis. *Clinical Psychology & Psychotherapy*, **21**(6), 495–507. https://doi.org/10.1002/cpp.1854

Leaviss, J., & Uttley, L. (2015). Psychotherapeutic benefits of compassion-focused therapy: An early systematic review. *Psychological Medicine*, **45**(5), 927–945. https://doi.org/10.1017/S0033291714002141

LeDoux, J. (1998). *The emotional brain: The mysterious underpinnings of emotional life*. Simon and Schuster.

Lee, D., & James, S. (2012). *The Compassionate Mind Approach to Recovering from Trauma: Using Compassion Focused Therapy*. Hachette UK.

Lee, R., Geracioti Jr, T. D., Kasckow, J. W., & Coccaro, E. F. (2005). Childhood trauma and personality disorder: Positive correlation with adult CSF corticotropin-releasing factor concentrations. *American Journal of Psychiatry*, **162**(5), 995–997.

Leibovich, M. (1975). An aspect of the psychotherapy of borderline personalities. *Psychotherapy and Psychosomatics*, **25**(1/6), 53–57.

Leiderman, L. M. (2020). Psychodynamic group therapy with hispanic migrants: Interpersonal, relational constructs in treating complex trauma, dissociation, and enactments. *International Journal of Group Psychotherapy*, **70**(2), 162–182.

Lewis, G., & Appleby, L. (1988). Personality Disorder: The Patients Psychiatrists Dislike. *British Journal of Psychiatry*, **153**(1), 44–49. https://doi.org/10.1192/bjp.153.1.44

Lilienfeld, S. O., Waldman, I. D., & Israel, A. C. (1994). A Critical Examination of the Use of the Term and Concept of Comorbidity in Psychopathology Research. *Clinical Psychology: Science and Practice*, **1**(1), 71–83. https://doi.org/10.1111/j.1468-2850.1994.tb00007.x

Linehan, M. (2014). *DBT? Skills training manual*. Guilford Publications.

Liotti, G. (2012). Disorganized attachment and the therapeutic relationship with people in shattered states. In *Shattered states: Disorganised attachment and its repair* (pp. 127–156). Karnac Books.

Liotti, G. (2017). Conflicts between motivational systems related to attachment trauma: Key to understanding the intra-family relationship between abused children and their abusers. *Journal of Trauma & Dissociation*, **18**(3), 304–318. https://doi.org/10.1080/15299732.2017.1295392

Liotti, G., & Gilbert, P. (2011). Mentalizing, motivation, and social mentalities: Theoretical considerations and implications for psychotherapy. *Psychology and Psychotherapy: Theory, Research and Practice*, **84**(1), 9–25.

Longe, O., Maratos, F. A., Gilbert, P., Evans, G., Volker, F., Rockliff, H., & Rippon, G. (2010). Having a word with yourself: Neural correlates of self-criticism and self-reassurance. *NeuroImage*, **49**(2), 1849–1856.

Lorentzen, S. (2013). *Group analytic psychotherapy: Working with affective, anxiety and personality disorders*. Routledge.

Lucre, K. (2022). Compassion Focused Group Psychotherapy for people who could attract a diagnosis of personality disorder. In *Compassion Focused Therapy: Clinical practice and applications*. Routledge/Taylor & Francis Group.

Lucre, K., Ashworth, F., Copello, A., Jones, C., & Gilbert, P. (n.d.). *Compassion Focused Group Psychotherapy for attachment and relational trauma: Engaging people with a diagnosis of personality disorder*.

Lucre, K., & Clapton, N. (n.d.). The Compassionate Kitbag: A creative and integrative approach to compassion-focused therapy. *Psychology and Psychotherapy: Theory, Research and Practice*, e12291.

Lucre, K. M., & Corten, N. (2013). An exploration of group compassion-focused therapy for personality disorder. *Psychology and Psychotherapy: Theory, Research and Practice*, **86**(4), 387–400.

Lyddon, W. J., & Sherry, A. (2001). Developmental personality styles: An attachment theory conceptualization of personality disorders. *Journal of Counseling & Development*, **79**(4), 405–414.

Lyons, E. E., & Coyle, A. E. (2007). *Analysing qualitative data in psychology*. Sage Publications Ltd.

Main, M. (1995). Recent studies in attachment: Overview, with selected implications for clinical work. In *Attachment theory: Social, developmental, and clinical perspectives* (pp. 407–474). Analytic Press, Inc.

Malat, J., Cheng, S. E. T., & Tay, A. T. S. (2020). Group Psychotherapy. In A. Tasman, M. B. Riba, R. D. Alarcón, C. A. Alfonso, S. Kanba, D. M. Ndetei, C. H. Ng, T. G. Schulze, & D. Lecic-Tosevski (Eds.), *Tasman's Psychiatry* (pp. 1–36). Springer International Publishing. https://doi.org/10.1007/978-3-030-42825-9_37-1

Mangione, L., Forti, R., & Iacuzzi, C. M. (2007). Ethics and Endings in Group Psychotherapy: Saying Good-bye and Saying it Well. *International Journal of Group Psychotherapy*, **57**(1), 25–40. https://doi.org/10.1521/ijgp.2007.57.1.25

Marks-Tarlow, T. (2012). The Play of Psychotherapy. *American Journal of Play*, **4**(3), 352–377.

Martin, J., Cummings, A. L., & Hallberg, E. T. (1992). Therapists' intentional use of metaphor: Memorability, clinical impact, and possible epistemic/motivational functions. *Journal of Consulting and Clinical Psychology*, **60**(1), 143–145. https://doi.org/10.1037/0022-006X.60.1.143

Matos, M., Duarte, C., Duarte, J., Pinto-Gouveia, J., Petrocchi, N., & Gilbert, P. (2022). Cultivating the Compassionate Self: An Exploration of the Mechanisms of Change in Compassionate Mind Training. *Mindfulness*, **13**(1), 66–79. https://doi.org/10.1007/s12671-021-01717-2

Matos, M., Duarte, J., Duarte, C., Gilbert, P., & Pinto-Gouveia, J. (2018). How One Experiences and Embodies Compassionate Mind Training Influences Its Effectiveness. *Mindfulness*, **9**(4), 1224–1235. https://doi.org/10.1007/s12671-017-0864-1

McCarthy, K. L., Carter, P. E., & Grenyer, B. F. (2013). Challenges to getting evidence into practice: Expert clinician perspectives on psychotherapy for personality disorders. *Journal of Mental Health*, **22**(6), 482–491.

McMurran, M. (2012). Readiness to Engage in Treatments for Personality Disorder. *International Journal of Forensic Mental Health*, **11**(4), 289–298. https://doi.org/10.1080/14999013.2012.746754

McMurran, M., Huband, N., & Overton, E. (2010). Non-completion of personality disorder treatments: A systematic review of correlates, consequences, and interventions. *Clinical Psychology Review*, **30**(3), 277–287. https://doi.org/10.1016/j.cpr.2009.12.002

McMurran, M., & Ward, T. (2010). Treatment readiness, treatment engagement and behaviour change. *Criminal Behaviour and Mental Health*, **20**(2), 75–85.

Meares, R., & Stevenson, J. (1992). An outcome study of psychotherapy for patients with borderline personality disorder. *American Journal of Psychiatry*, **149**(3), 358–362.

Meuldijk, D., McCarthy, A., Bourke, M. E., & Grenyer, B. F. S. (2017). The value of psychological treatment for borderline personality disorder: Systematic review and cost offset analysis of economic evaluations. *PLOS ONE*, **12**(3), e0171592. https://doi.org/10.1371/journal.pone.0171592

Mikulincer, M., & Shaver, P. R. (2007a). *Attachment in Adulthood: Structure, Dynamics, and Change*. Guilford Press.

Mikulincer, M., & Shaver, P. R. (2007b). Boosting attachment security to promote mental health, prosocial values, and inter-group tolerance. *Psychological Inquiry*, **18**(3), 139–156.

Miller-Bottome, M., Talia, A., Eubanks, C. F., Safran, J. D., & Muran, J. C. (2019). Secure in-session attachment predicts rupture resolution: Negotiating a secure base. *Psychoanalytic Psychology*, **36**(2), 132–138. https://doi.org/10.1037/pap0000232

Mitchell, A. J., & Selmes, T. (2007). Why don't patients attend their appointments? Maintaining engagement with psychiatric services. *Advances in Psychiatric Treatment*, **13**(6), 423–434.

Molina, J. D., López-Muñoz, F., Stein, D. J., Martín-Vázquez, M. J., Alamo, C., Lerma-Carrillo, I., Andrade-Rosa, C., Sánchez-López, M. V., & de la Calle-Real, M. (2009). Borderline personality disorder: A review and reformulation from evolutionary theory. *Medical Hypotheses*, **73**(3), 382–386.

Moreno, J. L. (1987). *The essential Moreno: Writings on psychodrama, group method, and spontaneity*. Springer Publishing Company. https://books.google.co.uk/books?hl=en&lr=&id=dIAJWORz1JIC&oi=fnd&pg=PR5&dq=moreno+1987&ots=NzPt3GySqx&sig=mvMvaDOLo44HN_BOgFr-W0hVtzo

Mosquera, D., Gonzalez, A., & Leeds, A. M. (2014). Early experience, structural dissociation, and emotional dysregulation in borderline personality disorder: The role of insecure and disorganized attachment. *Borderline Personality Disorder and Emotion Dysregulation*, **1**(1), 15. https://doi.org/10.1186/2051-6673-1-15

Mullen, G., Dowling, C., Doyle, J., & O'Reilly, G. (2020). Experiences of compassion focused therapy in eating disorder recovery: A qualitative model. *Counselling and Psychotherapy Research*, **20**(2), 248–262. https://doi.org/10.1002/capr.12283

Mundt, J. C., Marks, I. M., Shear, M. K., & Greist, J. M. (2002). The Work and Social Adjustment Scale: A simple measure of impairment in functioning. *British Journal of Psychiatry*, **180**(5), 461–464. https://doi.org/10.1192/bjp.180.5.461

Music, G. (2018). *Nurturing Children: From Trauma to Growth Using Attachment Theory, Psychoanalysis and Neurobiology*. Routledge.

Naismith, I., Guerrero, S. Z., & Feigenbaum, J. (2019). Abuse, invalidation, and lack of early warmth show distinct relationships with self-criticism, self-compassion, and fear of self-compassion in personality disorder. *Clinical Psychology & Psychotherapy*, **26**(3), 350–361. https://doi.org/10.1002/cpp.2357

Narvaez, D. (2020). Ecocentrism: Resetting Baselines for Virtue Development. *Ethical Theory and Moral Practice*, **23**(2), 391–406. https://doi.org/10.1007/s10677-020-10091-2

Narvaez, D., & Bradshaw, G. A. (2023). *The evolved nest: Nature's way of raising children and creating connected communities*. North Atlantic Books. https://books.google.co.uk/books?hl=en&lr=&id=3gB_EAAAQBAJ&oi=fnd&pg=PR13&dq=darcia+narvaez+the+evolved+nest&ots=EBwoXH5dd2&sig=zpauoOZ-7LCxaJxH4ThSP5rZ984

National Collaborating Centre for Mental Health (UK). (2009). *Borderline Personality Disorder: Treatment and Management*. British Psychological Society. http://www.ncbi.nlm.nih.gov/books/NBK55403/

Navab, M., Dehghani, A., & Salehi, M. (2019). Effect of compassion-focused group therapy on psychological symptoms in mothers of attention-deficit hyperactivity disorder children: A pilot study. *Counselling and Psychotherapy Research*, **19**(2), 149–157. https://doi.org/10.1002/capr.12212

Nitsun, M. (1998). THE ANTI-GROUP: Destructive and Creative Forces in Groups. Mikbatz: *The Israel Journal of Group Psychotherapy* / מקבץ: כתב העת הישראלי להנחיה ולפיטול קבוצתי, **4**(1), I–XVIII.

Nitsun, M. (2014). *The anti-group: Destructive forces in the group and their creative potential*. Routledge.

Nitsun, M. (2015). The anti-group: Destructive forces in the group and their therapeutic potential*. In *Foundations of Group Analysis for the Twenty-First Century*. Routledge.

Norton, P. J., Klenck, S. C., & Barrera, T. L. (2010). Sudden gains during cognitive–behavioral group therapy for anxiety disorders. *Journal of Anxiety Disorders*, **24**(8), 887–892. https://doi.org/10.1016/j.janxdis.2010.06.012

Ogden, P., & Fisher, J. (2015). *Sensorimotor psychotherapy: Interventions for trauma and attachment* (Norton series on interpersonal neurobiology). WW Norton & Company.

Ogden, P., Minton, K., & Pain, C. (2006). *Trauma and the Body: A Sensorimotor Approach to Psychotherapy* (Norton Series on Interpersonal Neurobiology). W. W. Norton & Company.

Panksepp, J. (1998). The periconscious substrates of consciousness: Affective states and the evolutionary origins of the self. *Journal of Consciousness Studies*, **5**(5–6), 566–582.

Panksepp, J. (2004). *Affective Neuroscience: The Foundations of Human and Animal Emotions*. Oxford University Press.

Panksepp, J. (2007). Can PLAY Diminish ADHD and Facilitate the Construction of the Social Brain? *Journal of the Canadian Academy of Child and Adolescent Psychiatry*, **16**(2), 57–66.

Panksepp, J. (2015). Give Play a Chance. *The Handbook of the Study of Play*, **2**, 477.

Panksepp, J., Siviy, S., & Normansell, L. (1984). The psychobiology of play: Theoretical and methodological perspectives. *Neuroscience & Biobehavioral Reviews*, **8**(4), 465–492. https://doi.org/10.1016/0149-7634(84)90005-8

Paterson, R. J. (2022). *The assertiveness workbook: How to express your ideas and stand up for yourself at work and in relationships*. New Harbinger Publications. https://books.google.co.uk/books?hl=en&lr=&id=_P9bEAAAQBAJ&oi=fnd&pg=PT12&dq=the+assertiveness+workbook+randy+paterson&ots=49e031D-h5&sig=Wng4R0nwE6BFhlHQFer_eCRwYMw

Payne, P., Levine, P. A., & Crane-Godreau, M. A. (2015a). '*Somatic Experiencing: Using interoception and proprioception as core elements of trauma therapy*': Corrigendum.

Payne, P., Levine, P. A., & Crane-Godreau, M. A. (2015b). Somatic experiencing: Using interoception and proprioception as core elements of trauma therapy. *Frontiers in Psychology*, **6**, 93.

Pearce, S., & Haigh, R. (2008). Mini therapeutic communities–a new development in the United Kingdom. *Therapeutic Communities*, **29**(2), 111–124.

Pearlman, L. A., & Courtois, C. A. (2005). Clinical applications of the attachment framework: Relational treatment of complex trauma. *Journal of Traumatic Stress*, **18**(5), 449–459. https://doi.org/10.1002/jts.20052

Penlington, C. (2018). Exploring a compassion-focused intervention for persistent pain in a group setting. *British Journal of Pain*, 2049463718772148. https://doi.org/10.1177/2049463718772148

Pepping, C. A., Lyons, A., McNair, R., Kirby, J. N., Petrocchi, N., & Gilbert, P. (2017). A tailored compassion-focused therapy program for sexual minority young adults with depressive symotomatology: Study protocol for a randomized controlled trial. *BMC Psychology*, **5**(1). https://doi.org/10.1186/s40359-017-0175-2

Pistole, M. C., & Watkins, C. E. (1995). Attachment theory, counseling process, and supervision. *The Counseling Psychologist*, **23**(3), 457–478. https://doi.org/10.1177/0011000095233004

Porges, S. W. (2011). *The polyvagal theory: Neurophysiological foundations of emotions, attachment, communication, and self-regulation (Norton Series on Interpersonal Neurobiology)*. WW Norton & Company.

Porges, S. W. (2017). Vagal pathways: Portals to compassion. *The Oxford Handbook of Compassion Science*, 189–202.

Rihacek, T., & Roubal, J. (2017). Personal therapeutic approach: Concept and implications. *Journal of Psychotherapy Integration*, **27**(4), 548.

Robles, T. F., & Kane, H. S. (2014). The attachment system and physiology in adulthood: Normative processes, individual differences, and implications for health. *Journal of Personality*, **82**(6), 515–527.

Rogers, C. (2015). *The Institute of Group Analysis > Members & Students Areas > Students Area > Students Area > London > Foundation Course > Lecture timetable > 15/10/15 Dynamic Administration*. https://www.groupanalysis.org/MembersStudentsAreas/StudentsArea/StudentsArea/London/FoundationCourse/Lecturetimetable/151015DynamicAdministration.aspx

Rogers, C. (2017). 'Just don't get involved': Countertransference and the group – Engaging with the projective processes in groups. In *Introduction to Countertransference in Therapeutic Practice*. Routledge.

Roulston, K. (2001). Data analysis and 'theorizing as ideology'. *Qualitative Research*, **1**(3), 279–302.

Rüsch, N., Lieb, K., Göttler, I., Hermann, C., Schramm, E., Richter, H., Jacob, G. A., Corrigan, P. W., & Bohus, M. (2007). Shame and Implicit Self-Concept in Women With Borderline Personality Disorder. *American Journal of Psychiatry*, **164**(3), 500–508. https://doi.org/10.1176/ajp.2007.164.3.500

Sabo, A. N. (1997). Etiological significance of associations between childhood trauma and borderline personality disorder: Conceptual and clinical implications. *Journal of Personality Disorders*, **11**(1), 50–70.

Safran, J. D., Muran, J. C., & Eubanks-Carter, C. (2011). Repairing alliance ruptures. *Psychotherapy*, **48**(1), 80–87. https://doi.org/10.1037/a0022140

Sanislow, C. A., & McGlashan, T. H. (1998). Treatment Outcome of Personality Disorders. *The Canadian Journal of Psychiatry*, **43**(3), 237–250. https://doi.org/10.1177/070674379804300302

Schlapobersky, J. R. (2016). Structure: Dynamic administration, composition, selection. In *From the Couch to the Circle*. Routledge.

Schlesinger, H. J. (2013). *Endings and Beginnings: On terminating psychotherapy and psychoanalysis*. Routledge.

Schore, A. N. (2015). *Affect regulation and the origin of the self: The neurobiology of emotional development*. Routledge.

Seppälä, E. M., Simon-Thomas, E., Brown, S. L., Worline, M. C., Cameron, C. D., & Doty, J. R. (2017). *The Oxford Handbook of Compassion Science*. Oxford University Press.

Sheehan, L., Nieweglowski, K., & Corrigan, P. (2016). The Stigma of Personality Disorders. *Current Psychiatry Reports*, **18**(1), 11. https://doi.org/10.1007/s11920-015-0654-1

Sheridan, M. A., & McLaughlin, K. A. (2020). Neurodevelopmental mechanisms linking ACEs with psychopathology. In *Adverse childhood experiences* (pp. 265–285). Elsevier. https://www.sciencedirect.com/science/article/pii/B9780128160657000136

Silva, C., Ferreira, C., Mendes, A. L., & Marta-Simões, J. (2019). The relation of early positive emotional memories to women's social safeness: The role of shame and fear of receiving compassion. *Women & Health*, **59**(4), 420–432.

Sloman, L., & Taylor, P. (2016). Impact of Child Maltreatment on Attachment and Social Rank Systems: Introducing an Integrated Theory. *Trauma, Violence, & Abuse*, **17**(2), 172–185. https://doi.org/10.1177/1524838015584354

Smith, A., Pedersen, E. J., Forster, D. E., McCullough, M. E., & Lieberman, D. (2017). Cooperation: The roles of interpersonal value and gratitude. *Evolution and Human Behavior*, **38**(6), 695–703.

Speer, D. C. (1993). 'Clinically significant change: Jacobson and Truax (1991) revisited': Correction.

Spong, A. J., Clare, I. C. H., Galante, J., Crawford, M. J., & Jones, P. B. (2020). Brief psychological interventions for borderline personality disorder. A systematic review and meta-analysis of randomised controlled trials. *Clinical Psychology Review*, 101937. https://doi.org/10.1016/j.cpr.2020.101937

Sroufe, L. A. (1986). Appraisal: Bowlby's contribution to psychoanalytic theory and developmental psychology; Attachment: Separation: Loss. *Journal of Child Psychology and Psychiatry*, **27**(6), 841–849.

Steele, K., Van Der Hart, O., & Nijenhuis, E. R. S. (2001). Dependency in the Treatment of Complex Posttraumatic Stress Disorder and Dissociative Disorders. *Journal of Trauma & Dissociation*, **2**(4), 79–116. https://doi.org/10.1300/J229v02n04_05

Steindl, S., Bell, T., Dixon, A., & Kirby, J. N. (2023). Therapist perspectives on working with fears, blocks and resistances to compassion in compassion focused therapy. *Counselling and Psychotherapy Research*, **23**(3), 850–863. https://doi.org/10.1002/capr.12530

Stiles, W. B., Leach, C., Barkham, M., Lucock, M., Iveson, S., Shapiro, D. A., Iveson, M., & Hardy, G. E. (2003). Early sudden gains in psychotherapy under routine clinic conditions: Practice-based evidence. *Journal of Consulting and Clinical Psychology*, **71**(1), 14–21. https://doi.org/10.1037/0022-006X.71.1.14

Strauss, J. L., Hayes, A. M., Johnson, S. L., Newman, C. F., Brown, G. K., Barber, J. P., Laurenceau, J.-P., & Beck, A. T. (2006). Early alliance, alliance ruptures, and symptom change in a nonrandomized trial of cognitive therapy for avoidant and obsessive-compulsive personality disorders. *Journal of Consulting and Clinical Psychology*, **74**(2), 337–345. https://doi.org/10.1037/0022-006X.74.2.337

Swart, S., Wildschut, M., Draijer, N., Langeland, W., & Smit, J. H. (2020). Dissociative subtype of posttraumatic stress disorder or PTSD with comorbid dissociative disorders: Comparative evaluation of clinical profiles. *Psychological Trauma: Theory, Research, Practice, and Policy*, **12**(1), 38.

Tangney, J. P., & Dearing, R. L. (2003). *Shame and Guilt*. Guilford Press.

Taylor, J., & Hocken, K. (2021). People hurt people: Reconceptualising criminogenic need to promote trauma sensitive and compassion focussed practice. *The Journal of Forensic Practice*, **23**(3), 201–212. https://doi.org/10.1108/JFP-04-2021-0015

Terr, L. C. (1991). Acute responses to external events and posttraumatic stress disorders. In *Child and adolescent psychiatry: A comprehensive textbook* (pp. 755–763). Williams & Wilkins Co.

Thomas, P. M. (2005). Dissociation and Internal Models of Protection: Psychotherapy With Child Abuse Survivors. *Psychotherapy: Theory, Research, Practice, Training*, **42**(1), 20.

Tomasulo, D. J. (1998). *Action methods in group psychotherapy*. Ann Arbor, MI: Braun-Brumfield.

Tomko, R. L., Trull, T. J., Wood, P. K., & Sher, K. J. (2014). Characteristics of Borderline Personality Disorder in a Community Sample: Comorbidity, Treatment Utilization, and General Functioning. *Journal of Personality Disorders*, **28**(5), 734–750. https://doi.org/10.1521/pedi_2012_26_093

Topa, W., & Narvaez, D. (2022). *Restoring the kinship worldview: Indigenous voices introduce 28 precepts for rebalancing life on planet earth*. North Atlantic Books. https://books.google.co.uk/books?hl=en&lr=&id=ffE3EAAAQBAJ&oi=fnd&pg=PR17&dq=darcia+narvaez+kinship+worldview&ots=vtMbiJjqJd&sig=DRLeNslQEHKeZeHJWAOaDouBxKY

Twomey, C. D., Baldwin, D. S., Hopfe, M., & Cieza, A. (2015). A systematic review of the predictors of health service utilisation by adults with mental disorders in the UK. *BMJ Open*, **5**(7), e007575. https://doi.org/10.1136/bmjopen-2015-007575

Tyrer, P., Crawford, M., Mulder, R., Blashfield, R., Farnam, A., Fossati, A., Kim, Y.-R., Koldobsky, N., Lecic-Tosevski, D., Ndetei, D., Swales, M., Clark, L. A., & Reed, G. M. (2011). The rationale for the reclassification of personality disorder in the 11th revision of the International Classification of Diseases (ICD-11). *Personality and Mental Health*, **5**(4), 246–259. https://doi.org/10.1002/pmh.190

Van der Kolk, B. (2014). *The body keeps the score: Mind, brain and body in the transformation of trauma*. Penguin UK.

Van der Kolk, B. A. (2015). *The body keeps the score: Brain, mind, and body in the healing of trauma*. Penguin Books.

Wallin, D. J. (2007). *Attachment in psychotherapy*. Guilford press.

Warren, R. (2015). *Emotion regulation in borderline personality disorder: The role of self-criticism, shame, and self-compassion*.

Webb, D., & McMurran, M. (2009). A comparison of women who continue and discontinue treatment for borderline personality disorder. *Personality and Mental Health*, **3**(2), 142–149. https://doi.org/10.1002/pmh.69

Weekers, L. C., Hutsebaut, J., & Kamphuis, J. H. (2021). Client and clinical utility of the assessment of personality disorders. *The Journal of Nervous and Mental Disease*, **209**(11), 846–850.

Weinberg, H. (2020a). Online group psychotherapy: Challenges and possibilities during COVID-19—A practice review. *Group Dynamics: Theory, Research, and Practice*, **24**(3), 201.

Weinberg, H. (2020b). Online group psychotherapy: Challenges and possibilities during COVID-19—A practice review. *Group Dynamics: Theory, Research, and Practice*, **24**(3), 201.

Willig, C. (2013). *Introducing qualitative research in psychology*. McGraw-hill education (UK).

Wingenfeld, K., Spitzer, C., Rullkötter, N., & Löwe, B. (2010). Borderline personality disorder: Hypothalamus pituitary adrenal axis and findings from neuroimaging studies. *Psychoneuroendocrinology*, **35**(1), 154-170. https://doi.org/10.1016/j.psyneuen.2009.09.014

Wingenfeld, K., & Wolf, O. T. (2014). *Stress, Memory, and the Hippocampus*. https://doi.org/10.1159/000356423

Winnicott, D. W. (1991). *Playing and Reality*. Psychology Press.

Woodger, K. (2020). Drop the disorder! Challenging the culture of psychiatric diagnosis by Jo Watson (ed)(2019). *Journal of Psychosocial Studies*, **13**(2), 219-222.

Yalom, I., Brown, S., & Bloch, S. (1975). The written summary as a group psychotherapy technique. *Archives of General Psychiatry*, **32**(5), 605-613.

Yalom, I. D. (n.d.). With Leszcz, M.(2005) *The Theory and Practice of Group Psychotherapy*. New York: Basic Books.

Yalom, I. D. (1995). *The theory and practice of group psychotherapy*. Basic Books (AZ).

Yousif Ali, A. (2015). Personality & Personality Disorders: Evolutionary Entrances and Exits. *International Journal of Emergency Mental Health and Human Resilience*, **17**(3). https://doi.org/10.4172/1522-4821.1000276

Zaleski, K. L., Johnson, D. K., & Klein, J. T. (2016). Grounding Judith Herman's trauma theory within interpersonal neuroscience and evidence-based practice modalities for trauma treatment. *Smith College Studies in Social Work*, **86**(4), 377-393.

Zuroff, D. C., Santor, D., & Mongrain, M. (2005). Dependency, self-criticism, and maladjustment. *Relatedness, Self-Definition and Mental Representation. Essays in Honour of Sidney J. Blatt*, 75-90.

Case study characters

Here are the short biographies of the five group members, printed here for ease of checking back as you go through their journeys in the book.

Louie

Louie is a 54-year-old man of mixed heritage, whose referral to psychotherapy services preceded years of reportedly unsuccessful short-term cognitive behavioural interventions.

Louie grew up in a large, instrumentally violent family, all of whom suffered with significant emotional and mental health difficulties and alcohol dependency. He was excluded from school for repeated absence and violent incidents.

He was involved with criminal gangs from a young age, but avoided prison, stating that he 'got away with it'. There was some suggestion in his notes that he may have posed a risk to his intimate partners. He came to CFGP stating that this was the 'end of the road'.

Adam

Adam is a 35-year-old white English man, whose referral to psychotherapy services was his first despite being in the prison system for many years.

He had a significant history of physical abuse, neglect and sexual trauma, which services seemed to 'turn a blind eye' to despite it being evident at school. Adam had no siblings and never knew his father. He had a daughter from a committed relationship in his early adulthood that ended abruptly following a serious incident of domestic violence.

Adam hurt and punished himself, for example pulling the hair from his beard and hitting himself, often with objects. He came to CFGP unclear about what, if anything, could be offered or would be helpful, or even if he had the right to ask for anything.

Sherelle

Sherelle is a 38-year-old woman of mixed heritage, who was referred to psychotherapy services having been involved in social care and health services her entire life.

She spent her early life scattered across multiple failed foster and care-home placements with sporadic contact with her parents until their early alcohol-related deaths. She lost touch with her two younger siblings who were placed in different homes and eventually adopted by the same family.

Sherelle's early and adult life involved repeated experiences of intrusion and abuse, with many violent and controlling partners and five children who were all taken into the care system, which she fought tirelessly. She has had many admissions to inpatient services following impulsive overdoses and taking herself to a local car park, where she considered jumping.

Dalvinder

Dalvinder is a 28-year old individual of Pakistani heritage, who came to the psychotherapy service in the midst of a conflict and rupture with their mental health care team, which seemed to be part of repeating pattern.

Dalvinder was a carer for their mother from an early age. Dalvinder's father had been authoritarian, abdicating all responsibility for the care of his wife to Dalvinder before leaving the family in dire financial straits. In Dal's early life their own needs had been subjugated and feelings of anger or injustice, including their gender identity as non-binary, were not permitted.

Dalvinder was sexually abused by a school support teacher, which created further fragmentation with the approach-avoidance conflict, with this teacher being one of the first people to take an interest in and provide support for them.

Jane

Jane is a 60-year-old, retired, white English woman, who lived alone for all of her adult life. She was referred to psychotherapy services following the completion of CBT to treat depression.

Her early life had been characterised by heavily critical and physically harmful parents, who had insisted on her admission to inpatient services at the age of 14 years, where she remained on and off until the age of 17.

Despite graduating from her medical training with honours, she was never able to sustain work as a doctor. Jane struggled with binge-eating difficulties and found it almost impossible to throw anything away, to the point where only one room in her home was accessible.